Group Work in Schools

Group Work in Schools

PREPARING, LEADING, RESPONDING

SECOND EDITION

Anne M. Geroski
Jane E. Atieno Okech
Kurt L. Kraus

University of Vermont

cognella®

SAN DIEGO

Bassim Hamadeh, CEO and Publisher
Amy Smith, Senior Project Editor
Abbey Hastings, Production Editor
Jess Estrella, Senior Graphic Designer
Stephanie Kohl, Licensing Coordinator
Natalie Piccotti, Director of Marketing
Kassie Graves, Vice President of Editorial
Jamie Giganti, Director of Academic Publishing

Cover image: Copyright © 2017 iStockphoto LP/monkeybusinessimages.

Printed in the United States of America

This book was previously published by Pearson Education, Inc.

3970 Sorrento Valley Blvd., Ste. 500, San Diego, CA 92121

This book is dedicated to three counselor educators who mentored us in the sound practice of group work: Dr. Peg Carroll, Dr. Diana Hulse, and Dr. William Kline. These talented counselor educators and group leaders have left indelible marks in our knowledge and passion for group work, and we, in turn, hope to pass on their legacies to our students and practitioners in the field through this book. We also dedicate this work to our current and former students at the University of Vermont and Shippensburg University of Pennsylvania, as well as those with whom they work in their internship placements—we learn as our students learn. Finally, we dedicate this book to our children, who have inspired us in everything we do: Jocelyn, Emily, Monica, Ian, Curtis, Youl, Griffin, and Maxwell.

BRIEF CONTENTS

CONTENTS

PREFACE

We write this text from a variety of positions. The three of us have worked as teachers and school counselors, mental health counselors, and counselor educators. From these positions, we have developed a deep appreciation of the challenges inherent in conducting groups with youth and particularly in school settings. Our reason for writing this textbook is to share with counselor educators, graduate students, and practicing school counselors clear, concise, and well-exampled directions for culturally responsive ways to lead groups in school settings. Our goal is to help school counselors understand the multicultural and diverse school contexts in which they may work and to adapt, expand, and strengthen their personal and professional command of group leadership skills.

In preparation for writing the initial *Group Work in Schools* text, we debated what school counselors needed to become competent and confident group leaders. To this end, we searched through our own experiences as classroom teachers and school counselors leading groups in schools, our extensive training in group leadership, our experiences as trainers and supervisors of emerging group leaders, and a multitude of texts and articles on the subject. We also reflected on the experiences of our graduate students as they worked alongside school counselors running groups in their internship placements. The initial book, we believe, was solid. But, as we noted in the preface of that book, it did leave some "stones unturned." In planning this revision of the *Group Work in Schools* text, we saw a need for more depth in the sections on theories, skills, and working with a variety of group types in schools, and, importantly, we saw a need for a more meaningful focus on culturally responsive group work practice. We were grateful that Dr. Okech agreed to join our project, bringing her extensive knowledge and experience in all of these areas to the project.

More specifically, *in this second edition of* Group Work in Schools, *you will see an intentional focus on group leader cultural responsiveness*. Throughout this text, we urge group leaders to pay close attention to their personal work in cultural and social identity development, their worldview, and their cultural and social values, and to attend to the impact that these have on how they lead groups and how they respond to issues emerging among students and their school communities. Examples throughout this book come from a wide variety of social-cultural backgrounds and identities. The examples lend themselves to the creation of a very unique book that is intentional about creating group environments that demonstrate cultural responsiveness.

Also, *in this edition, we remain dedicated to the principles of group work—to the core principles of what makes groups work*. The group development and intervention theories we discuss in an expanded form in this edition of the text provide leaders with perspectives on how groups develop and the significance of contextual factors on the development of groups. Because these theories are sensitive to unique systems and dynamics of group functioning, they provide a solid foundation for leaders to plan and facilitate their groups with intentionality. *In this edition, we also include a chapter on learning theories*. Grounded in educational principles, these theories are intended to help school counselors plan and conduct their groups with an understanding of how to best promote student learning. Together these group and learning theories provide a theoretical and evidence-based foundation for the practice of a variety of types of groups in schools. The tables and case studies we use throughout the text offer further direction for the implementation of these theories and principles in schools.

The structure of this new edition shifts from three to two parts: planning groups and leading groups. The nine chapters within these two sections still provide a dual focus on theory-guided and evidence-based concepts, along with, as much as possible, concrete instructions for planning and leading groups for youth in schools. Chapter 1 offers an introduction to the kinds of groups that are typically conducted by school counselors and also focuses on critical issues for planning groups, including developmental and social-cultural considerations and ethical mandates. Chapters 2 and 3 are the theory chapters. We begin with learning theories in Chapter 2. This chapter outlines key concepts from behavioral, social learning, cognitive, and constructivist theories. The intention behind this chapter is for group leaders to be thoughtful in the planning of their groups so that their practices are aligned with what is known about how children learn. In Chapter 3, the focus is on theories that guide the practice of conducting groups. Here we review the concepts of process and content and therapeutic factors in group work. We also identify important components of systems theory and group stage theory. These theories together offer direction for what leaders can expect and plan for when they run their groups. We end this chapter with a discussion about leadership styles and the concept of "discipline," as used in school settings.

Chapters 4, 5, and 6 in Section I move into the concrete practice of group work with youth. Chapter 4 focuses on critical issues related to group membership and outlines strategies for planning groups. Here you will find helpful discussions on goal setting and drafting group lesson or session plans. Goal assessment is discussed in Chapter 5. Establishing this as a discrete chapter in the larger discussion of group planning helps to emphasize the importance of regularly assessing the goals we establish for our groups. We end this section on planning with a discussion in Chapter 6 about how to plan group strategies and activities so that they are engaging and meaningful. In this chapter, we discuss how leaders can scaffold learning by planning content that helps children develop models for concept development. We also review the principles of *Bloom's Taxonomy* and Vygotsky's *Zone of Proximal Development*. We end the chapter by circling back to group session/lesson planning with an emphasis on the importance of drafting concrete group plans in advance of conducting groups. The underlying point in these three chapters is that group work begins with *intentionality*.

Part II of this text focuses on group leader skills and strategies. Chapter 7 contains a comprehensive list of group counseling skills that are used by leaders to carry out the goals they have set for their groups. We describe each skill with examples to help illustrate how they are put into practice. We then move into the important practices of establishing appropriate group norms and rules—this is the focus of Chapter 8. In this chapter, we also outline practices for starting groups and introduce a model navigating critical group process dynamics so that they enhance rather than interfere with the learning that happens in a group. The final chapter—Chapter 9—emphasizes specific strategies that group leaders can use to keep group members focused on learning goals and help them respond to challenges that may arise in their groups. The range of responses discussed within these chapters extends from quiet attention to increasingly more assertive strategies, including ways to unhook from power struggles, setting limits, using time-out, writing behavior contracts, and eventually culminates with a description of de-escalation strategies. Lesson plans that illustrate the planning suggestions outlined in Section I of the book are included in Appendices A–F.

As you can see from this brief outline, this book doesn't claim to answer every question, fill every void, or address every challenge associated with groups in schools. We doubt any one book could "do it all" for the obvious reason that group work is simply too complex, too varied, and too demanding. We do hope, however, that this book will transport readers to a place of preparedness, enthusiasm, confidence, and skill for leading culturally and socially relevant groups in their schools. We concede that this edition of the book may still leave some stones unturned. But those stones we leave to be turned by others—by you, the reader. It is your creativity, your passion, your skills, and the knowledge you have of your school community and the social-cultural context within which it resides that will bring the important practices we discuss here to life. And, too, it is your experiences that will reveal the stones that have yet to be moved.

We end with a few additional comments that seem important to mention. First is the obvious point that this text has been written by the three of us. Among us is a wide variety of life experiences—both personal and professional. While we have the utmost respect for the unique experiences each of us brings to writing this text, we have attempted to meld our collective voices into one. But we often see issues from different perspectives; the mental models we have established to formulate our own understandings about the world are different, each of us teaches in different ways, and, truth be told, we don't lead groups identically either. In the writing of this text, we did not always see things the same way. But when we were stuck on how to convey an important point or deliver an important concept, we talked, we listened, and we yielded to each other. With this in mind, we ask that you, the reader, be tolerant of the varying and sometimes seemingly contradictory positions advanced in this text. We encourage you to use this text to develop your own style of working with youth in groups in schools.

Second, we offer a few words about our writing style. By following our inclination to be conversational, we have attempted to simplify and reduce the professional jargon as much as possible, making room for clear understandings and practical information for carrying out the complex practice demands of leading groups in schools. This is important information; we hope that our style of writing makes it accessible.

Third, and finally, the first edition of this text relied on the windows and mirrors metaphor, introduced by Emily Style (1998), to talk about how school counselors must make their groups accessible for diverse school populations. In conceptualizing this edition of this text, we were clear that this metaphor was important but also not strong enough, not instructive enough, and not comprehensive enough to explain and emphasize the importance of being a socially and culturally competent group leader. A brief look at the world beyond the pages of this text reminds us that we are not living in a just society where all students have equal access to education and opportunity. We are living in a world that is shaped by power, privilege, and injustice; by some having and others not having; and by the experiences, beliefs, values, and practices of some valued over the experiences, beliefs values, and practices of others. And all of these inequities are alive and well in our school communities. In fact, it is difficult to imagine a realm where diversity is more vivid than in schools— where children arrive daily with the joys and weights of differences that are very personal and quite political. Culture—be it race, faith, ethnicity, class, ability, sexual orientation, gender identity, or another phenomenon that resides under this one broad roof we call culture—is inescapably present in schools and, of course, in the groups that happen every day in those schools. So, while we still believe that groups conducted in schools must provide window and mirror opportunities for all group members, we assert that group leaders must be competent to lead their groups in ways that bring forward and truly honor difference, that level inequities, that invite dissenting voices, and that ensure that there will be learning opportunities for each and every student in their groups and their larger school communities. We take seriously the role of school counselors as advocates, and this position is an undercurrent throughout the new edition of this text.

Ultimately, it will be your application of best practices—in this case, best group practices—that will afford each and every student in your school the opportunity to maximize their potential for healthy growth and development. We offer you the foundation; now the work is yours. Go out there and make a difference in the lives of others.

ACKNOWLEDGMENTS

Many people have helped us produce this book—too many, really, to name here. A special thanks to University of Vermont Counseling Program alumni Jena Zuckerman, Gavin Santacross, Nicole Lewis, Kristin Dickerson, and Lindsey Kearns for contributing their work so that we could adapt it for the group plans in the appendices of this text. Thanks also goes to Kevin Davis and Meredith Fossel of Merrill/Pearson for having confidence in us and publishing the first edition of this text. Thanks, too, goes to the readers of this new edition of *Group Work in Schools* (Christopher Belser, University of New Orleans; Barbara Fitzgerald, Arizona State University; Chris Hennington, Lubbock Christian University; Samantha Klassen, University of Texas, Permian Basin; Ashley J. Luedke, St. Bonaventure University; Mary G. Mayorga, Belmont University; Kimberly N. Mudd-Fegett, Campbellsville University; Emily Sallee, University of Montana; and Robert Walrath, Rivier University) for all of their helpful feedback and suggestions. We want to offer a special thanks to Kassie Graves at Cognella Publishing, who supported the second edition of this text with an abundance of patience, goodwill, helpful feedback, and brilliant insight paired with gentle support, kindness, and warmth. Thanks, too, to Amy Smith and Abbey Hastings at Cognella for their patience and careful attention to detail in the copyediting process, and to everyone else who worked behind the scenes at Cognella to support this project. Thank you. Thank you. Thank you.

Planning Groups

CHAPTER ONE

Introduction to Group Work

Introduction

There is a very practical rationale for why school counselors seek to develop and master their group skills: just about everything that happens in schools happens in some sort of group format. In fact, we might say that groups form the operational structure of schools; they are an inherent part of school culture. And, of course, much of the work of school counselors happens in groups as well.

An obvious strength that school counselors bring to their work in school systems is their training in group work, which, for most school counselors, is based on the standards of best practice set forth by the American School Counseling Association (ASCA, 2019) and the Association for Specialists in Group Work (ASGW; *Professional Standards for the Training of Group Workers*, ASGW, 2000; Thomas & Pender, 2007), the curricular requirements set forth by the Council for Accreditation of Counselor Education and Related Programs (CACREP; *2016 CACREP Standards* (Council for Accreditation of Counselor Education and Related Programs, 2019), and the competencies articulated by relevant codes of ethics published by the ASCA (*ASCA Ethical Standards for School Counselors*, ASCA, 2016) and the American Counseling Association (ACA; *ACA Code of Ethics and Standards of Practice* (ACA, 2014) that govern the practice of counseling and group work in and out of schools. With that being said, school counselors engage in a distinct form of group work—a hybrid form of counseling and psychoeducation—that is strongly influenced by teaching principles and practices. This is why, throughout this text, we borrow from theory, research, and practice in both the fields of counseling and education.

Beginning here in Chapter 1, we start with some foundational concepts. We introduce the types of groups that school counselors conduct and discuss important situational and cultural considerations for group work in schools. We also offer an overview of developmental considerations—how working with youth is different than working with adults, particularly when conducting groups. From there we move into an important discussion about the ways in which social status and social location play out in schools. We will introduce the language of discursive positioning and discuss how privilege, oppression, and marginalization affect the school climate. This is the start of a conversation about how school counselors must be careful not to replicate systemic oppression in their work as they are charged with providing safe working spaces for *all* students, regardless of race, gender, sexual orientation, religious beliefs, social and economic status, or other social, cultural, or identity markers. We then turn to some additional ethical issues related to group work in schools. The chapter ends with some final points related to conducting groups in the unique setting of schools.

This first chapter is intended to offer a general background for the chapters and discussions that follow throughout this text.

Types of Groups in Schools

The ASGW conceptualizes four distinct types of groups conducted by counselors: (1) psycho-educational, (2) counseling, (3) task/work, and (4) psychotherapy groups (ASGW, 2000). Our focus in this text is on the first three of these groups because these are the group types that largely appear in schools (Paisley & Milsom, 2006/2007); these are identified by ASCA as classroom, small, and large groups (ASCA, 2019).

Image 1.1

It is important to point out that the distinctions between all of these group types can be a little fuzzy; there is often overlap between psychoeducation, counseling, therapy, and task groups. For example, counselors may use psychoeducation in their counseling and therapy groups, and they often find that a focus on group process dynamics in task groups can benefit the work of the group. This overlap between group types is also apparent in school group work practice. For example, leaders of small and large counseling groups in schools often incorporate psychoeducation into their work, and leaders of more content-focused classroom groups often engage students in here-and-now group process dynamics, similar to the processes used in therapy groups. School task and work groups typically have a psychoeducational component—they are intended to teach something specific or impart information on a particular topic, but they may also focus on group process dynamics. Further confusing these concepts, task and work groups in schools may be conducted as classroom, small, or large group formats. So while we offer brief descriptions of the types of groups outlined by both ASGW and ASCA here, keep in mind that these categories are meant to describe a scope of group work practice; they are not strict, rigid categories. Hybrid groups are more the norm than the exception in schools.

This point about how group work looks in schools touches on larger discussions around the definition of counseling and how counseling is implemented in schools. For example, many school counselors assert that their work in schools may be "counseling" but definitely *not* "therapy." Others simply describe their work as "teaching." The ASCA model for school counseling programs emphasizes practices that promote student success by working in the areas of academic, career, personal, and social development (ASCA, 2019). In this model, group work is focused on school counseling program goals in these domains, but it is also designed to be responsive to individual student needs (that may be met in groups).

Psychoeducation and Classroom Groups

According to the ASGW (2000), *psychoeducational groups* are aimed at promoting personal and interpersonal growth and development, and they are also used to address goals related to prevention (ASGW, 2000). This is similar to the ASCA (2019) concept of *classroom group work*. According to ASCA (2019), classroom groups focus on developing mindsets (e.g., beliefs and attitudes that promote learning, health, and success), learning strategies (e.g., decision making, creativity, time management, motivation), self-management strategies (e.g., responsibility, self-control, coping skills), and social skills (e.g., empathy, cooperation, assertiveness).

When used in a school setting, these classroom or psychoeducational groups tend to be instructional—providing specific information with a topical focus delivered sequentially over a specified period of time and for a specific purpose (Gitterman & Knight, 2016). For example, a school counselor may offer a 4-week classroom-based psychoeducational group focusing on the topic of bullying to third graders in an elementary school.

School counselors often work from a blend of teaching and therapeutic counseling practices to promote development in these areas. They may develop their own curriculum and materials, or they may use the curriculum already available and marketed for these kinds of groups. It should be pointed out that when group work is conducted in a classroom, it is intended for *all* students in the class. School counselors and other personnel sometimes refer to these groups as "developmental guidance" groups; in this text, we will use the terms classroom or classroom-based psychoeducational groups in reference to these types of groups.

It is important to mention here that classroom group work is not always used for prevention nor implemented with preplanned developmental curriculum; it may also be used in response to a specific issue that has arisen in a particular school. For example, a school counselor offered a series of psychoeducational sessions in a classroom following the death of a fifth-grade student. Although this latter topic may at first appear to be more appropriate to a small counseling group rather than a classroom-based group, the purpose of this particular group was to be informative and really needed to include all of the children in the class since they were all affected by the death. Children who desired (or those whose teachers' or parents' thought they would benefit from additional support after the death of their peer) were also given the opportunity to participate in a small counseling group, as this was also a part of this school's protocol in responding to this level of crisis.

It is significant that students are not specifically selected for membership in classroom groups; they consist of everyone who is already in the class. So many of these groups are relatively large—many classrooms have over 20 students, perhaps even more. Counselors can expect that students will bring a wide variety of life experiences and learning needs into these groups, and they can assume that not all of the students will be interested in or in need of learning about the topic or focus of a particular classroom group lesson. Added to this, classrooms typically have their own group dynamics that have developed over time and that existed long before a school counselor entered the room. A common challenge for school counselors leading classroom groups is navigating these complex group dynamics, balancing process and content, and assessing the effectiveness of their group interventions. These challenges highlight the importance of careful group planning, discussed in Chapters 4, 5, and 6, and other principles related to facilitating groups discussed in this text.

Image 1.2

Counseling Groups

The ASGW (2000) promotes the use of *counseling groups* for people who may experience transitory or episodic (rather than chronic) personal or interpersonal challenges or for those who are at risk for developing such challenges. According to the ASCA model (ASCA, 2019), *small counseling groups* are conducted for four or more sessions with a range of three to 12 students. They are typically designed to address issues that are in line with the overall framework of the school's counseling program (i.e., focused on student academic, career, personal, and social development), or they may be used to respond to specific academic, attendance, or discipline needs of a small group of students. Examples of these kinds of groups include a small group for fourth and fifth graders whose difficulties coping with divorce are interfering with their academic focus, kindergarten children who are struggling with being in school for the first time, or high school students who are feeling stressed about academics or the college application process.

The topics of counseling groups tend to be selected based on the specific needs of their members, and members are often encouraged to engage in active interpersonal interactions, personal sharing, and feedback exchange (Kline, 2003; Sink, 2005). So students in these groups are likely to be emotionally engaged with each other and invested in the topic of the group. For these reasons, membership in counseling groups is based on a screening process to determine the appropriateness of the match between the student and the group (ACA, 2014, 2016; Thomas & Pender, 2007). This helps ensure that the group addresses the specific and individual student member needs, as well as the psychological, emotional, and physical safety of group members. The screening process, which is an ethical responsibility of group leaders (ASCA, 2016) involves informing students (and their parents/guardians) of the purpose of the group, gathering information about the student and their experiences related to the intended topic of the group, and, of course, informed consent and student assent, which are discussed later in this chapter.

Task/Work and Large Counseling Groups

Task/work groups are purposeful groups designed to accomplish a particular goal or project. They tend to be time limited with a specific focus, and members are selected based on their knowledge, skill, and experience related to the group's focus (ASGW, 2000; Gladding, 2003). School-based examples of these types of groups include being an adviser to a school club, working with students on a special project (e.g., end-of-year prom planning), or facilitating a training to a select group of students on a particular topic (e.g., leadership). *Large counseling groups* in schools are described in the ASCA model (2019) as specific planned experiences for student development. For example, they may include a school tour, a career informational meeting, or specific training on leadership for a selected group of students.

Beyond their direct work with students, school counselors are also expected to engage in leadership, advocacy, and systems change activities, as well as collaborative work with school personnel on a variety of instructional and school culture–related projects (ASCA, 2019). One important way that they engage in these aspects of their school counseling program is to facilitate and participate in task or work groups (Paisley & Milsom, 2006). Examples of these task/work groups include department, team or grade-level meetings, Individualized Education Program (IEP) meetings, and curriculum committees.

Image 1.3

Developmental Considerations

Nowhere in the counseling profession is developmental range more apparent than in elementary, middle, and secondary school counseling programs. The distance between the cognitive abilities of kindergarteners and third graders, for example, is immense, as are the physical differences among students in any middle school. This developmental context of childhood and adolescence shapes the practice of counselors working with youth in some very important ways. For example, Vernon (2010) pointed out that young children tend to have concrete thought processes, limitations in abstract reasoning and problem-solving abilities, and typically have a short attention span. Vernon cautions practitioners not to make assumptions about the maturity of adolescents based on physical appearances, as they may appear physically mature but have lags in development in some of these other areas. Also, the type and range of issues or topics that are relevant and/or of concern for youth vary by developmental level and are different than those of interest and concern to adults (Vernon, 2010). For example, early adolescents may struggle with problem solving and decision making; younger children may grapple with fears or events in their lives over which they have little to no control (Vernon, 2010). Adolescents may be confused about their newfound interest in romantic relationships and sexual intimacy, and they are often also short on information and experience related to engaging in healthy sexual relationships. And while they have many questions, many adolescents are simultaneously seeking independence from adults and resist or appear to be reluctant to receiving help. As a result, it can sometimes be challenging for counselors to build meaningful relationships and engage adolescents in therapeutic processes (Martin, 2003).

It is also tempting but shortsighted to imagine that all students within a particular chronological age or social and cultural background will be developmentally identical. As an illustration, allow us to draw a parallel between leading groups and teaching math. A competent classroom teacher will recognize that within a classroom there will be those students for whom the material–say learning their multiplication facts—will be accomplished quickly and seem effortless. Others will inevitably take much longer to accomplish the same task and do so with great struggle. This range, although well within the developmental range of "normal," can produce numerous effects. For example, students who wiz through memorization of multiplication tables may scorn students who "hold the class up," while students who struggle may find inappropriate humor or oppositional behaviors preferable to "looking slow" in the eyes of their peers. The consequences of these variations are obvious. Teachers must be vigilant and responsive to the wide range of abilities, achievements, and behaviors of the students in their classes to best meet the needs of all of their students. This is also true for school counselors conducting groups in schools.

Play and Planned Activities

One of the most helpful and productive ways in which counselors accommodate the cognitive, emotional, social, and behavioral characteristics of children is to engage them in concrete and playful interventions rather than traditional talk therapy (Vernon, 2010). Play-based interventions typically fall in different places on the continuum of structured and nonstructured applications of play therapy. The more structured play-based interventions include counselor-planned and directed activities designed to focus on a particular topic or concern (Jones et al., 2003). Less structured play-based interventions invite the child to take responsibility for the direction of the work in therapy and are based on the premise that given appropriate nurturing conditions, children's innate capacities will direct them toward healthy growth and development (Guerney, 2001). While the nondirective approaches are, indeed, therapeutic for many children, it is important to note that children from families or cultural contexts where they are more accustomed to being given directions may need additional scaffolding in the play therapy process. Nondirective play therapy also tends to be a more long-term approach to counseling and for that reason is sometimes not used in school settings. Our point here, however, is to just point out that these various play therapy approaches to counseling children can also be used in group work. We will discuss the use of activities and exercises in groups with youths in schools in more detail in Chapter 6.

Structure and Content in Groups

Structure is an important consideration when planning groups with youth, particularly groups conducted in school settings. Students are largely accustomed to a content-oriented or agenda-driven instructional practices in their school classrooms, so structure and content-focused groups that mirror the pedagogical practices of their teachers may be most comfortable for children in school counselor–led groups. Structure may also be helpful in groups with a large number of children and when working with a wide variety of abilities, interests, cultures, behaviors, and temperaments. For these reasons, counselors often design activity-based lesson plans for their classroom-based groups. Highly structured approaches may not work as well in smaller counseling groups, however. This is because the structure of an activity or an exercise can inhibit spontaneous interaction among members or may prevent students from focusing on their own specific needs and challenges. The point here is that group leadership style and approach, including the use of play, activities, and structure, must be responsive to the developmental needs of the children present, the social-cultural context of the group members, and the aims and goals of the group.

In addition to the level of structure that is appropriate for a particular group, there is the issue of content. In using the term *content*, we are referring to the topic of the group. Group content, whether delivered through structured activities or through less structured discussions, should always be designed so that all of the students in the group are meaningfully engaged at an appropriate level of difficulty and in ways that relate to their own lived experiences. To these ends, content must be inclusive with respect to the various cultures represented by the members of a group, cognizant of student language knowledge and expertise, and match the cognitive and developmental needs of the students in the group. Remember that the school counselor's clientele is *every* student in the school.

Flexibility

Finally, we want to point out that classroom cultures vary extensively. There are enormous between-classroom differences across seemingly similar groups of students. A psychoeducational group lesson that works masterfully in one second-grade classroom may bomb in another right across the hall. Also, situations or events will inevitably arise in groups that have the potential to thwart the leader's intended direction or interfere with what a leader expected to accomplish during a specific lesson. The thought that leaders have full control over what transpires within their groups is, unfortunately, naive. Here we underscore the importance of flexibility and quick decision making when leading groups, especially in groups with youth in schools.

Group work always requires a precarious balance between staying with the session objective and spontaneously moving in a different direction because that is what is needed in the moment. Advanced contingency planning is an important way to be prepared for spontaneous changes, and we encourage group leaders to always have a plan B.

Social Status and Social Location in Schools and School Groups

"Given the current sociopolitical climate in the United States," Guth et al. (2019) reminded us, "it is more critical than ever for helping professionals to advocate, foster, and support the promotion of diversity, equity, inclusion, and acceptance" (p. 3). One of the important ways that these issues can be nurtured and promoted in schools is through group work. Here we want to invite counselors working in schools to understand this charge in terms of recognizing, respecting, and promoting diversity, as well as enacting social justice through education and advocacy. We begin with a discussion about the concept of social status and how status plays out in schools. Then we move to a discussion focused more directly on status as it relates to social location. Finally, we focus on the important topics of school counselor cultural competence and responsive group work practice.

Social Status

Meier (2002) asserted that schools matter "even more than TV" (p. 10) in telling children who they are and who they can be. Children keenly understand the unspoken hierarchical structures that relegate notions of popularity and competence according to perceived academic ability, athleticism, and attractiveness, as well as the categories associated with race, social class, gender, etc. (Cohen, 1994). The social ordering that exists in regard to these variables is an undercurrent in most school communities; social status functions according to unspoken rules with powerful implications. In schools, social status influences how students feel invited into and are able to participate in learning tasks; the relative influence that students have on others; the ways in which students are treated by peers, teachers, and counselors; and students' own expectations regarding performance and competence (Cohen, 1994). For example, students with lower levels of social status are often reluctant to participate in group discussions; if they do, their contributions are sometimes ignored or passed over by peers in favor of contributions from higher status peers. Also, students with lower socioeconomic status, which typically translates to a lower social status among peers, may lack access to learning materials, resources, or information. As a result, they may have difficulties completing tasks, especially homework, and be characterized as passive learners or students who do not really care. We also know that students with lower social status are not picked for teams and small group activities as frequently as their peers. Groups have the potential to offer youth opportunities to acquire knowledge and skills to create the ways that they want to be with others and in the world; they also have the power to condemn youth to the social roles that have inhibited their growth in their school communities. The group leader holds the reins for influencing group norms, member roles, and group dynamics, thus leading the group to either destiny (Okech & Rubel, 2007; Yalom & Leszcz, 2005).

Classroom and counseling group work offer school counselors a variety of opportunities for attacking status perceptions. First, groups can be designed to invite youth to intentionally deconstruct social conventions related to social status. For example, groups can provide a venue for students to discuss conventional notions of attractiveness, gender roles, and behaviors. These discussions help students become critical consumers of ideas. Second, when a group is facilitated in ways that offer every group member a valued role, and when the group tasks are interesting, engaging, and organized in ways that require different abilities and different student strengths for participation, students will come to value the various strengths of all of the members of the group (Cohen, 1994). Third, maintaining a no-tolerance stance toward hurt and hate and upholding group norms of respect and fairness play an important role in dismantling the presence of status in groups (we will discuss group norming processes later in Chapter 8). Fourth, students must be adequately prepared with the requisite social skills for participating in groups.

Some students need special instruction and coaching to be able to adequately participate in and benefit from a group experience. Without this preparation, they may flounder in ways that create or reinforce a position as someone who does not have a meaningful or respected presence in the group. Opportunities for success go hand in hand with opportunities for status elevation in groups and in schools more generally. Students can be scaffolded toward successful group participation when group roles and tasks are made explicit, when learning tasks take into account the varied abilities of all members of the group, and when the group leader is active in assigning competence to all members of the group (Cohen, 1994). *Cooperative Learning* (Johnson et al., 1994), *The Responsive Classroom* (Charney, 1991), *Complex Instruction* (Cohen, 1994), and *Experiential Learning* (Luckner & Nadler, 1997) are teaching models that offer approaches to structuring learning environments and experiences to enhance the strengths of all group members.

Social Location

We know that culture, ethnicity, religion, gender, age, sexual orientation, ability status, gender identity, and socioeconomic status are important features of identity. We also know that these identity markers influence how people are perceived by and treated by others (Pieterse et al., 2013; Sue & Sue, 2003). The term *social location* is often used in discussions about identity because it attempts to capture the idea that one's social, racial, or ethnic group affiliation is part of a larger structure of social stratification (Kubiak, 2005; Pearlin, 1989). Schools, of course, are a critical place where social location dynamics play out. While most school counselors know that the way children are viewed by others has an important influence on how they come to view themselves, social location affiliated with race, ethnicity, and other identity markers also affect social interactions and future opportunities. Monk et al. (2008) reminded us that "it's not enough to just celebrate the rainbow of colors of diversity without taking seriously the ways in which cultural divisions lead to differential opportunities in life" (p. 49).

The term *discourse* was used by Foucault (1972) in reference to structuring ideas within a particular culture or social context that shape our common understandings about the world around us and how we see ourselves and others. As such, discourses have a norming influence on behavior. For example, contemporary discourses about gender are represented in color-coded fashion norms on display in department stores across America. They invite us to perceive gender from a limited binary perspective and as a code for how girls and boys should dress and, we argue, behave. *Discursive practice* is a term used for when discourses shape how we think and behave.

Another example of a discourse that has common currency in many schools across the United States these days is the idea of the "helicopter parent." This discourse is typically used to describe some version of "hovering parents who are potentially over-involved in the lives of their child" (Padilla-Walker & Nelson, 2012, p. 1177). As a discourse, helicopter parent references a set of parenting behaviors that everyone presumably can identify. It is also used, typically, as a derogatory comment about parents, as it unquestionably suggests that their behaviors are inappropriate. Without weighing in at this point on appropriate parenting practices, we just point out that the helicopter parent discourse represents one of many mixed messages delivered to the parents of children in our schools—in this case, we want parents to be involved in the lives and schooling of their children but not too involved. What?

We introduce this concept of discourse as a way of discussing one of the subtle ways in which the stratification of social location happens in schools. Again, quoting from Monk et al. (2008), "It would be nice if all the social groups to which people belonged were equally valued in our communities. ... A moment's reflection on life in the United States at the moment, however, is enough to see that this situation does not exist" (p. 141). Discourses are not neutral; they are formulated in complex and unequal societies where some groups are privileged over others (Drewery, 2005). Getting back to the example of the helicopter parenting discourse, Geinger et al. (2014) argued that parenthood is enacted under an "omnipresent gaze" (p. 498) of social, political, and moral discourses that give rise to a "booming industry" (Jensen, 2010, p. 176) of parenting advice. Yet this advice, based on contemporary parenting (particularly mothering) discourses, promotes a view of parenting that is based largely on white, heterosexual, middle-class norms (Rolfe, 2008), which are not accessible nor, perhaps, desirable for all.

Even when discourses around race, class, and status are not explicit, they are always present within student interactions, student-teacher interactions, and school-community relations. *Cultural racism*, which refers to the messages and images in society that reinforce the notion of white privilege, "is like smog in the air" according to Tatum (1997, p. 6). Tatum went on to describe this smog:

> Sometimes it is so thick it is visible, other times it is less apparent, but always, day in and day out, we are breathing it in. None of us would introduce ourselves as "smog-breathers" (and most of us don't want to be described as prejudiced), but if we live in a smoggy place, how can we avoid breathing the air? (p. 6)

One of the major ways in which cultural racism appears in school hallways and classrooms, despite the best intentions of school personnel, is in the enactment of *microaggressions*. Microaggressions are the "brief and commonplace daily verbal, behavioral, or environmental indignities, whether intentional or unintentional, that communicate hostile, derogatory, or negative racial slights and insults toward people of color" (Sue et al., 2007, p. 271). Three types of microaggressions identified by Sue (2010) include *microassaults*—intentional and explicit racial denigrations, *microinsults*—subtle racial putdowns that are likely to be unintentional, and *microinvalidations*—denying the lived experiences, thoughts, feelings of people of color. Microaggressions are often expressed by individuals who are situated in dominant or privileged social groups (Sue 2010; Smith et al., 2014). Because they are part of a conditioning process of bias and prejudice that is widely permeated within our culture to the point of being normalized (Sue et al., 2007), they often go unquestioned. Also, microaggressions can be so nuanced that they are sometimes difficult to comprehend, and they can be so subtle that recipients are sometimes confused about whether they actually happened (Smith et al., 2014). This is why many people, including school personnel, may commit microaggressions without even being aware of it. Regardless of intention, microaggressions can be deeply damaging and may have far-reaching effects on students' social and identity development, as well as academic performance in schools (Darvin, 2018).

Discursive practices that give rise to school climates that are replete with (subtle and overt) experiences of marginalization for some of the children and families in the community are challenges that school counselors face in their attempts at creating a learning climate that promotes learning for all (Darvin, 2018). The larger point we are getting to, and this is a position forwarded by the ASCA in the ASCA model (ASCA, 2019) and leaders in the field (e.g., Dahir & Stone, 2012; The Education Trust, 2009; Holcomb-McCoy, 2004), is that school counselors are well positioned to address the needs of historically marginalized social groups as they are increasingly being called upon to act as leaders and advocates in their schools (Paisley & Milsom, 2006/2007). As leaders and advocates, school counselors encourage individuals to maintain their ethnic, cultural, and personal identities, and they work to create cohesive and respectful school communities across these differences so that everyone has a seat at the table or a place in the group.

When we speak of cultural competence in schools, then, we are referring to many things: an environment that scaffolds critical thinking skills, perspective taking, and socially just decision making and empowerment; a curriculum that offers contributions from multiple perspectives and opportunities for all; and policies and practices that confront racism, injustice, and hate. All school constituents need to participate in the process of creating an inclusive environment that is characterized by cultural competence—this includes students, teachers, staff, and administrators and, equally important, parents or guardians. And circling back to the focus of this text, much of this work in schools can happen in groups: classroom psychoeducational groups, counseling groups, and task, work, and large groups, such as clubs, meetings, and workshops.

Cultural Competencies and Responsive Group Practice in Schools

We start with a brief clarification of what we mean by cultural competence. Very generally, counseling scholars use the term *cultural competence* in reference to attitudes, knowledge, and skills that counselors need to work appropriately with clients from diverse cultures (e.g., Arredondo et al., 1996; Collins & Arthur, 2010; Hogan-Garcia, 1999; Hook et al., 2016; Sue et al., 1992; Sue & Sue, 2003). Cultural competence is also required in work with individuals who locate in diverse social locations, including race, ethnicity, age, ability status, sexual orientation, gender identity, religion, language, and socioeconomic status—individuals who locate in marginalized social locations. Sue and Sue (2003) point out that cultural competence (they use the term *multicultural competence*) must go beyond a discussion about sameness and difference; it must also include the ability to acknowledge and address the influence of existing systems of power and privilege that benefit individuals from various social locations unequally (Anderson et al., 2004; Pieterse et al., 2013). A final point we raise about this concept of cultural competence is that the term is sometimes used in a way that suggests it is a definable stage or specific level of achievement. Competence is simply not that concrete. We invite you to think of competence more as a transformational process.

Holcomb-McCoy (2004) outlined nine areas of competence for school counselors so that they can best serve a diverse student population. These competencies focus on the awareness, knowledge, and skills that school counselors need to work with a diverse student body. They include understanding the diverse ways in which students seek help, understanding the context of and fallout from racism in school communities, and using racial identity theory in providing counseling and other services to youth in schools. The Holcomb-McCoy competencies also compel school counselors to respect the variety of parenting styles and family networks or kinship relationships that may exist within their school communities and to work to nurture family-school-community partnerships across differences. Finally, these competencies highlight the important role of school counselors to act as advocates and agents of change. The Holcomb-McCoy competencies are supported by the work of others in the field and constitute a call to professional counselors to serve in the roles of counselor, educator, and advocate with regard to diversity issues (for more on this topic, see *ACA Multicultural and Social Justice Counseling Competencies*, Ratts et al. (2015), *Advocacy Competencies for Professional Counselors*, Trusty & Brown (2005), *ASGW Multicultural and Social Justice Competence Principles for Group Workers*, Singh et al. (2012), *The ASCA National Model*, ASCA (2019), *ASCA Ethical Standards for School Counselors*, ASCA (2016), and *ASGW Best Practice Guidelines*, Thomas & Pender (2007)).

In terms of their work in groups, school counselors need to be intentional about constructing groups so that *all* members have a place, as well as an opportunity, for identification and growth in the group—this is what we mean by planning for windows and mirrors, which will be discussed shortly. Because identity characteristics associated with race, ethnicity, gender, socioeconomic status, sexual orientation, age, and physical and mental ability exist in polarized contexts of status/advantage/privilege, a minority voice in a group of dominant-group others can easily be silenced. A student who stands apart on one aspect of the aforementioned characteristics may not *feel*—and may not *be*—safe in the group. As a result, students whose experiences in life are different from the others in the group may feel censured, may censure themselves, or may feel like unvalued and token representatives from particular identity categories. Not only does this mean that they are not likely to benefit from being in the group, but it is also likely that the group could be potentially harmful to these students.

We sometimes like to think that "diversity issues" are variables that smooth over with inclusion; on the contrary, inclusion does not happen if these issues are smoothed over. Groups with a diverse membership have the potential to offer a rich array of perspectives into the learning and therapeutic process, but that potential is only realized when students feel that they have a place in the group and that their voices are wanted, worthy, and respected. We emphasize that it is the responsibility of the group leader to assure that all members feel and truly are safe in their groups—that they are protected from "physical, emotional and psychological trauma" (ACA, 2014, p. 6).

Guth et al. (2019) call upon school counselors to engage in culturally competent work through counseling, education, and advocacy. They offer the following suggestions for promoting equity, inclusion, and diversity in groups (these strategies are discussed in more detail in Guth et al.'s aptly named article, "Ten Strategies to Intentionally Use Group Work to Transform Hate, Facilitate Courageous Conversations, and Enhance Community Building" (2019), approved by the ASGW in 2018):

1. Acknowledge that culture and power are always present.
2. Develop multicultural and social justice competencies.
3. Be brave and affirming and create humanizing spaces where conversations about injustice, inequity, and social change can happen.
4. Be purposeful in processing the experiences of group members.
5. Cultivate cultural humility.
6. Intentionally engage in unity building.
7. Facilitate with mindfulness and reflexivity.
8. Lean into difficult conversations.
9. Consider possibilities for action.
10. Always assess the effect of the group experience on individual members, the group as a whole, and larger communities.

Windows and Mirrors

Getting at the issue of educating students to respectfully understand others and to create and maintain school climates that support diverse perspectives and lifestyles is at the heart of Style's (1998) metaphoric concept of *windows and mirrors*. Style said,

> Education needs to enable the student to look through window frames in order to see the realities of others and into mirrors in order to see her/his own reality reflected. Knowledge of both types of framing is basic to a balanced education which is committed to affirming the essential dialectic between the self and the world. (p. 150)

Image 1.5

Creating *windows* in a group refers to the creation of experiences that help group members see and respect multiple lifestyles (a window to see through to the life of others) and multiple perspectives of others. Windows expose group members to the lived experiences of students who are not like them with the intent of enhancing perspective taking, empathy, and creating a basis for developing genuine relationships across differences. So, one of the inherent benefits of using group work as a medium for learning in schools is that it has the potential to offer individuals a window into the lives of others.

When creating window experiences in groups, however, group leaders must also be open to exposing students to the realities of racism, classism, sexism, and heterosexism, which are also a part of the experience of those who locate in marginalized social locations. For one to see clearly through windows, the shades of privilege must be raised. McIntosh (1998) reminded us that acknowledging privilege—that is, acknowledging one's personal privilege, acknowledging the ways in which privilege works its way into the lives of others, and noting how privilege permeates curriculum in institutions of education—makes one newly accountable for the benefits that are granted to those who are in positions of power. This means that understanding how cultures are situated within systems of power is an important part of the windowing experiences that school counselors can bring into their work in school groups. We emphasize here that school counselors must engage in windowing without making it the responsibility of colleagues or students in marginalized locations to educate and sensitize the privileged majority.

For Style (1998), holding up *mirrors* refers to helping students see themselves represented in the community and the collective knowledge of the group. This includes seeing their contributions validated and their experiences valued by others, as well as exposing students to all of the possibilities of what they can do and who they can be. Style (1998) pointed out that school curricula have traditionally privileged dominant cultural experiences and views, relegating individuals from minority groups to the repeated experiences of windows of others with little validation of what is their own truth and experience. The point here is that groups have the potential to provide an opportunity for all of the students in the group to see mirrors of themselves as strong and healthy individuals—and this should happen in all of the various group types that occur in schools.

Opening up the content in the group to account for the experiences of a diverse population of students also allows students with less social capital (i.e., those who are members of underprivileged or socially marginalized groups) to witness their own experiences as having a place in the group. Representation communicates that one's truths are respected as valid rather than minimized or ignored. Groups that offer windows and mirrors to all students set a precedent for privileging the voices of every member of the group and fits with learning and therapeutic goals in almost every area of development that is addressed in school counseling programs. Articulating in your group plans how you will assure that you are offering both windows and mirrors in your group ensures that this will happen. Case Study 1.1 offers an example of how one group leader offered a first-pass window into the experiences of discrimination in her elementary classroom group.

CASE STUDY 1.1 Windows and Mirrors

The goals for all of the classroom groups in a semi urban elementary school included the expectation that students will learn about perspectives that are different than their own and that they will develop acceptance and appreciation across differences. The rationale for this goal was linked to the state harassment law, which articulates the wide range of protected categories that are addressed by this particular protective legislation. Part of the comprehensive developmental program in the school also included helping students understand what is meant by a "protected category" and why one group may warrant special protections under the law.

Working towards this goal, all of the students in a fifth-grade studied the concept of family with the objective of understanding different experiences of family; this happened in a classroom "developmental guidance lesson" conducted by the school counselor. The idea was that family includes children who are living with aunts and uncles, grandparents, and siblings, as well as with foster families, same-sex parents, heterosexual couples, and divorced and blended families. In carrying out this objective, the counselor used the film and discussion series *That's a Family* (Cohen, 2002; Logan et al., 2002) to expose children to multiple family types. She also used the book *And Tango Makes Three* (Richardson & Parnell, 2005), which exposed children to the true story of two male penguins at the Central Park Zoo who fell in love and raised a baby penguin together.

We emphasize that the content of the group described in Case Study 1.1 is not—and should not be—designed to encourage students to adopt values that are different than their own; it is designed to have students become aware that there are other perspectives and other ways of experiencing the world. As Style (1998) said, "For me, the beauty of the classroom gathering lies in its possibility for seeing new varieties of Beauty [*sic*]" (p. 150). Written plans that specifically outline discussion questions and comments that bring forth these other levels of learning can be used to invite students to examine the information presented at an ever-increasing level of cognitive complexity. For example, a discussion after the film and book can help students connect the new information about different family types to social-context issues, such as societal norms, or to school-experienced behaviors, such as bullying and teasing. Students might be asked to think about how they make decisions about others based on judgments, thus learning how to critically evaluate information that is presented to them. All of these represent higher level learning tasks designed to offer windows and mirrors for various group members.

We recognize that school counselors might struggle to facilitate these group processes, especially if they have not engaged in the intensive personal growth processes of examining their own privileged or marginalized status and its impact on their personal and professional lives. This is hard work; yet, it has the potential to create a richer and more equitable learning and therapeutic experience for students. So, with this is a call for school counselors to be diligent in their own personal and professional development towards cultural competence.

Facilitating Intercultural Competence Among Students

Thus far, we have discussed the importance of the intentional work that school counselors do to assure that the students in their groups are exposed to the worldviews of others and are able to see themselves mirrored in positive and successful ways. This requires that counselors have an awareness of social status and social location issues in their schools and, especially, in their groups and that they work to equalize status hierarchies in their groups. Shortly, we will discuss how this work translates to becoming advocates in their school communities. But first, we want to introduce the concept of *intercultural competence* to emphasize the important role that school counselors play in promoting students' abilities to work with others in complex and diverse learning and group communities.

The concept of intercultural competence, arising largely from the study of Americans living in other cultures, most generally refers to an ability to cross effectively into unfamiliar cultures (Leung et al., 2014). It is a concept that is understood and described differently by scholars and researchers and in diverse fields of study, and it is sometimes used interchangeably with other terms, such as cross-cultural adjustment or awareness, intercultural effectiveness, and cultural competence (Taylor, 1994). Intercultural competence is described by Sorrells (2013) as the development of critical and reflective thinking and acting that "enables us to navigate the complex and challenging intercultural spaces that we inhabit interpersonally, communally, and globally" (p. 15). For Sorrells, it is a way of thinking, analyzing, reflecting, and, importantly, acting. Koester and Lustig (2015) described intercultural competence as acquiring social judgment and a way of being in the world. They said it is "not something one does but rather something that one is perceived to be" (p. 20). For Taylor (1994), intercultural competence is a transformational process that evolves from sensitivity and communication abilities and leads to a "higher state of consciousness and a more discriminating and integrative world view" (p. 392).

These definitions are indeed powerful concepts to consider when thinking about how to prepare oneself and others—children—to engage in respectful intercultural interactions and relationships.

And they are important. Intercultural competence is a way of being, thinking, and doing with others that is respectful, adaptive, and life transforming. Again, we want to mention our earlier caution against conceptualizing the notion of competence as a static state or final accomplishment. That is, intercultural competence is a process and an engagement, not an end point.

The reason we are discussing intercultural competence here is because it is linked to teaching models that invite educators to think about how to promote awareness, sensitivity, and adaptation among their students as they engage in cross-cultural relationships. Taylor (1994), for example, offered a model for teaching intercultural competence that initiates with *contact*—the (new) experience of being with someone who is culturally different. This, he suggested, causes a disruption in one's familiar lens of understandings or, as he puts it, a disruption in one's "uncritically accepted cultural or personal ideologies" (Taylor, 1994, p. 401). From this initial contact and disruption is the potential for *critical reflection*. When students become aware of something that is new, different, and/or confusing, there is a potential for the evaluation of their commonly held assumptions and perspectives. It is an opportunity to question those perceptions, and this is where teachers and school counselors can do much to begin the process of helping children develop intercultural competence. Taylor (1994) cautioned, however, that experience and critical reflection alone do not translate into intercultural competence. For competence to develop, students need to engage in *exploration*, *experimentation*, and *action*, all of which, he asserted, occur when one is engaged in *dialog* with others. When they are engaged in relationships and discussions, students can try out new roles, gain new information, and receive feedback, leading to new perspectives, new understandings, and new ways of being with others.

Similarly, in Sorrells's *Intercultural Praxis Model* (Sorrells, 2013), interpersonal competence arises from a complex process of engagement that includes curious inquiry, framing or perspective taking, positioning awareness, and engagement in dialogue, reflection, and action. Beginning with *inquiry*, Sorrells believed that interpersonal competence arises from an initial desire and interest in knowing, asking, and learning. It is based on a genuine curiosity, suspended judgment, and a willingness to take risks, allowing one's own views to be challenged and, perhaps, changed. *Framing*, the next entry point in Sorrells model, is based on the idea that our views are always experienced through a set of frames that give rise to our perspectives, as well as our views of self and others. These frames, importantly, are based on our own specific individual, cultural, national, and regional experiences and instruction. In Sorrells's model, the point is that it is critical to become aware of the frames through which we see and experience the world. This means that we need to understand the context of our perspectives. With this understanding, Sorrell argued, we develop the ability to "zoom in" and "zoom out," altering our perspective so that it takes into account the differently based experiences and perspectives of others.

Next in Sorrells's model of intercultural competence (Sorrells, 2013) is *positioning*. This is based on positioning theory and refers to the location in which one stands within an "intersecting web of socially constructed hierarchical categories" (p. 12). Positioning theory is described by Harre and his colleagues (see Harre & Moghaddam, 2003; Harre & Van Langenhove, 1991) as a way of examining how social interactions unfold according to local and typically unspoken rules of engagement and the processes by which individuals construct meaning (Harre & Moghaddam, 2003). These rules are situated in social and cultural contexts that are governed by discourses and structures of power and privilege. In the Sorrells model, positioning refers to the ability to understand how one's own positioning—the stand and speech actions one takes—affects intercultural communications. This understanding compels us, she asserted, to "interrogate who can speak and who is silenced" (p. 18) in intercultural exchanges, and it "demands that we question whose knowledge is privileged, authorized, and agreed upon as true and whose knowledge is deemed unworthy, 'primitive,' or unnecessary" (p. 18).

Reflecting on the etymology of the word *dialogue* to describe the next entry point in her model, Sorrells (2013) noted that dialogue is a communication within an interpersonal connection that has the potential to change people. It is not something that just happens between two individuals;

it is something that passes through and across individuals who are engaged in a relationship. In the intercultural praxis model, dialogue entails respect for the perspectives of others and invites the possibility of shared understandings and new meanings. This is critical, she believed, for true intercultural understandings and relationships. *Reflection* is the next point of entry in Sorrells's model. Here she referred to one's ability to learn from introspection, to be able to observe oneself in relation to others, and to alter one's perspectives and actions based on these observations and reflections. This, too, according to Sorrells, is a critical component of being able to navigate complex and challenging intercultural spaces. The final point of entry into intercultural engagement in the intercultural praxis model is *action*. Here Sorrells reflected on the work of Paulo Freire in arguing that individuals who have engaged in the processes mentioned in this model will have an increased understanding that compels them to take action to make a difference in the world. That is, intercultural competence includes the responsibility for creating change. In the words of Sorrells, action refers to an informed responsibility "to create a more socially just, equitable and peaceful world" (p. 20). These components of Sorrells model of intercultural competence are summarized in Figure 1.1,

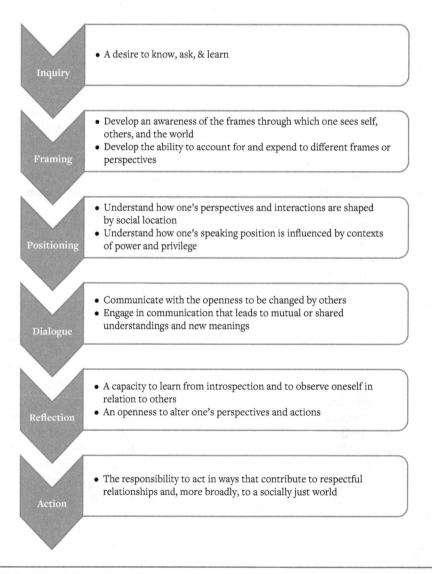

FIGURE 1.1 Facilitating Intercultural Competence

and can be adapted for group work by school counselors who hope to promote cultural competence among their students.

The Role of School Counselors as Advocates

Some of the discussions so far in this chapter may have raised uncomfortable and, perhaps, controversial ideas. We realize that talking about race or acknowledging same-sex partnerships or nonbinary gender identities, for example, may be deemed "unspeakable" in some communities. Perhaps it is also unspeakable from the lips of some counselors and group leaders? To this discussion, we add two very important points.

The first is about the role of counselors as advocates and agents of change. Nieto (2000) asserted that institutional racism and other systemic forms of discrimination may inflict *greater* damage than individual acts of discrimination. This is because, she believed, institutions (such as schools) wield extensive power that reinforces and legitimizes oppressive policies and practices. "Interethnic and intraethnic biases and personal prejudices," Nieto said, "while negative and hurtful, simply do not have the long-range and life-limiting effects of institutional racism and other kinds of institutional discrimination" (Nieto, 2000, p. 36). Indeed, there is a loud call in the profession for school counselors to take on the role of agents of change in their schools, their communities, and in the lives of the children and families they serve (ASCA, 2019; Paisley & Milsom, 2006/2007; Trusty & Brown, 2005). "It is critical," Bemak and Chung (2005) concluded, "for school counselors to become advocates who challenge old paradigms and power structures" (p. 197).

Second, we remind you of the very important duty we have as counselors to assure safety for *all* students in our schools. Challenging inappropriate structures of power and privilege is an important goal for all schools to embrace, but it should never come at the expense of compromising the safety of minority and potentially marginalized students. It is the job of the adults in the school to facilitate important discussions and to provide meaningful learning experiences, and it is also their responsibility to do so in a caring, respectful, thoughtful, and, especially, safe way.

Cultural competence, then, refers to the intentional work of school counselors, and here in this text, we are speaking about the work of school counselors as group leaders—to help students (as well as parents and colleagues) see and respect multiple perspectives; to scaffold students' abilities to understand and confront racism and injustice; to intentionally teach students to make thoughtful decisions and become critical thinkers; to model, encourage, and support multiple possibilities for all students; and to speak out and become agents of change in contexts that are composed of colleagues, parents, and members of their communities. Creating these kinds of experiences for students through group work requires self-reflection and personal growth in the area of cultural competence, careful attention to planning, intentional leading in the group, and thoughtful responses to problems in the group.

Image 1.6

Ethical Mandates for Group Work in Schools

While a thorough review of ethical considerations relevant to counseling children and adolescents is beyond the scope of this book, here we mention these important principles related to group work with youth in schools: informed consent, confidentiality, protection from harm, and mandated reporting.

Informed Consent

Informed consent and student assent are important pre-group processes for student participation in counseling groups in schools. *Informed consent* refers to providing information to students and their parents or guardians about the counseling services offered (Wheeler & Bertram, 2012). This includes explanations regarding the purpose, techniques, goals, and other information related to counseling processes (including confidentiality and duty to warn) and potential outcomes. Seeking parental consent for students to participate in small counseling groups is an ethical mandate for school counselors (see *ASCA Ethical Standards for School Counselors*; ASCA, 2016); it is incumbent upon all school counselors to be informed about their school policies in this regard.

Student *assent* refers to a process of informed consent for minors. From a legal point of view, students under the age of 18 cannot grant legal consent for participation in school-related activities, as this privilege of consent is afforded only to adults (although there are important state-specific and federal exceptions to this point). For this reason, parents or guardians must give consent (in most cases) for their children to be involved in counseling groups while at school. However, students of all ages can (and should) be asked to assent—meaning that they have a voice in whether they would like to be members of a particular counseling group. Counselors should always respect students' decisions to participate or decline to participate in a group. In the long run, a counseling group that was formed by coercion (in its many overt and subtle forms) is not likely to be productive to anyone—not to the members nor to the group leader. Those who are assigned membership without assent may bring defensiveness, reluctance to engage, or anger with them into the group. Students who have made an informed decision about being in a group, on the other hand, are likely to stick with the group, support its established goals, and actively engage in group learning activities and processes.

Seeking assent from students requires that the purpose and process of the group be presented in developmentally and culturally appropriate language so that those who are invited to be members can determine if they wish to make that commitment. To this end, counselors should plan a pre-group informational meeting where invited students are informed (individually or in a small group) about the group (and as mentioned, parents/guardians, too, must be informed about the purposes of the group prior to being asked for consent). Skipping this critical step in the composition of a group has the potential to increase the complexity of the counselor's leadership role and could easily put members in danger of physical, emotional, and psychological harm. But most importantly, screening for participation in small counseling groups is an ethical mandate for school counselors (ASCA, 2016). In regard to seeking informed consent for classroom and large group counseling, as well as task/work groups, school counselors should inform parents or guardians about the nature and techniques that will be used in all of these educational opportunities, and parents/guardians should have the opportunity to opt their children out of participation if they desire. Here again, school counselors should be informed about their school policies relevant to these situations.

Of course, complexities sometimes make the informed consent process challenging. For example, if you intend to lead a small time-limited, supportive counseling group with students who are experiencing a parental divorce, it might be quite challenging to obtain parental or guardian permission because of custody issues. In cases where a legal guardian is not assigned or not involved, from which parent should you ask permission? Can the parents function cooperatively to grant permission that would be in their child's best interest? Are there good reasons for why seeking permission from one or the other is unwise? Or, what if a parent insists on having their child participate in a particular counseling group, but the child does not want to participate? An important variable in making these decisions has to do with the legal guardianship and custodial arrangements that are in place. The parent/guardian with legal custody typically has the right to provide permission for participation in counseling groups (but, of course, sometimes both parents may share legal custody of the child). Even in the process of contested custody, one or both of the parents or a separate legal guardian will have custody in the interim. Schools should have child guardianship and custody information, as these legal agreements also dictate permissions related to education records, emergency contacts, etc. Violations of these important parental (or guardian) rights could result in a student being withdrawn from participation in counseling services or, possibly, ethical and legal consequences for the counselor. We cite the *ASCA Ethical Standards for School Counselors*

(ASCA, 2016), the *ACA Code of Ethics and Standards of Practice* (ACA, 2014), and the *ASGW Best Practice Guidelines* (Thomas & Pender, 2007) as the ethical road maps for these decisions. School counselors should also engage in consultation and supervision practices to help them negotiate these and other complicated quandaries that may arise when trying to balance child- and school-specific needs and legal and ethical obligations.

Confidentiality

Confidentiality is a cornerstone of ethical counseling practice and maintaining confidentiality in regard to student disclosures is a fundamental aspect of the practice of counseling in schools, whether one is working with students individually or in a group (ACA, 2014; ASCA, 2016). The general rule concerning confidentiality is that counseling processes are confidential except in cases of potential harm to self or others. However, this is sometimes complicated in situations involving youth. As mentioned, parents are typically the legal guardians of children and adolescents, and they are the ones who (in most cases) provide consent for services. It makes sense that parents may sometimes want to know what is discussed between a counselor and their child in individual or group counseling sessions. When this happens, though, the dual needs of protecting student confidentiality

Image 1.7

and informing parents can be rather tricky (ASCA, 2016). Most counselors who work with youth try to negotiate the terms of confidentiality (with both the students/clients and their parents) at the start of their work together. They also try to align with the principles of respect, transparency, and ethical practice, sharing only what they have consent to share and only on a need-to-know basis. It is always a good idea for school counselors to seek supervision or consultation with other professional counselors when questions arise related to confidentiality.

The issue of sharing information with other professionals in the school (e.g., teachers, administrators, paraprofessionals, other therapists who work in the school) can also be challenging for group leaders who work in schools. School counselors often find themselves being asked questions that touch on confidential student issues in meetings and even sometimes in public spaces, such as lunchrooms, playgrounds, and school hallways. The general rule used by most school counselors is that information shared with other professionals should only include very general information; it should be limited to a brief as-needed professional exchange of information; and if information is shared, it should be communicated, of course, in a private setting. Otherwise, sharing confidential information must be preceded by parental consent and student assent (ACA, 2014; ASCA, 2016).

Having mentioned these challenges, we point out that maintaining confidentiality among group members is even more complicated. School counselors can never ensure complete confidentiality to group members because they are not able to control what children say and do outside of the group. Because of this, the *ASCA Ethical Standards for School Counselors* (ASCA, 2016), *ACA Code of Ethics and Standards of Practice* (ACA, 2014), and *ASGW Best Practice Guidelines* (Thomas & Pender, 2008) all recommend that group leaders be perfectly clear and culturally and developmentally sensitive about this risk to group members. That is, group participants need to know that what they say in a group can slip out of the group at any time. Ideally, group leaders and members should also develop a plan to address concerns that emerge from violation of group confidentiality by group members.

Discussions with students about these confidentiality caveats should also focus on the importance of respecting others and managing one's own personal boundaries concerning self-disclosure. These conversations should occur during the screening, informed consent, and group norming processes.

Reminders about confidentiality should also be given at critical times in the group. That is, if a leader has concerns about a potentially impactful or perhaps inappropriate self-disclosure, he should raise the issue of confidentiality again with the students in the group. At these times, it would be helpful to talk with the students (in developmentally appropriate language) about why confidentiality is so critical in this particular situation. Even in classroom psychoeducational groups, school counselors will likely need to help some students with decisions regarding self-disclosure and the kinds of boundaries they want to establish for personal sharing. Students should never be encouraged to share personal information that will later leave them feeling inappropriately vulnerable around their peers. The bottom line is that it is the executive function responsibility of the group leader to oversee group members' safety—regardless of group type—and this extends to monitoring the level and content of personal sharing in the group.

Mentioning confidentiality raises a final important point to address here: If a student expects that no one in the school will know that they are spending time with the school counselor—individually or in a group—that expectation is unrealistic. School counselors are typically located in office spaces that assure availability to all students in the school, and this means that almost anyone can see who is coming in and out of the counselors' offices. This is also true for students who need teacher consent to leave the classroom for a meeting with a counselor or to participate in a counseling group. It may be important for counselors to help some students find a way to articulate to their teachers or others about why they are spending time with the school counselor. An example of successful communication between Mrs. Ahadi, a eighth-grade science teacher, and Ms. Lebowitz, a middle school counselor, is outlined in Case Study 1.2.

CASE STUDY 1.2 Negotiating What to Say

Pavan is an eighth-grade student newly transferred from a school in another state. His science teacher, Mrs. Ahadi, had mentioned at an eighth-grade team meeting that she was worried that Pavan was making a poor adjustment to the new school. Others concurred, and Ms. Lebowitz, the school counselor, agreed that she would meet with Pavan and invite him to participate in a group for new students at the school.

When Ms. Lebowitz met with Pavan in a short screening and invitation session, she mentioned that Mrs. Ahadi had expressed concerns about how he was doing in class. Pavan seemed to appreciate Mrs. Ahadi's concern, and he told Ms. Lebowitz that he really liked Mrs. Ahadi, but he did not know how to tell her that he was having difficulties adjusting to the new state and school, as well as some family changes at home. Ms. Lebowitz agreed that it could be difficult to talk to teachers about difficult things, and she invited him to participate in the new student group, as there were likely other students who would like to discuss the topic of how to communicate with their teachers about difficulties. After gaining consent from Pavan's parents for him to participate in the group, and with Pavan's assent, he joined the group. Ms. Lebowitz asked Pavan for permission to allow her to mention to Mrs. Ahadi that he had accepted an invitation to participate in the group. Pavan told her that would be great.

The group entailed rich discussions among students lasting several sessions. The students also rehearsed how to approach teachers for help (this played out in a very funny role play among the group members). As a result of sharing these feelings and rehearsing how and what to share with his teachers, Mrs. Ahadi very willingly offered to help Pavan in whatever way she could.

However, the story continues. Mrs. Ahadi sought out Ms. Lebowitz in the hall one morning and asked—with good intention, as well as with some sense of urgency—"What exactly is going on with Pavan's family? How can a mother uproot such a sweet kid? How selfish and horrible divorce is—and ..."

Ms. Lebowitz listened and replied, "You really have such strong feelings about this and really care deeply for Pavan—and I know he appreciates your care. I'm so thankful that you raised your concern about Pavan with the team last month—that has really helped us figure out how to support him. Unfortunately, I'm not able to share any details about Pavan's home life, but I can tell you that things are becoming okay. It also is clear that Pavan seems to really value you and your class, and I think your relationship with him is helping him adjust—that is what he needs right now."

Fortunately, Mrs. Ahadi recognized the limits set by Ms. Lebowitz. "Okay, I understand," she said. She also continued to engage in a strong relationship with Pavan, and she continued to check in from time to time by asking if things were still okay and later noted that things seemed to be getting better.

Protection From Harm, Harm to Others, and Mandated Reporting

Protection from harm refers to the ethical and legal mandates that school counselors have to protect the safety of students who may present a threat to themselves or are potentially a victim of harm by others (ACA, 2014; ASCA, 2016). The words *may* and *potentially* are intentional here: these mandates dictate that counselors must act to protect children, even if there is uncertainty about actual harm. Counselors have an "obligation to act in the best interest of the client" (Wheeler & Bertram, 2012, p. 15) using a *standard of care* that is consistent with their level of training, skill, and the ethical practice of professional peers. When there are suspicions that a student is in danger of self-harm, a harm assessment must be conducted by the school counselor or another professional who is trained to conduct such an assessment. The mandate is clear: school counselors must act to protect the safety of their students, including being in contact with professionals and family members who are able to offer appropriate protection (ASCA, 2016).

In cases of *potential harm to others*, school counselors must follow school protocol, which will typically include an assessment conducted by a trained professional, procedures for contacting law enforcement authorities, and the duty to notify any identifiable potential victim of harm. These mandates concerning protection from harm (i.e., harm to self, harm by others, harm to others) refer to all of the children and adolescents that the school counselor is in contact with: students in the hallways and playgrounds, students they talk to individually, and students who are in their groups.

Mandated reporting is the duty-to-warn requirement that states school counselors and others working in schools have to inform appropriate authorities when they have suspicions that a child is a victim of abuse or neglect. Here "appropriate authorities" refers to state social service agency personnel who are in the position to receive such reports—typically those working in the child divisions of state departments of human services, as well as local state and federal law enforcement officers. Importantly, mandated reporting requirements are about *suspicions*, not certainties; it is up to the appointed child protective services authorities to investigate, substantiate, and, if substantiated, to take appropriate action on these reports. Specific reporting procedures vary by state, and school counselors should keep up to date with these legal state and federal mandates. There are legal consequences for mandated reporters who fail to report suspicions of abuse or neglect (Barnett & Johnson, 2015; Brown et al., 2008; Sommers-Flanagan & Sommers-Flanagan, 2007; Welfel et al., 2000), and failure to adhere to these legal mandates may be adjudicated in either state or federal courts. Again, this is relevant to students in any of the groups conducted by a school counselor, as well as any other youth that school counselors come in contact with.

Coordinating With School Personnel

We want to end this chapter with a few points regarding the implications of conducting groups in the unique setting of schools. Here we will discuss the importance of providing information about services offered to school personnel, as well as teachers. We will end with a brief discussion about physical space—where groups are conducted in schools—as counselors working in schools often work in shared spaces.

Information About Services

Education in schools happens as a result of coordinated efforts on the part of teachers, counselors, administrators, and a wide variety of staff. What one professional does affects and how others work. School administrators have the role of overseeing educational processes, as they are accountable for everything that happens within their school. They are expected to know about everything that is taking place under their supervision, and they often field questions from parents, district administrators, and, sometimes, school board members about activities and incidents that are happening in their school buildings. This accountability and need for informing others can put them in a weighty and untenable position if they are not aware of what their staff members are doing. It is important, then, for school counselors to keep their administrators informed about the various components of their work—very generally, especially if concerns arise.

Sometimes the content of school groups is subject to questioning from parents, guardians, teachers, and administrators; on occasion, they may wonder whether some topics really are school "business." We firmly believe that the litmus test to relevance is always found in the answer to this question: Does this group assist students in maximizing their chances for success in school? If this question is applied to, say, a counseling group for students whose parents are recently divorced and the goal of the group is to assist students in navigating such a difficult personal adjustment, then we believe that the group would probably be very appropriate—in fact ideal. Being clear about the focus of their interventions and the larger mission of their school counseling program helps counselors navigate important decisions regarding the services they offer to the youth and families in their school communities.

School counselors tend to use a variety of methods for informing the administration, as well as parents and guardians, about the work they are doing. These include phone or in-person conversations, newsletters, school websites, and other paper or electronic venues for nonconfidential updates, news briefs, and invitations. Please do not misunderstand this public communication as unethical—of course, that which is confidential must remain confidential. However, since school counselors are generally afforded much autonomy in regard to how they carry out the responsibilities of their work, people often do not see or understand it. We believe, as the ASCA model (ASCA, 2019) recommends, that good school counseling programs are inextricably linked to the overall vision and mission of their school communities and that transparency is a key to the kind of collaborative practice that is necessary for program success. Most experienced school counselors will submit an annual report to the school administrator and community that articulates the nature of individual and group counseling services offered through the year (respecting, of course, their ethical mandates to protect confidentiality), the number of students and families contacted, and an analysis of the effect of the school counseling program on the overall interpersonal and academic performance of students and the school.

Physical Space Considerations

The issue of physical space—where the group is held—is relevant to all group work. Ideally, counselors will seek spaces for their groups that are relatively comfortable, that maintain confidentiality (when this is important and relevant to members of a particular group), and that provide an adequate venue for the activities that will be used in the group. For example, some activities require space for movement, and others require big tables, computers, access to water, or other materials. Also, it is important to remember that some students work best in rooms that are relatively free of distractions, so ideally, the group space would also be one that will help students maintain focus. All of these considerations are relevant to groups with youth of all ages.

Group leaders who work in schools must take into consideration some of the constraints that are inherent to the school setting. One such constraint experienced by some school counselors is that they do not have adequate space in their offices to conduct groups. Many school counselors find that they must work in and around spaces provided by others—conference rooms, for example— and when they are conducting classroom groups, most counselors work directly in the students' classrooms. In these shared spaces, it is important, of course, that counselors respect their guest or cohabitation status. Being a guest or a cohabitant in spaces that ostensibly belong to others requires being vigilant that the room is clean and in order at the end of the group, that others' belongings are not disrupted, and that the room is given back to its other inhabitants promptly at the end of the allotted time. Following these simple "guest rules" will go a long way toward fostering collaborative relationships with other staff members in the school.

We also point out that some activities used in groups may have the potential to be noisy or otherwise distracting to the classrooms nearby. So school counselors may need to seek out creative space solutions or alternative planning for some of their group sessions. Sometimes, for example, counselors may decide to conduct a session outdoors when they are using activities that require a lot of space or that make a lot of noise. If this is the case, their planning should include ensuring that the outdoor space is really available and not disruptive to others in the building; they should have a "rainy day" alternative space; also, they will need to, of course, take into consideration any school policies related to taking students out of the building.

Reflection Questions

1. Sit for a moment and brainstorm all of the different groups you felt you belonged to through your education to this moment. Which would you categorize as psychoeducation, counseling, and task groups?
2. In this chapter, it was mentioned that group work in schools provides an opportunity to introduce students to other perspectives and other cultures (windows) and to offer opportunities for students to see themselves mirrored in strong and positive ways. It was also discussed that groups are an excellent opportunity for engaging in discussions about issues of marginalization, power, and privilege. What pre-group planning will be necessary to carry out these goals so that they are successfully addressed in a (or a variety of different) group(s)?
3. How might you intervene in a group if it is discovered that one of the children or adolescent members of the group broke confidentiality?

CHAPTER TWO

Learning Theories for Group Work Planning

Introduction

Some may argue that "grand theories" of learning or epistemologies of education are far removed from the practice of classroom teaching. This is sometimes referred to as the "theory-practice gap" (Runesson, 2015, p. 186). Runesson, however, argued that theoretical knowledge (knowledge acquired from scholarship and education) offers "critical lenses" (p. 191) for synthesizing practical and formal knowledge around the practice of teaching. More simply stated, theory has the potential to deepen teachers' knowledge and practice in the classroom (Thorsten, 2015). The importance of using theories to inform practice is also highlighted in the profession of school counseling where counselors are called upon to use human development and learning theories and evidence-based practice to guide their work in supporting student success and achievement (ASCA, 2019).

It was John Locke who first articulated the novel idea (at the time) that infant minds are like blank slates ready to be filled or formed by their experiences in the world (Kirylo, 2016). While this suggests a somewhat passive idea about how young children learn, Locke's ideas called attention to the importance of actively creating learning environments to promote development. In this chapter, we discuss some of the theories that inform the active work of teachers and group leaders in structuring learning environments that foster growth and learning. This review of theory is complemented by the group work theories outlined in Chapter 3. Together, these theories offer a rich array of ideas that are the foundation of group work planning and group management. We end the chapter with Case study 2.1, which includes application questions for you to think about the ways in which these various theories might explain and inform intervention in a school group.

Finally, we would be remiss if we did not point out that most learning theories that inform contemporary teaching and group work practice were written from a Western, white, male-dominant cultural perspective. In addition, most of the examples originally referenced within these theories arose within a gender binary perspective; they included few, if any, other diversity and demographic factors. This does not mean that these theories are not useful when one is working with a diverse population of students. But it is critical that school counselors are aware of the limited worldview and perspective of the authors of these influential theories and to take that into consideration while reviewing this literature. Most importantly, school counselors must always consider the diversity of the populations they serve in their schools and strive to incorporate relevant sociocultural perspectives into their group plans and interventions.

Behavioral Theories

Behavioral theories are based on the idea that human behavior is shaped by stimuli in the environment, and they focus on environmental conditions that promote and sustain observable behavior

(Guney & Al, 2012). Behaviorism emerged as a prominent 20th-century theory of learning in response to growing criticism that preceding theories of development needed a more scientific base (Bigge & Shermis, 1999), thus the razor-sharp focus in behavioral theories on observable behavior. When thinking about the two major branches of behaviorism described here, then, it may be helpful to remember that behavioral change is equated with learning. The aim of behavioral interventions is to change behavior, and that change represents a new learned behavior.

Image 2.1

Classical Conditioning

Ivan Pavlov's laboratory experiments with dogs in the early 1900s gave rise to the behavioral concept of *classical conditioning* (Kirylo, 2016). These experiments were then applied to human functioning by John Watson in what became known as the "Little Albert" experiments (Kirylo, 2016; Miller, 2002). The fundamental idea of classical conditioning is that learning begins with a biologically programed stimulus-response reflex system, which can be shaped through a conditioning process (Boyd & Bee, 2015). In Watson's experimental laboratory, a loud noise was paired with exposure to a gentle rat that a little boy named Albert enjoyed playing with. The result was that Watson was able to condition Albert to have a fear response associated with rats, and thus he no longer wanted to play with them. This human example of classical conditioning promoted the idea that individuals learn through establishing associations between various external events or stimuli (Berk, 2014; Miller, 2002). For example, a teacher walks into her classroom and rings a bell that is sitting on her desk. This is a cue, telling students to find their seats and be ready for instruction. The students in this classroom have been conditioned to associate the bell with the start of class. In a counseling group, students feel listened to and cared for. This experience, even if not intentionally designed to do so, conditions these students to feel comfortable with the school counselor and, potentially, any future invitations to participate in a counseling group with that school counselor.

Operant Conditioning

Skinner's concept of *operant conditioning* also has implications on group work practices. He called attention to the ways in which learning happens as a result of consequences. Here the idea is that what happens after a particular behavior is enacted (i.e., the consequence) determines if that behavior is likely to occur again (Berk, 2014). Examples of consequences are when a child is given an allowance for cleaning their room, a student studies hard and passes their driving license test, and a teen comes in after curfew and is not allowed to go out the following night. All of these consequences are designed to shape particular behaviors.

Reinforcers and punishers are two major types of consequences that shape behavior—these occur in classrooms and groups, as well as naturally in the environment. A *reinforcement* is something that follows a behavior and causes that behavior to continue or to be repeated; a *punishment* follows a behavior and causes it to cease (Boyd & Bee, 2015; Kirylo, 2016). For example, if a child does well on an exam and receives their paper back with a 100% and "Good Job!!!" written on it, that feedback is intended to reinforce the desired behavior of working hard or completing the task correctly. If a child is swatted for reaching for a cupcake off a table, their reaching behavior is punished by the swatting (an unpleasant experience), which is intended to teach the child not to take things without asking. In the first example, learning to study and do well is reinforced by good grades. In the second, learning not to take something without permission is promoted through the consequence of a punishment. Skinner's ideas were initially articulated with the goal of determining environmental events that control behavior and to shift conversations about learning to concrete observable events and situations (Mowrer & Klein, 1989).

While there is considerable debate about the appropriateness of using rewards and punishments to promote learning, what some refer to as the incentivization of learning (Kirylo, 2016), it is easy to see that consequences that shape our behaviors occur naturally in our everyday lives. For example, we may get uncomfortably wet when we go out in a heavy rainstorm, and from this, we learn to bring an umbrella the next time we go out in the rain. A child puts a handful of dirt in their mouth and quickly spits it out because it does not taste good, thus learning not to eat dirt. If a child learns to share or is able to regulate their impulses, the natural consequence is that other children will reinforce these behaviors through the extension of friendship. (Of course, we know that friendships are based on numerous other variables as well, but social rewards are an important shaping influence in how children make and keep friends.) All of these consequences—those that occur without intentional human intervention—are called *natural consequences*.

In behavioral terminology, a *logical consequence* is something that is implemented by an adult, teacher, or someone else for the purpose of shaping a particular behavior; it is a planned consequence. For example, I might plan to treat myself to a meal in a favorite restaurant at the end of a long week of work. In schools, a teacher might take their students out for recess after their work is completed. The point here is that these consequences are imposed by someone; they don't just happen. The *responsive classroom* model (Three Types of Logical Consequences, 2011; for more on the responsive classroom model, see Charney, 1991; Center for Responsive Schools, https://www.crslearn.org/history/; Responsive Classroom, https://www.responsiveclassroom.org/about/) recommends using the following three types of logical consequences in response to student misbehavior in a classroom: (1) "You break it, you fix it": The student must take responsibility for fixing a problem that they have created. (2) A loss of privileges: This refers to the child being prohibited from participating in a particular activity or using a particular material for a limited period of time. (3) Positive time out: Here the recommendation is to move a misbehaving child away from a situation so as to offer them time to calm down and regain self-control. These suggestions are discussed in more detail in Chapter 9.

Another common application of operant behavioral principles that we often see in schools is the offering of praise, attention, and material rewards (such as stickers and free time) to reinforce students' on-task behaviors. These are also discussed in Chapter 9. The *Positive Behavioral Interventions and Supports* (PBIS; for more on PBIS, see Goodman-Scott et al., 2018; OSEP Technical Assistance Center on Positive Behavioral Interventions and Supports, 2017; Ryoo et al., 2017) framework, commonly implemented in K–12 schools across the United States, is a school-wide approach to the prevention of and intervention in challenging student behaviors that is based, in part, on behavioral principles. PBIS promotes the use of prompting, modeling, practicing, encouraging, and rewarding positive behavior (OSEP Technical Assistance Center on Positive Behavioral Interventions and Supports, 2017). Research suggests that PBIS is effective in reducing behavioral challenges in schools, although evidence on its positive effect on student achievement is still inconclusive (Ryoo et al., 2017). Research also shows an increasing need for PBIS programs to be culturally responsive in schools that serve diverse populations (Banks & Obiakor, 2015).

We focus our attention on these programs and practices to point out that behavioral principles, particularly operant conditioning practices, are ubiquitous in schools. Understanding the ways in which consequences, particularly reinforcements, can be used in group work can help group leaders use them effectively to promote student learning in their groups. Again, we will talk more in Chapters 8 and 9 about how a variety of consequences can be used by group leaders to shape student behaviors and address challenges that may emerge in a group.

Social Learning Theory

Social learning theory focuses on influences on behavior that emerge from observational principles. It originally came from the work of Albert Bandura and his colleague, Richard Walters, who initially studied adolescents who were tasked with observing a model demonstrating particular behaviors. They found

that the adolescents in their study acted aggressively toward others if they witnessed role models behaving aggressively. This was even if the teens were not directly reinforced for the aggressive behavior (Bandura & Walters, 1959/1980; Bandura et al., 1961). From this work emerged decades of study and theory—largely based on the thinking of Bandura—about how modeling, observational learning, reinforcement, and motivation influence behavior and learning processes (Bergen, 2008). Initially called social learning theory, Bandura began to refer to this theory as *social-cognitive theory* (Bergen, 2008).

Observational Learning

As mentioned, Bandura and Walter's study of observational learning revealed that role models can be influential in teaching new behaviors (Bandura & Walters, 1959/1980). They found that *attention*, *retention*, *motor reproduction*, and *reinforcement processes* are key factors involved in imitation learning processes (Bandura, 1971, 1986). We will briefly review each of these here.

First, of course, one must *attend* to a role model for imitation to occur. Here Bandura indicated that certain characteristics of a role model may have particular salience in capturing the attention of an observer and thus influence whether the modeled behavior is repeated. For example, Bandura suggested that perceptions of social capital, desirability, or perceived prestige of a role model prompts imitation (Bandura, 1971, 1986). If a role model is popular or perceived to be "cool," for example, their behavior is more likely to be repeated by the observer. In fact, Bandura noted that "the effect of a model's prestige tends to generalize from one area of behavior to another and even to unfamiliar models who share characteristics with known reward-producers" (Bandura, 1971, p. 55). So, children are likely to imitate a wide range of behaviors modeled by a prestigious role model, and they are also likely to imitate the behaviors of models who look like or otherwise appear to be similar to a prestigious role model. We might speculate that this principle is in action in pop culture where we are witness to the proliferation of adopted codes of dress and performance (by children, teens, and adults) that are aligned with the appearance and behaviors of desirable or prestigious others. Bandura pointed out that in cases where children are not sure about the extent to which they will receive rewards and punishments for performing a particular behavior, they often rely on these perceived indicators of a model's status reflected in appearance and linguistic style, as well as age, gender, perceived likability, competence, and other markers of status (Bandura, 1971).

According to Bandura (1986), when a role model has the social power to *control and dispense rewards* to others, their actions will also be highly influential. That is, if a child knows that the role model can and may reward or punish them for imitating a particular behavior, the anticipation of this consequence will influence the likelihood that that child will imitate the modeled behavior. While *perceived similarity*, particularly around gender, also influences imitation, Bandura (1986) clarified that power inversions (i.e., the expectation that the role model will dispense rewards or punishments for imitating a particular behavior) override the influence of gender (or other kinds of perceived similarities). Bandura noted that the *expectation of a reward or punishment* for performing a modeled behavior is the most significant influence affecting imitation (Bandura, 1971). That is, Bandura found that modeled behaviors are replicated when the observer notices that the role model is rewarded for performing a particular behavior; they are less likely to be imitated if the role model is punished. This is because the observer anticipates receiving similar rewards or punishments related to the modeled behavior. In fact, these anticipated consequences are the most influential in determining if a modeled behavior will be replicated by an observer. Bandura used the term *vicarious reinforcement* in reference to when one's behavior is changed as the result of witnessing a model's actions being rewarded or punished (Bandura, 1971).

The second process Bandura identified in regard to the performance of imitated behavior is *retention* (Bandura, 1971, 1986). This refers to how well an individual is able to encode and retain in memory a modeled behavior. *Motor reproduction*, the ability of an individual to recall and motorically reproduce a modeled behavior, is the third process influencing whether a particular behavior will be imitated (Bandura, 1971, 1986). The fourth and final process is the *observational reinforcement process* (Bandura, 1971, 1986). This final characteristic goes back to the earlier point that imitation decision making is influenced by perceived potential consequences for exhibiting a particular behavior. If a child thinks that a particular behavior will be reinforced, they are more likely to imitate it than if they expect punishment.

As these processes suggest, *interpretation* and *motivation* are important variables in imitation performance decision making. Bandura indicated that the motivation to perform a modeled behavior is based on cognitive representation processes—the ability to think about or anticipate a consequence, goal setting, or self-evaluation (Bandura, 1977, 1986). Bandura believed that individuals evaluate themselves against a set of standards, and the belief that they can achieve those standards (having a positive outcome expectancy) leads to performance (Bandura, 1977); this is something we will get to shortly in our discussion about self-efficacy. But first, we pause here to offer the point that a major reason why school counselors conduct groups is to achieve academic, social, and emotional learning goals and to provide opportunities for students to learn from one another. Understanding the extent to which peers influence others based on these social learning principles compels group leaders to think carefully about group membership selection, which we will discuss in Chapter 4, and ways in which they can use group process dynamics to promote learning.

Self-Efficacy

Another important contribution from Bandura comes from his interest in the ways in which our beliefs in our abilities to accomplish something affect how we think, feel, and act (Bandura, 1977, 1986). Bandura used the term *self-efficacy* in reference to a person's ideas about their ability to carry out a particular action. He found that a person's ideas about their ability to accomplish a particular action affect whether they will even attempt the action in the first place.

Bandura (1977, 1989) identified these sources of efficacy beliefs: (1) *performance accomplishments* or *direct mastery experiences*: having direct experience in successfully performing a task encourages us to believe that we can perform that task in the future; (2) *vicarious* or *observational experience*: seeing someone we identify with persistently and successfully perform a particular task helps us believe that we can also perform that task; (3) *verbal* or *social persuasion*: when people who are important to us articulate their confidence in our abilities to perform a particular task, we believe them; and (4) *physiological* or *bodily and somatic states*: our emotional processes, such as depression, stress, tension, or happiness, affect our efficacy beliefs. Because these self-efficacy principles are so important to social learning and have implications on how group leaders can promote learning in groups, we have highlighted them in Figure 2.1.

Bandura and subsequent researchers suggested that self-efficacy, particularly academic self-efficacy, predicts academic and school success (e.g., see Bandura, 1993; Weiser & Riggio, 2010). Further elucidating this work, Weiser and Riggio (2010) highlighted these important classroom interventions, which support the development of academic self-efficacy: observations of adults articulating cognitive strategies while performing academic tasks (i.e., self-talk or self-coaching), offering students regular performance feedback, and attributing feedback and matching success to students' efforts rather than factors such as being smart. All of these strategies can, of course, be used in most groups to encourage the development of domain-specific (i.e., self-efficacy in the specific area that is the focus of learning in the group) self-efficacy.

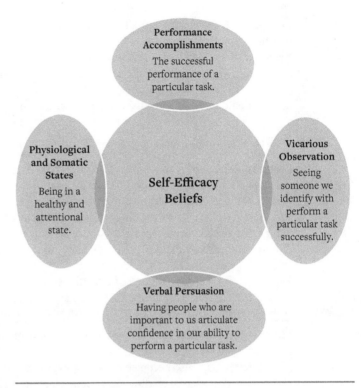

FIGURE 2.1 Sources of Self-Efficacy Beliefs

Cognitive and Constructivist Theories of Learning

Cognitive theories of development further expand our understandings of learning to an examination of the ways in which mental processes are involved in thinking and learning. In cognitive and constructivist theories, children are positioned as actively engaged in their environment, and learning is viewed as an internal process that involves symbolic mental constructs that are organized and processed within the mind (Guney & Al, 2012). These theories highlight the important role of interpretation and reflection in the learning process; they propose that new learning is built on how we make sense of existing knowledge and experiences. Within this category, we will discuss the work of Piaget, Vygotsky, and Bruner.

Piaget

Swiss psychologist Jean Piaget made an extensive impact on the ways in which we have come to understand and continue to think about cognitive development and teaching processes (Elkind,

1981; Singer & Revenson, 1997). Piaget believed wholeheartedly that children are actively engaged in learning (Smidt, 2011) and that "much of our knowledge about reality comes to us ... from within by the force of our own logic" (Elkind, 1981, p. 19). His descriptions of cognitive development offered an outward-to-inward model of learning; in this model, internal cognitive thinking processes are stimulated by experiences in the environment. These dual ideas are evident in his stages of cognitive development, as well as his discussions about cognitive schemas—both described next.

Stages of Cognitive Development

Piaget is perhaps best remembered for his stage model of cognitive development (i.e., *sensorimotor*, *preoperational*, *concrete*, and *formal observation* stages of development), which are described in Table 2.1. Piaget's ideas outlined in this model suggest that children engage in somewhat universal and characteristic patterns of interactions and attempts to control objects and others in the environment using the cognitive structures (these are sometimes referred to as schemas or mental models) that are presently available to them (Elkind, 1981). As children use these cognitive structures and

TABLE 2.1 Piaget's Stages of Cognitive Development

Sensorimotor (Infancy to Early Toddlerhood [Birth to 2 Years Old])

- Cognitive development initiates with a refinement of reflexive infant motor behaviors, such as tasting and reaching.
- Motor activity also becomes a basis for exploration/learning.
- Knowledge is based on direct experiences and interactions with objects and individuals in the immediate environment and trial and error experimentation.
- Object permanence develops toward the end of this stage (children learn that objects have their own existence).

Preoperational (Toddler/Early Childhood [2–7 Years Old])

- Use of symbolic representation through language—a child is able to represent ideas through mental images and symbols that are based on their own perceptions.
- Memory processes augment new cognitive functioning abilities.
- Egocentric thinking dominates cognitive processes (difficulty taking the viewpoint of others).

Concrete Operations (Middle Childhood [7–11 Years Old])

- Uses internal thought processes/mental operations (interiorized action—action performed in the mind).
- Understands conservation processes (substances remain the same despite appearance changes) and reversibility (understands that something can be added or subtracted).
- Able to classify objects by a particular characteristic and sequence objects in hierarchies.

Formal Operations (Early to Mid-Adolescence [11–16 Years Old])

- Uses abstract concepts and thinking processes (can think into the future and imagine the hypothetical).
- Uses logic to test hypotheses, engage in deductive reasoning, consider multiple perspectives, or solutions to problems.
- Thinking processes are flexible, rational, and systematic.
- This period marks the beginning of the development of an inner value system and engagement in moral judgment.

Adapted from Singer, D. G., & Revenson, T. A. (1997). A Piaget primer. How a child thinks. International Universities Press.

engage in new experiences, their cognitive capacities grow and change, thus prompting movement into stages of more advanced understandings and thinking abilities. This happens, according to Piaget, because new information and experiences cause existing cognitive schemes to adapt and change in reciprocal processes of *accommodation* and *assimilation*, eventually leading to new cognitive schemes (Bergen, 2008; Fox & Riconscente, 2008; Kirylo, 2016).

We will examine Piaget's important ideas about schemas in more depth next, but first, we highlight two important points regarding the relevance of Piaget's stage model of cognitive development to the work of school counselors and group leaders working with youth. First, as mentioned, Piaget highlighted the ways in which knowledge develops through internal thinking processes stimulated through engagement in the environment. This is particularly important for school counselors who are likely to be working with children who have experienced developmental trauma and adverse childhood experiences. Although Piaget's stages of cognitive development suggest that cognitive development is a somewhat uniform and universal process, we now know that when children's development is interrupted by experiences of trauma or when their experiences in the world are truncated by adverse living conditions, their cognitive development is disrupted. So, it is important for school counselors to remember that these experiences will likely affect children's emotional and cognitive development and functioning (for more on this, see Baron-Cohen, 2011; Cook et al., 2005; Johnson, 2005; Perry & Szalavitz, 2006; Siegel, 2012). This calls for counselors and group leaders to be attentive to the unique and varied experiences of the children in their groups and to understand how these experiences may affect their participation and performance in classrooms and school groups.

Second, Piaget's claims about universal stages of cognitive development, many argue, do not adequately account for the multiple social-cultural factors that shape children's cognitive processes (Arnett & Tanner, 2009). Children come to school with a huge variety of cultural and social experiences; we should be aware that assuming that there is a uniform pathway to cognitive development can cause us to make assumptions about children's abilities and lead to creating educational experiences that are not appropriate for some group members.

These points do not negate the important contributions of Piaget's thinking about stages of cognitive development, but they do remind us to be aware of the limitations of using this (and any) single model of understanding to frame the work we do with youth in schools.

Schema and Schema Adaptation

Perhaps most significant to our thinking about group work and learning processes is Piaget's description of the internal component of cognition as a mental structure that is capable of generalization and transfer of knowledge from one concept and experience to another (Elkind, 1981). This structure, which he referred to as a *scheme*, *schema*, or in plural form, *schemata*, might best be thought of as an organizing mental process that changes over time based on biological maturation and experience (Bergen, 2008; Boyd & Bee, 2015). Singer and Revenson (1997) described Piaget's schema as "a simple mental image or pattern of action, a form of organizing information that a person uses to interpret the things she sees, hears, smells, and touches" (p. 17). They offer the following examples of a schema: the smelling of a cup of hot cocoa conjures the image and concept of cocoa, thus tapping into a cocoa schema, and the schema of a "dog" that includes an image of a four-legged animal that wags its tail.

Piaget (1972) suggested that understandings develop through a process of schema adaptation (Bergen, 2008; Elkind, 1981; Singer & Revenson, 1997; Smidt, 2011). According to Smidt (2011), Piaget thought *adaptation* to be the most important principle of human functioning. Adaptation includes the two processes of assimilation and accommodation—processes that occur as children explore their environment. *Assimilation* refers to the mental processes that occur when a new object is encountered and incorporated into an existing schema. For example, if a child is introduced to a new food for breakfast, the name and flavors of this new food become assimilated into their existing understanding or schema of breakfast food. *Accommodation* occurs when a new encounter in the environment cannot be incorporated into an existing schema and thus causes the schema to change. An example of accommodation used by Bergen (2008) is when a baby uses a sucking schema to think about how to drink from a cup for the first time. The sucking schema, of course, is the tried and true understanding of how to feed, based on their experiences of breast or bottle-feeding. But when encountering a cup (instead of a nipple), the baby finds this understanding of feeding to be unsuccessful. This means that their feeding schema must adapt to accommodate this new require- ment of drinking rather than sucking.

Equilibrium (Bergen, 2008; Elkind, 1981; Singer & Revenson, 1997; Smidt, 2011) is the term Piaget used for the higher order thinking that governs the complex interplay of the assimilation and accom- modation processes leading to expanded forms of thought (Piaget, 1972). This underscores Piaget's point that knowledge is constructed from interaction in the physical world through the manipulation of objects and making comparisons between and among objects and ideas, and it is trans- mitted from others while engaged in the social environment (Bergen, 2008).

We highlight these processes here as they offer important insights into how group leaders can create productive learning environments for youth in their groups. Building on what children know, finding creative ways for them to expand their existing understandings, and offering them the opportunity to engage in their material and social environments are clearly learning tools that are applicable to group work. These ideas are captured in our discussions on group planning in Chapter 6.

Development Through Play

Piaget proposed that children use social language and play for assimilation and accommodation thinking processes (Bergen, 2008). That is, when engaged in social interactions and in play, children are busy relating their new experiences to an existing cognitive schema, and they are also changing these schemata as new information enters into their world. In very young childhood, Piaget proposed, children engage largely in *imitation* play (Singer & Revenson, 1997), which is an accommodation process—children are learning from observing others. From about 6 months to 3 years of age, Piaget noticed that children engage in what he referred to as *practice* or *mastery play* (Bergen, 2008; Singer & Revenson, 1997). Here they repeat similar play actions with gradual elaboration each time. This kind of play reflects the internal processes of cognitive accommodation and adaptation.

During this time, children also begin to engage in *parallel play*—they largely play by them- selves while in the company of other children who are similarly playing by themselves (Singer & Revenson, 1997). So, while they seem to enjoy the company of other children, this experience ends at any real social engagement. Yet the cognitive processes of schema accommodation and adaptation are at work. From about 2 to 5 years of age, parallel play slowly morphs into increasing social engagement and includes more complex symbolic play scenarios (Bergen, 2008; Singer & Revenson, 1997). In this stage of *symbolic play*, children engage in "role and perspective taking, social comparison, language narration, and social script knowledge" (Bergen, 2008, p. 101). Through symbolic play, children build increasingly elaborate play scenes and are involved in activities that rely on the cognitive representation of abstract objects and ideas. They begin to imagine symbols or images as representations for real people, events, or objects. For example, a doll is a friend, a stick is a gun. Underscored in these observations about children's play is Piaget's point that play is an important component of children's cognitive, emotional, and social development (Singer & Revenson, 1997).

Application of Piaget in Child Development and Education

There is an extensive application of Piaget's cognitive learning theories in contemporary teaching practices (Bergin, 2008). For example, in education circles, Piaget's ideas have influenced classroom practices of engaging children to be active participants in constructing knowledge. They have taught teachers to focus on stages of cognitive capacity, to design instruction at developmentally appropriate cognitive reasoning levels, and to structure learning opportunities to scaffold assimilation and accommodation learning processes. In short, Piaget's work has encouraged educators to think about the importance of matching curricular materials to the cognitive abilities of children in different stages of development (Elkind, 1981) and to create learning activities and environments where children are tasked to link new information to the knowledge they already have (Kirylo, 2016). We underscore here the importance of exposing children to a variety of cultures in these learning processes. For example, using books with characters of different racial and ethnic identities, dolls of different colors and genders, toys that represent different environmental contexts (e.g., tractors, snowplows, race cars, bicycles) enables children to adapt and accommodate their existing concepts of race and ethnicity, as well as environments, into more complex and nuanced concepts.

Vygotsky

Lev Vygotsky, a Soviet educator and psychologist working in the early 1900s, was the architect of what is sometimes called the *sociocultural theory of learning*. He believed that human behavior and mental processes are inseparable from their cultural contexts (Emihovich & Lima, 1995; Wertsch, 1985), that "the development of mind is inextricably linked to the social world" (Emihovich & Lima, 1995, p. 376). Vygotsky highlighted two important ways in which knowledge is socially constructed. First, he pointed out that psychological processes (i.e., cognitive processes) embody cultural artifacts (Bergen, 2008). By this he meant that thinking emerges from everyday engagement in social- and/or cultural-specific encounters and practices, objects, symbols, languages, beliefs, and values. These social and cultural artifacts, he believed, are the organizing processes for the development of mental structures. Second, Vygotsky believed that cognitive processes develop through children's social engagement with peers, parents, and other adults most directly in their social environments (Bergen, 2008).

Vygotsky's ideology about the dynamic connections between social engagement and internal cognitive processes, however, "does not simply assert that mental functioning in the individual somehow emerges out of participation in social life" (Wertsch & Toma, 1995, p. 162). Vygotsky was also very much interested in the ways in which the higher level cognitive processes of attention, memory, perception, and thinking moved from socially influenced to internally regulated thinking processes (Wertsch, 1985). For him, language is the primary vehicle for all of this complex mental functioning. In fact, Vygotsky saw the processes of thought and language "developmentally woven together" (John-Steiner, 2007, p. 137). This point is particularly critical to school counselors working with students who speak multiple languages and for

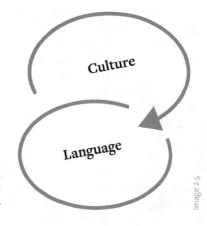

Image 2.5

whom English might not be their primary language. We will elaborate on these language-thought connections a bit more here.

Language Use and Metacognition

According to Vygotsky, this interwoven process of thought and language begins with prelingual (i.e., nonverbal) social exploration (John-Steiner, 2007). From infancy up to about 2 years of life, Vygotsky pointed out that communication occurs largely through crying, laughing, and social contact. But as children begin to use language socially, and especially to express their needs, Vygotsky noticed that they also begin to use language to plan their actions and describe their experiences. Communication in this period of development also becomes internalized; this is what Vygotsky referred to as *inner speech* (John-Steiner, 2007; Wertsch & Toma, 1995). Inner speech is an auditory self-coaching mechanism that helps children approach challenges, and it becomes more evident as children enter school, where they use it for structuring their engagement in activities. Vygotsky's concept of inner speech is described as a largely *egocentric* form of speech and is qualitatively different than the *social speech* that children use (at the same time) for interpersonal engagement and communication (Wertsch, 1985). Vygotsky proposed that inner speech guides increasingly complex metacognition and self-regulation of cognitive abilities, creating a seamless "ingrowth" (Bergen, 2008, p 108) of conceptual thinking. Although Vygotsky did not use the term *metacognition*, this is a contemporary expression for this kind of coaching speech.

Vygotsky argued that the process of cognitive complexity is a long process of internalization of language that is scaffolded by adults and others (including parents, teachers, or a more competent peer) in a child's environment (John-Steiner, 2007). This idea of *scaffolding* plays a key role in Vygotsky's ideas about teaching and learning. As we will discuss later in Chapter 6, scaffolding student engagement in learning, including engagement in group process dynamics, is a critical task of group leaders. The important point here is that speech is not only used for social functioning; it is also a part of our thinking processes (Fox & Riconscente, 2008; John-Steiner, 2007; Kirylo, 2016). Vygotsky's attention to inner speech and the role of language in thought processes calls our attention to the important ways in which group leaders can promote learning by encouraging social engagement among group members *and* by scaffolding tasks so that students can learn to self-coach through inner speech processes.

Zone of Proximal Development

Key to the idea of scaffolding is Vygotsky's notion of the *zone of proximal development* (ZPD). This concept is used extensively by educators across a wide variety of disciplines. The ZPD refers to the distance between one's actual developmental or knowledge level and one's potential that is realizable under the guidance of knowledgeable peers or adults (Bergen, 2008; Bigge & Shermis, 1999; Douthit, 2008; Kirylo, 2016). Here the idea is that teachers and other capable adults can promote increasing levels of cognitive complexity by planning educational practices and activities that are at a level just beyond what a child currently knows and is able to do but not so complicated that the challenge is inhibiting. Wertsch (1985) and Hedegaard (2005) suggested that the ZPD represents Vygotsky's most concrete ideas related to the interrelatedness of social and intrapersonal functioning. We get back to this idea in Chapter 6, where we discuss planning group strategies and, again, in Chapter 8 during our discussion of working within the *growth zone*.

Bruner

Jerome Bruner, referred to as a "contemporary cognitive interactionist learning and developmental psychologist" by Bigge and Shermis (1999, p. 133), also had an important influence on the field of learning theories. Bruner conceptualized learning as a transformational process where

new information results from a refinement of previous knowledge. Like Piaget, knowledge is constructed
through a process of relating new information to previously acquired understandings or frames of reference
(Bigge & Shermis, 1999). "Mental growth is not a gradual
accretion, either of associations or of stimulus-response
connections," Bruner (1966) asserted, "it appears to
be much more like a staircase with rather sharp risers,
more of a matter of spurts and rests" (p. 27).

Bruner expanded upon Piaget's concept of symbolic
thought, which, as you recall, refers to the ability to use
symbols or internal images to represent objects, people,
and events (Bergen, 2008). While not endorsing the
idea that children have different modes of thought at

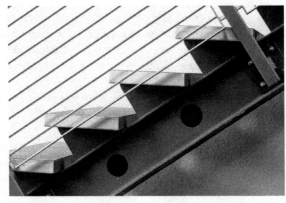

Image 2.6

different ages or levels of development, Bruner identified three modes of representational thinking
to describe how information is processed—how it is coded and stored in memory—for concept
understanding or meaning making (Bruner, 1966). The first of these is what he referred to as *enactive* representational processes. This mode focuses on the development of understanding through
action or doing. Enactive representation is very evident in the ways in which children learn about
the world through manipulating objects in their environment—largely in play (Bruner, 1966; Smidt,
2011). Bruner described play as a "means of improving intellect" (Bruner, 1983, p. 63). While this is
the primary mode of meaning making used by infants and preverbal children, we also see children
of all ages (and even adults) use action and performance to encode tasks into memory for learning
(Bruner, 1966). Because action and doing are such critical components of thought development for
children, many counselors use the medium of play for therapeutic goals in their work with children.
Along these lines, in Chapter 6, we emphasize the use of activities in group work with youth in schools.

Iconic representation is a second mode of thought identified by Bruner (1966). It refers to the use
of mental images for cognitive representation and meaning-making processes (Bruner, 1966; Smidt,
2011). Here Bruner was referring to the visual storage of information; the formation of a mental picture
of an object, person, or idea in our minds. For example, we visualize a black cat that looks exactly
like the cat we have at home when we think of the concept of a cat. As this example illustrates, this
type of visual representation can be very concrete and specific to one's own personal experience.

The final mode of concept representation identified by Bruner is *symbolic representation* (Bruner,
1966). Here Bruner points to the ways in which we are able to use words and language to represent
objects and people in the process of concept formation. For example, we know what cold means even
without having to visualize a cold snowy mountain. We also understand the symbolic meaning of
cold when it is used to describe a person; we may think of a "cold person" as someone who is a little
distant or nonresponsive to our gestures of friendship, for example. Symbolic representation is a
more abstract and language-dependent mode of thinking that requires the use of codes and symbols
for concept representation. Bruner suggested that symbolic representation helps us evaluate, make
judgments, and engage in critical thinking (Bruner, 1966; Smidt, 2011).

As is evident in these descriptions of modes of representational thinking, a central point for
Bruner was that symbolic systems used to construct meaning are "deeply entrenched in culture
and language" (Bruner, 1990, p. 11). Like Vygotsky, Bruner saw culture, language, and cognitive
meaning-making processes as intertwined. He said, "Human beings do not terminate at their own
skins; they are expressions of a culture" (Bruner, 1990, p. 12).

In summary, a major contribution to our understandings of cognitive development from Bruner
is his attention to meaning-making processes. Bruner proposed that people are interpretive beings—
always working to make sense of their experiences (Bruner, 1990) in a process of "negotiating and
renegotiating meanings" (p. 67) within a cultural context. Bruner described this process of meaning making to be "one of the crowning achievements of human development in the ontogenetic,

cultural, and phylogenetic sense of that expression" (Bruner, 1990, p. 67). For the purposes of this text, which focuses on group work in schools, the connection is obvious. Helping children engage with one another in the construction of meaning is a critical instructional process that is used in group work. We will return to this idea of meaning making in Chapter 6.

CASE STUDY 2.1

A new student has just been enrolled in your school's fourth-grade class. The student, Joshua, communicates through American Sign Language (ASL), as he has significant hearing impairment. Your school has invested in an interpreter service agency to support Joshua's integration and success in your school. The classroom teacher, Mr. Patel, has sought consultation with you, the school counselor, because of certain emerging concerns in the classroom. Despite multiple efforts to connect Joshua with the rest of the class, a number of the children in the classroom appear to avoid communication and do not play with Joshua. This pattern of exclusionary behavior was also been noticed by a couple of the ASL interpreters.

Using our discussions of behavioral theory, social learning theory, and the cognitive and constructivist theories of learning covered in this chapter, how might you conceptualize what's going on in the classroom from each individual theory? What social-cultural factors would you need to pay attention to in order to respond effectively to the emerging group concerns? Using concepts from each of these theories, what kind of interventions might be suitable as group interventions to address the class's group dynamic effectively? In what ways are these three theories effective, and in what ways might they be limited in their ability to aid in an effective response from you and Mr. Patel regarding the concerns in this classroom?

Reflection Questions

1. Consider the different factors you would need to take into account if you were running a psychoeducational group in a classroom where a third of the children speak multiple languages and English, the language of instruction at your school, is not their primary language. Which theory would guide your conceptualization of the group and which factors mentioned in this chapter would influence your choice of interventions?

2. In this chapter, it is mentioned that most of the learning theories discussed (and that inform U.S. contemporary educational thought) were written from a Western, White male dominant-culture perspective and that most of the examples referenced within these theories include few diversity and demographic identity factors. What demographic factors should you take into consideration when planning your group, especially when using one of these theories?

3. How might you approach a group with children of varied functioning in terms of cognitive complexity?

CHAPTER THREE

Group Work and Leadership Theories

Introduction

Next to the learning theories described in Chapter 2 that are used in planning instruction and managing classrooms in schools is an array of group work theories that help us understand and manage the complex and powerful dynamics that happen in groups. These group work theories offer unique insights into group processes and how group leaders can think about group goals, objectives, and activities and generally manage the variety of group types that are conducted in schools.

We begin this chapter with an introduction to the concepts of *content* and *process*. Group content refers to the topic or focus of a particular group, and group process refers to the interpersonal dynamics within groups. Together these terms describe dual threads in the weave of group functioning that is managed by group leaders. Next, we turn our attention to what is known as *therapeutic factors* in group work. These ideas, now the subject of countless research inquiries, arise from the work of Irvin D. Yalom whose text *Theory and Practice of Group Psychotherapy* (1995, 2005) is now in its fifth edition (with collaborator Molyn Leszcz in the most recent edition) and considered a seminal volume on group psychotherapy. One might ask, why would a psychiatric textbook be of interest to school counselors since school counselors don't do psychotherapy? As it turns out, many of these factors also have measurable effects on the functioning of classroom, counseling, task, and work groups conducted in schools.

The two key group concepts of *interdependence* and *equilibrium* are also important in our discussion of group work theories. These concepts are drawn from systems theories and frame group work as a unique venue for therapeutic work in the fields of counseling and psychology. They illuminate additional complexities that arise within group dynamics and are important considerations for group leaders who work in schools as well. The final theory related to group work that we discuss here is *group stage theory*. This is, perhaps, the most well-known group theory in the field, and it is used by many group leaders to map out their interventions within individual group sessions and throughout the group over time.

In the second part of this chapter, we take a brief dip into the waters of leadership theories. Here again, we emphasize the point that group leader orientation or philosophy will drive their actions and interventions. We initiate our discussion in this section of the chapter with a review of various group leadership styles, and we discuss how leadership style sits in juxtaposition to group types. We end the chapter with a discussion about the concept of discipline. We invite readers to think about discipline as a philosophical position that is taken up by group leaders (along with others in schools) and to be intentional about how it is enacted in their groups (and more generally in their work in schools).

Content and Process in Groups

We start by calling attention to what Jarvis (2006) refers to as the art and science of teaching. Here he points out that the *science of teaching* refers to the study of teaching methodologies—what one does in the classroom and other learning communities to facilitate learning. The *art of teaching*, on the other hand, has more to do with teaching style—how one goes about the complex work of teaching (Jarvis, 2006). These concepts have a parallel in the group work literature: group content and process.

Group *content* refers to the focus of a particular group. It is what the group is about, "what the group is working on" (Schwarz, 2002, p. 5), and goals, tasks, subject matter, or purpose of the group (Geroski & Kraus, 2002; Gladding, 2003). When a group leader is attending to group content, they are being sure that the group is focused on its intended focus, group, and member goals or the stated topic of the group.

Group *process* refers to the group dynamics—the interactions among group members and between members and the group leader (Geroski & Kraus, 2002). Yalom (1995) pointed out that when we attend to process, we ask, "What do these explicit words, the style of the participants, the nature of the discussion tell about the interpersonal relationship of the participants?" (pp. 130–131). Group process interventions, then, are those that draw attention to the ways in which individuals are interacting with each other in the group and with the group leader—how they work together or not, how communication occurs within the group, and how the work of the group moves forward.

Hulse-Killacky et al. (1999) asserted that "process facilitates content, and process needs to be balanced with content or a group will fail to attain its objectives" (p. 114). This is true, they suggested, across group types. The point they make is that attending to interpersonal group process dynamics is critical for group content goals to be met. This is because social and cultural influences within a group compel members to act in certain ways, and these behaviors influence whether and how individual and group goals will be achieved (Gladding, 2003). For example, students in school groups are often concerned about how they will be perceived by others, and this concern may shape how they behave in the group. For some, this means that they weigh their words carefully before talking, or they may silence themselves with peers who appear to hold more social capital in the group. This may occur, as mentioned in Chapter 1, when students are situated in marginalized social locations, such as lower socioeconomic status, minority racial or ethnic groups, or when they identify as lesbian, gay, bisexual, or transgender (LGBT). Reflecting back on the discussion of social learning theory in the previous chapter, we are reminded that people are easily influenced by those they perceive to have higher status, prestige, and power (Bandura, 1977). When students are in a group with others they know or with people they hold in high regard, they feel pressure to conform, and they are likely to be influenced by group dynamics (Gladding, 2003).

Case Study 3.1 illustrates how group content goals can be addressed through careful navigation through group process dynamics. You will see in this case study how the school counselor uses the skill of shifting the focus with intentionality to address the important group dynamic issue that is of concern and very much related to the content of the group. The skill of shifting the focus is discussed in more detail in Chapter 8.

CASE STUDY 3.1 Using Group Process to Facilitate Content

Mr. Nyal is a school counselor working with a middle school health classroom group for 6 weeks to address the topic of bullying and harassment. His lesson plan for this week called for reviewing the school harassment policy. The topic that had been discussed in the classroom previously was bullying. Students had defined bullying and role-played ways to respond when they saw bullying in the hallways.

Mr. Nyal started the group by asking students to subgroup into triads and review the written school policy on harassment. Realizing at once his mistake in not assigning the subgroups, Mr. Nyal watched helplessly as students scurried to form the small groups for the task. This task of forming small groups immediately revealed a number of exclusionary problems. One group insisted on taking in a fourth member, whispering to the extra member, "Come to our group, so you don't have to go over there with them. Mr. Nyal won't care," while two students appeared to be groupless.

Since the group had previously discussed how exclusion was one of the ways that bullying starts, Mr. Nyal thought that it would be important to use this teachable moment to help students see how quickly and seemingly unintentionally bullying can start. He called attention to the issue in a nonjudgmental and exploratory way. First, he used a conceptual group-level intervention (this type of intervention will be discussed in more detail in Chapter 8):

"Okay. Hold up. Let's stop for a minute." When students were listening, he continued, "I wonder if people sometimes feel left out, even if others don't mean to leave them out. Like in here, when I asked you to group up in threes, I noticed that students called out who they wanted to be with, and some students were left without a group."

He paused and then added, again keeping his interventions on a group level to avoid raising the intensity too much higher, "Let's take a minute to talk about how it feels to not be invited into a group—I know that all of us have had that experience."

After a few students talked about how it has felt for them in the past when they were left out of a group, Mr. Nyal asked, "How can something like a noninvitation lead to what we talked about last week: 'bullying climates'?"

These conceptual interventions remained on the group level as he did not want the students who experienced feeling left out to feel even more estranged from the group.

After students acknowledged that bully climates often started with exclusion, Mr. Nyal asked them to focus on what had just happened in their class.

David said, "I wasn't trying to be mean. I didn't think I was bullying, but now, I realize that Georgia may have felt that way."

Mr. Nyal translated David's comment into a larger point: that sometimes exclusion happens without us even realizing it or even when we don't do it intentionally. He added, "Next week, we will come back to this when we talk about implicit bias." He then wrote *implicit bias = an act of bias that is not yet in our awareness* on the blackboard. He continued, "But remember that not meaning to do something does not give us a pass. We may not have intended to do something, but it still happened."

"Yup. I'm sorry, Georgia," David said after a moment of silence in the group.

A few other students commented on how they did not mean to bully anyone, but they could see how they did things that could make their peers feel left out. A couple of students offered anonymously directed apologies to "anyone who might have been offended by what I did."

Mr. Nyal then asked the group to identify ways that they could try to be more inclusive in this group so that no one felt left out and to avoid creating a bullying climate. Although this teachable moment was not scripted into his lesson plan, taking the time to process what was happening in the group was an excellent way for Mr. Nyal to facilitate a process of interpersonal learning that tied into the content objective that he had for the group. In this case, Mr. Nyal used group process to facilitate content.

Group leaders know that decisions about whether to focus on group process dynamics in the moment versus staying focused on planned group content are quite complex. These decisions are influenced by who is in the group; the extent to which the group process dynamics might help the group better achieve its goals or, conversely, impede group functioning; and on the type and intent of group (Geroski & Kraus, 2002).

In small counseling groups, particularly when the goals for group members are related to intrapersonal or interpersonal development, leaders often use group process to facilitate content (Geroski & Kraus, 2002). In classroom and task groups, this can happen as well. However, Hulse-Killacky et al. (2001) pointed out that leaders of task groups often neglect group process and attend more to content goals (to the detriment of the group). These authors encouraged group leaders to "strike a balance between these themes [process and content focus] so that the goals of the group can be attained" (Hulse-Killacky et al., 2001, p 7). Similarly, school counselors often prioritize a focus on group content over group process in classroom groups as well (Geroski & Kraus, 2002; Gladding, 2003). This too can be detrimental. Throughout this text, we invite you to think carefully about how to adjust your leadership style so that attending to group process dynamics is inherent to promoting group content goals, regardless of the group type.

Therapeutic Factors in Group Work

The term *therapeutic factors*, originating in Yalom's extensive practice and research in group psychotherapy and originally called *curative factors* (e.g., Yalom, 1995; Yalom & Leszcz, 2005; Yalom & Yalom, 1990), refers to particular mechanisms and conditions that are known to make groups productive. They are conditions in groups that enable learning, growth, and change. Described in more detail in Table 3.1, Yalom's therapeutic factors are *universality, altruism, group cohesiveness, installation of hope, imparting information* (didactic instruction and providing direct advice), *development of socializing techniques, imitative behavior, catharsis, interpersonal learning* (learning input and learning output), *corrective recapitulation of the primary family unit*, and *existential factors*, which include accepting responsibility for one's decisions and living authentically (Yalom, 1995, 2005; Yalom & Leszcz, 2005).

TABLE 3.1 Therapeutic Factors (Yalom)

FACTOR	DESCRIPTION
Universality	When group members encounter others in the group who have had similar experiences and/or challenges, they feel connected and less isolated.
Altruism	When group members reach out to help and support others in the group, they learn that they have something to offer others; they feel more connected. Also, others experience them differently, and they begin to see themselves in new, positive ways.
Cohesiveness	This refers to the feeling of belonging within a group. When a group is cohesive, members have the opportunity to feel connected with and valued by others.
Instillation of Hope	When people who are grappling with challenges are witnesses to change in others who share their challenges, they become hopeful that they too can change. Also, when group members are acknowledged and celebrated by others in the group, they feel encouraged and hopeful.

FACTOR	DESCRIPTION
Imparting Information (Didactic Instruction and Giving Direct Advice)	The exchange of information that comes from the group leader and group members broadens understandings of the subject area that is the focus of the group. This exchange occurs in the form of direct teaching or advice giving. In addition, many groups offer members an opportunity to reflect on this information and practice what they have learned in the group.
Socialization	As group members engage with one another, they learn effective ways of interacting. The group gives them the opportunity to practice or try out new behaviors and receive feedback from others.
Imitation	Group members are exposed to group leaders and other members who role model certain behaviors in the group. From these role models, members can observe and experience new behaviors and practice emanating those behaviors with feedback and shaping within the group. In some groups, the learning, modeling, and practice of specific social skills is the focus of the group. In other groups, this learning is an added benefit of working with other group members.
Catharsis	The experience of sudden insight or understanding. This may come with a strong emotional expression often described as a release.
Interpersonal Learning (Learning Input and Learning Output)	Through the relationships established among group members and with the group leaders, members have the opportunity to learn about relationships. This may include experiencing honesty, intimacy, joy, open communication, etc. This occurs through participants sharing and offering perspectives to the group, as well as listening and learning from others and allowing themselves to be influenced by others.
Corrective Experiences	This concept is based on Yalom's concept of the "recapitulation of the family group," which refers to when one group member relates to another as if that person is a member of their family of origin with whom the group member has struggled in the past. But this projection is met by the reality that the group member is not the original family member and responds differently. This allows for learning different communication and relational patterns.
Existential Factors	The group provides members an opportunity to explore existential questions around identity (place in the world), meaning of life, loss, death, etc.

Adapted from Yalom I., & Leszcz, M. (2005). Theory and practice of group psychotherapy (5th ed.). Basic Books.

Yalom's therapeutic factors initially described therapeutic processes rather than specific group leader techniques (Bloch et al., 1981). However, in his later work (i.e., Yalom & Leszcz, 2005), there was a shift toward understanding these factors as therapeutic process *and* therapeutic techniques. For example, the development of *socializing techniques, imparting information,* and a focus on *interpersonal learning* are therapeutic factors and leader interventions that are used to promote learning, growth, and change. Regardless of therapeutic modality or group type (Marogna & Caccamo, 2014), the relative importance of and emphasis on one or a few of the therapeutic factors in a particular group depends on the type and purpose of the group, the stage of the group, and group membership (Kivlighan & Goldfine, 1991). It also depends, of course, on the group leader's ability to activate these factors into the group process successfully.

Over the years, Yalom's concept of therapeutic factors has captured extensive attention in the practice of group work, and they have also been the focus of extensive research. Multiple clinical and research studies have linked Yalom's therapeutic factors to healthy and well-functioning groups (American Group Psychotherapy Association, 2007). In research of groups with adolescents, for example, Akos et al. (2006) suggested that Yalom's notions of *group cohesion*, *universality*, development of *socializing techniques*, *interpersonal learning*, and *imitative behavior* are particularly relevant for promoting growth and change among this population. These findings underscore the important ways in which the social milieu created in a group promotes learning opportunities for all group members, and this may be particularly critical in groups with youth, as we know that their attention is highly attuned to peers and social interactions. They also remind us of the importance of careful attention to group membership, which is discussed in Chapter 4.

Shechtman (2007) reported that *relationship climate*, which includes experiencing support, care, and empathic listening in a group, was the therapeutic factor most valued by the children in the groups she studied, regardless of gender and group composition. Shechtman also indicated that group bonding—what Yalom would call *group cohesion*—was a critical therapeutic factor in the groups with children that she studied. In more content-focused, school-based, skill-building groups, Letendre et al. (2003) found that *therapeutic alliance* was a significant factor in promoting group participation, and this in turn led to an increase in the prosocial skills and decreased levels of aggression in the child participants. All of these studies underscore the importance of creating an appropriate group climate and culture that facilitates growth and change in group work with youth. However, Letendre et al.'s (2003) caution that therapeutic alliance alone was not sufficient in affecting change in the levels of aggression in the children in their study is important. These authors called attention to the important role of having *appropriate content or curriculum*, as this was also a critical variable in the positive outcomes reported in their study. This reminds us of the importance of attending to both group process and group content when leading groups with youth.

Our intent here is to offer just a small sampling of the group work research on these factors in relation to groups conducted with children as a way of emphasizing the importance of these factors in group work in schools. In summary, this literature suggests that *cohesion*, *universality*, *caring*, *support*, *imparting information*, and a focus on *socialization and interpersonal learning* are important factors for successful groups with children and adolescents. The main point here is that as students invest in the group, their participation enriches their group experience; group process dynamics influence group content learning.

Before moving into our discussion about systems theory, we briefly turn our attention to two important premises that accompany Yalom's concept of therapeutic factors for groups. The first is

that group members bring their preexisting perceptions of self, the influence of their primary family unit, their interactional patterns with others, and their personal understandings and experiences of and in the world into their social interactions within a group (MacNair-Semands & Lese, 2000; Yalom & Yalom, 1990). This tells us that children will engage with peers in their groups (and with the group leader) in ways that are similar to how they engage with others in their lives outside of these groups. Second is Yalom's point that the interaction and feedback that occurs within a well-facilitated group also transfers back

Image 31

into the outside social settings within which children function (Yalom & Yalom, 1990). That is, students grow and learn in groups (that are facilitated appropriately by the group leader), and they bring this learning into other social communities in and out of schools. This reaffirms why group work is such an important venue for realizing many of the academic, career, social, and emotional development goals of school counseling programs. It is an important reminder about the power and magic of groups.

Systems Theory

Systems theory helps us understand groups as complex multileveled processes that operate on a unique set of principles. Systems theory comes to group work from multiple disciplines—notably from the work of biologist Ludwig von Bertalanffy, social psychologist Kurt Lewins, and Gregory Bateson and others in the field of family therapy (Agazarian & Gantt, 2005; Connors & Caple, 2005). This work was translated into the field of group work by Helen Durkin and others in the early 1970s (Agazarian & Gantt, 2005). We have selected here two key systems theory concepts that are particularly salient for group work in a school setting.

The first of these concepts is the idea that systems or groups are *more than just a sum of their parts*. This idea was first introduced by biologist Ludwig von Bertalanffy, who in the 1940s studied structural similarities across biological organisms (Agazarian & Gantt, 2005; Connors & Caple, 2005). This notion later became foundational in the work of family systems therapists who observed that families do not change as a result of changes made by one individual family member (Connors & Caple, 2005). The point is that individuals within various social systems or groups (such as a family, a community, or any other organized group) are interconnected, and the functioning in one aspect of a system affects the functioning of other parts of that system (Connors & Caple, 2005). This underscores the *holistic nature of systems* (or groups). Group members do not operate in isolation; they are "dynamically interdependent" (Connors & Caple, 2005, p. 99). It is also related to Lewin's field theory concept that people's perceptions about themselves and their behaviors are an "output of the person's perception of his or her environment" (Agazarian & Gantt, 2005, p. 187).

In work with families, therapists observe how these dynamic interconnections are enacted in family alliances and rituals and influence patterns of enmeshment, disengagement, scapegoating, and parent/child relations (Connors & Caple, 2005). In school group work, these dynamics may be similar—the patterns of student interactions, alliances, and group rituals become established in the group and are influential to the behavior of individual group members. From a systems perspective, problematic interactional patterns are not seen as problems with any one student; substantial growth and change for individual group members is a function of a larger system change (Hawe et al., 2009; Vetere & Dowling, 2016).

This calls upon group leaders to engage in "'big picture' thinking" (Connors & Caple, 2005, p. 99). For example, when a particular group has established a pattern of off-task behavior, intervention with one group member will likely not be as effective as intervening with the group as a whole. Our discussion of the intervention cube in Chapter 8 offers an excellent model for thinking about these types of systemic interventions.

Von Bertalanffy also emphasized that systems (groups) have their own set of self-stabilizing dynamics—something that has since been called *homeostasis* (Connors &

Image 3.2

Caple, 2005). These dynamics, von Bertalanffy believed, cause systems to be in processes of self-organization and to evolve in complexity. In group work systems theory, this principle is referred to as *equilibrium*. Group members tend to organize themselves in stable and repeating patterns of behaviors, and groups move toward an equilibrium of order and stability (Day, 2007; Toseland & Rivas, 2005). Very generally, groups tend to favor adaptation over confrontation—particularly in the early stages of group development. Group members will look for ways to adjust and accommodate or to compensate when their peers in the group are not conforming to group norms or when the group is not functioning properly. For example, early in group development, a student may assume the role of always volunteering to speak first, and soon this becomes a pattern where others look to this one student to start group conversations. Other roles may also be established early on and remain unchallenged: one student may be the person who always complains about group tasks or processes, and silent members may be consistently silent.

As these examples illustrate, the implicit goal of maintaining homeostasis can be problematic in a group, as it sometimes prohibits individuals from taking risks, growing, and changing. It can also inhibit the group from achieving its goals. For example, if a student is acting in ways that are aggressive, off task, or nonparticipatory, the other group members will adjust their behavior accordingly. Some may shut down, stop working, or find other ways to avoid being drawn into the group dynamics. Others may become unfocused, tangential, vie for power, respond with aggression, step in to try to fix interactional patterns, try to take on the sole responsibility of completing the group task for the group, etc. When a group is consumed by these kinds of dynamics, leaders have a responsibility to intervene and assist the group in engaging with each other in more productive and effective ways. This requires a flexible attention to group content goals *and* group process dynamics, as well as being able to shift the focus between the two as needed (Geroski & Kraus, 2002; Kraus & Hulse-Killacky, 1996), especially when there is conflict in the group. The leadership principles and skills identified in Chapter 7 are some of the tools that group leaders use to facilitate these dynamic and nuanced processes.

The concept of equilibrium also has implications on how leaders think about group membership. In addition to thinking about what students can potentially learn from being in a particular group, leaders will need to consider the potential contributions that each student will bring to a group, and how they may be affected by others in the group (American Group Psychotherapy Association, 2007; Bernard et al., 2008; Connors & Caple, 2005; Schwartz, 2002).

Systems thinking has important implications for all types of school counselor-led groups. It reminds us that individuals are always making decisions about how to participate in groups, and these decisions are based on their perceptions of their role in the group, how others in the group are behaving, and overall group functioning, as well as the context in which the group is situated. We will revisit these ideas about holism and equilibrium again in the following discussion about group stage theory.

Group Stage Theory

A number of stage models of group development have been advanced in the field of group work to describe the ways in which group dynamics pass through a somewhat predictable process from start to end (Birnbaum & Cicchetti, 2005; Tuckman, 1965; Tuckman & Jensen, 1977). These models forward the premise that groups (and group members) must navigate the tasks and challenges that emerge within each phase to function well and achieve the intended individual and group goals, and these models are relevant for all group types conducted in and out of school settings (Berman-Rossi, 1993). Arguably, the first comprehensive and most-cited stage model of group development was drafted by Tuckman (1965) and further refined by Tuckman and Jensen (1977). This model, which we review next, is based on Tuckman's premise that groups must successfully navigate and move through each stage of group development (although not always happily or easily). The group leader has the responsibility to facilitate the group's navigation through the tasks and challenges of each stage in the model. Table 3.2 offers a concise description of each stage with recommendations for group leaders.

TABLE 3.2 Group Stages and Leader Tasks

GROUP STAGE	DESCRIPTION OF STAGE	LEADER TASKS
Forming	Members are getting to know each other and the leader, and they are oriented to the tasks of the group.	• Make introductions, welcomes, and set members at ease. • Facilitate connections between members. • Review group tasks and goals. • Establish rules. • Set limits, if necessary.
Storming	Conflicts emerge as members become more comfortable, begin to be honest, express themselves, and create an identity for themselves in the group.	• Provide space for all voices to be heard. • Assure safety. • Bring attention to interpersonal and group process dynamics. • Use process observers and facilitate feedback exchange, if appropriate.
Norming	As the group members express themselves and open dialog begins, there is a new process of creating norms. Cohesion and mutuality develop, and the interpersonal dynamics become cooperative and supportive among members.	• Encourage discussion and renegotiation of the rules, if needed. • Monitor member commitment to the new norms. • Encourage member participation. • Introduce new content or tasks (related to the group goals).
Performing	The new group norms give way to productivity, and the tasks of the group become the members' focus.	• Continue to monitor norms and encourage participation and interpersonal engagement. • Encourage members to use resources and make decisions. • Offer support and resources as needed. • Engage members to resolve conflicts, if necessary.
Adjourning	Group tasks or goals are met. Learning is summarized, and members consider the transfer of learning to outside of the group.	• Help members summarize and reflect on learning. • Encourage the transfer of learning. • Address any unresolved issues. • Lead the group in a process for expressing farewells.

Adapted from Geroski, A. M. (2019). Helping skills for counselors. Cognella.

The first stage in the Tuckman model is called *forming* (Tuckman, 1965; Tuckman & Jensen, 1977; Tuckman initially called this stage *testing and dependence*). In this starting phase, group members learn about the purpose or task of the group and begin to assess the relevance of this task to their own needs, perceptions, and levels of involvement in the group. As members begin to get to know others in the group, they carefully observe and make decisions about how they want to engage with others, as well as with the task or purpose of the group. This is a time when group members may have concerns about how they will be perceived by others. As a result, group members in this stage tend to engage in safe patterned behaviors, are reluctant to take risks, and tend to look to the group leader for guidance and direction. Problems can arise in the group during this phase if members do not understand the purpose of the group, if they perceive the group to be meaningless, when there is a lack of focus, and if they do not have a sense of belonging or influence in the group. Also, problems may surface if members are encouraged to engage in conversations that are premature or perceived to be too personally risky at this early stage of group development (Birnbaum & Cicchetti, 2005). For these reasons, group leaders working in groups that are just forming must set parameters around the nature of member interactions, including the level of sharing required for the group to succeed, the feedback exchange process, and the nature of support that members offer each other within the group.

Storming is the next stage in the Tuckman model (Tuckman, 1965; Tuckman & Jensen, 1977). Aptly named, this is a time of conflict in the group. After the initial forming, group members begin to express themselves more freely and engage more openly in the group, often leading to alternative perspectives, competing interests, and conflict. At this point in the group, we sometimes see member's patterned interactional behaviors manifest themselves in how they participate and interact with others outside of the group. This, of course, affects the group dynamics, and it reflects Yalom's idea of the group as a microcosm of how members interact in other (i.e., outside of the group) social relationships (Yalom & Yalom, 1990). In this stage of the group, students continue to gauge each other; they are making decisions about how to assert their own needs in the group. Harris and Sherblom (2005) pointed out that this is the time when group members begin to feel safe enough to be more authentic with others in the group. They may decide to try new behaviors or ways of interacting with others, vie for positions of power, or become anxious, resistant, defensive, and avoidant. Unaddressed conflict in the group at this stage may inhibit the group from effectively engaging with its intended purposes (Toseland & Rivas, 2005). It is also important to point out that the group leader can become the target of this storming phase as members raise questions about structure, power, competence, and control of the group (Gladding, 2003; Kline, 2003). All of these behaviors are normal in the storming phase, and most agree that the storming phase is necessary for the development of subsequent cohesion and cooperation in the group (Harris & Sherblom, 2005).

As a group begins to resolve some of the conflicts that arose in the storming phase, a sense of cohesion develops. This marks the entry into the next stage, which is called *norming* (Tuckman, 1965; Tuckman & Jensen, 1977). At this time, the group begins to refocus on its intended goals and members begin to demonstrate an appreciation for each other. Support and cooperation develop as the group begins to coalesce into a sense of "we." In counseling and psychotherapy groups, members become open, and honest personal sharing becomes the norm. In task/work and classroom or psychoeducational groups, there is an open exchange of ideas and opinions and a commitment to the task of the group. Across group types, there is a renewed level of investment, a willingness to take risks, and norms for cooperation and participation are solidified during this time.

As norms for engagement and task completion are established, the group is able to move into the *performing* stage (Tuckman, 1965; Tuckman & Jensen, 1977). This is also referred to as the *working stage* of the group (Day, 2007; Gladding, 2003). Here members are actively engaged, invested, and focused on the task or purpose of the group (Day, 2007; Gladding, 2003). Groups tend to be quite productive at this time (Tuckman, 1965). Any conflicts that might arise in the group during this stage are usually negotiated and resolved within the group, often with little intervention needed on the part of the group leader. In fact, the autonomy of group members that emerges in the working phase can only occur if members were allowed and, perhaps, guided to develop authentic and meaningful relationships. It should be pointed out that in groups with youth, members may need to be taught effective skills for authentic and productive interactions; this is a prerequisite for adequate functioning at this stage of a group.

When group tasks or goals have been met, the group then moves into the final *adjourning* stage (Tuckman & Jensen, 1977). While this stage was not included in the original Tuckman model, it is now included in virtually every group stage theory model that is used in the field. At the end of some groups, members feel satisfied, energized, and hopeful (Gladding, 2003). But it is also possible for members to feel indifferent, sad, disappointed, or angry about the ending of the group (Gladding, 2003; Toseland & Rivas, 2005). This may be especially true for members who were very invested in the group or in groups where the leader did not invest sufficient time into the termination process. In counseling and therapy groups, members who took many risks and who may not have adequate support and resources outside of the group may feel sad or disappointed when the group is at its end. Since this kind of outcome is potentially predictable, group leaders can take steps to ensure that sufficient time is invested in the termination process, appropriate referrals are made for those who need them, and members are provided with resources for support and additional counseling, should they need it.

It is important to note, of course, that not all groups are as linear and predictable as the stage models would suggest. Some of these stages may not be experienced in some groups; they may not follow in the order expected, and more often than not, dynamics of multiple stages can occur simultaneously in a group (Harris & Sherblom, 2005). Toseland and Rivas (2005) note that groups are often cyclic, moving from one stage to the next and then back again through earlier stages. However, most group leaders rely on group stage models for insight into complex group dynamics and for direction regarding group leader planning and interventions. We will be referencing these stages in the later chapters on group leader interventions.

Developing a Leadership Position

We use the term *position* to talk about the philosophical and relational stance from which group leaders interact with group members. It is a term that is used to describe how social interactions unfold according to spoken and unspoken rules of engagement and the processes by which individuals construct meanings within and from those social interactions (Harre & Moghaddam, 2003). Here our use of the concept of position emphasizes the importance of connecting one's leadership actions to underlying principles and ideas about leadership, growth, and change with youth.

The way in which school personnel engage with students in schools is informed by their beliefs, which are shaped by larger social discourses; their professional training and experiences related to adult-child relationships; and their roles and functions as teachers, administrators, school counselors, and other staff members in educational settings. For example, if we hold some version of the belief that children are blank slates ready to be imprinted on by knowledgeable adults, then our interactions with children will likely be shaped by efforts to provide them with plenty of information and advice. If we believe that children learn self-control through the imposition of clear and strict rules during the formative years, then we will do that as school staff members and group leaders. If, on the other hand, we believe that children learn best by being allowed to explore their environment uninterrupted by the adults in those spaces, then we are likely to avoid asserting ourselves too much into their work and play. These examples point to extremes, of course, but there truly are multiple and varied ideas and perspectives about how to best facilitate child growth and development. There are also tomes of literature outlining philosophical positions related to the practices of education, counseling, and group work with youth. The point is that our understandings and beliefs in all of

Image 3.4

these areas are not just in the background of our work; they are enacted in our everyday interactions with adults and youth in our schools.

Learning—whether it is about learning a particular concept or skill, about intrapersonal growth, or focused more on interpersonal development—does not just happen because students are together in a room with a common goal; learning happens as a result of intentional facilitation on the part of the group leader. Group leaders must be clear about the philosophies that guide their thinking; these ideas are the foundation for how they lead the various groups they conduct in schools. Here we will discuss leadership styles in relation to important leader functions, and we will end this chapter with a short discussion on the concept of discipline.

Leadership Styles

Kline (2003) described three leadership styles that influence the intervention choices that group leaders make in their groups. They are (1) *autocratic(authoritarian)*, (2) *democratic*, and (3) *laissez-faire*. We will describe each of these styles briefly next. These styles are anchored in the earlier empirical works of Lewin (1944) and Hansen et al. (1980) and conceptualized as existing on a continuum. That is, effective leaders constantly blend one or more of these styles in their work, depending on the context of the group and what the group or group members need at any given moment. Approaching leadership rigidly from only one of these styles is likely to impair a group's growth and development.

Autocratic (Authoritarian) Leadership

Autocratic leaders work from a philosophical position that group members are dependent on the group leader for learning and change. In line with this position, they tend to manage group members' personal or intrapersonal functioning and intrapersonal interactions fairly extensively in the group. The idea is that leader intervention is needed for member effectiveness within the group (Hansen et al., 1980; Kline, 2003). Autocratic group leaders are highly engaged—sometimes too highly engaged—in their executive function role. They tightly manage inter-member inter-actions and work hard to promote insight, learning, and growth. It is as if they believe, perhaps, that learning is not possible without the expressed intervention and involvement of the group leader. For example, in a large high school group visit to a local community college, the group leader insisted that all of the participating students submit their questions in advance, and they were subsequently asked by him (rather than the students). He also insisted that students be silent during the tour of the campus, and he ran the meeting afterward as a question-and-answer period rather than a group discussion.

While being actively involved in the group is sometimes needed at some point, overengagement can lead to member disengagement, a thwarted sense of agency, and a lack of motivation to work on goals. Why invest in the work of the group when the leader is doing it for you? Or when the leader is making all of the decisions?

Democratic Leadership

Leaders working from a democratic position are working from the belief that given the proper condi-tions, members have the capability to engage in effective personal functioning and can demonstrate interpersonal and intrapersonal effectiveness within the group (Kline, 2003; Hansen et al., 1980). As a result, democratic leaders are collaborative in their approach to leadership; they seek input and engagement from members in the development of group norms, rules, and goals, and they make an effort to solicit the input of group members in most critical group decisions (Kline, 2003). For example, the democratic leader of the aforementioned large group that was engaged in a tour of the campus of a local community college spent two pregroup meetings with students to engage them in a discussion process of why they were interested in college, why they were participating in the tour, and what they hoped to get out of it. During the tour, she sought consensus when questions were asked of the group about how long they wanted to stay on campus, and she initiated an open discussion for students to talk afterward.

While this is a desirable leadership style, democratic leaders need to be cautious about being over-reliant on collaborative and consensus-building efforts, as doing so may inhibit their ability to set boundaries and perform their executive function roles at times when these are needed in the group. That is, regardless of their preferred leadership role, group leaders must always be aware of their responsibility to perform executive function duties in every group that they lead. This point is critical, as sometimes group members who feel the unharnessed power of being in a majority can engage in harmful behaviors toward other group members. When this happens, the group leaders must be able to step in to protect minority or marginalized group members; stepping in to provide safety to group members who are scapegoated in the group, for example, can never be something that a leader leaves to group consensus or collaborative decision making. Leaders have an ethical responsibility to protect all of their group members, especially those who are marginalized in the group.

Laissez-Faire Leadership

Laissez-faire leadership is on the opposite end of the continuum from autocratic leadership. The working belief of laissez-faire leaders is that group members do not need group leaders' input to manage their personal functioning, nor are leaders needed to influence members' interpersonal effectiveness (Hansen et al., 1980; Kline, 2003). It is as if just being together in a group is enough for learning, growth, and change. As a result, laissez-faire leaders make minimal effort to be engaged in group member interactions, and they are equally disengaged in establishing member roles, group norms, and goal setting. These leaders resist setting boundaries around the nature and kind of interactions that are allowable or effective within their groups, and they give members full reign in terms of initiating interactions with each other, engaging in feedback exchange, and developing meaning-making and learning processes related to group content or process dynamics. For example, a school counselor had a sign-up sheet for a community college tour and sent out an email that told all of the interested students to meet in the lobby of the college at a particular time. After the tour, no follow-up was arranged unless students initiated individual appointments with the counselor to discuss their visit.

Elements of laissez-faire leadership deserve merit, however. Allowing group members opportunities and space to grapple with difficult personal and interpersonal ideas and experiences can be effective in creating agency and inviting students to learn from a challenge. However, many of the learning theories reviewed in the previous chapter and many of the leadership ideas that will be discussed later in Chapter 6 teach us the importance of using scaffolding, reinforcing, and other leader or teacher interventions to promote student learning. If leaders do not intervene to direct the focus of the group when it is off track, groups are at risk of becoming unfocused and ineffective. In addition, group leaders who operate solely from a laissez-faire style may endanger vulnerable group members by not stepping in to intervene when student behaviors are harmful to themselves or others. This gets us back to our earlier point that group leaders should operate from a continuum of leadership styles; intentionality rather than commitment to any one leadership style should always guide group leader actions within each group they lead.

Authoritative Leadership

Authoritative leadership is a term that is used in the teaching and parenting literature to describe an educational-oriented approach whereby the leader is clearly in charge or in control of the group but leads in a fair, warm, and caring way (Hughes, 2002). While it is sometimes difficult to translate a philosophical stance into observable behaviors, Larrivee (2005) suggested that authoritative group leaders convey a sense of being in charge of and caring for members by being attentive; by offering specific and direct comments, suggestions, instructions, and feedback; and through modeling. Authoritative group leaders articulate reasoned expectations for the group, encourage verbal interchange among members, encourage student self-regulation, set appropriate boundaries with group members, and enforce those boundaries and rules while also being flexible and attentive to specific situations and member needs (Hughes, 2002; Ingersol, 1996). Authoritative leaders have high and appropriate expectations for group members; they intervene to help members make appropriate choices whenever possible; they provide ample opportunities for success in the group; they establish and enforce fair rules in the group, making the reasons for these rules transparent when appropriate (Larrivee, 2005). Case Study 3.2 offers an example of this type of group leadership.

Be careful not to mistake authoritative for the authoritarian/autocratic leadership style—the two sound alike but are distinctly different! In contrast to the authoritative style, an *authoritarian* or *autocratic* leader establishes clear hierarchical divisions between the group leader and group members and often determines and controls almost all activities in the group with little input from group members. Hierarchy in itself is not problematic, of course, but it certainly is problematic when it is used (intentionally or not) to silence group members, to control the group process, and to limit group member contribution to the content, processes, and outcomes of a group.

CASE STUDY 3.2 Authoritative Leadership

In a sixth-grade classroom group early on in the school year, school counselor Mrs. Herrera noticed that in group discussions, students consistently raised their hands and waited for her to call on them before they would speak. They looked at her rather than at each other when they spoke, and their comments did not take into consideration what was stated before them. Along with this, the pacing was odd—it was as if the group discussion was regulated through her. The regular classroom norm of raising hands before talking was probably very effective for some of the academic discussions that happened in that classroom, but Mrs. Herrera thought that it interfered with students' abilities to more naturally enter into a discussion with each other in this group. She wanted students to feel more in charge of the group process, but she was also keeping in mind her role in leading the group toward the intended goals.

After two group sessions, Mrs. Herrera decided to present her observations to the group. She started with, "It seems that many of you have important things to say when we have discussions, but I'm thinking that it might work better if we didn't have to raise our hands to speak. That way, you could all talk to each other and not have to wait for me to call on you."

The students all agreed with this proposal and were ready to jump in and give it a go.

"However," Mrs. Herrera added, "I'm thinking that it might be a good idea to talk about how we can make this change from hand raising to non-hand raising and still be sure that everyone has a chance to speak if they want to. Sometimes when people just call out, they forget to clear a space for others to speak, and they get so focused on what they want to say that they forget to listen to others. Any thoughts on how we might do this successfully?"

As the group moved into a discussion about this, Mrs. Herrera intentionally worked to draw out some of the quiet members, and she reminded some of the more verbose members to hold back so that others could speak. In these ways, she was able to model the kinds of behaviors she expected from the students.

As the discussion came to a close, Mrs. Herrera asked students to reflect on how the group managed the discussion they just had, and if there were some ways that they could do better in the future. This question led to an interesting discussion about how some students were quieter in the group and others were louder. They moved into talking about ways in which they would notice the quieter voices and how to respectfully notice when they felt that someone was too domineering in the group. Some of the more active students seemed committed to making a space for others in the group, and the quieter students agreed to try to participate more in discussions.

In the end, the group decided that they would share spontaneously in group discussions rather than raise their hands before speaking. With the help of Mrs. Herrera, the following expectations were outlined: (a) student contributions will be relevant to the discussion, (b) they will not be hurtful to other members of the group, (c) students should not dominate the discussion (i.e., they should take turns and remember to clear a space for others), and (d) everyone will try to participate in group discussions.

While it may seem that the lengthy discussion about raising hands in the group discussed in Case Study 3.2 might be excessive if not tangential, we would argue that time spent early on in discussing group norms and creating appropriate rules and expectations is time well spent. In this case, not only did this discussion help to facilitate a group process that seemed appropriate for this particular group, but it also created an opportunity for students to think about the ways in which they and their peers interact with one another and contribute to collective discussions.

In the weeks that followed, Mrs. Herrera had to remind the group members of the rules from time to time, and, as one might expect, she occasionally had to respectfully cutoff a student telling a long and winding story. Mrs. Herrera also worked to find specific roles for members who seemed challenged to find a way to participate in the group. For example, she assigned students to be coleaders in group discussions and introduced other roles for students, including a time manager and materials captain (these are examples of executive functioning, and this concept comes to us from Cohen's work in the area of complex instruction [Cohen, 1994]). In these ways, Mrs. Herrera was able to capitalize on the strengths of all the students and step back from being too actively controlling of the group.

As Case Study 3.2 illustrates, the different ways in which group leaders interact with and relate to group members form group norms. This happens explicitly and implicitly. The group norms that come from the group leader's leadership style produce group dynamics that further define rules, roles, and member interactions, and they affect how group goals are being met. For example, if a group leader enters into a group using the *laissez-faire* leadership style, which may be perceived by members as disinterest in who they are or the goals or activities in the group, then the students may become disengaged; they may feel unimportant or unvalued; they may not invest in the group or in the intended learning opportunities. On the other hand, if a leader truly values the students in the group, really believes that they have important and valuable ideas, and believes that the members are capable of learning from each other, as is often demonstrated by a leader using a *democratic or authoritative* leadership style, then these beliefs and principles will be the norm in the group, and students will likely conduct themselves accordingly. Authoritative group leaders like Mrs. Herrera in Case Study 3.2 assert appropriate limits and controls and encourage independence, verbal dialogue, and debate. The focus of authoritative or democratic leadership actions is always on communicating the belief that each individual in the group is capable, and it is aimed at supporting each and every student (sometimes differently) so that those capabilities come forward.

Servant and Transformative Leadership

Moving away from the aforementioned leadership styles that are typically referenced in the field of group work, a leadership style that has emerged from the organizational and business literature (and more recently moved into the field of education) is the concept of servant leadership—a name and concept that was developed by Robert Greenleaf in the 1970s (Greenleaf, 1977). Servant leadership has its roots in faith-based and humanitarian organizations and is sometimes described as a transformational approach to leadership.

At the core of servant leadership is the idea that a leader's role is to serve the members of their organization. This happens by being invested in and working *for* them. The emphasis on service to others is based on the belief that organizational leaders—and we extend this to group leaders—are in the role of creating a better future, and they do this through a type of leadership that positions leaders in the role of service (Parris & Peachey, 2013). Servant leadership has two dimensions: one has to do with what leaders *do*, and the other is about who leaders *are* (Fields et al., 2015). The latter point is particularly salient in the servant leadership philosophy. According to Waterman (2011), "The concept of 'servant' is laden with symbolism that infers a state of being under the will of others or of giving selflessly" (p. 24), and these leaders are followed because others trust them (Ciulla, 2006). Servant leadership is embodied in the following characteristics and behaviors: listening, empathy, healing, awareness, persuasion, conceptualization, foresight, stewardship, commitment to the development of others, and community building (Fields et al., 2015; Waterman, 2011).

The concept of transformational leadership comes from the work of James Burns (focusing originally on political leadership) developed in the late 1970s. It currently enjoys a well-respected and influential position in contemporary leadership literature (Owens & Valesky, 2015; Price, 2008) that spans many fields of study, such as business, education, and health sciences. Transformational leaders are in the role of inspiring others, and most authors describe transformative leaders by who they *are* and how they *act* rather than what they *do* (Mason et al., 2014; Price, 2008). According to Mason et al. (2014), "Transformational leaders inspire followers to perform beyond expectations by developing, intellectually stimulating, and inspiring followers to transcend their own self-interests for a higher collective purpose, mission, or vision" (p. 175). Here, then, we might say that the focus is on inspiration, while in servant leadership, it is on serving.

The idea of transformative leadership is to engage others in a common cause where group functioning is based on shared values and shared aspirations (Owens & Valesky, 2015). According to these authors, this is typically implemented by empowering members to make decisions among themselves (according to a larger and shared mission) and with minimal authority on the part of the leader. In this role, the transformative leader typically acts as a facilitator or someone who makes recommendations or suggestions to, but not decisions for, group members. Leadership and group tasks are distributed among group members.

While servant leadership has gained a great deal of popularity, it, unfortunately, remains largely understudied (Parris & Peachey, 2013), with many scholars (including its founder) indicating the difficulty of operationalizing its principles and practices (Greenleaf, 1977; Parris & Peachy, 2013). Transformative leadership is often mentioned in the context of organizations (such as schools) rather than the smaller scale groups that we are discussing in this text (although it does run parallel to the democratic and authoritative leadership styles mentioned earlier). With that said, these two leadership styles are important, as their core characteristics are grounded in the principles of social justice and empowerment of clients. As we know, these principles are closely aligned with the fields of counseling, school counseling, and group work. So, while there hasn't yet been much in-depth discussion and research in the field of counseling and group work on the applications of servant and transformative leadership in school group work, they are worthy of further study.

Leadership Style Differences in Classroom-Based Versus Counseling Groups

Of course, classroom and small counseling groups are different. They differ in their purposes (their goals and objectives), in the number and makeup of their members, in how their goals and objectives are accomplished, and in how each group is facilitated by the group leader. These differences compel us to think about how group leader style and skills will need to adapt as the leader switches back and forth between these two distinct group types.

Let us start with the concepts of structure and directiveness. *Structure* refers to a group process that is organized and predictable. This is when the leader has planned (in advance) what they hope will happen, how they expect it to happen, and when it should happen in the group. Nonstructured groups are organized around more spontaneous group member input with less intentional focus on activities or plans. *Directiveness* refers to the ways in which a group leader is actively involved or engaged in structuring interactional and activity processes in the group. The extent to which a particular group needs structure and leadership will depend on a wide variety of factors, including group focus or goals; group member age, behaviors, abilities, and motivations; time and content; and a variety of other factors that may be present in the school and group context.

Generally, groups conducted in school classrooms tend to require higher levels of directiveness and structure than smaller counseling groups. This is due to multiple factors, but perhaps most significantly, these larger classroom groups have larger numbers of student members and a wider range of student abilities and behaviors. So there is more potential for a mismatch between group content or focus and student interest or need. Some participants may be less engaged than others.

It would be naïve to assume, however, that structure and directiveness are only required in larger classroom-based groups. Indeed, a leader must be exceptionally clear and may need to be extremely structured and every bit as directive in small counseling groups as well. In fact, almost all initial group sessions, regardless of group type, will need some level of structure and directiveness to establish norms (especially with regard to confidentiality) and direct student attention. Also, many school groups, regardless of type, will need leader direction to guide students to think about what they have experienced or learned at the end of each group session (DeLucia-Waack, 2006). Kline (2003) reminded us that while groups may not always need extensive directive structuring, the leader must be *ready* to provide direction as needed, regardless of group type. So it is not simply a matter of whether a leader is directive or not but rather different situations call for different levels of directiveness on the part of the group leader. The same is true for structure.

Another difference between the counseling and classroom groups is that classroom-based groups often do not deliver the metaphorical *depth* that counseling groups can elicit. We tread on thin ice here, as we try to further explicate this notion of depth from the professional discourses of what is considered therapeutic in counseling and what is considered appropriate for the school context. Our reference to depth here refers to the extent to which a particular issue can be personally explored in the group. To clarify, in this context, a lack of depth does not connote "not useful." The truth is that classroom-based groups that focus on delivering curriculum in the areas of academic, personal, social, and career domains tend to offer a broad, educationally focused group experience that only secondarily (and only sometimes) provides opportunities for extensive personal exploration. The curricular focus of classroom group work definitely should have the potential to be personally beneficial to students (we hope this happens for all students in classroom groups), especially when there is a logical connection between the goal of the group and the group delivery plan (Trusty & Brown, 2005), but it is often not what we might call *deep*. Again, this is not to say that students do not explore issues in-depth in classroom groups; it is just that they will probably not personally engage with the material in classroom groups in the same way that they might in the smaller counseling groups.

This notion of depth has huge implications on leadership style and group leader decisions for planning and leading classroom-based and counseling groups. First, because classroom-based groups tend to be aimed at eliciting broad, intellectual engagement with ideas and experiences or on concrete or specific skill building, leaders often use structured learning activities (which are discussed in Chapter 6) in these groups. Processing questions or discussions, typically after an activity has been used, is the method through which students are engaged in meaningful, thoughtful, and personal reflection and exploration about those activities. But largely, as mentioned earlier, classroom groups do not have the kind of depth that more often characterizes learning goals and processes of smaller counseling groups. Counseling groups, then, tend to focus on meaningful personal exploration and reflection on topics or learning goals that are more specifically suited to the specific needs of group members. In many counseling groups, leaders use less structure and direction; instead, they use group process dynamics as the medium for learning. However, some group leaders do use activities and process conversations in small groups to stimulate this focused and personal learning. This is particularly true in small groups with younger children or in groups where students lack adequate behavioral or emotional self-regulation abilities.

A Discipline Philosophy

As we know, groups do not always run smoothly. And when things go wrong in a group—as we can expect they sometimes will—leaders sometimes scurry to identify and label a particular student as the problem, and they remedy the problem by removing that individual who is deemed culpable. In response to this, we raise two points that are fundamental to the position we take in this chapter and related to this concept of discipline as it is often used in institutions of education. First, it is important to keep in mind, as systems theory teaches us, that most difficulties that arise in groups are not because of any one individual but the result of a group dynamic that is problematic for one or many individuals. When group leaders are able to manage groups so that students are engaged and supported to learn, when they devise group plans that are developmentally appropriate and engaging for students, and when they give students opportunities for feedback in regard to the skills and ideas they are learning, growth and learning can happen for all students in the group, and problems and misbehavior will be kept at a minimum. Second, not all "problems" in a group are problematic. Learning can happen when things go "wrong" in a group if leaders are intentional about harvesting learning opportunities from such challenges. Key here is the word *intentional*. Case Study 3.3 illustrates the value of these two points.

CASE STUDY 3.3 **Problems in the Group**

Patrick, an active boy with a 3-year reputation of being "challenging" (according to his teachers), was invited to participate in a 10-week counseling group. The group goal was "being the best we can be." The school counselor's screening and invitation process predicted that although Patrick might be a "handful" in the classroom, he seemed to really be interested in participating in the small group.

At the end of the first group session, which was extremely challenging to manage, the counselor concluded that they had "seen the light" and had "made a huge mistake inviting Patrick" into the group. Patrick's in-group behaviors demanded nearly constant attention; he was fidgety, loud, and bossy, and he seemed disinterested in engaging in the work of the group. Strangely, though, he seemed keenly aware of both the counselor's and his peer's frustrations with him in the group.

Initially, and quite understandably, we can see how the leader's attention immediately focused on Patrick being a bad fit for the group. In fact, the counselor framed the "disaster" as a nearly insurmountable and decided that if Patrick were not removed from the group, the remaining nine sessions would be a failure.

After consulting with a colleague, the school counselor considered this situation in light of systems thinking—that behaviors influence and are influenced by group dynamics and other group members. With this, the counselor began to focus on what Patrick might bring to the group—with all his challenges intact. Rather than blaming or lamenting, the counselor asked themself how the dynamic of Patrick's behavior could stimulate learning for all of the members in the group. After all, Patrick was present in a similar fashion with everyone in the third grade every day, so what they were experiencing in the group was an everyday occurrence in the regular classroom and in other settings in the school. As you might imagine, Patrick had perfect attendance!

With these thoughts in mind, the counselor decided to hold off on removing him from the group, at least for one more week. In the subsequent group session, the counselor focused on processing Patrick's behavior in the here and now, using exactly what was happening in the group instead of attempting to control Patrick's behaviors or others' reactions to him. For example, at one point, Alina asked for the counselor's assistance to put a book away. At that moment, Patrick jumped up, approached the counselor to display a picture that he had been drawing, and asked the counselor if they liked the picture. Alina called over again, asking for assistance a second time. Patrick turned to Alina, saying, "You can put that away yourself. Ms. P is helping me right now. Can't you see that?"

With this, the counselor stopped the group and said, "We are working on communicating respect in this group. Has anyone noticed a communication that has happened that may have felt disrespectful to another person in the room?" The counselor followed by directing Alina and Patrick to speak to one another about the interaction that had just transpired.

While Patrick's problem behavior became a major focus of the group members' interest—a real in-the-present enactment of "becoming the best we can be"—students developed skills (with group leader direction) in offering feedback to him and to each other. These exchanges offered students an opportunity to consider the importance of self-regulation for developing friendships. In the end, the group was a grand success, and although Patrick's behaviors were initially seen as disastrous, both he and the other members of the group demonstrated marked gains in both objective measures and members' subjective reports on how participating in the group benefited them.

It seems that at some point or another, most discussions about problems in a group and, even more broadly, discussions about the role of school counselors in schools raise questions about the position of school counselors with regard to *discipline*. And this circles us back to our earlier discussion about positioning—the philosophical stance from which school counselors and group leaders lead.

Some school counselors report being hesitant to "discipline" students in their schools (we use the term here as a teacher action in response to a particular incident) because they believe that doing so will compromise their ability to adequately develop counseling relationships with those students at a later time. Or they believe this precarious dual role will baffle students who will not be able to see the distinct differences between counselor and teacher. We know many school counselors, however, who have been able to adopt a school presence that is consistent and effective across the various roles they assume in schools, including classroom and small group work. They, like us, believe that discipline is about setting limits and that setting limits is not something that is inherently bad nor is it something that necessarily compromises their ability to develop supportive counseling relationships with students. As Jones and Jones (2001) said, "The main issue is not whether teachers should be less warm or friendly, but that they must simultaneously assert both their right to be treated with respect and their responsibility for ensuring that students treat each other with kindness" (p. 83).

We offer a metaphor for thinking about discipline as a guardrail: Imagine a road without guardrails that bridges a deep canyon. Crossing this road will be difficult and very scary for many drivers—not being able to clearly see where the edge of the road ends and where the fall begins. Putting guardrails on this road, however, lessens the anxiety and makes the journey across the canyon easier to travel. Like guardrails that provide drivers with a clear and secure barrier so that their vehicles can cross the canyon safely, limits allow students to know how close they are to the edge and protect them from falling off. Note that in this metaphor, cars are not supposed to crash into the guardrail to prevent them from falling into the abyss. Rather, the guardrail, like clear limits that uphold and enforce the rules and responsibilities of being a member of the school or a particular group, is intended to alert drivers that the abyss is very real.

Image 3.5

In schools, the guardrail is constructed from norms and rules that are clear, fair, and enforced—something we will discuss in more detail in Chapter 8. When the term *discipline* is synonymous with setting limits, then it is like the metaphoric guardrail that provides safety for crossing through difficult places. We would argue that when discipline refers to limits that are set with a focus on learning and imposed in ways that respect the integrity of others—as they always should be—then, yes, school counselors, like all professionals in schools, should use "discipline" with their students. You will notice that the interventions included in the second part of this text (Chapters 7–9) are offered from a position of providing guardrails to shape student behavior. They outline ways in which group leaders can intervene in increasingly direct ways (moving toward a more autocratic approach on the leadership style continuum as needed) to respond to problems that may be developing in their groups.

A few caveats warrant mention here. First, remember that not all roads have guardrails. Guardrails are only put along the roads that need them. This is true, too, for leaders who set limits in the group. Second, remember that guardrails do not attempt to steer individuals across the canyon. Group leaders should give students every opportunity to steer themselves successfully toward their desired destinations—the guardrails are just on the periphery to assure that the student is doing so safely. Third, well-marked guardrails allow for safe passage, but they do not usurp personal responsibility or self-control. Drivers must still work within the safety zone. Finally, we point out that consequences for venturing out beyond the rail must be clear, fair, and without discipline in a draconian sense. This is a delicate balance at times. Remember Patrick from Case Study 3.3? The school counselor had subjective urges of telling him to "sit down, pay attention, and don't ruin this group for those who really want to be here!" but that would have been "grabbing hold of the wheel" rather than maintaining the guardrails and allowing both Patrick and other members of the group to navigate the road appropriately and successfully. If, however, dangers had arisen in the group due to Patrick's behavior, the counselor would have needed to intervene more actively, and these actions likely would have included imposing consequences for his inappropriate behavior. As we have mentioned throughout this discussion on group leadership styles, group leaders need to be able to engage in various forms of leadership when responding to challenges in their groups.

Reflection Questions

1. Think about a class that you are currently enrolled in. What group dynamics have you noticed? How does the course instructor navigate those dynamics?
2. Systems theory describes the power dynamics that exist within systems and that influence the interactional patterns and outcomes of groups. Can you think of examples of power dynamics that exist in a class you are currently enrolled in or have taken in the past? Consider how interactional patterns within the course you named earlier may be influenced by the culture of the suprasystem within which your university, program, and course exists.
3. What interventions might a group leader use when strong cliques or subgroups appear to be inhibiting cohesion and group functioning in a school group with youth? Might these interventions be different in different types of groups (counseling, psychoeducation, task)?

Credits

Table 3.1: Irvin D. Yalom and Molyn Leszcz, "Therapeutic Factors," *Theory and Practice of Group Psychotherapy*, ed. 5. Copyright © 2008 by Perseus Books Group.
Img. 3.1: Copyright © 2012 Depositphotos/gunnar3000.
Img. 3.2: Copyright © 2015 Depositphotos/Oliver26.
Img. 3.3: Copyright © 2013 Depositphotos/ivelin.
Img. 3.4: Copyright © 2012 Depositphotos/zizar.
Img. 3.5: Copyright © 2010 Depositphotos/sovlinik.

CHAPTER FOUR

Group Planning

Membership, Goals, and Objectives

Introduction

The call for school counselors to be integral to the mission of their school communities by providing a wide range of services intended to support the academic success of students is, indeed, mighty. School counselors are asked to deliver curriculum and individual planning services to promote academic, career, social, and emotional development and to be prepared to meet immediate needs and concerns that may put some students in peril of academic success (ASCA, 2019). It is inconceivable to imagine that any school counselor could manage these hefty responsibilities without strong professional and personal organizational abilities. Being organized is the foundation for the group work practices described in this and the following two chapters.

We begin here with a discussion about group membership—factors to consider when making decisions about who might benefit from the different types of groups offered in school. This section on group membership is summarized in a series of questions in Figure 4.1 that are designed to guide group leader thinking on membership planning. We then focus on how goals and objectives can aid in meeting member needs and group purpose. Our point is that planning groups to address specific goals and objectives is essential to ensuring that a group is purposeful and productive. We pick up on this discussion in the following two chapters where we discuss planning assessment measures to ensure that goals have been met (Chapter 5) and planning strategies and activities to use in the group that are consistent with individual and group goals (Chapter 6). We end this chapter with an overview of how to write group plans. The advance spoiler for this and the following two chapters is this: groups work when they are planned well. Taking the time to carefully plan the hows, whats, and whys of how a particular group will unfold and using simple assessment tools to determine if intended goals have been met helps to ensure that school groups will be meaningful and successful.

Group Membership

Here we address the following important group planning questions: Who is in which group and why?

School counselors create various groups for a variety of purposes; it is the purpose of a particular group that determines their membership (Beebe & Masterson, 2015). That is, potential group members should be selected for membership in a group based on two things: (1) the extent to which they will likely benefit from the group experience, and (2) their potential to offer something to the group. The focus, topic, or content of a particular group must be matched to member need.

Groups thrive when members are generally interested in personal learning and change and display some level of openness to other perspectives (Schwarz, 2002). This speaks to the issue of motivation. Potential members should *want* to be in a particular group, or they should at least *want* the outcome that is the goal of being in a particular group. For example, if you offer a counseling group for elementary students on getting along with others, it is important to invite students who are trying to or, at the very least, who want to get along with others, even if they struggle with doing so. These intentions around interpersonal connection, then, would be congruent with the focus of the group. Let us say you have a group planned to teach anxiety reduction strategies and have selected for membership a number of students who appear to need these strategies. If these identified students are not motivated or interested in being in this group, even if we all agree that they *need* the anxiety management strategies, the group will likely fail. These points remind us of the importance of taking the time to help students understand the relevance of a particular group, finding ways to make a particular group interesting and meaningful to the student members, and highlighting the importance of screening potential members for small group experiences. Groups are more likely to be successful if there is a match between student membership and group purpose.

Classroom Groups

Classroom-based psychoeducational groups are typically designed to meet the curricular component of comprehensive developmental school counseling programs (Stone & Dahir, 2006) or the curricular dictates of a particular school (Schmidt, 2007; Sink, 2005). They typically focus on some aspect of cognitive, behavioral, social, or affective growth and development (the ASCA model highlights the domains of academic, career, personal, and social development [ASCA, 2019]). For example, a school counselor offered a 3-week group focusing on career readiness in sophomore English classes. Another facilitated a four-session psychoeducational classroom group on identifying, naming, and expressing feelings in an elementary school. Yet another school counselor conducted a 6-week,

Image 4.1

healthy relationships, classroom-based, psychoeducational group as part of the health curriculum for eighth-grade students in her middle school.

What is important to point out in regard to these and most classroom-based psychoeducational groups is that these types of groups are intended for *all* students in a particular class. This means many things. First, there is no screening or selection process involved in deciding group membership—everyone who is in the class will be a member of the group. Second, these groups tend to be fairly large. As teachers know, managing a large number of students at one time can be a challenge. Third, within each group, there will be a wide variety of student learning and behavioral styles, needs, motivations, and academic readiness. These groups are not typically structured around the needs of an individual student in the class and not all of the students will be equally interested in or in need of the particular content of the group. Finally, school counselors conducting classroom groups will enter into a room of existing classroom dynamics with all of their unique social patterns already fairly well established. For example, some students in the class may be in conflict with each other, some may be dealing with a difficult or frustrating instructional content, or there may have been a critical incident that happened earlier in the day. This means that there is much to attend to in classroom group work. Classroom group plans must accommodate a variety of learning needs, styles, and prerequisites, and leaders will need to be diligent about selecting topics and activities that are suitable for a range of students. This is not only a good idea but also an ethical mandate for school counselors (see ASCA, 2016). Also, entering into existing group dynamics requires a high level of leader awareness and a wide repertoire of intervention skills (such as those included in Chapters 8 and 9). In summary, because membership selection in classroom group work is usually not possible, planning classroom-based psychoeducational groups requires careful and creative forethought, and running these groups requires confidence and flexibility.

Counseling Groups

Counseling groups are another way in which school counselors are able to promote social, emotional, behavioral, and academic development or skills. School counselors also use these groups to address specific interpersonal and emotional issues, problems, and/or needs that are common to a small group of students (ASCA, 2019; Schmidt, 2007; Sciarra, 2004; Stone & Dahir, 2006). Examples of these kinds of groups include a small counseling group of fourth and fifth graders who are distracted by experiences of having a parent in jail or prison, a counseling group for middle school students who have difficulties asserting themselves, or a group for high school students who are in the process of exploring or asserting their sexual orientation.

The content of counseling groups tends to be designed around the specific needs of its members. When appropriately matched to a group topic, students will likely have a high level of motivation to be in these groups. For example, a student may struggle with asserting himself, but he really wants to be able to be assertive with his peers. So, in this example, the student is motivated, if not yet able, to achieve his goals. Counseling groups tend to be much smaller and less instruction focused than classroom-based psychoeducational groups, and the format of counseling groups typically encourages personal sharing and interpersonal interaction among members (Sink, 2005). While these groups may include psychoeducation or instruction, the smaller and member-focused goals of these groups really allow for the generative use of process to promote content.

In small counseling groups, membership is based on a screening process that allows for matching students to groups (and vice versa). Screening conversations typically involve informing students of the purpose of the group and gathering some information about the students and their experiences or expectations related to the intended focus of the group. The informed consent process for these groups also typically includes providing information about the group to parents or guardians and seeking their consent for services; again, seeking parental/guardian consent is an ethical obligation of school counselors (ASCA, 2016). Finally, screening also entails making the determination if a particular student has the requisite emotional development, behavioral skills, and knowledge to be able to participate in the group in a meaningful way. In other words, while a student may be interested in being in a particular group and may be in need of the content addressed in the group, if that student is not able to adequately participate as a group member with others in a group, the counselor may decide that placement is not appropriate. In this situation, the counselor may decide to work individually with the student to help them acquire the requisite interpersonal skills and then invite the student into a similar group at a later time. Or a counselor may find that a particular student is much younger or less mature than the others who are in a group and thus arrange for a different group for the student to participate in. We add here that even when students match well for a particular group, they will, of course, be different from their peers in other ways. For example, while all of the students in a grief group may share the common experience of loss, they may be different in the ways in which they experienced the loss, and the ways that their families responded to the loss will obviously be different. There likely will be differences in other areas as well, such as in reading level, the degree to which they are introverted or extraverted, cultural and experiential background, other abilities and skills, or temperament. This wonderful mix of differences means that all of the students have something to offer to the group. But for the group leader, planning efforts must account for different needs among group members, as well as ways in which the unique contributions of various members can be shared. We will be circling back to this discussion throughout this chapter, especially in our evaluation of heterogeneous versus homogeneous grouping and group member readiness.

Image 4.2

Large Counseling and Task/Work Groups

One of the defining features of task/work groups is that they tend to be focused on the accomplishment of a particular assignment, mission, or task (ASGW, 2000; Hulse-Killacky et al., 2001). Similarly, this is true with large groups, as described in ASCA (2019) as short-term groups planned with a focus on a specific topic or activity. According to Beebe and Masterson (2015), the goals for these groups will typically be related to generating an idea, information, or options; making a choice related to a larger problem; or putting an idea into action. Different than the aforementioned classroom-based psychoeducational and counseling groups, these groups tend to have a narrow focus on an outward accomplishment or product.

Examples of task/work groups for students in school communities include topic-specific tasks (e.g., forging LGBT welcoming practices in the school), committee or planning meetings (e.g., planning a school-wide event, such as a prom), discussion groups or study circles/groups (e.g., a study circle on gender equity among interested students and teachers), team meetings (e.g., a meeting of seasonal sports teams captains), clubs (e.g., Student Government Association, Honors Society, chess club, yearbook staff, school newspaper), or in the case of the ASCA (2019) described large counseling groups, college visits or training in a specific area. What all of these groups have in common is that they are focused on students coming together to accomplish a particular goal, with the assumption that each member has at least a minimal interest in the topic and some level of skill to offer in the work of the group. Some of these groups, such as the chess club, for example, may be largely activity based—they mostly just play chess when they meet—but they may have some fundraising functions, for example. And others may have a skill development component: A Team Captains Meeting group, for example, was designed to offer leadership skills but also to plan events and discuss sports-related policies that have been brought to the attention of the athletic director.

What largely selects for membership in task/work or large counseling groups is the task for which the group is intended. For example, a task group on climate will be appealing to students who are interested in climate issues. A service club will attract students who want to engage in community service. A college informational night will be for students interested in attending college. However, while all potential members will clearly have some connection to the purpose of the group and presumably something to offer toward task accomplishment, group leaders should not assume that all potential members share a similar level of investment in these groups. Nor should they assume that all potential members have the well-tuned skills that will assure the accomplishment of the group goal or intent. These points are particularly important because task/work groups are best conducted with group work principles in mind (Corey & Corey, 2006; Hulse-Killacky et al., 2001), meaning that interpersonal, social, and communication skills are some of the skills that benefit these groups.

When the leaders of task/work or large counseling groups have the ability to select students for membership, they should pick students who have something to offer in ways that complement the group (Paisley & Milsom, 2006) and that reflect the diversity of the student body as a whole. Using a specific application process is one way to accomplish this. For example, a short essay is required of students in a particular high school who are interested in joining the school's Honor

Society. Of course, applications are not always possible or appropriate for task/work or large counseling group membership. When leaders are not in a position of screening or deciding who will be joining these groups, they may need to rely on their strong planning and intervention skills to scaffold task accomplishment and ensure that all members have an opportunity to contribute and benefit from others. These leadership management skills are the focus of the second part of the book. We point out that the group leadership skills needed to facilitate well-functioning task groups are the same skills required to successfully lead other group types.

Homogeneous Versus Heterogeneous Grouping

An important question for group member selection is whether potential group members would benefit more from being in a group where there is a high level of similarity between them and their potential peer group members (*homogeneity*), or is it better for students to be in a group where they are different from their peers (*heterogeneity*)?

We offer the example of something that we often see in elementary schools to start this discussion: "friendship groups" that are designed to offer students the opportunity to learn and practice social and communication skills. Across the schools where we have witnessed these groups, we have seen two models. In some schools, these groups have students who are very friendly and thought to have excellent social skills grouped with other students who have difficulties establishing friendships. This is an example of a *heterogeneous* group—a group of students who are different on a key characteristic that is the focus of the group. In other schools, we see *homogeneous* friendship groups where all of the students in the group struggle with social skills—none of them are faring well in their friendships.

In the balance of these decisions is, on the one hand, the valid point that students can learn from people who are very different than them; diversity offers new perspectives and new learning opportunities. Yalom's principle of universality (Yalom, 1995, 2005) sits on the other side of this balance. The idea here is that students find comfort and learning opportunities when they are in groups with others with whom they share common experiences. In these groups, they feel safe to make mistakes and take risks, knowing that their peers are also grappling with the same challenges.

Using the friendship group examples mentioned earlier, we invite you to consider some key questions related to group homogeneity and heterogeneity. In the first group, the thinking is that a skilled "role model" student can demonstrate appropriate social skills, and within the group, they can help their peers navigate challenging interpersonal interactions. But how does a "model" student benefit from being invited into a group where the major reason for their presence is to guide or somehow help others? What is the goal of the group for that student? It could be argued, of course, that being in a friendship group as a role model offers a chance for the student to teach others. Or perhaps membership in this group provides the model student with an opportunity to experience benevolence or to develop patience with or tolerance for others? Perhaps the benefit is that this group offers the model student a window into the lives of other children or an opportunity to develop empathy? These goals may be very appropriate, but are these experiences needed, wanted, and made explicit for the role models in this group? The question here is, what is in it for the role model students? It is important to remember that there should be a potential benefit or learning opportunity for *all* members of a group.

Also, we must ask about the issue of using teacher- or school counselor–selected role models. Remembering the work of Bandura (1971, 1986) discussed in Chapter 2, we know students are more likely to emulate role models who are perceived (by the observer) to have prestige, who have the power to control and dispense rewards, who they believe will reinforce them for behaving like the role model (vicarious reinforcement), and, critically, who they perceive as similar to them in some important ways. This underscores the point that the selection of *who* would be an appropriate role model in a particular group is important. And once selected, Bandura (1971, 1986) reminded us that attention, retention, motor reproduction, and reinforcement processes are key factors involved in imitation learning processes. That is, the group leader must use the modeling opportunity in very intentional ways.

Finally, we must consider positioning theory (Harre & Moghaddam, 2003; Harre & Van Langenhove, 1991), as mentioned in Chapter 1, when making decisions about the inclusion of "role models" in our example of a heterogeneous group. Positioning theorists are particularly interested in how history, culture, and social context—communicated through social discourses—dictate the ways in which individuals are invited into and participate in social interactions (Geroski, 2019). Social discourses shape how individuals interact with each other; in fact, Drewery and Winslade (1997) argued that discourses are *prescriptive*. The danger of having "role model" peers in a social skills group is the potential for the reenactment of existing social hierarchies within the school community. That is, does the positioning of a student as a "good" role model among peers who are failing inadvertently set up or reinforce a dynamic of good versus bad students in the school? Clearly, avoiding this dynamic would require nuanced work on the part of the group leader who is using a role model approach to help students achieve interpersonal social skills.

And what about the second group in our example? Recall that this was the group of students who all struggle with interpersonal relationships. We must ask, does this homogeneous group actually provide students with an opportunity to see and learn new social skills when all of the members struggle with these skills? Will they actually learn these skills from each other? Will they

Image 4.4

even get along well enough in this group to make it productive? Will the students' lack of social skills make it difficult for the leader to even facilitate this group in the first place? Clearly, for this group, the leader will also have to be intentional in leading so that the group is productive for all of the members.

At the core of the responses to these questions is the point that membership decisions must be based on the overall purpose or the goal of a group and the specific needs and goals of each potential member. Groups need to be designed in ways that promote meaningful learning opportunities for *all* group members.

Also critical is the point that context determines group makeup and student needs. There are times when member similarity on one or a few key characteristics—member homogeneity—is clearly beneficial to the mission and functioning of a group and its members. For example, if the purpose of a group is to provide an opportunity for students to talk about the inherent stressors they experience from living in a racially dominant/ subordinate society, it is very likely that the student members will benefit more from a group comprised solely of peers who similarly identify with a racial group that is marginalized in the school and/or the larger community. As Tatum (1997) pointed out, many teens will gravitate toward this type of natural grouping anyway, thus providing insight into "why are all the black kids sitting together in the cafeteria?" (i.e., the title of Tatum's 1997 book).

Providing a space for students who experience marginalization to be able to talk about their experiences in a safe group with others who share the same racial or social identity is important. And having this group limited to only those students who similarly share these troubling experiences is usually best. While it might be informative for students who identify with the dominant racial group to witness and learn from the experiences of their peers who face challenges and barriers because of their identities (race, gender, sexual orientation, etc.), this education should *never* come at the expense of students who are already marginalized in their schools and communities. That is, marginalized students do not benefit from the experience of being asked to take on the responsibility of teaching other students about marginalization. If anything, such requests and experiences are ultimately harmful to the marginalized students themselves and to their relationships with their peers. We would argue that the goal of teaching students in the dominant group about the issues of power and privilege is an important goal for all schools to embrace, but the manner in which this learning happens deserves careful attention. It should be led by well-informed school counselors, teachers, and administrators and should never fall on the backs of the students who themselves experience marginalization.

In other cases, the diversity characteristic that separates some students from others may be less salient than the issue that is the subject of the group. In these cases, heterogeneous grouping may be very appropriate. For example, it may be appropriate for a student who uses a wheelchair to be in a group focused on anxiety reduction strategies if that student is grappling with anxiety. And, of course, excluding the student from this group because of the disability is obviously inappropriate. Here the inclusion variable is the common focus on anxiety. In these situations, ability status, race, socioeconomic status (SES), sexual orientation, gender identity, and other social location characteristics do not disappear; they just may not be the primary focus in this particular group. That does not mean that these differences and their related social implications are not significant. In fact, these differences will likely surface in the group, and when they do, they warrant due attention. For example, in the case of the student who uses a wheelchair, discussing the stress of using a wheelchair in a school that is not completely accessible is likely to be relevant to the topic of anxiety. It is not something that should be squelched because it might be uncomfortable for the members or for the leader to talk about. In fact, it may even be—and probably is—appropriate for the group leader to raise this issue of accessibility in the first place. Doing so is a way of signaling that the group is a place where disability-related challenges can also be voiced.

Broaching is a concept originally introduced into the counseling literature by Day-Vines and colleagues (2007) that emphasizes the importance of creating a space in counseling for clients to talk about their experiences related to their social or cultural identities. Knowing that silence is complicit with other forms of marginalization, Day-Vines and her colleagues emphasize that it is the counselor's responsibility to broach or initiate conversations about race and other social location issues and experiences. Broaching topics of difference, bias, and marginalization communicates that the school counselor or the group leader is open and available to hear and facilitate uncomfortable conversations. Broaching invites conversation in place of silence. It invites connection rather than isolation.

Finally, we want to mention a point of nuance in the seemingly dichotomous concepts of heterogeneity and homogeneity. In one of our examples, we referenced a group of students who shared a common racial identity and made use of a group to discuss their experiences with marginalization. Even in this group where members share a common racial identity, there will be a certain degree of heterogeneity—as members will have unique personal experiences and be in different places in terms of their racial identity development; they may even be different ages. We would argue that there is value to such heterogeneity, even within a homogeneous group, as heterogeneous groups tend to yield better outcomes for group members if one of the purposes of the group is to help one's peers (Marzano et al., 2001).

Group Member Readiness

A basic level of communication and self-management skills are needed for students—or anyone—to be able to participate in a group in a meaningful way (Schwarz, 2002; Toseland & Rivas, 2005). Of course, what exactly constitutes adequate requisite skills for a particular group is not always clear-cut, and different groups will have different prerequisite requirements. For example, kindergarteners will obviously not be appropriate for a content-heavy classroom group focusing on careers. Children with short attention spans may struggle in groups where they must sit and listen to others for long periods of time. Students who struggle to manage their aggressive impulses may not be appropriate for a group populated with peers who similarly struggle with impulse control, especially when there are many of these students in one group. We maintain that a minimal level of interpersonal competence and behavioral self-regulation abilities are needed for any student to be able to meaningfully contribute and benefit from a group experience.

When students are ill suited for a particular group, they may be unfairly asked to meet inappropriate expectations, and their presence in the group may have unwanted and detrimental consequences for them and the other group members. Clearly, consistent and significant disruptions in a group will affect the learning potential for all of the students in that group. This is true for classroom-based psychoeducational groups, smaller focused counseling groups, clubs, and other types of task/work or large counseling groups. While it is incumbent upon school counselors to work diligently to make their groups accessible to a wide variety of students and to be thoughtful and creative in planning their groups so that they address the learning needs of a variety of students, it is also true that not every student can benefit from group learning all the time. Inviting a student into a group for which they lacks adequate skills to participate and benefit in a meaningful way is a set up for failure for that student, for others in the group, and for the group leader. When they are able to make decisions about who is in the group, group leaders need to pay careful attention to group member selection processes.

When working in other group venues, such as classroom-based psychoeducational groups and open-member clubs, task or other large counseling groups, counselors will need to construct plans that enable them to accommodate students with diverse communication and emotion regulation skills, and they will need to use their group leadership skills (outlined in Chapters 7–9) to manage complex group dynamics. In some cases, seeking a coleader (this may be another counselor or a classroom teacher, instructional assistant, or another member of the school personnel) can be a good way to ensure that groups with larger or challenging membership run smoothly. The questions listed in Figure 4.1 are designed to help leaders think about group membership.

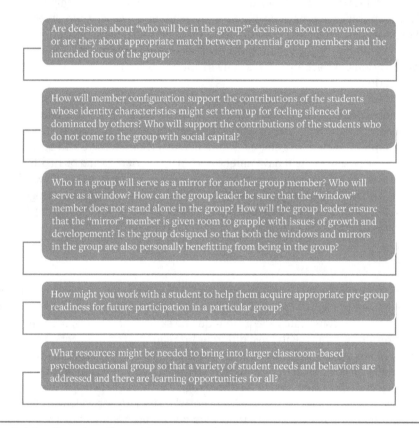

FIGURE 4.1 Guiding Questions Group Member Planning

Group Goals and Objectives

An important theme within the covers of this text is that of intentionality. Two of the critical ways in which groups function with intentionality is in the establishment of appropriate goals for the group and careful planning to assure that these goals are and remain in focus during the course of the group. According to Corey and Corey (2006), goal setting is at the core of group counseling because "in the absence of a clear understanding about the purpose of a group and meaningful goals for members, much needless floundering can occur" (p. 145).

Goals are an articulation of what one is attempting to accomplish—an "object or aim of an action" (Locke & Latham, 1984, p. 5). In the world of counseling, goals typically refer to the outcome expectations for a therapeutic experience—what clients hope to achieve as a result of a therapeutic intervention. Group goals, very generally, are the outcome expectations for the group. They are intended to provide direction and long-term plans for groups. In group work, individual and group goals are typically in alignment.

The term *objective* is sometimes used interchangeably with goal. We use the term here as recommended by MacLeod (2012) in reference to narrower, more specific, and concrete *subgoals* that direct group leader interventions or plans. In the model of group planning presented in this text, goals refer to the longer term accomplishment expectations for the group over time. Objectives refer to the short-term goals associated with an individual counseling group lesson, session, or meeting. Objectives, in our model, speak to the specific focus of each group lesson or session—the

Image 4.5

subgoals or steps that lead to the larger group goals. Both refer to the expectations of what we hope students in the group will accomplish as a result of our interventions. You will notice that the sample lesson plans in Appendices A–F include group goals in the unit plans and lesson/session objectives in the weekly plans. More on this shortly!

Goal-Setting Theory

According to O'Neill and Conzemius (2006) "although most of us acknowledge the power of goals in our own lives, they remain the single most underestimated and underutilized means of improving student learning" (p. 2). The reason that goal setting is such a powerful part of the learning process, these authors suggested, is because goal setting forces us to attend to learning—what we hope to accomplish as a result of instruction. "When we don't have a results focus," they went on to assert, "we have a tendency to keep adopting new programs and initiatives, never stopping to ask about the outcomes we are seeking to achieve" (p. 10).

Goal-setting theory (Locke & Latham, 1984) is a set of principles developed by Locke and Latham that help us understand why goals are so important to learning processes. Locke and Latham initiated their work from the premise that all human behavior is purposeful and regulated by individual goal setting. They describe goals as ideas for the future or desired end states, such as "intention, task, deadline, purpose, aim, end, and objective" (Locke & Latham, 1990, p. 2). In their research, Locke and Latham found that goal setting leads to a higher level of performance, especially when goals are *clearly articulated* and when the goals are somewhat *challenging or difficult* to achieve (Locke & Latham, 1984, 1990; Latham & Locke, 1991)—a finding that has been confirmed in subsequent research studies (Kleingold, van Mierlo, & Arends, 2011; Latham, 2016). This is because, Kleingeld et al. (2011) concluded, clear and somewhat challenging goals "initiate goal striving by directing attention, mobilizing effort and persistence, and encouraging development and use of task strategies" (p. 1290). That is, setting goals focuses our attention on their achievement.

Locke and Latham (1990) also indicate that cognitive factors, particularly *feedback* and *self-efficacy*, play a major role in goal-based performance outcomes. For example, they indicate that goals are more likely to be attained when feedback has been present; goals help translate feedback into action. Using Bandura's ideas about self-efficacy (as discussed in Chapter 2), Locke and Latham (1990) also offer research that indicates that people with higher levels of self-efficacy regarding goal attainment (i.e., holding the belief in one's ability to perform a particular task to achieve a particular goal) perform better than those with lower self-efficacy beliefs regarding goal attainment. Conversely, if students are asked to pursue and achieve goals that are too difficult—beyond their current ability or knowledge level—they will have difficulties accomplishing those goals (Winters & Latham, 1996). And when people experience failure, particularly repeated failure, their motivation to continue to work hard at achieving their goals diminishes. Recall that self-efficacy beliefs are based in large part on performance accomplishments (Bandura, 1977, 1993).

Related to this, Locke and Latham (1990) pointed out that a person's *commitment* to achieving a particular task or goal is critical for its achievement. But this relationship between commitment and achievement is complicated by goal difficulty and influence by others. When goals are too difficult, one's commitment to attain them declines, and this, in turn, affects the likelihood that they will be achieved. These authors also, however, underscored the role of *influence* by someone who has "legitimate power or authority" (p. 257) in promoting a commitment to goal achievement. That is, a person's commitment to achieving a particular goal increases when they are in the presence of someone who holds power or authority. Here we point out that group leaders are in positions of authority in schools, and thus they have a large role to play in helping students remain committed to goal achievement.

In short, goal-setting theory and its subsequent research base tell us that support in a student's environment; a student's commitment, efficacy perceptions, and level of motivation; and a student receiving appropriate feedback are important factors that help youth accomplish their goals. In contrast, "no goals or low goals" (O'Leary-Kelly et al., 1994, p. 1289, as cited in Kleingold et al., 2011) or "do your best" (Kleingold, van Mierlo, & Arends, 2011, p. 1290) goals do not clearly articulate performance expectations and thus do not adequately generate motivation for accomplishment. The messages for group leaders are (1) goals need to be challenging but not discouraging, (2) students need feedback on their performance to continue in the direction of their goals, (3) students need to believe that they will be able to attain their goals, and (4) group leaders play an important role in engaging students in goal performance.

A final interesting component of goal-setting theory has to do with the distinction between performance and learning goals. *Performance goals* are objectives that are focused on a specific desired outcome (Latham, 2016; Winters & Latham, 1996). For example, an A on an exam is a performance goal, as it represents a single accomplishment. Accomplishing performance goals is typically dependent on having prerequisite knowledge or skill (Latham, 2016) that engenders motivation (Winters & Latham, 1996). *Learning goals*, on the other hand, focus on the development of a strategy or a process that is used for increasing (rather than achieving) performance (Latham, 2016; Winters & Latham, 1996). Latham's example involved learning five specific ways that a person can improve their putting ability on a golf course. Other examples included acquiring learning techniques for taking a penalty kick in football/soccer or understanding a variety of ways to solve mathematical word problems. The point that Latham and colleagues were making is that if someone does not have the requisite knowledge or skills to accomplish a particular task, no amount of hard work will enable its accomplishment. Instead, what they need to do is "work 'smarter'" (Winters & Latham, 1996, p. 237); their goal becomes a learning goal—learning how to accomplish that task rather than performing it. The shift here is from performance to learning how to perform. Learning goals may be more appropriate than performance goals in situations where one's ability or knowledge is lacking (Latham, 2016).

We consider this distinction between performance and learning goals relevant to our earlier discussion of goals versus objectives. We suggest that unit goals be articulated as performance goals. Session objectives, however, are more like learning goals; they describe the specific steps and tasks needed for obtaining the larger performance goals.

Individual and Group Goals

Before moving forward, we want to call attention to our references so far in this text to *group goals*. Groups are typically planned to address common outcome expectations for all of the members in a particular group; the group goals are the outcome expectations of the group experience. However, group goals are typically articulated as individual group member accomplishments—what students will be able to do as a result of being in the group. And, as we will allude to in the next chapter, individual member goals are often used to assess group outcomes (Garrett, 2005). For example, the goal of a small group for middle school students was "students will be able to identify three time-management strategies." In this example, the goal of the group was articulated as an individual learning goal statement. Assessment entailed student's pre- and post-group ability to manage their time effectively.

While group goals are set for the group as a whole, there may also be additional goals articulated for specific individuals in that group (Kleingeld et al., 2011). For example, in a classroom group, the group goal was for increased effective communication among students. Within that group, the implicit goals for a few of the students were related to speaking up, and for others, it was holding back or waiting their turn. So, in this example, the goal was set for the group as a whole, and students in the group had different individual learning goals for accomplishing the larger group goal. Beebe and Masterson (2015) pointed out that when individual and group goals are matched, the group is more likely to be productive. These authors argued that the "paradox of group membership" (p. 60) is that while people tend to join groups to achieve personal goals, those goals must remain secondary to the larger group goals in order for the group to be successful. Group leaders must remain focused on the collective needs of the group rather than putting too much attention on members' individual goals. This is the difficult balance that leaders face when planning groups—providing opportunities for individual goals (whether implicit or explicit) to be met while remaining focused on the collective needs (and goals) of the group.

Not all group goals, of course, are articulated as or based on individual student goals and accomplishments. Many groups are solely focused on a group accomplishment. This is particularly true for many tasks and some psychoeducational groups. For example, the goal of a student-led task group in a regional high school was to create a formal Gay-Straight Alliance in that school. In that school and district, this effort was a yearlong project involving an extraordinary amount of support and advocacy on the part of the students, as well as a school counselor and teacher at the school. The goal of the group was to achieve this particular accomplishment (as a first step). While this task group goal may have been related to some of the individual needs, hopes, desires, and goals of some of the students in the group, the group was focused on the accomplishment of this larger task. As another example, the goal of an 8-week classroom group in another school was to create a classroom climate that was kind, caring, and supportive. This goal was accomplished through a variety of developmental guidance lessons delivered by the school counselor. In this case, while individual students benefited, the group was planned around a larger goal related to classroom climate.

Image 4.6

Positive Interdependence and Individual Accountability

Many counselors attempt to structure their group learning environments so as to provide opportunities for individual, as well as group goals to be met. One example of this is Johnson and Johnson's (2004) cooperative learning model, which introduced the concepts of positive interdependence and individual accountability. *Positive interdependence* refers to a learning task in which group performance is highlighted and individual accomplishment is a function of how well the group does (Johnson et al., 1994). *Individual accountability*, on the other hand, is focused on individual achievement rather than on a collective group goal or performance (Johnson et al., 1994).

Positive interdependence can be facilitated by inviting students to work together on tasks that are oriented toward and measured by collective group success. For example, a challenge exercise where all of the students must make it across the room walking on mats that are spaced apart requires students in the group to plan and work together to accomplish the task. It also requires that all of the students be involved in the task in order for it to be realized. Assigning student roles in these tasks can facilitate group interaction and is also an excellent way to neutralize social status differences among group members (for more on how to work with social status hierarchies in classroom group work, see Cohen, 1994). For example, having one student in the group be the "materials manager" responsible for getting the materials before and after the activity, and another the "note taker" helps engage all students by giving them important roles in the group.

Learning tasks that focus on *individual accountability* require students to individually demonstrate learning or proficiency in some way. A good way to facilitate individual accountability in counseling and classroom groups is to encourage individual goal setting. By inviting students to consider what they think will be personally relevant to them with regard to a particular topic or task, each student is able to work toward attaining their unique goal while participating in the group experience. Individual goal setting can be formalized by asking students to document their personal goals and having the leader review them periodically and/or at the end of the group. It also can happen more informally and in a more abbreviated way by asking students to consider what they might personally hope or expect to learn from a particular activity as that activity is being introduced.

Counseling and Classroom Group Goals

In small counseling groups, goals tend to be designed around a particular theme that is common to all of the students of the group. In these groups, by their very nature, group and individual goals tend to be matched closely. For example, students are selected for a self-management group based on their individual needs for personal self-management skills.

In classroom groups, however, individual and group goals may not be so closely aligned. This is because the goals for these larger psychoeducational groups are typically framed around the broader school- or district-identified goals. Many are based on the academic, career (vocational), and personal/social development instructional domains set out by the *ASCA National Model* (ASCA, 2019), or they are developed in response to a school or classroom-specific need or concerns. As mentioned, they are not typically designed around the needs of a specific student in the group. Thus the goals for these groups may not correspond directly with students' individual goals in the ways that they might in small counseling groups.

Having said that, it is probably safe to say that there will always be at least a few and hopefully many students in every classroom who are especially in need of developing competency in the area that is the focus of the classroom psychoeducational group. For example, learning to resolve conflicts was an identified curricular goal addressed in one fourth-grade developmental guidance curriculum in a local school. As it turns out, there were two students in the two fourth-grade classrooms who were particularly challenged in managing themselves when in disagreement with others. Indeed, for both of these students, the acquisition of conflict resolution and self-management skills were documented goals in their individualized education plans. So, in this situation, the psychoeducational group goals overlapped with the individual needs and goals of these particular students in the group. Our point is that while classroom-based psychoeducational groups are not typically designed around the individual needs of a particular student in the group, these groups may indeed meet the goals developed for individual students. However, the leaders of these groups must remain focused on the collective needs of the group rather than putting too much attention on any one member's individual goals.

This leads us to a reminder about the role of motivation in goal achievement (as pointed out in our earlier discussion of goal-setting theory). Generating motivation to work toward group goals can be a challenge when the group includes a wide variety of student abilities, skills, and interests. So, in groups where there is not an option to select for membership, one of the tasks of the group leader—and this is not always an easy task—is to enhance student motivation so that all of the students in the group can benefit from the group experience. Kleingold et al. (2011) recommended a "tell and sell" (p. 1291) approach to generating motivation that includes explaining the goals to all of the group members ("tell") and including a rationale for why those particular goals are relevant and appropriate for all of the members of the group ("sell"). This kind of transparency, these authors suggested, is likely to result in better group performance.

A second approach we offer here to increase motivation toward goal achievement is based on Latham and Locke's (1991) point out that when people think more intensely about a goal, they are more likely to be committed to action toward that goal. Student engagement in goal-setting discussions works toward this end, and this applies to engagement in either personal goal setting or engagement in setting group goals. In fact, group decision making in regard to group tasks and goals is also associated with increased intergroup communication and motivation (Kleingold et al., 2011). Counselors can initiate their skill groups, then, by having students begin by setting personal goals related to the topic of the group. They can ask students to identify markers of goal achievement, and later at the end of the group, to assess their own progress toward their identified goals. This process, we believe, encourages students to think carefully about and become responsible for their own learning vis-à-vis the larger group intent.

We end with a related point emphasized by Kerr and Nelson (1998): Whenever possible, students should be encouraged and given opportunities to provide input into what they are learning, and they should be invited to work with the leader to determine how the content of the group is relevant to them. This input can be elicited at the beginning of the school year, at the beginning or end of a particular topic or group, or periodically as curricular objectives change throughout the year. On a larger level, student, teacher, and parent input should always be solicited in curricular goal-setting processes for developmental school counseling programs in schools and/or at the broader district level. To this end, we see school counselors consulting advisory boards that include students and teachers, as well as working with their peer colleagues when planning curricula for their school counseling programs. Of course, communicating often and effectively with parents, guardians, teachers, administrators, and the school board also promotes engagement.

Task and Work Group Goals

Most of our earlier discussion related to goal setting actually emerges from the task group literature. So it is, of course, relevant to task/work and many larger classroom groups conducted in schools. Kleingold et al. (2011) pointed out that *task interdependence* is a defining characteristic of task group work. That is, student engagement with group member peers in information exchange, the sharing of materials, expertise, etc., affects group functioning and task completion. So the balance between individual student needs and goals, on the one hand, and those of the larger group on the other is important. For example, students in a work group planning a fund-raiser for a community organization might be assigned different tasks, and they have specific goals and deadlines for each of those tasks. The group cannot accomplish its larger goal without each student or each subgroup doing their part.

When members come to these kinds of task groups with *egocentric individual goals*—goals that are focused on their own self-interests (and we do not use this term in a derogatory way; it is just to identify their goals as personal rather than group related), the performance of the group may be compromised (Kleingold et al., 2011). For example, if one student in the aforementioned task group is determined to be seen as the leader of the group and insists on participating in each and every subgroup activity, then the group may be slowed down as it waits for this student to find time to plan and participate in each subgroup task.

Kleingold et al. (2011) pointed out that when members' individual goals are *group centric*, meaning that they are largely focused on the collective group performance; group performance is enhanced. So, in our example, if this individual student who wants to be seen as the leader of the group recognizes the value of having each subgroup accomplish its task on its own according to a group-determined deadline and instead avails herself as a "support person if needed," then the group may function more efficiently. This point about egocentric versus group-centric goals again highlights the importance of the match between student (group member) needs and group intent and the screening processes used to determine group membership. It also highlights that leaders may sometimes need to engage and help motivate members to become involved in and committed to larger group goals—something that might be accomplished by establishing positive interdependence and individual accountability when conceiving the group plans.

SMART + Goals

The concept of SMART goals is not new—educators, corporate trainers, planners, and even motivational speakers have used it for decades to identify how to articulate goals in productive or achievable language (MacLeod, 2012; O'Neill & Conzemius, 2006). The SMART acronym stands for setting goals that are specific, measurable, achievable/attainable, relevant, and time bound. The concept of SMART goals is based on two initial studies underscoring the importance of goal setting for later achievement; these studies have been subsequently supported by a large body of research (MacLeod, 2012). The first of these studies asked graduates of Yale University in 1953 if they had goals for their future. At that time, only 3% of those asked had set future goals for themselves. Then in a follow-up study 20 years later, researchers found that 97% of those initial 3% who had reported having future goals had accomplished more personal financial wealth than 97% of all of the graduates combined. MacLeod reported that a similar study of Harvard Business School graduates yielded similar results. Over the years, the SMART goal characteristics have been refined to articulate the qualities of goals that are particularly helpful in shaping achievement expectations. Here we have adapted the SMART acronym to SMART+ to include a few additional goal characteristics that school counselors can use to help guide their group goal-setting processes. All of these qualities are summarized in Figure 4.2.

Specific is the first SMART goal category (MacLeod, 2012; O'Neill & Conzemius, 2006). When writing a goal—whether for a group or an individual—it is important to be as specific as possible about what you hope to accomplish as the result of the group or learning experience or intervention. As illustrated in the unit goals in the appendices, the goal should be an articulation of who will be able to do what and when as a result of the group experience. To be specific and clear, Price and Nelson (2007) suggested leaving out nonessential or tangential words and information and remaining focused on the specific, concrete performance accomplishment expectations. The point is that writing clearly articulated and specific goals will allow you to later determine if a particular goal has been met.

This brings us to the second quality in the SMART acronym: *measurable* (MacLeod, 2012; O'Neill & Conzemius, 2006). The focus here is on defining the criteria that will be evidence of goal accomplishment (Price & Nelson, 2007). For example, "students will be able to identify three mindfulness or calming strategies."

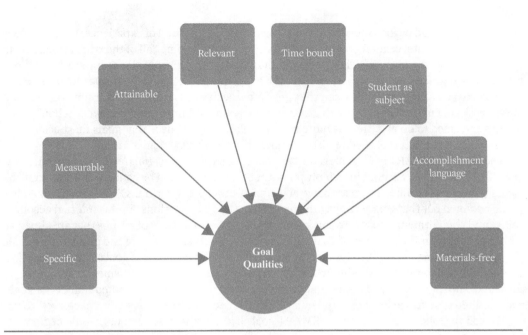

FIGURE 4.2 Goal Qualities

This clarifies that we are looking for three strategies, not one, five, or some unidentified quantity. It also identifies the accomplishment criteria as "mindfulness" or "calming" strategies, which are terms that are understood among counseling practitioners. Thus this goal is clear and measurable.

Goal specificity and measurability get at the important question that all group leaders have: "How will I know if this goal has been accomplished?" Key to answering this question is the verb that is used to articulate each goal statement. For example, "students will *recognize* ..." may be more challenging to assess than "students will *demonstrate*. ..." When goals and objectives are clearly written in specific, concrete, measurable, and, as much as possible, behavioral terminology, it is easier to assess their accomplishment, and it also helps us plan strategies designed to meet those goals (Price & Nelson, 2007). Remember that when you are able to demonstrate that the goals of a group are being met, you are more likely to garner support for your work from parents, teachers, and the administration.

The A in SMART goals reminds us to plan goals that are realistically *achievable* or *attainable* (MacLeod, 2012; O'Neill & Conzemius, 2006). The point here is that individual and group goals should also be realistic or doable. That is, given the member, time, and resource parameters inherent to a particular group, is there a realistic opportunity for goal achievement? Recall our earlier discussion of goal-setting theory underscoring the importance of motivation in goal achievement. When we perceive that the goals set by or for us are attainable—within what Vygotsky referred to as the ZPD—than we are more likely to work toward their accomplishment (for more on the ZPD, see Chapter 2; Bergen, 2008; Bigge & Shermis, 1999; Douthit, 2008; Kirylo, 2016).

Goals must also be *relevant* to the focus of the group and the needs of the individuals in the group. The R in SMART goals represents this element (MacLeod, 2012). In the words of MacLeod (2012), we do not want group members to be spending too much time "'doing the wrong things' or 'being in the thick of some very thin issues'" (p. 70). Group members should be in groups that are applicable to their needs and accomplishment expectations.

The second point here is that group goals (and what happens in those groups) should also be in alignment with or relevant to the expertise of the group leader. This is reflected in the ACA Code of Ethics (ACA, 2014, C.2 Professional Competence), which mandates that counselors do not engage in practices that extend beyond the boundaries of their training and level of experience. For example, a school counseling intervention geared toward the goal of, say, helping "all of the students pass their math exams at a 90% level or higher" is an admirable goal but probably inappropriate for a school counselor–led group because it is not within the expertise of the school counselor to prepare the students to pass a math exam, nor can they guarantee such a pass rate no matter how skilled they might be. A goal more related to math anxiety, however, is within the realm of what school counselors are trained to do and, thus, is more relevant. The bottom line is that goals must accurately reflect what can be accomplished realistically and ethically in a particular group.

The final T in SMART goals represents the concept of a goal being *time bound* (MacLeod, 2012; O'Neill & Conzemius, 2006). This simply points out that goals should be conceived as accomplishments that can be attained in a reasonable and agreed-upon point in time. O'Neill and Conzemius (2006) pointed out that goal setting with appropriate time expectations "builds internal accountability and commitment" (p. 17). To this point, we advocate for a series of groups that are aimed at accomplishing a limited number of goals that can be assessed at the end of the group rather than planning long-term "forever" groups that attempt to achieve a wide range of goals over a long period of time. When planning for time-limited, specific, goal-focused groups, assessment can be made at the end of the time frame and a subsequent group can be planned with a limited number of goals and a limited time frame for those students who might need additional work on unachieved goals.

We add the following points to the SMART goals list. First, goal statements should begin with *"students" as the subject* (e.g., "The students will. ...") so as to correctly position the focus on the people who are the intended beneficiaries of the group experience. Second, they should be worded in *accomplishment language.* That is, goals should be articulated as the expectation of what will be accomplished as a result of the group experience rather than, for example, what students shouldn't do anymore. Consider these examples: Students will learn conflict management skills. Students will have a better understanding of the grief process. Students will identify three ways to de-escalate when they are angry. These are far clearer and more motivating that than goals such as students will not be in conflict anymore or students will not hurt others.

We realize that it can sometimes be challenging to articulate a goal or an objective in positive language when they are designed to address the things that are not going well or what students are not yet able to do. The *miracle question* is a tool used by many counselors to reframe deficit-based goals into realistic potential accomplishments. This technique, a part of the practice of solution-focused brief therapy, is designed to help clients focus on future possibilities and to think broadly about the potential for change (De Jong & Berg, 2008). Basically, the miracle question sets up a hypothetical scenario where the student is asked to imagine that they fall asleep and while sleeping a miracle occurs and erases the problem from their life. The student is then asked what life would look like without the problem—what they would be thinking, doing, and feeling if the problem was no longer present. This then becomes the goal.

Case Study 4.1 illustrates how to shift from problem to goal-setting language. In this case study, the math teacher asked the counselor for help with regard to a particular issue in her class. While the teacher was able to identify a legitimate concern, translating it into a desired outcome accomplishment (i.e., a goal) was a bit challenging. The counselor needed to know what the teacher hoped she would accomplish in the group before she could actually plan the intervention. The counselor's knowledge about the learning process and anxiety helped her develop an appropriate goal statement and helped her identify the smaller group objectives that would be used toward accomplishing the goal.

CASE STUDY 4.1 Articulating Goals as Potential Accomplishments

A math teacher in a middle school asked the school counselor to work with her students because they were "very anxious" about their upcoming final exams. When the counselor asked what the teacher hoped would be accomplished in the classroom group, the teacher said, "Could you help make them be less anxious?"

The counselor wanted to have a sense of what the students would be doing or experiencing if they were not anxious during the test. She wanted to know what "less anxious" looked like. When she asked the teacher clarifying questions, the teacher expressed that the students would be able to do better on the test if they could focus on the exam rather than on their anxiety about it.

Drawing from this and her own knowledge in the areas of self-regulation and academic behaviors needed for success, the counselor developed a classroom group goal that the students would acquire test-taking skills. This goal was broken down into three smaller objectives: (1) learning self-calming strategies, (2) learning multiple-choice test response strategies, and (3) learning proper study habits. They were written as follows:

Goal: Students will acquire test-taking skills.

Objective 1: Students will learn and use three self-calming strategies when they are anxious.

Objective 2: Students will learn and use three multiple-choice test response strategies.

Objective 3: Students will develop and demonstrate three helpful study habits.

These plans were developed so that each objective was addressed as a separate group session, and the group ran for 3 sequential weeks for 30 minutes in the class math block.

Finally, we advocate for goal and objective statements to be written in *generic* or *"material-free" language* (Price & Nelson, 2007). This is not to say that the *plan* should not include the names of the specific materials that will be used, but we emphasize that *the goals and objectives* should be stated material-free. The reason for this is so that the leader can articulate what the student is expected to learn without having to track down specific materials and ascertain the intent of those materials. For example, a goal (or objective) that students will complete the Best-Ever Career Interest Inventory does not clearly articulate the desired goal of students developing a list of current, personal career interests. Even if the Best-Ever Career Interest Inventory will be used to achieve this goal of awareness around career interests, it is best considered as a means toward a goal, not the goal itself. Having said this, you should also include the names (and locations) of all materials that will be used in the weekly plan for the group in the group plan, which will be addressed shortly.

In summary, regardless of group type, students need to be clear about the expectations for the group they are in, and groups need to be facilitated in a way that allows students to participate fully and have the opportunity to meet the intended goals. It is up to the leader to structure the group toward these ends. Written group plans outline and structure how this will happen. Allow us to add a final important point alluded to earlier: plans are not laid in concrete. We do not advocate that you adhere so austerely to your plans so as to limit students' spontaneity, which can flourish in counseling, classroom, and work groups. While thoughtful planning allows counselors to facilitate the overall direction of the group, serendipity can invite unplanned learning opportunities. We would be naïve to believe that only one road leads to a desired end point. Case Study 4.2 offers an example of the importance of being flexible when following group plans.

CASE STUDY 4.2 Flexibility With Group Plans

A counseling group met for approximately four sessions with a group goal focused on physical fitness. This group was cofacilitated by the school counselor and physical education teacher during lunchtime 1 day a week. Most of the fourth and fifth graders in the group had received poor performance evaluations in physical education for a wide variety of reasons. The specific objective for this particular group session was to build a list of physical activities as alternatives to inactivity; it was called "The To-Do List."

At the beginning of the lesson, one student seemed to bear the brunt of others' giggles and subtle mocking over how she had outgrown the clothes she was wearing that day. Although the counselor loved the lesson planned for the day, it was obvious that this teasing issue needed immediate attention (and, of course, in many ways, it was related to the larger group content and the experiences of the group members). The To-Do List plans for the day were adjusted to focus on the taunting that happened in the group. Not surprisingly, it turned out that these kinds of taunts were experienced at some point and in one way or another by all of the students in the group. Consequently, the discussion was rich and beneficial. The original group goal was kept in sight, but the ways in which the group would reach those goals proved to be flexible and beneficial.

Group Planning Documents

In this section of the chapter, we will offer an outline for written group planning. This outline is also summarized in Figure 4.3. This model includes two components: (1) the unit/overall plan and (2) the lesson/session plan. The unit/overall plan is the general outline of the group over the course of multiple group sessions. It lists the rationale, goals, and general information about the group but does not include the specific strategies or activities that will be used each week. The lesson/session plan is the outline of each weekly lesson or session. This planning format is used in the sample classroom and group plans included in Appendices A–F.

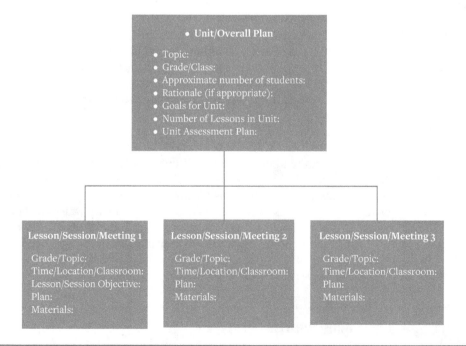

FIGURE 4.3 Model for Unit and Session/Lesson/Meeting Plans

The model we offer here is designed so that the written plans for a group are essentially the same for the classroom, counseling, and task groups. However, some task groups may require far less structure: a service club, for example, may not require detailed weekly planning documents. You may also notice that we make liberal use of teacher terminology and sometimes refer to teaching practice in this discussion (as well as the related discussions in Chapters 5 and 6), particularly in regard to psychoeducational and classroom group work. We firmly believe that there are profound differences between what school counselors and teachers do. Yet we also believe that there is much in the practice of professional teaching that can enhance the practices of professional school counselors, particularly in regard to group planning.

Finally, we want to emphasize that the best plans are those that are easily accessible for the group leader. School counselors are very busy—often running from one task to another—and, as all teachers know, managing a large group of children or adolescents can be tricky. School counselors should not be focused on trying to decipher a plan that was written some time ago while they are also focused on managing a group of enthusiastic children with boundless energy! Having all the information for leading the group available in clearly articulated simple steps is extremely helpful. The message here is (1) keep it simple, and (2) don't make it so simple so that you are left wondering what to do during the group.

The Unit Plan

As mentioned, the unit plan outlines what will occur in the group over time. It begins with general information about the group: the grade or age and number of students, the topic of the group, and the rationale (the articulated reason for the existence of the group). The unit plan also includes the goals, the number of lessons or sessions planned to address the topic over time, and a brief outline of how the goals will be assessed.

When the group goals fit with the curricular components of the school or district developmental school counseling plan, this can be referenced in a rationale statement. For example, the classroom-based psychoeducational group plans in Appendices A, C, and E reference the comprehensive school counseling program district plans for the school where those plans were implemented. Unit plans for counseling and task groups do not typically include standards-based rationales; a brief statement clarifying the purpose of these group plans typically serves as the rationale, as illustrated in Appendices B, D, and F. We understand that school counselors often do not document extensive rationales in their group planning documents, but we do recommend at least a minimal articulation of why the group has been established, as this can be helpful for school counselors who are asked to describe or justify their work to parents, administrators, or larger school boards or advisory committees.

The assessment component of the unit plan is the articulation of how the group leader will measure the extent to which the group goals have been met. The assessment of group goals is the subject of the next chapter. Here we will just point out that in some cases, school districts have specific benchmarks or student competencies that are targeted in school counseling developmental guidance programs. For example, a school district may establish a target benchmark of fewer than 10% unexcused absences per quarter in each school. Designing a classroom group intervention with the goal of decreasing classroom absences for a particular class with high truancy might fit within this broader district mission. However, we caution you to think carefully about the importance of selecting appropriate goals and assessment measures for your group work. In the example of classroom group work and truancy, we know that multiple and complex factors account for student truancy, and the assumption that a classroom group intervention alone will have a measurable effect on this larger issue may not be realistic. In this case, it would be far more appropriate to identify smaller and specific goals for this classroom group—goals that are associated with or are a part of a larger school-wide intervention plan related to the truancy issue. And it would also be best to measure these more realistic goals at a proximal level. We call your attention specifically to the discussion in Chapter 5 regarding distal and proximal assessment measures.

The Lesson/Session/Meeting Plan

The group lesson, session, or meeting plans are the outlines of what will happen each time the group meets. Each unit typically has a number of lessons, sessions, or meetings that are designed to accomplish the unit goals. Notice here our language: lesson, session, or meeting plan. Typically, the classroom-based groups are called *lessons*, matching the educational intent of these groups. Counseling groups are more often referred to as group *sessions*. Task groups are often referred to as *meetings*. Again, our model for planning is intended for use across these group types.

Lesson/session/meeting plans typically list the specific objectives for each session and the specific actions that the group leader will use toward the accomplishment of these objectives. The strategies used to meet these objectives are articulated under the section called *plans* (which are discussed in more detail in Chapter 6). Lesson plans should also identity needed materials and any advanced preparation that might be required to conduct the group—the specific names of any videos, books (including page numbers), games, etc., that might be used to achieve the objectives. While it may seem like a tremendous amount of time is required for drafting these plans, we assert that careful group planning is a key component of assuring that your group will be effective, and it is ethical group work practice (Thomas & Pender, 2007).

Reflection Questions

1. Discuss factors to consider when determining whether a group should include homogenous or heterogenous members? What challenges might you run into with each of the groups? What steps might you take to mitigate the aforementioned challenges?
2. Discuss finding the balance between writing detailed group plans—including writing potentially lengthy rationales for the group, sifting through numerous activity books to find the right activity for a particular group, and carefully drafting processing questions—and managing the pressures that school counselors have regarding time. It is worth taking the time to write detailed group plans? Why or why not?
3. In Case Study 4.2, did it seem like a good idea to postpone the plans in the middle school group rather than proceed with the activity planned for that day? Why or why not?

CHAPTER FIVE

Assessment of Group Goals

Introduction

In the previous chapter, our focus was on planning and writing group goals and objectives that give direction to group work in schools. Here we focus on goal assessment—determining if the intended goals and objectives of a group have been met—as this is a critical component of the group planning process. This focus on goal assessment is aligned with current practice in the field of counseling, which emphasizes the importance of using data-driven assessment measures to evaluate learning, growth, change, and, more generally, assuring school counseling program accountability (ASCA, 2019; Brown & Trusty, 2005; Sink, 2009; Young & Kaffenberger, 2015). Here we review key assessment concepts that can help group leaders develop useful group assessment plans. We begin with a discussion about the different purposes of formative and summative assessment practices. Then we turn to an important discussion about types of assessment data that can be used to determine the achievement of group goals. Here we highlight the difference between proximal and distal assessment measures and the match between assessment measures and types of goals. We end with a review of ethical considerations for planning assessment practices in group work.

Formative and Summative Assessment Practices

Goal assessment begins with having a well-articulated outcome expectation (Cobia & Henderson, 2007); we recommend, as discussed in the previous chapter, establishing SMART+ goals that are articulated and documented in concrete, specific, and measurable goal language. Goals articulated in these ways allow for more accurate assessment, which then informs decisions regarding continued intervention (or not), and assessment also promotes accountability. These two purposes of assessment are accomplished through formative and summative assessment practices.

Formative assessment is used at various times throughout the implementation of a specific intervention or program to assess how learning is being accomplished (Bennett, 2010; Black & William, 2009; Puddy et al., 2008). For example, a group leader may ask students to participate in an oral check-in by articulating something that each of them has learned, writing a reflection or journal entry regarding their recent group experience, or responding to a scaling question related to something that has been discussed in the group. The purpose of these kinds of formative assessment practices is for the group leader to get a sense of what the students have learned in a particular group session or over the course of a few sessions. Formative assessment is used to gather evidence that is used for instructional or therapeutic decision making and to determine if the students are learning as hoped or if adjustments are needed in future group sessions. More generally, formative assessment is used to facilitate improvement (Bennett, 2010; Black & William, 2009; Puddy, et al., 2008).

In contrast, *summative* assessments are used to evaluate what a student has achieved or learned as the result of—and usually at the end of—instruction or a group experience. Rather than focusing on assessment to inform ongoing practice, summative assessment is typically used to determine if a particular goal has been met (Bennett, 2010; Puddy et al., 2008). It is an assessment that usually occurs at the end of an intervention. For example, students may be rated on the performance of a particular task that they have been taught in a classroom group. They may take a "test" on the major concepts presented in a large counseling group. Or, using a more distal assessment measure, behavior incident reports of students before and after a group intervention may be used to determine if a particular intervention was effective.

CASE STUDY 5.1 Formative and Summative Assessment Practices

Mr. Ellis conducted a 6-week counseling group to address shared challenges of some of the sixth-, seventh-, and eighth-grade students in his school. The group was focused on issues related to weekend visits to their noncustodial parents' homes. He designed the group to address the following goals:

a. Students will have strategies to lessen the effects of stress related to living in two separate and sometimes very different homes.
b. Students will have strategies to smooth their adjustment between homes.
c. Students will feel less isolated and be able to share (articulate) their stresses related to parental divorce.
d. Students will feel more optimistic and be able to share (articulate) the benefits of living in two separate homes.

Several outcome assessment measures were designed to assess these goals:

1. Students responded to a four-item, self-report, scaling question asked at the end of each session. This questionnaire asked students to rate (on a scale of 1–10) the extent to which they believed that they acquired a stress-reduction strategy, had ideas about managing the transitions between their two homes, felt more optimistic about their transitional processes between their parents' homes, and felt that others understood their divorce-related stressors.
2. At the end of the 6 weeks, Mr. Ellis used what he called the 3-2-1 assessment: He asked each student to identify three stress-relief strategies they learned, two ideas they had for managing transitions between homes, and one new person who understands them.
3. Mr. Ellis also asked the group members for suggestions regarding the group experience.

Student responses on the 3-2-1 questions were compared to their baseline responses to those same questions. This was a *summative* assessment, as it was an attempt to determine the extent to which each student accomplished the goals of the group. Notice that this assessment was closely linked to the specific group goals—the questions that students were asked to respond to were related to the goals of the group, making it a *proximal* outcome measure.

In contrast, the scaling questions that were used each week were part of a *formative* assessment process that allowed Mr. Ellis and the students to determine each week if they appeared to be on target toward achieving the group goals. From this data, Mr. Ellis (or the students) could make adjustments when needed.

Similarly, by asking group members to offer suggestions about the group experience at the end of the group, Mr. Ellis was able to gather additional information for future group planning. In this case, every member of the group suggested that the groups be segregated by grade (i.e., a separate group for sixth-, seventh- or eighth graders)—because they felt that the stresses and concerns were very different for members of each grade.

There is some debate in the field of educational research regarding the distinction between formative and summative assessment processes and the relative benefits of each (Puddy et al., 2008). For example, Puddy and his colleagues pointed out that some promote the use of formative evaluation practices because of their potential for a direct effect on instruction. That is, formative assessment helps instructors and group leaders regularly adjust their work so that the group is effective in achieving its goals. Others argue the opposite—that summative evaluations yield more meaningful information and can also be used to inform teaching practice (Puddy et al., 2008). We believe that understanding both formative and summative assessment enables group leaders to think carefully about their assessment intentions and to align their work accordingly. For example, formative assessments have the potential to provide immediate feedback to students, group leaders, and parents/guardians, and because of this, their usefulness in informing educational and clinical decision making is invaluable (Puddy et al., 2008). If the intent of assessment, on the other hand, is to offer evidence of a program's success or justification for a particular intervention or program that has been implemented, than summative assessment measures may be more beneficial. The ASCA, for example, emphasizes the importance of using summative assessment measures for assessing school counseling program effectiveness, informing stakeholders, and ensuring school counselor accountability. The national model offers a number of examples of how school counselors can use assessment to determine program effectiveness and improve program design and delivery (ASCA, 2019).

Image 5.1

Proximal and Distal Outcomes and Assessment Measures

Brenner et al.'s (1995) proximal-distal continuum for assessing health status outcomes offers another helpful framework that is applicable to our discussion on goal assessment for school groups. *Proximal outcomes* are assessment processes that rely on objective signs and symptoms that are closely related to the goals of a particular intervention. For example, asking students who participated in a 3-week mindfulness group conducted for students with test anxiety to rate their pretest anxiety before and after participation in the group would be a measure of a proximal outcome. This is because this assessment protocol of pre-post comparison data is directly related to the specific group goal of decreased anxiety, and it is connected to the specific focus of the group. *Distal outcomes*, on the other hand, are broader indicators that are more distantly related to specific interventions and intervention goals. Collecting participant test scores or end-of-semester grades as an assessment of data points for the mindfulness-anxiety reduction group is an example of a distal outcome measure.

We point out that numerous sources of data are used to assess learning, growth, and change in schools. These include student grade point average, class/course progress/failure, attendance and truancy rates, vandalism incidents, discipline referrals, parental involvement, teacher attendance rates, standardized test scores, extracurricular activity and community service involvement, higher education choice data (Johnson et al., 2006), and various rating scales (Corey & Corey, 2006;

Gladding, 2003). Many of these are distal outcome measures because the outcomes indicated in these assessment results are not directly related or clearly linked to a single intervention—they are outcomes that are related to numerous variables.

Javdani and Allen (2011) pointed out that many large-scale efforts in promoting change are difficult to measure in practice, especially when the outcome expectations are broad and difficult to define. While it is possible that the mindfulness group mentioned earlier had a positive effect on student test scores or end-of-semester grades, we know that test scores and grade point average are also reflective of a number of other variables. For example, these scores and grades will reflect whether the students went to class, received relevant instruction, paid attention during instruction, did their homework, etc. A related example of using distal measures inappropriately is offered by Brown and Trusty (2005) in their example of using high school graduation data as a measure of the success of an academic tutoring program. Here again, there are multiple factors that affect graduation outcomes and a particular tutoring program may or may not be one of them. Using a distal measure, especially when it is a single data point, for an outcome assessment in a complex web of multifactorial cause-and-effect variables linking intervention to outcome is obviously problematic.

The point is that assessment measures for interventions should be closely linked to the intervention goals and strategies or processes that unfold in the group. In terms of assessment of individual and group goals, we suggest that formative and summative assessments based on proximal outcomes will likely offer more meaningful information in terms of goal attainment. We recommend that if you are using distal assessment measures, they should be used in conjunction with other more proximal measures.

Sources of Assessment Data

Johnson et al. (2006) pointed out that outcome data can be collected *verbally* (e.g., articulation of what has been learned), in *writing* (e.g., tests, worksheets, behavior reporting), and through *demonstration* (e.g., role play, real-life applications). All of these types of data can be collected through self-report (Bloom et al., 2009). *Verbal self-report* may, for example, entail asking students to respond verbally to questions about something they have learned or experienced in the group. *Written self-reports* are, obviously, the written version of this. For example, students may be asked to monitor their own progress toward intended goals by writing in daily logs or structured diaries (Garrett, 2005), or they may be asked to write a reflective comment ("exit card") or paragraph at the end of a group session. Students may also be asked to complete a pre-post questionnaire or assessment or to complete a more formal assessment measure, such as, for example, a depression inventory, at the end of a unit (DeLucia-Waack & Gerrity, 2001). You will notice that the middle school classroom group plan in Appendix C lists a pre/post body image questionnaire to assess all of the goals in the unit. The high school counseling group assessment plan in Appendix F makes use of a brief questionnaire, as well as small group discussion comments for the assessment of goals in that group.

Image 5.2

Self-assessment is an important source of data for goal assessment. Also valuable is input on goal attainment provided from the perspective of others. Many teachers and counselors use *observational information* or seek comments (i.e., *collateral information*) from teachers or parents to assess goal attainment. For example, Garrett (2005) recommended observing group member behavior in the group itself or engaging students in role plays, which can be useful ways to assess performance goals. Teachers, parents/guardians, and administrators are frequently called upon to produce collateral data or testimony regarding student learning outcomes (Garrett, 2005). While it can sometimes be difficult to obtain feedback from teachers and parents/guardians—as we know, parents, guardians, and teachers are usually very busy—their unique perspective can provide valuable input.

Some examples of assessments that invite others to assess student goal attainment are included in the sample group plans in the appendices. The elementary counseling group assessment plan in Appendix B, for example, makes use of a variety of assessment tools, including a teacher report linked to the second and third group goals. Similarly, the assessment plan for the middle-level counseling group in Appendix D indicates that a follow-up with referring teachers will be used as one of a number of assessment data points in that group. In both of these groups, and all of the assessment plans included in the appendices, a variety of data sources are identified in relation to the various groups' goals. This is intentional on our part, as we believe that having a variety of data points for outcome assessment has the potential to offer a richer picture of how the group has or has not been able to meet intended group goals.

We diverge for a moment to point out that there is a secondary reason for inviting parents/guardians to provide assessment information. Not only does it provide a perspective from someone who interacts with students in a different setting but also inviting parent or guardian involvement in assessment may promote the transfer of learning from the group experience to home. For example, asking parents/guardians to comment on the extent to which their children learned a particular concept taught in a group invites an opportunity for another round of student exposure to the content—an opportunity for spiral learning, which we will discuss in more detail in the next chapter. In addition, reaching out to parents/guardians to provide information or act as a source of expert knowledge about their children, gives us more information to work with in planning how to help the students we work with. It may also serve to strengthen parental/guardian involvement in school activities and could build public confidence in the work that happens in comprehensive school counseling programs. This is important, as Whiston (2007) pointed out that parental involvement is related to student success in counseling, especially for low or underachieving students. Of course, not all parents/guardians will be available or willing to complete survey instruments or provide comments and feedback. So multiple sources of input to assess goal attainment are ideal.

Image 53

Assessing Cognitive, Affective, and Behavioral Goals

Here we want to focus on being intentional about selecting an assessment measure that addresses the specific domain of a particular learning goal. By domain we mean whether the desired learning was about information or knowledge acquisition or thinking processes (*cognitive domain*), feelings (*affective domain*), or doing (*behavioral domain*). For example, giving students a multiple-choice test on steps in conflict mediation will help identify how well the students have memorized the conflict mediation steps that were taught in the group. This is an assessment of information; it sits in the cognitive domain. But it will not yield data about how well the students use the steps to resolve conflict in a role play or "real-world" situation. If the group goals are related to particular actions rather than acquired information, then the outcome measure should probably focus on behaviors. However, since cognitive knowledge often precedes action, it might be most effective to offer instruction and then assess for learning in the cognitive before looking at performance goals. This conversation speaks to the complexity of assessment, and it is a good reminder to think carefully about intended learning goals and objectives when planning assessment measures. We will speak to each domain briefly here.

Cognitive Goals

We use Bloom's *Taxonomy of Educational Objectives* (Bloom, 1956), which is a classification framework for educational or learning objectives, to discuss ways in which group leaders can assess cognitive goals. (This is usually just referred to in the shortened form of *Bloom's Taxonomy*.) Here we will start with a brief introduction to *Bloom's Taxonomy* and then offer suggestions for how to assess learning in various and increasingly complex cognitive categories. We will return to this discussion about *Bloom's Taxonomy* in regard to lesson planning in Chapter 6.

Although Benjamin Bloom's name is associated most prominently with *Bloom's Taxonomy*, the taxonomy was initially developed by Bloom and a number of colleagues in the 1950s (Krathwohl, 2002; Seaman, 2011). Since then, it has been used extensively in the field of education for instructional planning and assessment, and it has even been translated into 22 languages (Gershon, 2013; Seaman, 2011). *Bloom's Taxonomy* was originally conceived with the intent of classifying student behavior in terms of intended learning outcomes (Bloom, 1956)—what students would be doing, thinking, or feeling as a result of instruction—which is why we introduce *Bloom's Taxonomy* here in our discussion about assessment of learning goals. But it is currently used extensively in the field of education for instructional planning as well. Also, interestingly, the original intention of Bloom and his committee was to develop taxonomies for cognitive, affective, and psychomotor domains of learning, but the committee concluded that there was so little existing research in the affective and psychomotor domains of learning that their work in these areas would not be productive (Bloom, 1956). So the focus of the committee's work was limited to producing a framework for learning objectives in the cognitive domain; the identification of learning outcomes in the other areas remains undeveloped.

In the original *Bloom's Taxonomy*, six domains of cognitive learning were identified in order of complexity and moving from concrete to abstract learning. These included *knowledge, comprehension, application, analysis, synthesis*, and *evaluation* (Bloom, 1956). Anderson, Krathwohl, and Wittrock, working with additional colleagues in the early 2000s, undertook a revision of the taxonomy (Krathwohl, 2002). This revision led to changes in the terminology, structure, and emphasis (Gershon, 2013; Krathwohl, 2002; Seaman, 2011). According to Krathwohl (2002), the revision includes additional complexity in the original *knowledge* category (it now distinguishes *factual, conceptual, procedural*, and *metacognitive* knowledge); the original subcategories were renamed (the knowledge verb was changed to *remember*, comprehension became *understand*, and the verb forms of application, analysis, and evaluation became *apply, analyze*, and *evaluate*); the ordering of categories shifted (e.g., *synthesis* became *create* and was reordered after *evaluate*). But the taxonomy continues to use a hierarchical order of these learning categories. The intent of the change in category names from nouns to verbs was to use a more accurate action-oriented description of what students are doing within each category. The revised version of the taxonomy is outlined in Figure 5.1, and the discussion that follows focuses on outcome measures or assessment suggestions for each category in the taxonomy.

As indicated in Figure 5.1, the first category in the taxonomy is *remember*. At this level, learning tasks focus on the recall of facts and information (Armstrong, n.d.; Forehand, 2011; Krathwohl, 2002). Outcome measures for remembering may include articulating, demonstrating, or documenting specific facts, concepts, methods, or procedures; behaviorally, students may be asked to recite, define, tell, label, or name a particular fact, idea, or concept (Price & Nelson, 2007).

The second category is *understand*. Here students are tasked with simple meaning-making processes regarding oral, written, and graphic communications (Armstrong, n.d.; Forehand, 2011;

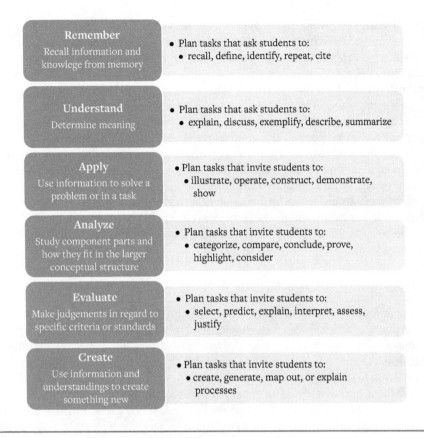

FIGURE 5.1 *Bloom's Taxonomy* (Revised Version)

Krathwohl, 2002). For example, they may be asked to interpret, exemplify, classify, summarize, infer, compare, and explain (Armstrong, n.d.; Forehand, 2011; Krathwohl, 2002). In terms of assessment, students could be invited to restate or rewrite a concept, offer an example, or summarize, paraphrase, describe, or offer a conclusion in regard to something they have learned (Price & Nelson, 2007).

The next category is *apply*. Here students are expected to use information that has been recalled, remembered, and understood (as per the earlier two categories). Verbs that describe this task are executing and implementing (Armstrong, 2016.; Forehand, 2011; Krathwohl, 2002). To assess learning in this area, students may be asked to demonstrate the correct usage of a particular concept or to predict, solve, operate, or construct something related to the topic or subject of learning so as to demonstrate their knowledge (Price & Nelson, 2007).

The fourth category in the revised taxonomy is to *analyze*. This requires the ability to divide information into its various constituent parts and detect relationships among those parts, as well as their relationship to the overall purpose or structure. Verbs to describe these tasks include differentiating, organizing, and attributing (Armstrong, 2016.; Forehand, 2011; Krathwohl, 2002). Student behaviors that might demonstrate learning in this area are to compare or contrast two ideas; distinguish between facts and inferences; categorize, diagram, or outline a concept; offer an analysis of a concept; or make decisions regarding the relevancy of data or ideas that the students have been exposed to (Price & Nelson, 2007).

Next is *evaluate*. Here the learning tasks are to check and critique. This category asks learners to make judgments about information based on available criteria and standards (Armstrong,

2016; Forehand, 2011; Krathwohl, 2002). Assessment tasks may include offering rationales; making judgments regarding the accuracy, relevancy, or appropriateness of a particular concept or idea; selecting, predicting, explaining, or rating something; or offering interpretations and support for one's conclusions (Price & Nelson, 2007).

The final category in the revised model is *create*. This category speaks to putting together pieces to make up a coherent whole or to create an original product based on the actions in earlier steps in the model. Verbs that describe this task are generating, planning, and producing (Armstrong, n.d.; Forehand, 2011; Krathwohl, 2002). Price and Nelson (2007) suggested that this level of cognitive understanding can be demonstrated through the production of a research paper or a project, where students are asked to produce, design, devise, compose, or reorganize and combine ideas to create something new or articulate their understandings.

In summary, we focus on *Bloom's Taxonomy* in this and the next chapter because it is an important part of planning lessons that allow students to be engaged in learning with increasing cognitive complexity and because it is a good guide for the assessment of learning, even when that learning occurs in a group format.

Affective Goals

Group goals that focus on affective learning are notably difficult to assess (Gronlund, 2000). Remember the *Bloom's Taxonomy* committee's initial and subsequently abandoned attempt to create a learning taxonomy related to affective goals? The reason for the challenge in assessing affective goals is largely because it is virtually impossible to make definitive interpretations about how someone else is feeling. Arguably, an important way to determine how someone feels or what they value or believe is to ask them. Yet even while student self-report regarding affect is probably the best source of information regarding student's feelings (as well as their motivations and attitudes), the truth is that self-report is not always entirely accurate. This is in part why Garrett (2005) recommended using collateral information sources for affective goal assessment.

Standardized assessment instruments, such as depression inventories or commercial anxiety scales, are sometimes used (with varying accuracy) in clinical counseling work with children (e.g., see DeLucia-Waack & Gerrity, 2001). But these tools are not often used by counselors working in school settings. Instead, school counselors typically invite student self-report about their affective states by, for example, asking them to comment on or rate their feelings. They also rely on parent/ guardian or teacher perceptions and reports for this information. The "Middle-Level Body Image Classroom Group Unit" in Appendix C is an example of a self-report tool that was designed to surface emotional responses from students regarding body image.

Behavioral Goals

Some groups, as mentioned, focus on having students learn or perform a specific skill. Here we are talking about group goals that focus on behavior or behavior change. The assessments of these types of goals are aptly called behavioral or performance assessments.

By now, we guess that you are recognizing the ways in which cognitive, affective, and behavioral goals are interconnected. Without discounting the important role of operant conditioning (e.g., reinforcement and punishment) in the learning process, we propose that many behavioral goals actually do initiate with cognitive processes. That is, knowing what to do and knowing how to do it—having a cognitive understanding about a particular behavior—often precedes being able to willfully perform that behavior. In support of this idea, we call your attention to the final *creating* category in *Bloom's Taxonomy*. The taxonomy model suggests that cognitive understanding typically culminates with a student's ability to create or produce something (Armstrong, n.d.; Forehand, 2011; Krathwohl, 2002).

This idea of knowledge preceding action is also high-lighted in goal-setting theory, discussed in Chapter 4. Latham (2016) argued that if a student does not have the requisite knowledge or skills to accomplish a particular goal, they will have difficulties achieving it. Locke and Latham (1990) made the point that cognitive factors (par-ticularly feedback and self-efficacy) play a major role in successfully attaining performance-based goals. And, of course, goal-setting theory was influenced by social learn-ing theory and, especially, Bandura's concept of self-efficacy (Bandura (1977, 1989). Direct experience and feedback are important factors in developing self-efficacy, and self-efficacy provides motivation for students to attempt challenging tasks and continue to be motivated to achieve difficult goals. So cognitive and behavioral goals are inex-tricably interconnected. For this reason, we recommend that the assessment of behavioral goals should initiate with an assessment of the requisite knowledge and skills needed to perform those goals.

Image 5.4

Let us assume now that we have completed an assessment of knowledge and are assured that a particular student has acquired the knowledge to perform a particular behavioral goal. Next, we want to assess that performance ability. One way to do this is to ask students to perform the desired behavior in the group itself. For example, the "refraining from comment" goal—in this case a behav-ior of not responding—is theoretically predicated on a thorough understanding of the sociological context of body image in the "Middle School Classroom Group Unit Plan" in Appendix C. In the elementary counseling group, Appendix B, students will be asked to demonstrate the cooperation and turn-taking skills they are learning—and the counselor leading the group will assess their performance—in the various cooperative group activities planned over the course of the group. Arguably, observing students enacting the desired behaviors in a naturalistic or nonstructured setting would be a better assessment of goal attainment than observing the skills in a role play or structured activity scenario. However, naturalistic setting assessments can be challenging to con-duct in schools both because of the high demands already placed on teachers and school counselors and because instances of problematic behaviors, such as bullying, often arise spontaneously and outside of the presence of adults.

A *functional behavioral assessment* (FBA) is a fairly simple tool that is sometimes used in schools to map behavior in the context of its antecedent and consequent events (Floyd et al., 2005; Gresham et al., 2001; Waguespack et al., 2006). It can be used in unstructured (e.g., playground) and classroom settings, and despite the challenges mentioned, an FBA is something that can be conducted by the school counselor who is leading a group. The FBA assesses the antecedent or triggering events, as well as the consequent or reinforcing/punishing actions that condition particular behaviors. It can also be used to assess the performance of behaviors related to a particular expectation. Many rec-ommend using additional assessment tools to complement the FBA, such as behavior rating scales, questionnaires, interviews, self-report or self-monitoring instruments, and direct observation in a naturalistic setting (e.g., see Floyd et al., 2005; O'Brien & Carhart, 2011; Waguespack et al., 2006).

Teachers and parents/guardians can provide additional anecdotal and collateral data that can offer important insights in regard to the attainment of behavioral goals. For example, in a brief conversation at the end of a planned group experience, a counselor can ask a teacher, parent, or guardian if improvements have been made. To make this request more focused and thoughtful, these informants could be asked to rate problematic behaviors on a simple pre-/post-questionnaire. Additional school-collected data can also be used as collateral information in the assessment of individual or group behavioral goals. For example, a comparison of the number or type of disciplinary reports collected about a student before and after the group experience can point to meaningful change. However, keep in mind that this is a somewhat distal measure, as multiple unidentified variables could also have affected student disciplinary reports, so this type of assessment measure should not be used in isolation.

Again, there is a limitation in goal assessment measures that rely solely on behavioral performance. For example, if a student displays a poor behavioral performance, it remains unresolved whether cognitive learning actually occurred or if the difficulty was just in the performance. This is why we pointed out earlier that it is best to pair the behavioral or performance assessments with a knowledge assessment. Another limitation of using behavioral assessment tools is that teachers and counselors sometimes feel overwhelmed by a large amount of paperwork that they have to complete in the regular course of their jobs, so they may not be open to completing a survey or checklist. Similarly, parents/guardians may be quite busy and not able to complete forms and checklists. So be realistic and fair in what you ask and expect others to do.

Responsible and Ethical Assessment Practices

School counselors are guided by professional and ethical obligations to demonstrate accountability for the intended outcomes of the groups they run, as well as to the ways in which they measure

Image 55

those outcomes. The codes of ethics of the ASCA (2016) and the ACA (2014) offer important guidelines regarding assessment practices. These guidelines highlight the importance of being careful in the selection of assessment measures; engaging in culturally and developmentally appropriate assessment practices; protecting student and family confidentiality, particularly in the reporting of outcome data; and being mindful of assessment limitations, particularly in regard to the reporting results. These guidelines caution us to think carefully about our assessment practices, even if they are small-scale practices that we believe pose little risk to the members of our groups.

One factor that requires careful consideration is the extent to which the students feel comfortable or safe in a group and with the counselor/group leader and how this issue of safety affects assessment results. This issue of safety is particularly salient in situations where students are asked to provide feedback to group leaders regarding their experience in the group. Because of power differentials, it is likely that students will be concerned about the repercussions of providing negative feedback to a group leader. Many students would be reluctant to tell a group leader, for example, that they did not like a group experience that that leader so carefully planned for them. This issue of honest self-report may be particularly salient for students who identify in minority or marginalized social locations (Sternberg, 2007). For example, would a student who occupies a minority social location within a particular group be able to say that the group was boring and unproductive? That the peers in the group were not open, friendly, or inviting? Imagine how this issue would quickly become even more complicated if there are cross-racial or cross-other social category differences between the leader and this student. So it is incumbent upon the group leader to use assessment practices that do not leave some students feeling vulnerable, targeted, and unsafe or that do not inadvertently set up a situation where students are not able to provide honest self-report information.

This leads to our second point, which also has to do with ethics related to assessment practices with culturally diverse students. Sternberg (2007) pointed out that the very act of assessment has very real effects on student performance, largely because the meaning of assessment (as well as the meaning of the concepts of smart and intelligent) varies across cultures. Sternberg also cautions that the use of the term *test* may conjure expectations that are not consistent with our intentions. So group leaders should be aware of the language they use when introducing assessment processes to students in their groups. The second part of this concern has to do with a lack of culturally sensitive definitions of success in assessment tools. When assessment measures fail to take into consideration language proficiency limitations or cultural differences in self-expression—for example, cultural norms about the expression of sadness, anger, self-praise—the information yielded by such assessments will be misunderstood at best, incorrect at worst. Sternberg added that individuals from different cultures may think about concepts and problems differently than how they are conceptualized in instruction and assessment instruments, so inviting students to explain or describe their understandings rather than just indicating "yes" or "no" may be particularly helpful with a diverse population of students. Finally, group content that is far from the experience of the members of the group will probably require more time and instruction, and this means that assessment practices need to be timed with realistic expectations for student achievement.

Third, it is important to recognize that assessment results that fail to demonstrate concept proficiency—the goal of the group has not been met—may say more about the community of the learners or the instruction than about any individual within that group (Sternberg, 2007). Failure on a test or other assessment measure, for example, may reflect factors other than ability—factors such as poor health, a lack of understanding of the requirements of the assessment tasks, or instruction that is inadequate or inconsistent with the students' cultural frame of reference. And, of course, a lack of individual progress toward goals may also reflect a poorly designed or poorly conducted group experience. The point is that poor performance on outcome data may be related to any number of variables—variables that we are aware of and those that are beyond our immediate field of vision.

Of course, this discussion about bias is related to larger discussions about assessment and test bias in K–12 education and higher education. The issue of test bias in educational and psychological professional communities has long focused on race, gender, and SES/class group differences in standardized assessment results (for more on this, we suggest reviewing the FairTest website: www.fairtest.org) and unfair practices of student placement or tracking practices. This debate continues to raise questions about whether racial, gender, and SES differences in standardized assessment results are due to flaws in assessment instruments themselves or, instead, reflective of flawed educational settings that are inherently unfair and unequal. This compels us to think more broadly about the ways in which any assessment data is used in schools. While these debates tend to focus on standardized assessment practices, they also have relevance to the kind of nonstandard assessment measures that are used to assess goals in school-based groups. We must always ask what kinds of biases and blinders we bring into our practices of assessing the success of our groups and what kind of messages flawed data communicate to larger school and community stakeholders.

Another point is that while sharing assessment outcomes with parents/guardians, teachers, and school administrators can be helpful for obtaining feedback, any reporting of group assessment data to public sources should be provided in a way that protects student confidentiality. This extends,

Image 5.6

of course, to the distribution of assessment information in newsletters, quarterly or annual reports, and meetings with particular interested or invested parties (such as the parents/guardians or teachers of the students in your group). We also suggest that whenever possible, group leaders should share their assessment results with the student members of their groups. This allows them the opportunity to reflect on their learning and feel that they are a part of their learning process (i.e., that they help construct learning, it does not just happen to them). This provides an avenue for the leader to gain valuable student insights about the assessment and group process and for future directions with the group.

While it is affirming when the feedback from assessment indicates that our students have learned what we had hoped they would learn, we know that this does not always happen, even when we have worked hard to plan excellent learning experiences for our students. Cobia and Henderson (2007) pointed out that the "purpose of the evaluation is to determine the extent to which program goals are being met *and* provide information that will lead to program improvement" (p. 70, emphasis added). This reminds us to use assessment data in a formative way—to account for our program strengths, as well as our program weaknesses. If assessment data yields unfavorable information, that information can help us make changes to accomplish our original group goals. Where we are ineffective, we are obliged to take steps to improve group outcomes. This ends our discussion of the concept of assessment measurement *utility*. This term, offered by Bloom et al. (2009), refers to the extent to which a particular assessment measure is efficient, cost-effective, relatively easy or convenient to use, readily accessible, and relevant to intervention planning (i.e., the extent to which it offers formative information). If an assessment process is too complicated, it is likely that it will not be used effectively. Our final recommendation is that assessment measures should be realistic and usable. The point is, keep it simple.

Reflection Questions

1. Review the lesson plans in Appendices A–F. Do these lessons incorporate assessment measures that get at a range of cognitive complexity, as described by *Bloom's Taxonomy*? What additional assessment measures might be implemented to assess higher level cognitive understandings?
2. What should a group leader do if their assessment yields findings that some of the members have mastered a particular concept and others have not?
3. How might a group leader set up an assessment process that invites students to offer honest feedback in a way that does not also leave them feeling vulnerable or unsafe?

Credits

Img. 5.1: Copyright © 2012 Depositphotos/alexskopje.
Img. 5.2: Copyright © 2014 Depositphotos/tonodiaz.
Fig. 5.1: Adapted from R. E. Mayer, "Rote Versus Meaningful Learning," *Theory Into Practice*, vol. 41, no. 4. Copyright © 2002 by Taylor & Francis, and K. M. Price and K. L. Nelson, *Planning Effective Instruction: Diversity Responsive Methods and Management.* Copyright © by 2006 by Wadsworth Publishing.
Img. 5.3: Copyright © 2014 Depositphotos/artisticco.
Img. 5.4: Copyright © 2018 Depositphotos/motortion.
Img. 5.5: Copyright © 2017 Depositphotos/ImageSource.
Img. 5.6: Copyright © 2013 Depositphotos/Aquir014b.

CHAPTER SIX

Group Planning

Strategies and Activities

Introduction

We have already discussed the importance of planning for groups so as to ensure that they are productive. Chapter 4 focused on group membership decisions and planning groups with clearly articulated goals and objectives. This was followed, in Chapter 5, with a discussion about establishing assessment systems to determine if a group was successful and to inform continued group planning. In this chapter, we focus on selecting strategies and activities that the leader will use to facilitate learning and goal achievement. We use the term *strategies* in reference to the specific activities, exercises, and concrete instructions that are planned for each group meeting (and documented in the lesson/session plans).

We want to call your attention to two important threads of our discussions in this chapter. The first is about *intentionality*. Here we reference the learning theory concepts discussed in Chapter 2 to invite you to think about how to engage students in increasing levels of cognitive complexity. The discussions in the first part of this chapter, then, are aimed at thinking about adding depth, promoting meaning making, and fostering skill development. Second, we call your attention to the dynamic balance between providing structure through careful group planning and being *flexible*. Group plans are critical, but equally important are opportunities for in-the-moment spontaneous learning that often arises from interactions and critical incidents that emerge in the group. This is the beauty of group work: it allows group members to learn from each other; structure should not inhibit this critical learning potential.

Scaffolding Cognitive Depth and Intentional Meaning Making

When we talk about *meaning making*, we are referring to an aspect of learning where concepts and ideas are transformed into meaningful information that the learner can make sense of and then build upon, act on, or somehow become moved or changed. Recall that Piaget (1972) used the terms *assimilation* and *accommodation* in reference to how individuals make meaning or learn from new material. Assimilation involves incorporating new ideas into existing cognitive structures, and accommodation means changing those cognitive structures as a result of the new information. Learning requires a balance, or in Piaget's terms, *equilibrium*, between these processes.

To further locate what we mean by meaning-making processes, we also bring your attention to Vygotsky's emphasis (also discussed in Chapter 2) on the roles of language and culture in cognitive development. He argued that all cognitive functions originate in and are products of social interactions (for more on Vygotsky and the roles of language and culture in cognitive development, see Bergen, 2008; Champe et al., 2013; Emihovich & Lima, 1995; Wertsch, 1985). Vygotsky argued that learning is not merely an active process, as Piaget explained, but also a social process. This is encapsulated, too, in the social constructionist perspective of knowledge, offered here by Vivian Burr:

> It is through the daily interactions between people in the course of social life that our versions of knowledge become fabricated ... what we regard as "truth" ... is a product not of objective observation of the world, but of social processes and interactions in which people are constantly engaged with each other. (Burr, 1995, p. 4)

In our notion of meaning making, then, we want to convey this social constructionist premise about learning: Knowledge is not merely transmitted to individuals—it is constructed and reconstructed in a learning process. Learning implies an active engagement by and with the learner.

Group work affords rich opportunities for students to be engaged in meaning making because it provides a venue for members to "negotiate and re-negotiate" (Bruner, 1990, p. 67) knowledge, experiences, and meanings together. Further, group leaders play a critical role in facilitating these meaning-making processes (Wheelan, 1990). This happens when there is intentional planning for complex thinking and through attention to and navigation of group process dynamics. Lieberman et al. (1973) argued long ago, and most group leaders still agree, that helping group members make sense of what is happening in the group is linked to positive group outcomes. Here we discuss how leaders can intentionally facilitate the construction of meaning by working with mental models and spiral learning.

Mental Models

Tileston (2004) highlighted the ways in which learners use mental models for understanding new concepts and ideas. A *mental model*, according to Tileston, is a cognitive representation of an idea or concept that is formed from existing information and experience. Mental models become a referent for thinking and reasoning and thus serve as a base from which new concepts are constructed; something that Piaget referred to as *schemata*. The idea is that meaning is erected from linking new concepts to existing knowledge and from reflection on experience.

There are a number of ways group leaders can stimulate the use of mental models to help students grasp new concepts and ideas. One is *mapping*. Sequencing learning tasks according to a logical order or mapping connections between concepts helps students construct a model for understanding. Leaders can then verbally *remap* that sequence or connections between concepts at the beginning of each session. This remapping serves as a reminder and helps students recall the concept model they have been building. Presenting information in a *variety* of ways and *cuing* student attention to key concepts or ideas are additional ways of stimulating the formation of mental models. Students can also be presented with *steps* for learning a particular skill and then be asked to *self-coach* or *self-verbalize* these steps as they *practice* or *enact* the skill. Tileston (2004) also suggested that teachers (group leaders) *pause periodically* and *invite students to stop and think*, as this allows students the time that they need to make connections between new information and existing experience and knowledge. These suggestions are incorporated in Figure 6.1.

Spiral Learning

Learning does not happen through a single exposure to information; most of us must study new information over and over again to really understand it. Bateson (1994) proposed that "lessons too complex to grasp in a single occurrence spiral past again and again, small examples gradually

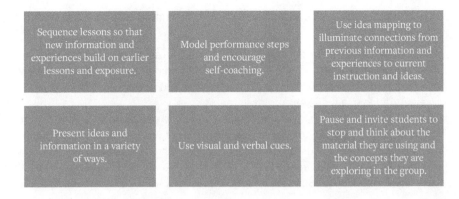

Sequence lessons so that new information and experiences build on earlier lessons and exposure.	Model performance steps and encourage self-coaching.	Use idea mapping to illuminate connections from previous information and experiences to current instruction and ideas.
Present ideas and information in a variety of ways.	Use visual and verbal cues.	Pause and invite students to stop and think about the material they are using and the concepts they are exploring in the group.

FIGURE 6.1 Creating Mental Models

revealing greater and greater implications. … Spiral learning moves through complexity with partial understanding, allowing for later returns" (p. 30–31). So, providing students with multiple and varied exposures to information is an important way of facilitating understanding.

Learning objectives can be spiraled in group work in a variety of ways. For example, information can be presented to students through didactic instruction. Then students can be encouraged to engage in an activity where they must apply that information; this spirals students through the information a second time. Encouraging students to discuss the topic as they are working creates an additional pass. Structuring these discussions by asking strategic questions aimed at stimulating critical thought can introduce more complex thinking and draws attention to certain aspects of the topic that may require additional attention. Ending a group or lesson by asking students to personally reflect on the concept or what they have learned spirals them again through the information. Case Study 6.1 offers two examples of spiral learning.

Image 6.1

CASE STUDY 6.1 Intentional Meaning Making Through Mental Models and Spiral Learning

EXAMPLE 1

Mrs. Morrissey, a middle school counselor, planned to facilitate meaning making in her counseling group focusing on conflict mediation. During the first two group sessions on the topic, students were taught some basic communication skills and a conflict mediation process. Over the next 2 weeks, students were assigned to work in small groups to draft real-life conflict scenarios that they would then mediate. During the fifth and sixth weeks, students performed their conflicts and mediations in the group. After each conflict scenario, Mrs. Morrissey spiraled the learning by asking these processing questions:

- Why is it important to ask the protagonist's (the central character) to share their opposing positions in the conflict before moving on to the brainstorming options phase of the process?
- How was it for you to use these strategies? What did and did not work? How come?
- Have you ever tried to use these strategies in real life?
- What might be/are the strengths and pitfalls when you try to use them in real-world settings? How might you have to adapt them? What other skills might you need to call into play?
- What other strategies have you used to mediate conflict in the past, and how have they worked?
- What is the hardest part of mediating conflict in real-life situations? Can these skills help? What else will you need to be successful?

There is no one correct answer for these questions. They are primarily designed to scaffold depth through repeated exposure to the concepts under study and to invite critical thinking about solving conflicts. The leader's expectation for the group was that students would be engaged in the learning, and she believed that they would more likely use the conflict resolution steps in their own lives if they were repeatedly exposed to them, if they had an opportunity to practice them in the group, and if they had a chance to brainstorm in advance what challenge they might face during implementation.

EXAMPLE 2

Mr. Garcia was planning a unit on feedback exchange in his work with a fifth-grade teacher who hoped her students would learn better ways of communicating with each other, especially when they were in disagreement. He planned four classroom group sessions where students would learn steps in meaningful and effective feedback exchange. The first step would involve introducing and discussing the value of feedback and increasing student's motivation to acquire effective feedback skills— this he would do with some selected materials and an activity. Next, he would instruct students on a specific feedback exchange model, clearly describing and demonstrating the steps (these steps are outlined later in this chapter). The third step would then involve structured role plays where students would work in triads to practice the feedback skills with a peer in the role of process observer who would then provide them feedback (using the feedback model they were learning). At the end, Mr. Garcia planned to revisit the discussion on the value and role of feedback in a group, and he intended to use a final round and exit card assessment to have students reflect a final time on the skills they had learned and practiced.

As these examples demonstrate, spiral learning stimulates and engages students in slightly different ways. In both examples, the group leader spiraled through the material in a variety of ways. The repeated exposure to the information was intended to provide students with multiple opportunities to make meaning and learn with increasing complexity. Planning learning opportunities in these ways will stimulate complex thinking, increase the likelihood that group goals and objectives will be met, and offer strong promise for the application and retention of learning.

Bloom's Taxonomy

Recall our discussion in Chapter 5 regarding *Bloom's Taxonomy* (Bloom, 1856), which is used extensively by educators for promoting cognitive complexity through planned instruction. As mentioned earlier (Gershon, 2013; Krathwohl, 2002; Seaman, 2011), the revised taxonomy focuses on learning tasks that engage students in *remembering, understanding, applying, analyzing, evaluating,* and *creating.* These categories were summarized in Figure 5.1 in the previous chapter. While that discussion focused largely on assessment processes, here we revisit the taxonomy with a focus on planning group strategies to facilitate complex learning.

Taxonomy Learning Task Components

According to *Bloom's Taxonomy*, the simplest learning process is information retrieval or *remembering* (Mayer, 2002). Learning tasks, exercises, or activities aimed at this level of cognitive understanding invite students to recognize, define, tell, name, label, match, recite, locate, or recall information (Hunter, 2004; Price & Nelson, 2007), "but not necessarily understand that information" (Hunter, 2004, p. 103). Examples of a remembering task in groups conducted by a school counselor are to have students identify five steps in problem solving, define what is meant by metacognitive skills, or find and bookmark the online College Board (or any other) college search engine. While Hunter's point about understanding is important, Mayer (2002) pointed out that remembering learning processes are essential for engagement in subsequent and more complex knowledge tasks.

Shifting learning tasks from simply remembering to more complex information processing moves us to *understanding*. This stage in Bloom's Taxonomy refers to determining meaning from instructional messages, making connections between concepts, and incorporating new information into existing schemas (Mayer, 2002). Instructional practices aimed at increasing concept understanding include asking students to classify, paraphrase, exemplify, describe, summarize, compare, infer, or explain information or concepts (Mayer, 2002; Price & Nelson, 2007). For instance, in the classroom group on feedback exchange in Case Study 6.1, Mr. Garcia's plan was to ask students to describe the group's feedback exchange model and explain why it was important. He also planned to ask students to discuss why each step of a problem-solving process was important. These were his ways of prompting understanding.

Information and understandings are particularly useful when they can be used in or applied to a particular situation (Hunter, 2004). This is the next level of cognitive understanding in Bloom's Taxonomy: *applying*. Learning tasks such as asking students to make predictions, solve equations, think through potential solutions to a problem, or illustrate, operate, or construct are all examples of application tasks (Price & Nelson, 2007). For example, after asking students to bookmark the College Board website on their computers, the school counselor asked them to explore the site for about 5 minutes on their own. Then the counselor demonstrated the college search engine feature, using a particular college search. Next, the students were asked to find three small colleges with under 5,000 students and a Division 3 soccer program that offer majors in communications and media studies or a related discipline.

The next level of complexity in Bloom's Taxonomy is *analyze*. This entails investigating and studying the various components of a concept and grasping how each of these parts play a role in the larger conceptual structure (Hunter, 2004; Mayer, 2002). Mayer (2002) pointed out that analysis requires (1) being able to ascertain the key points or components of a task, message, or concept; (2) understanding how these points configure together; and (3) understanding the underlying purpose of a particular message or concept—something he refers to as *attribution*.

Learning tasks aimed at this level of cognitive processing include asking students to distinguish, categorize, outline, and/or diagram concepts; compare and contrast juxtaposing ideas and concepts; articulate conclusions with supporting evidence; distinguish between relevant and extraneous information; and identify underlying or implicit assumptions (Mayer, 2002; Price & Nelson, 2007). An example of an analysis thinking task is when the group leader working with students on the College Board search engine asked them to compute the costs of one semester of tuition and room/board of a college they are interested in and to compare that to the costs of an alternative college presented by the counselor. Another example surfaces in a small group project examining racism, where students were introduced to the concept of implicit bias and then later asked to examine a list of videos and statements taken from social media to identify instances of implicit bias.

Evaluate refers to the processes of appraising or making judgments using specific criteria or standards (Mayer, 2002). This, according to Mayer, is at the core of critical thinking. It is a process that requires the prerequisite abilities of understanding, applying, and analyzing (Price & Nelson, 2007). Evaluative learning tasks include asking students to select, predict, rate, explain, interpret, assess, and justify (Mayer, 2002; Price & Nelson, 2007). We have examples of this process as well. In a spontaneous group that was assembled by a school counselor to process a fight that broke out in the school cafeteria, the leader took the students through the steps that led up to the incident, helping them see how the incident unfolded in some nuanced ways. The intention was for the students to analyze the incident carefully. She then asked the students to reflect on and evaluate their own reactions to the incident, thinking carefully about how their own reactions fit into the chain of events, again, in some nuanced ways. In Mr. Garcia's group mentioned earlier, asking students to verbally reflect on their experience of receiving feedback by identifying the content, as well as their thought process and emotional reactions to the feedback they received, would have been a good processing sequence aimed at generating evaluation thinking skills. In the college information group previously discussed, students were given a hypothetical college budget for a year and then asked to evaluate the cost/benefit analysis of the school they selected in comparison to the example offered.

The final component of the revised Bloom's Taxonomy is to *create*. Based on the category of synthesis in the original Bloom's Taxonomy, this level of cognitive complexity entails being able to use existing information to construct something new (Price & Nelson, 2007) or to reorganize information or concepts into a new configuration (Mayer, 2002). For example, students in the college exploration group were asked to create a list of colleges they are interested in attending, organize their choices in order from one to five, and be prepared to offer a rationale for their ratings (including the cost/benefit analysis mentioned earlier). In another example, students and teachers in a high school advisory board task group were asked to analyze and evaluate the existing scheduling process at the school and then to brainstorm a new process that might be more effective. In line with Mayer's (2002) point that *create* can also entail the application of procedural knowledge, another task group of team captains was asked to develop a draft policy for the school's athletes, which outlined steps or procedures that students could take for registering concerns related to their athletic teams and coaches. This task emerged in response to concerns that arose the previous year, as students felt they did not have a voice when it came to concerns about their sports teams after a challenging year of parental complaints about a particular coach who was subsequently fired. Mayer (2002) suggested that create tasks be broken into the following steps: (1) identification of the problem and brainstorming of potential solutions, (2) planning for an identified solution, and (3) actually carrying out the solution.

Dimensions of Knowledge

Keep in mind the point made in Chapter 5 that the revised Bloom's Taxonomy now refers to knowledge as a multidimensional concept that includes factual, conceptual, procedural, and metacognitive knowledge. Each of these is subjected to the learning tasks across the remember, understand, apply, analyze, evaluate, and create process domains just discussed (Forehand, 2011; Krathwohl, 2002).

Factual knowledge is closely related to how many of us define knowledge; it refers to the basic elements of understandings or concepts that students need within a particular discipline (Krathwohl, 2002). Examples of factual knowledge include knowing basic mathematical concepts in a math class or asking a student to define what is meant by bully, victim, and bystander—concepts that were taught in a classroom guidance group. Within this domain of factual knowledge, higher level learning tasks can be used to encourage deeper understanding—students can be invited to engage in application, analysis, evaluation, and creation.

Conceptual knowledge refers to the interrelationships of basic elements within a common structure (Krathwohl, 2002). This has to do with classifications, categorizations, theories, principles, and generalizations. Within the conceptual knowledge domain, students can be encouraged to engage in tasks with increasing complexity (e.g., remember, understand, apply, analyze, evaluate, and create). Chapters 2 and 3 of this book offer examples of theories of learning and group work that we believe are fundamental to the practice of group work in schools; these are examples of conceptual knowledge. In a school context, students in a natural leaders training group studied depression—the reasons some people develop depression, symptoms of depression, how depression can sometimes lead to suicide ideation, and what students can do if they know someone who is depressed and potentially suicidal. Here students needed to learn more than just definitions; they needed to understand how depression develops and how to help their peers. The group leaders also believed that truly understanding these concepts would help these natural peer leaders engage empathically with peers who were experiencing depression.

Procedural knowledge refers to understanding subject-specific skills, practices, and processes (Krathwohl, 2002). For example, in an anxiety-reduction group, students learned the steps of centering as a component of self-management. These skills, then, can be analyzed, evaluated, etc., for deeper understanding and inquiry.

Metacogntive knowledge, which is something that has received a great deal of attention recently in the field of counseling, refers to having awareness of and knowledge about one's own thinking processes (Krathwohl, 2002). Helping children develop metacognitive skills is a core component of self-regulation instruction. For example, teaching students about triggers and providing them with a simple mindfulness activity that they can implement themselves in the moment of being triggered relies on the ability of students to be able to self-coach or self-talk themselves through each mindfulness step. This example parallels an example in the area of math where we might self-coach ourselves through each step in solving a complex math equation. Within this domain of metacognitive knowledge, Krathwohl (2002) pointed out that increased complexity can be stimulated through tasks in the areas of understanding, application, analysis, evaluation, and creation (Krathwohl, 2002).

Our point in calling attention to this aspect of the revised taxonomy is to remind you that many forms of knowledge are required for skill and concept development. While all of them are important, acquiring conceptual, procedural, and metacognitive knowledge may be the most salient component of the work that school counselors attempt in groups. Being intentional about planning for learning across these domains is something that happens in the group planning phase of group work.

Scaffolding and the Zone of Proximal Development

A scaffold is a temporary platform that is designed to support individuals who are working on a project; construction workers standing on a scaffold while working on a building project may come to mind here. Two operative words in this description of a scaffold that are relevant to our discussion are *temporary* and *support*. Temporary highlights the point that the intent of a scaffold is to provide assistance for as long as it is needed but not permanently. Support refers to the kind of assistance needed: it is active engagement that sits somewhere between doing for and standing in the

Image 6.2

background. A scaffold model of instruction also assumes that the kind of support that is needed by students will change over time and according to specific task demands.

The concept of scaffolding as we use it here references the instructional practices inspired by the cognitive and constructionist learning theories of Piaget, Vygotsky, and Bruner—the structuring of learning environments to provide opportunities for higher level learning and enhanced cognitive complexity. Productive learning environments, these theorists have told us, are ones in which teachers and group leaders design appropriate learning objectives and where learning is promoted through demonstration; coaching, prompting, offering cues, and reminders; and using other strategies to promote learning and success. In these learning spaces, teachers and group leaders do not simplify learning tasks so that students will easily be successful, nor do they leave students to fend for themselves in the face of complex learning concepts and tasks. Scaffolding is based on Vygotsky's notion of the ZPD (Bergen, 2008; Bigge & Shermis, 1999; Douthit, 2008; Kirylo, 2016), introduced in Chapter 2, which states that learning happens when students are challenged at an appropriate level and when they have access to temporary support or guidance, if needed, provided by knowledgeable peers, adults, and others in their environments.

In terms of planning, this reminds us to select activities and exercises that challenge students but also offer adequate support for learning. To this end, leaders should use tools and practices that address the learning needs of diverse students, select activities that offer varied roles or avenues for engagement, provide clear instructions, ask probing and facilitative questions while students are engaged in activities, and fully process activities at the end of instruction (using some of the processing questions and models discussed later in this chapter).

Vygotsky helped us understand that learning happens in interactions between individuals in a particular environment (Bergen, 2008; Dann, 2018). And groups, of course, provide a superb opportunity for students to create new understandings through their interactions with one another. So beyond thinking about how to create group plans that scaffold concept instruction, we also point to the ways in which group leaders can scaffold interpersonal interactions within their groups to help students acquire important social and intrapersonal skills. To this end, many group leaders use the skills outlined in the following chapter to draw out quiet members and open up discussions about the here-and-now group process dynamics. They also use linking, clarification, paraphrases, and even cutting off skills to help students engage with each other in productive and, for many, new ways. The important point that we want to emphasize here, though, is that scaffolding is an intentional intervention. It is up to the leader to intervene in ways that provide temporary support for new learning.

Social-Emotional Skill Development

Social-emotional development generally refers to a child's ability to understand the feelings of others, to control their own feelings and behaviors, and to get along with peers. Most parents, teachers, and school counselors also work to help students develop trust, confidence, and pride in their abilities and to regulate and express emotions in socially and culturally appropriate ways. Helping children acquire these skills is an important part of the work of school counselors operating within the contemporary framework of the ASCA National Model (2019), and these skills are seen as a critical component of school success (Ashdown & Bernard, 2012). While school counselor–led groups offer a unique venue for the structuring of these kinds of learning experiences, they do not happen without intentional planning. Here we rely on the field of education and skill-focused teaching practices to highlight critical components of social-emotional skill development instruction for group lesson/session planning. Our goal is to encourage school counselors to draft group plans that include activities, exercises, and processes that reflect the explicit instruction, structured learning, and feedback exchange principles described next. These ideas are summarized in Figure 6.2.

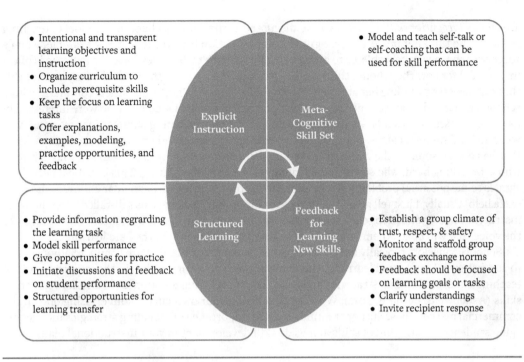

- Intentional and transparent learning objectives and instruction
- Organize curriculum to include prerequisite skills
- Keep the focus on learning tasks
- Offer explanations, examples, modeling, practice opportunities, and feedback

Explicit Instruction

- Model and teach self-talk or self-coaching that can be used for skill performance

Meta-Cognitive Skill Set

- Provide information regarding the learning task
- Model skill performance
- Give opportunities for practice
- Initiate discussions and feedback on student performance
- Structured opportunities for learning transfer

Structured Learning

Feedback for Learning New Skills

- Establish a group climate of trust, respect, & safety
- Monitor and scaffold group feedback exchange norms
- Feedback should be focused on learning goals or tasks
- Clarify understandings
- Invite recipient response

FIGURE 6.2 Skill Development Strategies

Explicit Instruction

We are all familiar with the colloquial statement "practice makes perfect." While this is a popular idea, cognitive and constructionist learning theorists teach us that practice *alone* does not make perfect. They highlight, as we have discussed, the important role of scaffolding in the instructional process. This idea of scaffolding is an important part of what is known as *explicit instruction*. Explicit instruction is a skill-building instructional model that encourages students to be actively engaged in their learning while the teacher provides structure and a level of control over the learning environment (Goeke, 2009). It is used to help students develop social-emotional competence for improved social-emotional well-being and academic success (Ashdown & Bernard, 2012).

According to Goeke (2009), explicit instruction begins with being transparent with students in regard to learning objectives and instructional practices. That is, students should know what they are expected to learn and how instruction will unfold each class, lesson, or week. To this end, teachers typically work from a structured framework in each lesson that begins with direction, instruction, and explanations. Explicit instruction also emphasizes the importance of modeling and practice (Goeke, 2009). After the initial introduction, the teacher then demonstrates or models the skill that is the focus of the learning. This is followed by time for students to practice the skill with feedback. The provision of feedback (corrective and affirmative) is a critical component of the skill practice sequence, as it helps students develop a clear sense of what they know and do well and what they still need to master. Teachers engaging in explicit instruction also work to keep the focus on the identified learning tasks during instruction; it is intentional, focused, and clear. Finally, explicit instruction is based on a model of instructional sequencing. Later lessons build on basic prerequisite skills that are taught early on in the instructional sequence (Goeke, 2009).

Goeke (2009) emphasized that acquiring a particular skill requires that students are able to demonstrate the physical components of that skill *and* that they are able to engage in the "invisible mental processes that underlie" (p. 69) the skill production as well. These invisible mental processes are the *metacogntive skills* or self-talk we discussed earlier in this chapter. For Goeke, teaching students the thinking processes that guide skill production is also explicit. For example, when a soccer coach teaches her athletes to always look for an outlet when they have the ball, she is offering a model for how they should think as they work their way down the field. She may prompt this thinking process by telling her athletes, "Always ask yourself: Where's an outlet?" Similarly, a high school teacher and school counselor were working with a group of students who were interested in learning de-escalation skills—skills they could use in their upcoming summer jobs working with youth in local summer camps. The group leader told her students, "When there has been an incident that has gotten some of the children revved up, I am always looking around to see who is jittery, who is breathing hard, who seems to be having trouble downregulating. This is critical because it signals to me potential problems and helps me focus my attention on particular children who need extra help. Usually, I just tell myself, 'Always scan the group.'" Voicing this self-talk during the skills instruction was intended to teach the high school students how to focus attention and internalize the voice that will coach them later as they begin to use the new skill they are learning.

School counselors typically use a variety of curricular programs that are commercially available to address social-emotional learning, and many of these programs highlight the important role of teaching children thinking strategies and self-talk in developing emotion and behavior regulation skills (Ashdown & Bernard, 2012). Whether developing your own curriculum or using one on the commercial market, these authors remind us of the importance of including strategies for encouraging students' metacognitive skills alongside skill development in your instructional plans.

Structured Learning

Structured learning is a psychoeducational- and behavioral-oriented model of social skill instruction that is based on the principles of structured learning therapy developed by Goldstein (Goldstein, 1973; McGinnis & Goldstein, 1984). Like explicit instruction, structured learning consists of providing information about the skill to be learned; modeling, providing opportunities for students to practice or role-play the skills, and offering students feedback on the performance of the skill; and providing opportunities for skills generalization (Begun, 1995; McGinnis & Goldstein, 1984). We will review some of the basic components of structured learning here. They are also summarized in Figure 6.3.

In the structured learning model, students first receive *explicit instruction* on the skill they are learning, which is then followed by *skill demonstration*. The demonstration component of this approach is key and based largely on the observational learning concepts in social learning theory, which, you will recall, were discussed in Chapter 2. Here, McGinnis and Goldstein (1984) pointed out that role models should display the behaviors they are demonstrating in a clear and detailed way, with progression from easy to more difficult, and they should display the behavior repeatedly with few distractions. These authors also recommend using multiple models for new skills instruction.

Social learning theory reminds us that learners also need to be positioned in certain ways to be available for learning from role models (Bandura, 1971). To this end, McGinnis and Goldstein (1984) pointed out that imitation of a model is more likely when the child is instructed to do so, when the child is friendly toward or likes the model, and when the child anticipates being rewarded for emanation of the desired behavior. We know from social learning theory, and McGinnis and Goldstein (1984) reminded us, that skill modeling is more effective when the model appears skilled at the behavior being performed, is considered to be of high status, appears friendly and helpful, is perceived to be similar to the observer in some important ways (i.e., gender, age, race, social status), and when the model is rewarded for their performance of the particular behavior they are modeling.

Given this emphasis on model prestige and model-observer match, we immediately can see the challenges that may arise when using role model instruction in skills groups with diverse membership. When group members perceive that the role models who are demonstrating the desired skills are unrelatable, the effectiveness of the modeling pedagogy is potentially compromised. That

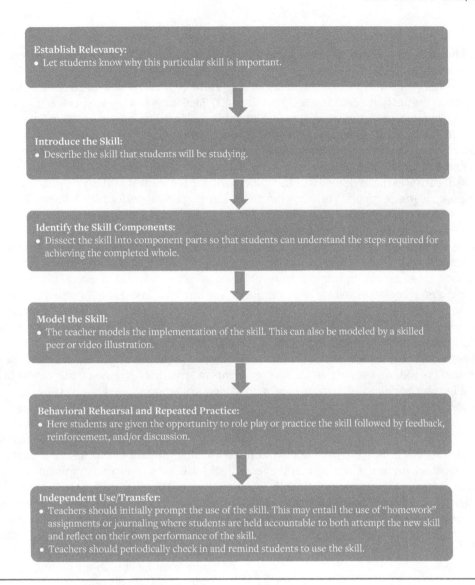

Establish Relevancy:
- Let students know why this particular skill is important.

Introduce the Skill:
- Describe the skill that students will be studying.

Identify the Skill Components:
- Dissect the skill into component parts so that students can understand the steps required for achieving the completed whole.

Model the Skill:
- The teacher models the implementation of the skill. This can also be modeled by a skilled peer or video illustration.

Behavioral Rehearsal and Repeated Practice:
- Here students are given the opportunity to role play or practice the skill followed by feedback, reinforcement, and/or discussion.

Independent Use/Transfer:
- Teachers should initially prompt the use of the skill. This may entail the use of "homework" assignments or journaling where students are held accountable to both attempt the new skill and reflect on their own performance of the skill.
- Teachers should periodically check in and remind students to use the skill.

FIGURE 6.3 Structured Learning Steps

is, what happens in groups where the "model" seems very different and thus irrelevant to some of the members of the group? This point brings us back to the concept of windows and mirrors, discussed earlier in this text—the point that group membership should include opportunities for *all* of the students to feel that they belong and are valued and that *all* members have an opportunity to learn from the group experience. Leaders must be thoughtful about who they select to model the skills they are teaching in their groups. In situations where the model—whether it is the group leader himself, a selected student in the group, or models on display in videos or other instructional materials—does not match the race, gender, or other experiences or identities of some of the group members, the group leader should be transparent about this mismatch. This can happen by first broaching the difference—the fact that the model doesn't look like some of the students in the group. From there, the leader can brainstorm with the students in the group how the skill might look if it was modeled by someone from a different cultural or racial group, gender, etc. Acknowledging differences in personal, social, and cultural experiences is key to developing the kind of trust and confidence that can allow cross-cultural modeling to be effective. This point is critical to keep in mind when serving a diverse group of students and in situations that require cross-cultural interactions among students.

Skill performance (often conducted as a role play) is the next component of structured learning instruction (Begun, 1995; McGinnis & Goldstein, 1984). McGinnis and Goldstein asserted that skill performance is most effective when a student is given a choice regarding participation (i.e., they are not forced to engage in a role play), when the student's commitment to learning a particular new behavior is publicly reinforced, when the role play includes improvisation, and when there is some kind of reward for role-play performance. They also indicate that repeated (correct) performances of the skill enhances the likelihood that the student will use the learned skill in everyday life outside of the group learning context (i.e., the transfer of learning). Skill performance should be paired with *performance feedback*; this is considered essential for learning in the structured learning model (McGinnis & Goldstein, 1984). McGinnis and Goldstein (1984) also emphasized the importance of providing material and social reinforcement to students after their practice performance of a new skill.

Research suggests that social-emotional learning programs that include explicit structured instruction are beneficial in helping young children acquire social skills, especially those that begin at the preschool level and are of long duration and intensity (Ashdown & Bernard, 2012). The long-popular structured learning curriculum called *Skillstreaming* is an example of a structured learning model of social skills instruction that can be used for young children (McGinnis & Goldstein, 2003), elementary-aged children (McGinnis, 2011a), and adolescents (McGinnis, 2011b). It involves the learning sequence of instruction, modeling, and practice described earlier. While this curriculum is good, we believe that these components of structured learning really can be incorporated into any social skills program used with students in schools.

Feedback

Since feedback is a critical component of structured learning, we turn our focus to the important topic of feedback exchange. Noting that the term feedback is used in a variety of technical, colloquial, and professional settings and disciplines, we begin with Dann's (2018) definition of feedback: feedback is "'something' (information, chemical, biological, electrical) that has been received which can subsequently be used for/or causes change within a cycle, gap or system" (p. 35). Dann added that feedback is intended to "reduce the gap between what is not known and what is known" (Dann, 2018, p. 37). Feedback is "dialogue developed to support learning in both formal and informal situations" (Askew & Lodge, 2000, p. 1).

In counseling and group work focused on interpersonal skill development, feedback offers students information related to their behavior; it helps them see how they are perceived by others and invites them to understand the effects of their behaviors on others (Claiborn et al., 2001; Gladding, 2003; Hulse-Killacky et al., 2006; Kline, 2003). In the field of education, feedback is identified to have a powerful and critical effect on learning and achievement (Askew & Lodge, 2000; Hattie & Timperley, 2007; McGinnis & Goldstein, 1984). However, as Askew and Lodge (2000) pointed out, "It is common to talk about 'giving' and 'receiving' feedback,

Image 6.3

but feedback is not always a 'gift' from one person to another" (p. 2). We believe that feedback can be a gift for students learning new skills—whether it comes from teachers and group leaders or from their peers—but for this gift to truly be productive, feedback exchange needs to be structured and planned carefully.

Types of Feedback

Feedback can be *descriptive* (i.e., it describes what one sees, hears, experiences, or assumes), or it can be *evaluative*, such as when it is used in a performance review or final examination. *Positive feedback* focuses on what has been done well or correctly; *negative feedback* is aimed at mistakes or problems— what has not been done correctly and needs to change (Askew & Lodge, 2000). The term *corrective feedback* references Yalom's point that group members learn from the perceptions and reactions of other group members; corrective feedback refers to providing information to group members on how their behavior is perceived by others (Alexander & Hulse-Killacky, 2005). In groups, feedback may be given to group members by the leader or by other group members, typically with the intent of inviting self-examination. When the group leader delivers the feedback, it is often accompanied by suggestions or instructions on what can be done differently in the future.

Feedback exchange refers to a process facilitated by a group leader that structures the productive exchange of these types of feedback among group members. For example, Ciara told Abraham that she noticed he rolled his eyes when she spoke and that she was offended because she assumed that he did not care about what she had to say. With the help of the group leader, Abraham responded that he heard and understood the feedback and that he did indeed care about what Ciara had to say. Then, following the steps in feedback exchange taught to the group (and listed next), he asked Ciara if she was open to hearing feedback that may explain why he rolled his eyes.

Models of Feedback

Askew and Lodge (2000) discussed three models of providing feedback to students, each located in a different teaching pedagogy. The first is feedback given by teachers in the *receptive-transmission model* of teaching. Here feedback is typically evaluative, aimed at the gap between what a student currently knows or does and the desired outcome. They point out that feedback in contemporary everyday use (outside of education) tends to align with this conceptualization of feedback. The idea in this model is that when feedback is given with the expectations that it offers new information to the recipient—something they do not already know—and that the recipient wants to hear the feedback, believes that it will be helpful, and if the recipient follows the feedback, improvement is inevitable.

Feedback embedded in a *constructivist model* of teaching focuses more on higher level learning, such as making connections, exploring understandings, and describing and discussing options. Feedback in this model moves away from evaluation and is more formative; it is information provided by a knowledgeable other (i.e., a teacher) in a way that invites the recipient to think, consider, reflect, and make decisions. A *co-constructivist model* of teaching, which is the third model of feedback discussed by Askew and Lodge, shifts responsibility for learning toward a collaborative process. In this model, feedback is conceptualized as dialogic and informative—a piece of information to consider rather than a directive or truth delivered from someone with more power or knowledge. It aims to stimulate critical investigation and analytic, interpretive, reorganizational, and reflective learning processes.

Askew and Lodge (2000) suggested that feedback delivered from the receptive-transmission model is not always helpful in yielding deeper understandings and higher-level learning. In fact, they point out that despite the feedback giver's best intentions, this kind of feedback can easily block learning. This happens especially if too much feedback is offered at one time, if the delivery is overpowering, and when it is not consistent with the ways in which the recipient is thinking or doesn't match their present understandings or perceptions. They suggest that feedback is most effective when it invites discussion and reflection and when it provides direction for how the recipient can incorporate the new information so as to change, learn, or grow.

Before moving ahead, we want to dip our toes into the murky water that distinguishes feedback from rules, limit setting, or "discipline." Our use of the term *discipline* refers to the articulation of behavioral expectations that require a certain level of compliance for further participation in the group; typically, this would have to do with the violation of a basic group rule related to respect for self, others, and property and places. For example, a counselor was using the classroom of an English teacher for a group meeting because there were no other spaces readily available in the school building at that time. At the start of the third group session, a student in the group sat at the teacher's desk and began looking through the contents of its drawers. The group leader responded immediately by moving toward the student and asking them to respect the teacher's belongings, to stop looking through the drawers, and to return to the group immediately. We consider this interchange to be disciplinary rather than a feedback exchange process as it entailed setting limits and reinforced previously discussed group rules. It was not aimed at instruction related to skills, nor was it focused on a specific group or individual goal. Even if this particular student was in the group to work on issues related to engaging in respectful relationships with others, the primary intent of this particular intervention was to get the student to stop looking through the teacher's desk drawers and to reengage in the content or task of the group. In this example, the group leader allowed the student to make the appropriate behavioral correction (i.e., the student closed the drawers and returned to the group) without requiring the student to engage in a discussion, without requiring the student to issue an apology, and without even having to verbally respond to the request. If this limit setting was followed by a discussion related to respectful relationships or if it included a private follow-up with the student at a later time, it could then be used as a "teachable moment" with the student in (or out of) the group. Our distinction between feedback and discipline, then, is that discipline in the group is something we think more of as "setting limits" and has to do with enforcing the norms, rules, and parameters of the group. The intent of feedback, on the other hand, is to promote learning related to intended goals. This admittedly obscure distinction, we believe, rests on intention.

Principles for Feedback Exchange

Group leaders play an important role in structuring feedback exchange in their groups; this structuring role is what enables feedback to be a powerful learning experience for group members. In fact, this attention to the important interpersonal dynamics surrounding feedback exchange is not only good leadership form but also a component of ethical (ACA, 2014, A.9.b. "In a group setting, counselors take reasonable precautions to protect clients from physical, emotional, or psychological trauma") and responsible leadership practice. Students are protected from harm when leaders are able to carefully manage "the flow of communication, addressing safety and pacing of disclosure" (Thomas & Pender, 2007, p. 116) as group members engage in feedback exchange. We offer the following principles as guidelines for structuring feedback exchange in groups with youth; they are also summarized in Figure 6.4.

First, it is important to remember that the focus of feedback should always be *related to a particular learning objective, goal, or tasks of the group* (Dann, 2018); it should never be a personal or social critique. That is, whether delivered by a teacher, group leader, or even one's own peers, feedback should be aimed at helping a student achieve a particular goal, receive important and relevant information, or, in the case of a task group, be pertinent to the accomplishment of the group task.

Second, the *context and manner of how feedback is delivered* are what determine if it is helpful. Feedback is not productive when it is given in a hurtful way, which is something that sometimes

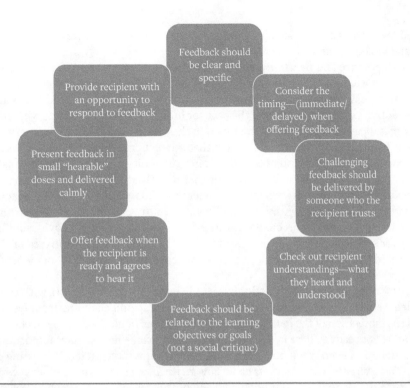

FIGURE 6.4 Principles for Feedback Exchange

happens when people are angry or reactive. For example, if Ciara in our earlier example had blurted out, "You're a jerk" to Abraham in response to his eye rolling, it is unlikely that further interaction between the two of them would have been productive. Providing feedback to students and engaging them in feedback exchange processes in groups requires a group climate of safety, respect, and trust, "particularly if disconfirmation and corrective feedback at any level is to be welcomed and used by the students (and teachers)" (Hattie & Timperley, 2007, p. 100). Classroom norms, which will be discussed in the next chapter, are an important way that group leaders facilitate safety in the group.

Patterson and Welfel (2000) reminded us that feedback is typically difficult to receive, and it often takes time to internalize, especially when it is not consistent with the recipient's preexisting self-perceptions. For this reason, they recommend that feedback be *presented "in small doses"* (p. 62). It is also important to remember that the recipient of feedback may have particular cultural beliefs, priorities, experiences, and understandings that lead to unintended understandings and reactions to feedback (Dann, 2018). This reminds us to always *check out recipient understandings* and reactions to the feedback that they have received. Patterson and Welfel (2000) also pointed out that feedback is typically easier to receive when it is *provided by someone who is considered to be a trusted ally* and when it is *offered calmly, clearly, and with concrete and specific information.*

Another important aspect of feedback exchange has to do with the frequency, timing, and valence (negative vs. positive) of feedback (Dann, 2018; Hattie & Timperley, 2007). While *immediate feedback* is helpful in correcting errors before they become habit or stored incorrectly in memory, *offering feedback at a later time* may actually be more effective—when the person is in a position to hear the feedback. This waiting may be more likely to facilitate the transfer of learning from the immediate situation to others (Dann, 2018). Delayed feedback may also be more helpful when the recipient is engaged in a complex task, as this does not interrupt other components of the task, and it allows for processing time (Hattie & Timperley, 2007). Shute (2008) summarized this advice by saying that delayed feedback is often more effective in response to challenging tasks, whereas immediate feedback tends to be better for easier tasks.

While both positive and negative feedback have been shown to be effective, Hattie and Timperley (2007) reported that the effects of each are complex. They point out that positive feedback in regard to personal attributes or self-regulation can increase the likelihood that students will persist in an activity. This is particularly the case for highly efficacious students who interpret the feedback as an indication of their talent or ability. In these cases, the feedback may serve as a buffer in the face of future disconfirmatory feedback that students may receive. That is, knowing that you can do part of a task well bolsters confidence in your ability to persist when the task becomes more challenging. These authors also point out that negative feedback can have an unfavorable effect on the motivation and performance of students with lower levels of self-efficacy. One way to avoid this impact is to *pair negative feedback with corrective information or instruction* on what to do differently; this helps the recipient put the feedback into use and provides an immediate opportunity for subsequent success. Finally, feedback should always be *delivered in clear, immediate* (i.e., related to something specific that has happened in the moment), *and behavioral terms* (Hulse-Killacky et al., 2001).

Dann (2018) reminded us that the "final 'learning power' of feedback rests with the agency of individual learners" (p. 115). That is, the potential for learning and changing from feedback really depends on the motivation of the recipient. Feedback is not particularly effective in eliciting change if the receiver is not ready to hear it. This reminds us that even when we have important feedback to offer a student and even when our message is consistent with a student's learning goals, it is always *up to the receiver to make decisions about how they will respond* to the feedback we give them. We cannot force people to follow our good advice! For this reason, Patterson and Welfel's (2000) point that feedback should always be *presented for consideration* "not as indisputable truth" (p. 62) is important.

Steps in Feedback Exchange

As mentioned, group leaders should be mindful of structuring feedback exchange processes in their groups, especially if they intend to have students giving feedback to each other. We recommend that group leaders establish feedback norms and be prepared to coach students when they are giving feedback to their peers by using the following steps:

1. **Begin by asking the recipient if they are open to hearing feedback.**

   - Example: In a counseling group and with the group leader encouraging him, Sam said, "Lia, I wanted to give you some feedback. Would you like to hear it?"
   - If the recipient says "yes" to being open to hearing feedback, the group leader or the student offering the feedback may need to request that the recipient listen and not respond until they have had a chance to think about what they have heard.

     o   For example, following the feedback guidelines discussed in an earlier group, Sam said, "Okay. Would you be willing to just hear me out before you respond to what I tell you?"

   - Sometimes the recipient may need prompting, coaching, and reminders to listen respectfully and not respond to the feedback until the person giving the feedback has finished talking.
   - For example, the leader said, "Lia, Sam asked for you to hear him out before responding. That seemed like a reasonable request, so I'm going to ask you to hold your comments

until he is done and then for you to take a minute to think about what you've heard before responding. Thanks."

  o If they indicate that they are not open or ready for feedback, that option must be respected. The leader can check to see if the student is ready for the feedback at a later time.

2. **Feedback should be delivered in a clear statement, including concrete information as much as possible. The feedback giver should be encouraged to tell the recipient how they were specifically affected by the behavior of concern.**

  - Example: "When I brought up the thing about my sister, you didn't say anything to me and then just started talking to Leonel. It felt so cold."
  - Feedback should be about something that was directly experienced, heard, or observed; it should be articulated clearly and concretely, as much as possible and delivered in small "sound bites" of limited focus.
  - Feedback should not include accusations about intent, feelings, thoughts, "character traits," or reiterations of conversations based on hearsay. If the person giving feedback includes some of their assumptions (based on their observations or experiences) in their feedback, it is important that the recipient has a chance to respond to those assumptions.
  - The group leader may need to intervene during this part of the process so as to keep the feedback focused on what was observed and what was felt and to cut off any hurtful or interpretive statements or reactions that may be stated in anger.

3. **After the feedback has been given, the counselor should thank the giver for providing the feedback and thank the recipient for respectfully listening.**

  - Example: "Thanks, Sam, for letting Lia know that. It took courage to say that. And thanks, too, Lia, for hearing him out. It can be hard to hear feedback."

4. **Clarify recipient understanding.**

  - Example: "Lia, I just want to be sure that you heard Sam's feedback correctly. What did you hear him say?"
  - The leader may need to clarify any misunderstandings and provide cultural or social context if this would help clarify the feedback for the recipient.

5. **The leader should ask the recipient if they would like to respond.**

  - Example: "Lia, please take a minute to think about what, if anything, you want to say to Sam after hearing his feedback."
  - If the recipient chooses to respond, the leader should invite them to think "for one full minute" before responding.
  - Just before the recipient responds, the leader may want to remind the original feedback giver to listen quietly and respectfully to what the recipient has to say. (And the leader should do this themselves if they are the one being offered the feedback.)

    o For example, the leader commented, "Sam, it looks like Lia wants to talk with you about what you said. I just want to remind you to listen carefully and respectfully when she is talking."

- Sometimes gentle support is needed to help the recipient shape their response so that it accurately reflects what they are thinking or feeling.
- If the recipient chooses not to respond to the feedback, the leader should respect that decision and probably follow-up with the recipient at a later and more private time. Follow-up with the recipient is important in case they need help making meaning of what has been said and in selecting an appropriate response.
- Keep in mind that some youth are likely to take in feedback and make appropriate changes to their behavior without verbal exchange or response. While this may not be most desirable in terms of establishing a conversation about the feedback and promoting prosocial conversations, it is important for group leaders to remember that receiving feedback can be very embarrassing, and saving face in front of peers is extremely important for many children and adolescents. In these cases, it is best to avoid *requiring* the recipient to respond, particularly in the group, as doing so may lead to a power struggle or further embarrassment. The counselor can work slowly toward an open exchange of feedback in the group, understanding that when working with youth, this will be a process that takes time.

Activities and Exercises

It is not surprising that school counselors often use structured activities or exercises as tools to achieve specific goals or learning objectives in their groups with children. This is because children tend to have a shorter attention span than adults; they may have limited abstract thinking abilities and trouble with verbal expression; and because children sometimes display limited perspective-taking abilities and behavior control (Shechtman (2014). Activities provide a flexible medium for communication and expression; they stimulate attention, motivation, and engagement; and activities have the potential to promote learning in a nonthreatening way, particularly in the early stages of

Image 6.4

a group (Gladding, 2003; Trotzer, 2004). They also tend to increase comfort levels and set a tone of having fun in the group (Jacobs et al., 2005; Kees & Jacobs, 1990).

While adolescents may have fewer challenges with self-management and self-expression than children, counselors leading groups with teens sometimes use activities to mitigate dynamics related to authority and power, which Shechtman (2014) pointed out may adversely affect teen/group leader interactions. Structured group activities are also used by group leaders to facilitate depth and focus on meaningful relationships and experiences, to prompt interactions among members, and, sometimes, to facilitate closure at the end of the group (Trotzer, 2004). While the use of activities in groups with youth seems intuitively appropriate, the literature suggests that the effectiveness of using structured group activities is not altogether straightforward—too much structure or too little structure in a group can be ineffective (Nitza, 2014). Trotzer (2004) invited us to think of group activities as a means to an end; they "are not intended to be ends in and of themselves" (p. 77). He went on to say that the purpose of using activities in a therapeutic group is not for entertainment; group activities are "only valid if selected and used in the context of effective group process and a defined group purpose" (p. 77). What makes a particular group activity appropriate for a particular group, then, is the match between the activity and the goals and objectives of the group or group members, the type and stage of the group, and membership needs and characteristics.

Activity Selection

A variety of activities can be used in group work with youth. Creativity is the limit! For example, Gladding (2003) recommended using puppets, music, and artistic activities to promote self-understanding and to help children understand others. Others recommend using written exercises (e.g., sentence completions, journals, lists, therapeutic cards), movement exercises (e.g., family/classroom sculpting; trust exercises; relaxation training; high- or low-level adventure-based activities; dance), arts and crafts activities (e.g., drawings, collages, clay sculpting, phototherapy), readings (e.g., read by leader/read by members), music, fantasy and guided-imagery exercises, play, group decision making, phototherapy, and therapeutic activity cards or games in groups (e.g., Jacobs et al., 2016; Kees & Jacobs, 1990; Shechtman, 2014).

Determining which activity to use when and in which group is an important part of group planning. It requires matching potential activities to the appropriate developmental milestones, ages, cultural and social contexts, abilities, and expectations of the group members. Activities also must be matched to group type and setting (in this case, the school setting). As an example of this latter point regarding setting, a school counselor we know was once besieged by disgruntled parents when he led a middle school classroom group through a guided-imagery activity. A few parents initially interpreted the activity as some form of hypnosis. Although this was an innocent misunderstanding, the principal of the school was not amused by the miscommunication. Trotzer (2004) suggested selecting activities for inclusion in a group session according to their potential to facilitate *process* and *purpose*. In terms of process, he suggested that activities can enhance group member interactions, stimulate group process dynamics, and engage group members in reflection. By using the term *purpose*, he means that activity selection should be based on the extent to which it addresses the purpose or goal of the group.

We end our discussion here with another important ethical consideration: It is important to select and facilitate activities that are within your own experience, knowledge, and ability levels. Do not lead group exercises that you are not trained or experienced to facilitate or that require more supervision or skilled facilitation than you can provide in the school setting. This is an ethical mandate that is clearly articulated in the ACA (2014) Code of Ethics (see C.7.c) and the ASCA (2016) Ethical Standards for School Counselors (see A.7.h.). Related to this, it is important to become familiar with each and every activity, game, and book that you plan to use *before* using it in the group. That is, read the books, play the games, and preview all visual and audio media in advance of using them in the group. Finally, ensure that the materials you intend to use are available (and easily accessible) on the day you want to use them in your group. The questions listed in Figure 6.5 can be used for decisions regarding activity selection.

Timing and Delivery of Activities

Because group process dynamics change over the course of the group, it is important to match group activity with the group stage, membership, and setting (Nitza, 2014; Trotzer, 2004). Important in this decision is the level of risk required in a particular activity. This is especially important when

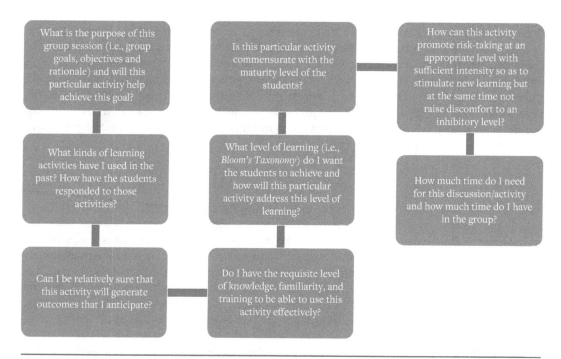

FIGURE 6.5 Questions to Consider for Activity Selection

working in larger classrooms and with sensitive or uncomfortable topics since larger numbers of students and a lack of group screening are variables that the group leader often does not have control over in these types of groups. This is a point that is underscored in the ASCA Ethical Standards, which states that school counselors should "select topics for groups with the clear understanding that some topics are not suitable for groups in schools and accordingly take precautions to protect members from harm as a result of interactions with the group" (ASCA, 2016, A.7.f). While some activities are excellent for fostering group cohesiveness and trust, others require trust and cohesion for them to work well in the group.

Remember that risk is individually defined. Although a particular activity may appear to be emotionally and physically safe to the counselor who planned it, personal circumstances, such trauma history or limited social capital, affect students' sense of vulnerability and perceptions of safety. Even when students are aware of their limits, the power differential between counselor and student may also leave some students feeling compelled to participate in a group activity at a level for which they are unprepared, and that is potentially harmful. For example, Shelia, a ninth-grade student participating in a Student Leadership Summer Academy that was designed by the administration and the counseling department, had what some referred to as a "panic attack" during a trust walk activity. She was participating in the trust walk with a peer when she, as the blindfolded partner, began to scream, tear at the blindfold, and run frantically away from her partner. Even though Shelia had consented to participate in the activity, and even though she was a superb young student leader, something about the activity triggered an unexpected reaction. Once the school counselor and a ninth-grade peer in the group managed to calm Sheila down, she was able to recover from the panic attack and get back with the group. Shelia agreed to spend some time with the counselor afterward and to talk with her parents later about the experience. The outcome was beneficial, but our purpose here is to insist that contingencies be made for such unexpected events, that alternatives always be presented to student participants in any activity, and that school counselors ensure that sufficient resources (in this case other professionals) be available if needed. Again, the point is that school counselors must consider their ethical obligations in selecting and implementing activities with their groups.

In general, introductory activities and activities that require less personal risk taking are good for early groups but using these types of activities later in the group may be unproductive or may stall group progress. As group cohesion increases, activities that require more self-disclosure or personal risk taking can be introduced. As group members begin to demonstrate high levels of motivation and take on more responsibility for their learning, group leaders may find that they need to take on a less active role in structuring the group, and many move away from the use of activities altogether, instead prompting discussions among group members.

Another aspect of timing has to do with being able to accurately predict how long a particular activity will take. When activities are very engaging for students or when they require careful attention from the group leader, it can be easy to lose track of the time. When this happens, the intended learning from the activity is easily lost in the scramble to rush through to the ending or to wrap up quickly. Rushing through an activity so that it can be completed in a short amount of time has the risk of rendering it ineffective, especially if the meaning-making part of the activity is cut. So it is important to plan activities that fit within the time allotted for the group—time that also includes properly processing the activity so as to promote meaning making. One way to help with this is to document in the lesson plan the expected time you will need for each part of the activity, including how much time is needed for meaning making or group processing after the activity is done. There may be situations where you may need to negotiate for more time for a particular group session, or you may need to consider dividing the activity into two sessions if extra time is needed. Some counselors have been able to work with classroom teachers to integrate their learning objectives into the academic curriculum, thus allowing them to use activities that require more time.

Processing Group Activities

While activities may make groups fun, remember that they are used in groups to advance the intended learning goals and objectives. According to Nitza (2014), "It is the carefully selected and planned use of an activity, targeted for a specific purpose within a specific group, and processed effectively that is likely to be useful in promoting change" (p. 95). The point, again, is that group activities are a *means* for addressing a particular goal; they are not *the* goal. Meaning making is what group leaders do to coax learning from group activities.

The term *processing* is used in counseling group work literature to describe the ways in which group leaders explicitly work to help group members learn from the exercises, activities, interactions or experiences in the group. Kline (2003) described processing as involving "stopping the group after significant interaction or series of interactions and directing members to discuss their emotional and cognitive reactions" (p. 239). This concept comes from the early work of Lieberman et al. (1973) who used the term *meaning attribution* in reference to ways in which group leaders help members make meaning from what is happening in the group. These illustrious group scholars emphasized the role of the group leader in facilitating group processing or meaning making, and it is a continued emphasis in contemporary group work. Ward and Litchy (2004) reminded us that it is the responsibility of the group leader to facilitate an atmosphere in the group where processing is expected. Underscored in all of these comments about meaning making is the notion that group members should not be passive recipients of fun activities; group activities should be used to help members learn, change, and grow.

A number of models are presented in the group work literature to describe ways in which counselors can facilitate group processing. For example, Glass and Benshoff (1999) offered what they refer to as the PARS model (PARS is the acronym for process, activity, relationship, and self). In this model, the group leader invites members to reflect on what has happened in the group (either interpersonal interactions or a group activity) by reviewing the details of what has unfolded, and then members are asked to explore how they understand the event and to consider how what has happened in the group is relevant to their interactions and experiences outside of the group. Similarly, Stockton et al. (2000) presented a model for group processing that includes identifying and examining the critical events that transpired in the group, inviting group members to explore their

Image 6.5

reactions to those events, and this model also includes a transfer of learning component where group members are invited to apply these understandings to circumstances in their lives outside of the group. Smead (1995) suggested that the focus of processing discussions be in the following four areas: (1) intrapersonal learning (i.e., an examination of the individual member's experience), (2) interpersonal experience (i.e., what happened between members of the group), (3) new thoughts or learning (i.e., a focus on what was learned in the group), and (4) application (i.e., a focus on how the new information or knowledge will be used). Figure 6.6 offers a synthesis of these models of group processing.

These processing steps can be done in a variety of formats. Borrowing from the work of Luckner and Nadler (1997), youth can be engaged in processing group experiences and activities in small or large group discussion formats, journal writing or prompted questions/activity sheets, with process observers, or through production activities (i.e., where children are asked to create something that represents their learning). These authors also recommend prompting critical thinking and group processing conversations by *framing*—providing information and thinking points prior to the group experience so as to guide focus and thinking for later conversations. They also remind us that it can sometimes be helpful to give group members a chance to think for themselves prior to engaging in processing discussions, especially when a particular group activity or exercise was very intense.

Strategies for Various Group Types

We conclude this chapter with some final comments about the use of group strategies, activities, and exercises in various group types conducted in school settings.

Classroom Group Strategies

In general, learning through content is a common emphasis in classroom-based group work in schools (Geroski & Kraus, 2002). That is, leaders of classroom-based psychoeducational groups often rely on

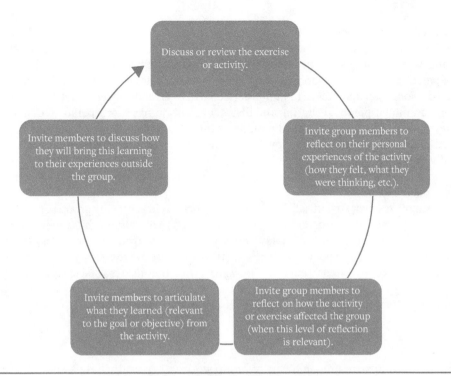

FIGURE 6.6 Questions to Consider for Activity Selection

educational strategies that provide structured learning experiences. School counselors use activities to, for example, promote interpersonal communication, problem solving, or decision-making skills and to teach students study habits or anxiety-reduction strategies. However, even in psychoeducational groups, Nitza (2014) cautioned against an overreliance on the use of activities so that the group does not become "a circle of people completing a series of exercises rather than a functioning group" (p. 98). Geroski and Kraus (2002) pointed out that while a focus on process dynamics may look different in classroom groups, it is *not* less important. Their research supports the idea that inviting spontaneous interactions between members—group process dynamics—is an important learning tool in psychoeducational and classroom group work.

The curriculum used by school counselors planning classroom-based psychoeducational groups is sometimes determined by the district and/or school level to address academic, career (vocational), and personal/social development instructional domains set out by the ASCA National Model (ASCA, 2019). Numerous publications and commercially produced "lesson plans" are used by many school counselors to achieve these goals. This means that in some schools, counselors have little say over the plans and activities they are using in their groups—particularly in their classroom group work. However, it is our observation that many school counselors have the freedom to "pick and choose" from these various programs and to be intentional about developing their own group plans. This, we believe, is desirable so that group activities, exercises, and instructional processes are matched to the specific needs of a particular classroom.

Counseling Group Strategies

As mentioned, counselors working in schools tend to approach much of group work, including small counseling groups, from a psychoeducational lens. This means that they often use structured activities and rely heavily on teaching strategies in their groups. While activities and instructional strategies can be meaningful to achieve counseling group goals, Nitza (2014) emphasized the use of process-oriented, here-and-now approaches over structured activities in small counseling groups. Similarly, Schechtman (2014) cautioned that activities and other types of structuring should be used "only when necessary" (p. 172) in counseling groups with children. This is because personal sharing and spontaneous engagement are critical ways in which intrapersonal and interpersonal skills are learned and practiced. An overreliance on structured educational activities can inhibit personal sharing and distract attention from interpersonal dynamics. For example, students in a group designed to address interpersonal communication skills may best be served through group plans that allow for spontaneous interaction and feedback that are only minimally prompted by exercises or activities. A group of new American students may need time to talk about their experiences and how to adjust more than they need to engage in a particular activity, game, or exercise.

There are times when structured activities can be helpful in achieving group goals in counseling groups, of course. For example, Nitza (2014) suggested that younger children may need more structure, while older children and adolescents seem to benefit from and enjoy less structure in counseling groups. Nitza also points out that activities can be used in the early stages of a counseling group to reduce anxiety related to being in a new group, and they also may be used at various times later in the group to provide focus. Finally, as mentioned earlier, explicit or structured learning formats are helpful ways of teaching specific skills, especially social skills.

Task, Work, or Large Counseling Group Strategies

Task and work groups are unique forms of group work and typically have a specific charge or mission that is a focus of the group. Members are sometimes selected or voted on by staff or peers to be a part of these groups; these selections are often based on student leadership skills, personal experiences, social identities, and/or knowledge of the subject matter. In other cases, however, task and related groups may form organically, and they may have open membership. For example, in one high school we know of, a school counselor worked alongside a group of students who advocated for and finally accomplished the establishment of a Gay-Straight Alliance. This group was initially formed by students who approached the school counselor and a teacher for support in accomplishing their mission. Both the teacher and the school counselor were engaged in a variety of roles, including facilitating, brainstorming, and advocating, but they rarely drafted group plans and did not use structured activities or exercises in any of their work with this group. School counselors may also be asked to participate in or lead task or work groups for teachers, guardians, parents, or other adults in the school community. While activities and exercises are sometimes used in task or work groups, in general, these groups tend to require much less structured planning. Instead, the role of the group leader is often focused on helping the group remain focused on its task.

Documenting Strategies in Lesson/Session Plans

We conclude our discussion about planning strategies and activities by emphasizing the importance of having written group plans that outline the various strategies that will be used to promote group content goals. Carefully spelled out group plans enable group leaders to be clear and focused on the group goals and objectives each time the group meets. They also free group leaders up to be more fully present in the group and respond to here-and-now group dynamics. While drafting written plans requires advanced detail and effort, once plans are drafted, they can be used over and over again. Written lesson/session/meeting plans also facilitate accountability, which is particularly helpful when stakeholders inquire into the implementation of a school's counseling program.

We recommend the following sequential approach (and included in Figure 6.7) for writing strategies of weekly lesson/session/meeting plans. This approach can be used for documenting

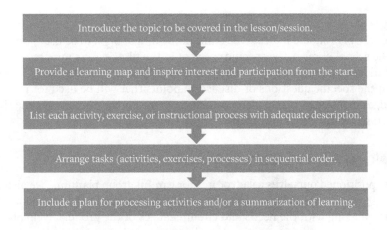

FIGURE 6.7 Questions to Consider for Activity Selection

plans for classroom-based psychoeducation groups, small counseling groups, or larger counseling, task, or work groups.

1. Begin the group with an *introduction* to the topic. The introduction should include a brief learning map, as well as strategies that can be used to inspire student interest and participation.
2. Next, include a *description of the activities, exercises, or any other instructional processes*, including the specific processing questions that will be employed for meaning making, that will be used to address the learning objectives of each session. These should be arranged sequentially according to how they will be introduced in the group.
3. Finally, group plans should *outline ending processes*—how you will close the group each session. This is a time to summarize the learning that has occurred. This may involve specific processing questions or engaging students in a closing round, for example, where they are invited to identify what they have learned. Keep in mind that inviting students to think about what they have learned stimulates thought processes that facilitate the transfer of learning. It is also useful as a tool for assessing the extent to which students reached the intended session objectives. When the time does not allow for extensive student input at the end of the group, the leader can offer a brief summary, linking what was discussed or done in the time together to the intended learning objectives. Also, while undue attention need not be drawn to the final moments of the group, it can be helpful to offer members advanced notice when the time is almost up so that students can prepare for the group to end.

The level of detail needed in the plan will vary from plan to plan and from leader to leader, and you will notice that the level of detail in group plans varies widely among the sample plans found in the appendices. This is intentional on our part. We want to communicate that there is considerable room for variability in how group plans are written. While some leaders like to write down what exactly they should say in various places or times in the group session, others may prefer to just note the topic, general theme, or a simple prompt. The topic of the group will also determine the level of detail needed in the group plans. For example, complex content probably requires more detail, as does content that is less familiar to the counselor leading the group. More detail may be needed in situations when the group is planned well in advance (thus helping the counselor remember what they had intended to do), when the group is planned by someone who is not actually leading the group, or when the counselor anticipates group management challenges.

In cases where more minimal notes are preferred, we suggest that the plan at least include the name of the material that will be used and a note regarding the relevant themes that are addressed through the use of the activity. If you are using a particular section of a popular film or a specific page in a book, the plan should indicate the name of the film or book to be used, where it is located (e.g., X is in the school library), the specific cue spot in the film (e.g., 34 minutes from the start of the movie), and how long the clip should be played (e.g., play for 5 minutes). It is also important to write down the specific questions or discussion points that will be used for processing group activities, and, as mentioned, group plans need to account for the amount of time that is needed for this important meaning-making process.

A Final Word About Group Plans

Having clearly positioned ourselves as advocates for careful group planning, we also caution that working well in groups, especially groups with students, requires flexibility and a willingness to change and adapt along with the needs and circumstances of the group. Group plans are useful guidelines; however, when they are used as law, the group can become more about the counselor's need for member conformity than about the members' experiences. This can be a formula for disaster. There is great power and value in following the path charted by students in the group rather than steering them back to where you wanted them to be. This concept is delicate, of course, as we would hate for any reader to misinterpret this to mean that a school counselor should stray with every distraction in classroom groups. Our point is that group leaders should know where they are going (i.e., what they hope to accomplish each session) but not allow that plan to cause them to lose other spontaneous and equally important opportunities for student growth.

Reflection Questions

1. We have stated in this text that even within apparent homogenous groups, there will be diverse learning needs. How can counselors plan to meet the diverse needs of students in their groups without drafting complex plans that will be difficult to carry out?
2. Students' experiences of receiving and giving feedback are often influenced by the dynamics of feedback exchange in their families of origin and previous experiences of feedback exchange in groups and classrooms. Discuss factors to consider when planning the introduction of a feedback exchange model to your group of students. Given the illustration provided in this chapter of effective feedback exchange contexts and processes, what challenges might you run into with the groups? What steps might you take to mitigate the aforementioned challenges?
3. We made the point that counselors often don't draft written plans for task groups. Think about/ discuss circumstances that may warrant the drafting of written plans for these types of groups in a school setting.

Credits

Img. 6.1: Copyright © 2014 Depositphotos/Kasza.

Img. 6.2: Copyright © 2014 Depositphotos/simazoran.

Fig. 6.3: Adapted from *Ready to Use Social Skills Lessons and Activities for Grades PreK-K.* ed. R. W. Begun. Copyright © 1995 by John Wiley & Sons, Inc.

Img. 6.3: Copyright © 2017 Depositphotos/IgorTishenko.

Img. 6.4: Copyright © 2019 Depositphotos/HayDmitriy.

Fig. 6.5: Adapted from J. P. Trotzer, "Conducting A Group: Guidelines for Choosing and Using Activities" *Handbook of Group Counseling and Psychotherapy* ed. J. L. DeLucia-Waack, et al. Copyright © 2004 by SAGE Publications.

Img. 6.5: Copyright © 2018 Depositphotos/ArturVerkhovetskiy.

Fig. 6.6: Adapted from N. L. Kees and E. Jacobs, "Conducting More Effective Groups: How to Select and Process Group Exercises," *The Journal for Specialists in Group Work*, vol. 15, no. 1. Copyright © 1990 by Taylor & Francis Group.

Leading Groups

CHAPTER SEVEN

Basic Group Work Skills

Introduction

The second part of this book is focused on what group leaders actually do in their groups to maximize the potential for learning. In the next few chapters, we will discuss general practices and suggestions that are effective for establishing norms, helping members develop an awareness of their roles in groups, facilitating group process, navigating challenges, and intervening when problems arise in a group. All of these come to us from the fields of counseling and teaching, and they are implemented through the intentional use of counseling and communication skills. So we begin in this chapter with an outline and description of these skills—basic group work skills.

Our intent here is to offer a brief description of these basic skills. While we call them *basic*, we invite you to think of them instead as *foundational*, not to be confused with simple or easy to implement. Many of these skills are, in fact, quite nuanced and complex. Thus, they can be challenging to use. Also, they are often used in combination with one another—not as discrete separate skills. Noting that our articulated intent is to offer brief discussions of these skills, we admit that the descriptions and reviews in some sections of this chapter are more expansive than others. This lack of uniformity reflects the fact that some of these skills do not easily lend themselves to concrete descriptions, and many are surrounded by important cautions. What we hope you will take away from this chapter is that these skills, with all of their complexities and with the appropriate cautions, can be used in a variety of ways to accomplish a variety of purposes. But the guiding principle of their use is *intentionality*. Again, the guiding principle is intentionality. Finally, we want to point out that the skills listed here are arranged alphabetically; please do not misinterpret those early on the list as easiest or the most basic and those late more difficult or advanced.

Active Listening

Active listening refers to attending to verbal and nonverbal communication among group members. It requires the group leader to be open, truly focused and listening, working to make sense of what they hear, and communicating their understandings back to students. In this way, it is an *active* engagement—a back and forth and co-construction of meaning.

We offer the following example as an attempt to describe what active listening might look and sound like: When Sabrina was talking in a group about an incident that happened to her in the community, Ms. Rios turned toward her, made eye contact, put the materials she had in her hands down, and focused on what Sabrina was saying. When there was a short break in the story, Ms. Rios summarized what she had heard Sabrina say, tentatively added an observation that Sabrina seemed discouraged, and then asked, "Did I get that right, Sabrina?" When Sabrina nodded that it was correct, Ms. Rios asked a question that directed Sabrina back to the place in the story where she had left off. In this example, we see that Ms. Rios did not just look at Sabrina; she also dropped what she had in her hands that might have been distracting (or that might have communicated that she was not fully listening). She then communicated her understanding to Sabrina to ensure that what she had heard and understood were accurate. Ms. Rios then invited Sabrina to add more information and returned the conversation to where

Sabrina had left off rather than just moving on to another topic. These actions had the effect of validating the significance of what Sabrina was saying. Also, Ms. Rios refrained from offering her own interpretation, frame, or advice. In this example, the active listening was a full-circle communication process that empowered and respected the student and her experience.

Active listening is typically demonstrated through nonverbal listening postures (e.g., facing the speaker, leaning in, and making eye contact), through minimal verbal responses such as uh-huh and mmmm, and, as illustrated in the example, paraphrasing what the listener heard and checking to see if it is accurate (Geroski, 2017). When listening actively, group leaders are not just attending to the verbal messages—what is said—but also listening to voice, tone, inflections, word choice, and speech quality, as these offer cues to the affective content of the communication. Because they sometimes can distort what they are hearing and how they respond to group members, group leaders must also monitor their own reactions and expressions (verbal and nonverbal) that occur during the active listening process.

It is important to remember that the context of what students communicate—that is, the student's everyday experiences, beliefs, and social and cultural practices—is what renders their experiences significant. Being aware of these context variables enables group leaders to understand group member communications more fully (Geroski, 2017). In the example, Ms. Rios was aware that there had been incidents of bias in the community, and she was also aware of how the students in this particular group were affected by these experiences. This understanding of context helped Ms. Rios more fully comprehend the present concern that Sabrina was discussing, as well as how Sabrina might have been feeling as a result.

While actively listening, group leaders will also want to pay careful attention to the ways in which students make meaning of their experiences—how they interpret and understand their experiences and how these understandings shape their interactions with others. As discussed in Chapter 1, it is important to understand these communications against a backdrop of socially constructed meanings and discursive positioning (Geroski, 2017). For example, social discourses on beauty shape the ways in which many students talk about popularity, their bodies, their identities, and how they may reference their own self-esteem. So when Bennett, who uses a wheelchair, sometimes expresses feeling left out (despite his active engagement in a number of school activities), the group leader may understand this sentiment in the context of gender expectations and stereotypes for men that communicate strength and attractiveness in ways that rarely highlight men who also have a visible physical disability.

In short, all of these—words, feelings, expressions, and context—give nuance and meaning to the communications that happen within the group. The point here is that active listening entails being attentive to what is being said, how it is being communicated, and the meanings of these communications—all of which sit within broader social and cultural contexts.

Blocking and Cutting Off

Blocking and cutting off are two skills that are used by group leaders to structure member sharing, to regulate what is said in the group (Gladding, 2003), to keep the group on track, to limit how

much time someone "takes up" in the group," and they are also used as an intervention to address situations in which the behavior of a group member is interfering with group functioning (Geroski, 2019). In these cases, the leader metaphorically steps in or stands in the way to prevent something from happening in the group. For example, Mr. Acharya raised his hand as a stop signal when Ope was about to jump in to complete Momo's sentence. This intervention was discussed between them in an earlier group session, and both had agreed that Mr. Acharya would signal Ope when it appeared that he was having difficulties giving others space in the group. In another example, Ms. Matusse intervened when the discussion in a psychoeducational group she was leading diverged significantly from the intended topic. Directing her comments to Jenna, who was off topic, she said, "Excuse me, Jenna. I am sorry to interrupt, but we seem to be a little off task, and I wanted to stop you here since we have a limited amount of time left today."

Blocking and cutting off are nuanced skills, but they need to be clear and direct in the communication of their intent. This is because some members may be offended or shut down if they feel unfairly blocked or cut off. Also, some group members may have concerns if a leader cuts off something that one of their peers is saying—they may feel that the peer is not being treated fairly by the group leader. So when using these skills, it is best to be clear, straightforward, respectful, and transparent, whenever possible. Notice in the previous example that Mrs. Matusse offered a brief explanation for why she cut off Jenna. In the same vein, Mr. Acharya and Ope had an earlier conversation about this intervention. These are examples of what we mean by communicating the intent of blocking or cutting off. It is important to add, however, that sometimes giving an explanation in the moment for why you are using these skills may not be possible, especially if you need to intervene in a situation where harm or safety are core concerns. When this is the case, it may be helpful to revisit the situation at a later time and give group members time to talk about (to "process") what happened and why the group leader intervened as they did.

Finally, we want to emphasize that after blocking, it is important to shift the focus back to the initial topic as soon as possible. This helps the group return to its intended focus and prohibits the problem (and the leader's intervention) from hijacking the group altogether. In the example, after cutting off Jenna, Mrs. Matusse said, "Jenna, we were talking about the change in application guidelines. Can you start us off on that?" In another example, Mr. Jacinda noted, "I'm sorry, Tony, for cutting you off, but I needed to intervene quickly to ensure that John was doing okay. Thank you for responding promptly to my signal. We were talking about the concept of 'microaggressions.' Can you start us off on that again?" These interventions, again, are intended to give context to an intervention that might be perceived as somewhat abrupt and to help return the group to the topic at hand.

Clarification

A clarification is a paraphrase or restating of something that a group member has said. The purpose of clarifying is to explicate something that has been said in the group and to ensure that group members' comments are understood. For example, "When you said, 'Back off,' it sounded like you were saying that you were finished with answering questions about this and wanted to talk about something else. Did I get that right?" As illustrated in this example, clarifications should typically be followed by a checking statement that invites the original speaker to verify or change the leader's paraphrase. This is important, as it ensures that students have been accurately heard. Another version of this skill is a clarifying question. This can be used when the group leader is confused about what a student has said. For example, "I wonder if I understood that correctly. Could you help me understand what you meant when you said ...?"

Confrontation

Confrontation is used by group leaders to address discrepant, confusing, unhelpful, or destructive statements, behaviors, or issues that may arise in a group. The idea is to provide feedback to a student so that they can see the effects of their behavior on themselves or others (Claiborn et al., 2001; Morran et al., 1998). Confrontation is used across many counseling modalities to address a wide variety of issues with powerful and effective results. But it has a long and controversial history (Polcin, 2003; Strong & Zeman, 2010) largely because when it is not delivered well, confrontation has the potential to cause unnecessary turmoil and harm. In fact, Geroski (2019) calls confrontation a "formidable and complex therapeutic skill" (p. 193) because power is enacted when one is confronting another person. This is true whether the confrontation is given by the group leader or is part of a feedback exchange process enacted among group members.

Maslow (Maslow, 1967) advocated for counselors to be honest, clear, and straightforward when offering a confrontation. In his words,

> People are very tough, and not brittle. They can take an awful lot. The best thing to do is get right at them, and not to sneak up on them, or be delicate with them, or try to surround them from the rear. Get right smack into the middle of things right away. (p. 28)

Maslow's point, we believe, is that confrontation should be clear and direct but not an attack. Indeed, the potential for confrontation to be therapeutically productive is best realized when it is asserted from a "power with" rather than a "power over" (Strong & Zeman, 2010, p. 333) position. This means that confrontation should never appear as a command or ultimatum, it should not be a put-down or social criticism, nor should it be a thinly veiled way of communicating advice. Instead, it should call one's attention to something and provide feedback. According to Strong and Zeman (2010), the idea is to engage group members in a "dialogic" process (p. 332). As the following examples attempt to illustrate, confrontations should be delivered in ways that prompt thought and discussion.

Our first example is set in a middle school conflict mediation training weekly meeting. Here the group leader confronts one of the students who was not meeting his group responsibilities:

"Achmed, you agreed last week that you would lead the exercise this week. Remember, we wrote it down in our 'next week' plans? Now you are saying you didn't know that you were supposed to lead this week and that you don't want to do it. I hear that, but this happened two weeks ago as well. I imagine that there is a reason why this is happening. Would you be willing to talk about what is happening that makes it hard for you to follow through on this commitment?"

Notice the respectful way that the group leader acknowledges that there is probably a reason for this behavior rather than punishing or criticizing Achmed for what he has done (or in this case for what he has not done). The group leader is curious about whether this is a follow-through difficulty, if there might be a group dynamic issue that causes Achmed to be reluctant to serve in the leader role in this group, or something else. Of course, there are any number of possibilities for this behavior; exploring those possibilities is the point of this leader's confrontation. Essentially, confrontation is intended to open dialogue that leads to a resolution of an emerging concern and not to shut down group conversation or reprimand a group member or the group as a whole.

In a middle school group focused on communication skills, Chloe abruptly interrupted as Amara was talking. This silenced Amara, who then said nothing as she granted the speaking space to Chloe.

"Let's stop a minute here," the leader intervened. "We have been talking in this group about 'speaking with clarity and respectful listening,' and I noticed that something just happened that did not meet this standard. Can anyone tell us what they just saw happen?"

Another student reported her observations on the dynamic between Amara and Chloe, commenting vaguely that this has happened before. The group leader then intervened with a confrontation for both Amara and Chloe.

"I have a few questions," she said. "What happened for you, Chloe, that you couldn't wait for Amara to finish? What happened for you Amara that kept you from saying something to Chloe about being interrupted?" She added, "Let's take a few minutes to have you two think about these questions, and then I'll invite you to respond to them in a minute."

Anticipating that Amara might have difficulties speaking up and that Chloe might become defensive, especially if others jumped to Amara's rescue, the group leader decided to further structure this conversation by adding, "I will ask the rest of you in the group to listen quietly as Chloe and Amara speak, and I also want the rest of you to think about what happens for each of you when you are interrupted. We will talk about your thoughts and feelings afterward."

The leader's intent was to provide an opportunity for both Amara and Chloe to practice the communication skills they had been learning and to introduce a discussion among group members about the complexities around using these skills in real situations. She foreshadowed this later intention by inviting the others in the group to think about these complexities and observe while she briefly worked with Amara and Chloe.

Confrontations can invite group members to reflect on their behavior in the group and to make decisions and choices about future behavior. But, as Oyum (2007) pointed out, "To know how to confront, and at the same time be respectful and inviting, is both necessary and difficult" (p. 42). The value of confrontation rests in "what the recipient does with it" (Strong & Zeman, 2010, p. 335). Leaders should remain engaged with a student who has been confronted—engaged in a way that maintains the relationship and that invites them into a process of understanding the source and purpose of the confrontation.

Our point is that the use of therapeutic confrontation is an assertion of power—whether it is delivered on the part of the group leader or between group members. So it must be used with intentionality. The steps outlined in Figure 7.1 represent the process that group leaders can use to structure their confrontations with students. We also recommend that group leaders teach students in their groups to follow the steps of feedback exchange outlined in Chapter 6 as a model for how they confront their peers.

Confrontation Cautions

Group leaders must be thoughtful around the use of confrontation in their groups. Their confrontations should never (intentionally or unintentionally) leave a student feeling an inappropriate sense of guilt, embarrassment, anger, or shame. In their role of protecting the safety and welfare of the students in their groups, leaders must also monitor and structure between-student encounters, including how they confront one another. To this end, group leaders may need to scaffold between-student confrontations so that they are appropriate and do not leave some students feeling unsafe.

We want to point out that students may sometimes feel vulnerable, guilty, embarrassed, or angry after a confrontation, even when every caution was taken to provide safety. These reactions may be due to a variety of factors, some of which may have little to do with the leader or the group. For example, family of origin dynamics, a history of trauma, experiences with bullying or scapegoating (especially when these have happened in groups), and other circumstances may

1. Point out the problem or discrepancy with appropriate tentativeness, a position of power-with, and with respectful curiosity.

- Use a paraphrase or reflection to identify the discrepancy.
- Speak clearly, respectfully, and with empathy.
- Do not interpret the discrepancy, merely point it out for further examination.
- For example: "Antonia, you told Genevieve that you're not angry but I noticed that your voice was raised—you were yelling at her."

2. Invite discussion and exploration. Invite the student into meaning-making.

- Invite the student to explain or make meaning of the problem or discrepancy before you offer an interpretation. This communicates respect and sets a tone for a continued conversation. It also lowers the intensity of the confrontation and thus may bypass any resistance, embarrassment, or anger that may initially be part of the student's reaction. Also, inviting a student to make meaning or consider why she has said or done something promotes agency.
- For example: "Help me understand whats happening, Antonia?" "What do you think that means?" "I wonder if we could talk about this some more?"

3. Offer your hypothesis or explanation when and only if appropriate.

- After the student has had an opportunity to think about and try to understand the problem that was pointed out, it is sometimes helpful for the group leader to offer a tentative interpretation of what happened. This may be necessary when you observe that an issue you think is critical has not surfaced in the conversation, when you want to expand the possibilities or invite group members to think in a new direction, or when the person is not able to offer a hypothesis or asks for your input.
- Because we can never really know what someone else is thinking and feeling, it is always appropriate to offer their hypotheses with tentativeness and to invite the person to disagree.
- For example: "I wonder if. ..." "Correct me if I'm wrong but ..." "Could it be that ..." "Do you think that maybe its because. ...?" Also, a simple, "What do you think?" or "Is that right?" after offering your input communicates that you are open to discussion about your assertion.

FIGURE 7.1 Steps in Confrontation

position students to be especially reactive to confrontation—whether it is delivered by the group leader or occurs between students during a group. Confrontation and feedback are also difficult to receive when they are delivered in a context of unequal power in relationships. For example, when a "popular" student confronts his "less popular" peer or when a teacher or the group leader is delivering the feedback, this feedback may leave the recipient student feeling especially vulnerable. All of this is further complicated in groups where such confrontations are delivered under the gaze of peers. These situations remind us of the importance of structuring confrontation so as to put recipients in a position of agency and relative openness. (We recommend using the steps outlined in Figure 7.1 or to follow the feedback exchange model reviewed in the previous chapter.) When students react to feedback in ways that are unproductive—shutting down or lashing out, for example—it is up to the leader to help them remain receptive, learn from the feedback, and, perhaps, find a productive way to save face.

Another potential landmine around the use of confrontation is that it can sometimes rupture relationships (Scaturo, 2002; Strong & Zeman, 2010). If a confrontation given by a group leader results in a relationship rupture, the leader must work to repair that relationship in a way that conveys genuineness and empathy, restores trust, and promotes learning. For example, if a student perceives a confrontation delivered by the leader to be hurtful, incorrect, or inappropriate, the leader must take responsibility for addressing the effect of this confrontation. This does not mean that the leader takes back or otherwise neutralizes the feedback (unless doing so is appropriate);

it means that the leader immediately works to establish a connection with the student, helps them make sense of the feedback delivered in the confrontation, and guides them in figuring out how to incorporate the feedback into their interactions or intrapersonal functioning. Helping students learn how to engage in constructive conflict and to navigate difficult conversations models a skill that is important for all students to learn.

Along these lines, if a confrontation between group members has gone bad and the students are unable to resolve the resulting fallout, the group leader will need to help those members work to repair the rupture. This will likely entail helping the students be in conversation with each other about the confrontation. Helping students engage authentically with each other about a confrontation and facilitating an opportunity for them to learn from the process is important interpersonal learning. This begins with requesting that the students listen carefully and respectfully to each other. While the students are talking and listening to each other, the leader can invite and support the recipient to understand and be open and responsive to the feedback that was delivered within the confrontation, even if the confrontation was difficult to hear. At the same time, the leader can help students in the group think about how, in the future, they can deliver challenging information or feedback to others in a way that is hearable. To this end, the student who delivered the confrontation can be helped to respond with empathy when their peer is reactive to their feedback and to offer apologies, if appropriate. This structuring helps students think about and take responsibility for the delivery of their confrontation (even if the content was valid) and to be aware of their effect on others. We believe that engaging students in feedback exchange processes, especially when feedback is delivered through confrontation, will help students develop skills more broadly in maintaining relationships through conflict. Here we reference, again, the steps in feedback exchange outlined in Chapter 6.

We end this topic with a reiteration of an important point. When a confrontation is delivered well, the recipient may still not respond as hoped. Students may not agree with the feedback or observation; they may not want to engage in further conversation; they may feel vulnerable, ashamed, or angry; or they simply may not be ready to hear the feedback or to change. When confrontation does not yield our hoped-for outcomes, we must meet the recipient student's response with empathy and respect, continue to engage them in the learning process, and, importantly, we must be patient. Learning how to offer others feedback through confrontation and learning how to engage in difficult conversations has important learning implications for all group members. But this learning typically requires careful group leader facilitation.

Cueing

Cueing refers to prompting appropriate behavior by restating directions, giving nonverbal signals, offering reminders, and controlling proximity (i.e., standing nearby escalating or problematic behaviors). Whenever possible, it is best to cue students in ways that do not draw undue attention to them or to the misbehavior, as doing so may unintentionally reinforce the problematic behavior. The point of cueing is to direct and support appropriate or expected behavior. Keep it simple, direct, and brief. For example, call out a student's name as they become distracted, periodically remind the group of the task they are supposed to be doing, or write the steps of an activity on the board and remind students of those instructions.

Drawing Out

In fast-moving discussions, space is not always available for reluctant or quieter members. And, of course, issues related to social power and privilege are always alive in groups, thus inviting some group members more readily into discussions while effectively silencing others. Group leaders sometimes need to intentionally create openings and invitations for less verbal or marginalized members to participate more fully in a group. This is what is meant by drawing out.

There are many ways to do this. One is to call on quieter members directly. For example, Ms. Strongbear said, "I wonder what you are thinking as you listen to this conversation, Joaquin?" In another group, Mr. Jacobs said, "Okay, so let's just take a pause here to give everyone a chance to collect their thoughts. We will start up in a minute or two with Aja's comments about what happened."

Another way to draw out members is to ask them to help with a particular task. To this end, a leader could ask a student in the group to hand out a worksheet, collect something, or start a response round. For example, Mr. Kargbo saw that Cyrus was often silent during group meetings, so he assigned Cyrus a group task. His intent was to help Cyrus feel invited into the group and to make Cyrus's presence more visible to others.

"Cyrus," he said, "can you start us off by selecting which mindfulness activity we will use today?"

In this case, Mr. Kargbo was aware that Cyrus had been fairly engaged in the group mindfulness activities, so he had a good idea that this particular request would be something that Cyrus could accomplish. But to be sure, Mr. Kargbo asked Cyrus to select rather than lead the mindfulness activity. Since this was his first attempt to draw Cyrus out in the group, he wanted to begin with a relatively low-risk proposition.

Mr. Kargbo also asked Justina to be in charge of passing out and later collecting the materials they were using that day. This was a way of drawing her out as well.

Leaders can also use rounds to draw out quieter members. A round is when the leader asks the members of a group to respond to a particular prompt in a leader-directed, predetermined, and fairly orderly way. For example, Ms. P said, "Let's take a minute to rate our anxiety here. We'll start with Jean Luc and move around the group in this way (pointing to the right). Jean Luc, can you tell us the number that describes your level of anxiety in this moment?" When using rounds, it wise to start the round with a group member who will respond in a predictable and expected way so as to set an appropriate response set for others in the group. In this example, Ms. P selected Jean Luc to start the round because she had a good sense that Jean Luc understood how to scale emotions and would be comfortable being the one to speak first. The "popcorn" version of a round is when members are invited to share their responses to the prompt in whatever order they decide.

Image 73

Empathy

In his seminal book, *A Way of Being* (Rogers, 1980), Carl Rogers described the state of empathy, or being empathic, in this way: "To perceive the internal frame of reference of another with accuracy and with the emotional components and meanings which pertain thereto as if one were the person, but without ever losing the 'as if' condition," (p. 140). This concept of empathy has been the foundation for many scholars, counselors, and group practitioners.

Building from Roger's work is Baron-Cohen's in-depth study of empathy (Baron-Cohen, 2011). Baron-Cohen defined empathy as an ability "to identify what someone else is thinking or feeling, and to respond to their thoughts and feelings with an appropriate emotion" (p. 12). Notice in this definition that Baron-Cohen outlines a two-step process of empathy that includes both *recognizing* the experiences of another person (in line with Roger's concept) and *communicating* that empathic awareness. Wynn and Bergvik (2010) added another step to this process. They describe the expression of empathy to be a three-part process that includes (1) an initial expression or communication from a client, (2) an empathic response that is felt by the counselor and then communicated to the client, and (3) the full-circle feedback loop where the client lets the clinician know (verbally or nonverbally) they felt the counselor's empathy. An underlying theme in these two models is that empathy doesn't happen unless the client feels it (Baron-Cohen, 2011; Wiseman, 1996; Wynn & Bergvik, 2010). We highlight that the Wynn and Bergvik conceptualization includes the additional step of confirmation that the empathy expressed was received and was accurate. This third step is really important because research on empathy indicates that counselors (and other professionals) are typically inadequate judges of empathy—that is, they are often not able to determine accurately if their clients experience them as empathic (Norcross, 2010). The primary way to determine if the counselor has been empathic is to ask the client (Frankel, 2009; Norcross, 2010).

What makes our task in this chapter of describing empathy as a skill so very complicated is that it is extremely difficult to pinpoint what exactly empathy looks like as a concrete behavior. For example, Rogers (1951) suggested that empathy has to do with creating a warm, nonthreatening, and accepting atmosphere that includes nonjudgmental engagement and an attempt to understand the feelings and ideas of others (in all of their complexities). But how does this look when it happens interpersonally or in a group? We translate these conditions into therapeutic responses that include *emotional engagement* (with appropriately regulated emotion), *respectful curiosity*, and being *responsive*—that is, actually responding to the cognitive and affective messages and experiences that have been communicated.

For example, in a small support group for students who were experiencing their parents' divorce, students were talking about feeling sorry for their custodial parent who was left with all of the work while the other parent, they thought, "did nothing to help." Shamus quietly commented—almost whispered—that he "didn't feel sorry" for either of his parents. He then added that he "didn't care" how they felt.

The group leader responded by saying, "That makes sense, Shamus. And it may be hard to even say that. I am thinking that it can be hard to be sympathetic when we feel like our own needs are not being met—which is also hard to say. I might be wrong, but I wonder if that might be part of what you are saying, Shamus—that your needs sometimes aren't being met in this new divorce arrangement? Is that right?" In this sentiment, the group leader hoped to communicate that she understood the dilemma that Shamus articulated (probably speaking for many of the children in the group as well)—that students may want to and, perhaps, even truly do feel empathic toward their parents, but they also may simultaneously feel somehow slighted by their parents' actions. But being aware that she does not really know what Shamus is thinking or feeling, the leader was careful to keep empathy in the forefront of what she was trying to communicate. She also wanted to promote insight about this complexity that Shamus seemed to be articulating. She did this through an interpretation issued as a question rather than a definitive statement. (We will talk more about interpretations shortly.)

According to Wiseman (1996) and Norcross (2010), empathy is a critical factor in what makes counseling work. In fact, Norcross (2010) found that empathy accounts for one third of the changes associated with therapy. This is likely because empathy helps people feel heard, valued, acknowledged, and respected (Baron-Cohen, 2011). This important finding on the value of empathy compels us to stay connected to the students in our groups, even when we feel disappointed about the choices that they may make, and even if we feel frustrated with the lack of progress in the group. It requires us to remain present and nonreactive, even when we feel challenged. And, finally, having empathy means that we must be able to withhold judgment, in spite of our own personal values and life decisions. Empathy requires us to be centered on the needs of the students and to be engaged in a therapeutic relationship with them, even when that is difficult to do.

Executive Function

The term executive function, discussed earlier in Chapter 3, refers to the administrative aspects of running a group (Lieberman et al., 1973). Executive function begins with careful group planning so that the group is aimed at reaching identified group goals and objectives and includes member selection and screening as appropriate for the group type. In addition, the maintenance of appropriate documentation for group functions, including group plans, assessment plans, informed consent, and group counseling session notes (ACA, 2014), are all part of the leader's executive function role. This, too, extends to making referrals to other counselors, teachers, or related professionals when appropriate.

Moving beyond these aforementioned tasks, we will focus our discussion on the executive function role of leaders that happens in the group when the group is running in real time. Here executive function refers to decision-making processes and direct interventions that ensure that the group is functioning appropriately, and is beneficial to all of its members. To this end, group leaders establish and manage the parameters of the group through the enactment of rules and limits; they provide appropriate structure so that members are heard, respected, and feel physically and psychologically safe to engage and take appropriate risks in the group (ACA, 2014; American Group Psychotherapy Association, 2007; Bernard et al., 2008; DeLucia-Waack, 2006; Okech et al., 2016). When a group member is being inappropriately targeted with criticism or feedback, when a group is developing culturally marginalizing and oppressive dynamics, or when group members feel unsafe in the group for other reasons, it is the responsibility of the group leader to intervene; this action is part of their executive function role. Along these lines of safety, group leaders working in schools need to ensure that the content and level of personal sharing in their groups is appropriate to the developmental stage of the student members, as well as the purpose and format of the group. According to the American Group Psychotherapy Association (2007), the group leader's primary function is to "monitor and safeguard the rational, work-oriented boundaries of the group, ensuring that members experience it as a safe, predictable and reliable container with an internal space for psychological work to occur" (p. 37).

The role that Mr. Cordera takes in leading the task group through a conflict in Case Study 7.1 is an example of a group leader stepping into the executive function role to help the group be safe for all of the members and to guide it into being productive and on task. (Case Study 7.1 is outlined later in this chapter after our discussion on the use of questions.) It is critical for us to point out that a safe group is one that allows for both physical and psychological safety in an environment that also encourages authentic engagement, risk taking, and expression of a myriad of emotional experiences and emotions, ranging from sadness, anger, and happiness, to anxiety, fear and crying. The concept of safety by no means implies the avoidance of interpersonal or emotional experiences that may evoke discomfort, fear, or sadness and that may require courage for members to embrace them and respond (Okech & Rubel, 2009). But we also caution that standards of acceptable safety vary according to group membership, type, and context.

Finally, within their executive function role, group leaders also set and maintain an appropriate pace in the group to ensure that students are learning or growing as intended in the group goals and objectives. This includes managing time (so the group begins and ends on time and the tasks of closure are met) and intervening if the group moves away from the content goals or topic. All of the skills mentioned in this chapter—especially drawing out, cutting off, redirecting or shifting the focus, informing, setting limits, and using questions—are tools used by group leaders to perform these executive functions.

Informing

In their research study of group work in schools, Geroski and Kraus (2002) noted that some group leaders may engage in teaching or informing as a part of their enactment of executive function duties in their groups. Here we use the term *informing* for its obvious reference to information. It is the offering of information to group members. For example, a leader of one group taught his students a five-step problem-solving model. Another group leader working with students on the topic of post-high school employment helped her students locate resources.

While seemingly simple, group leaders must be thoughtful about using this skill of informing. First, they need to be careful not to undermine student agency by, for example, offering students unsolicited advice or assuming that students need more help than they actually do. School counselors and group leaders also need to be sure to impart valid, updated, and relevant information. It is far better to say that you do not have an answer or to engage students in finding an answer with you than to pass off a guess or an opinion as a fact.

Immediacy

Immediacy is the counseling skill of calling attention to what is happening in the group in the moment. For example, a classroom group of second graders lost its focus and then lapsed into uncontrollable giggles when a parade of fifth graders walked by the open door singing happy birthday in very loud voices. The school counselor conducting the developmental guidance lesson/classroom group with the second graders called attention to this by saying, "That singing grabbed our attention, and now we're having trouble getting back to the feeling drawings we were working on." In a task group focusing on planning a school event, two students refused to work with each other. "That conflict from geometry class seems to be getting in the way of you two being able to work together in here today," the group leader commented. As these examples suggest, immediacy calls attention to dynamics affecting a group by offering feedback and is often used with confrontation and other advanced intervention skills (Claiborn et al., 2001).

Immediacy is typically used as a therapeutic intervention to promote insight about a particular issue or situation, to address relationship challenges, and, sometimes, to model how clients can be assertive in their communications with others outside of the group (Wheeler & D'Andrea, 2004). Like confrontation and feedback, immediacy has the potential to arouse a great deal of intensity (Hazler & Barwick, 2001). For this reason, immediacy should be used when you are sure that the student or the group can handle the intensity that may ensue and in the context of a solid group leader/member relationship. Also, like with confrontation, the therapeutic value of immediacy rests largely in its effectiveness in creating a meaningful conversation or engagement in meaning making. We recommend the steps in Figure 7.2 for using immediacy in groups.

Interpretation

An interpretation is a hypothesis, possible explanation, or a statement that is intended to promote understanding. It is typically offered in response to something that has been said, implied, or suggested by a group member. Interpretations are used to promote insight, especially in regard to how internal thoughts, behaviors, conflicts, and past experiences affect present relationships and personal well-being (Caper, 2001; Johansson et al., 2010).

According to Schermer (2011), a phenomenological approach to the therapeutic use of interpretation is for the counselor to share her experiences or ideas and then invite discussion. The therapeutic value of interpretation, like with confrontation and immediacy, largely happens in the dialogue that occurs *after* the interpretation is offered. Again, the aim is to promote awareness in a manner that invites new understandings. For example, Mr. T was working in a middle school classroom group focusing on test anxiety. Prior to the group, one of the students, Mac, had been in a conflict with his teacher. When Mr. T entered and started the group, Mac was uncharacteristically rude to Mr. T. Offering an interpretation to invite Mac to think about how he carried the conflict from one person to another, Mr. T said, "I might be wrong, Mac, but it sounds like you're still mad at your teacher and you are taking it out on me. Can you give that a thought, and we can talk about it later if you want?"

Interpretation is a tricky skill. It is easy to get it wrong. Even in our most insightful moments, we can never really know what others are thinking, nor can we fully grasp the significance of what

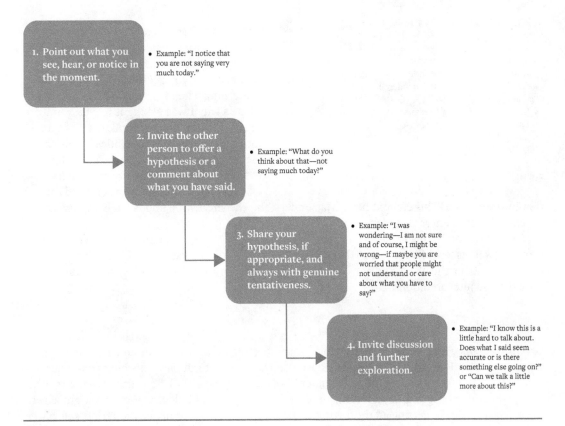

FIGURE 7.2 Steps in Using Immediacy

they say or do. And, of course, all of this is complicated by the power dynamics inherent to the leader-member and adult-youth relationships and the "public" nature of what happens in a group—something said to a student in a group is witnessed by all of the other group members. Within this context of power differentials, an interpretation may be taken as the gospel truth, even when it is not altogether accurate. As a result, an interpretation can easily convince a student to think about something in a way that does not fit or is not in correct alignment with their experiences, beliefs, or values. This is especially true when working cross-culturally or with vulnerable clients and in situations where the lived experiences of group members is far different than those of the group leader—think here about the experiences of race, ethnicity, and social class. We never want to suggest to a client that we know him better than he knows himself nor that his own lens for understanding himself or his experiences is somehow blurry or wrong. Instead, we want to use interpretations as an invitation to see another perspective or to think of new ways.

Remember, interpretation is a suggestion or an idea on offer rather than a truth.

For the reasons mentioned earlier, interpretations must always be delivered with caution. As we attempted to illustrate in our example with Mr. T and Mac, interpretations should be offered with the appropriate tentativeness and followed by a check-in to assess accuracy or to invite client input. According to Schermer (2011), even Freud himself cautioned against making inappropriate interpretations and suggested that valid interpretations are those that can be verified by client response—when the client is invited to determine if the interpretation is accurate.

Offering "evidence" or transparency is another way in which group leaders can use interpretations more effectively. When students understand how we have arrived at our ideas, they are better able to hear them, understand them, and accept them. For example, Mr. T could say something

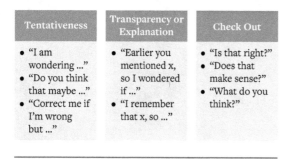

Tentativeness	Transparency or Explanation	Check Out
• "I am wondering …" • "Do you think that maybe …" • "Correct me if I'm wrong but …"	• "Earlier you mentioned x, so I wondered if …" • "I remember that x, so …"	• "Is that right?" • "Does that make sense?" • "What do you think?"

FIGURE 7.3 Interpretation Steps

like, "Mac, when you told me to shut up—well that isn't normally like you to say that to me, so I figured there was a problem. And then I realized that you seemed to be upset about something when I first came into the room. That is why I was asking if maybe you were mad at the other teacher and that was coming into the room with you." Notice in this example that Mr. T is providing a context for Mac to see how he came to the conclusion that Mac was actually mad at someone else and carried that into the room. This context helps Mac understand the suggestion and is likely to disarm any potential defensiveness that may arise.

Interpretation is an advanced therapeutic skill, especially when implemented in a group, and should only be used with appropriate therapeutic intention, a solid therapeutic alliance, and grounded knowledge about the client and the context of their life. Figure 7.3 offers suggestions on how to articulate an interpretation.

Leveling

Leveling entails using the skills of drawing out and cutting off to shift focus and attention among group members. For example, "Reg, let's have you wait a minute. Julian, let's hear from you." Or "Ravi, you have offered us a lot today, I wonder if we might check in with Tasha, who seems to want to say something." A group-level leveling intervention might be as follows: "Wow, the right side of the room seems to be getting all the airtime today—let's hear from someone on the left side of the room." (This is a group-level intervention because it is not directed toward any specific member of the group; the concept of intervention level is discussed in more detail in Chapter 8.)

It is almost always the case that some group members are more vocal or more participatory than others. Keep in mind that this dynamic is frequently a function of social capital in the group, but it can also be attributed to different levels of interpersonal awareness, skill, temperament, and confidence among group members. Status hierarchies in groups are apparent when group members regularly defer to one student for group decision making, follow one student's lead in tone and level of sharing, or appear reluctant to participate or participate in different ways when a particular student is present. Leveling is an intervention that can be used to equalize power within a group and is often employed during the norming and storming stages of group development (Gladding, 2003). It is critical to use leveling in the early stages of groups so as to set up a norm of equal engagement among group members. A group with level participation provides all group members with the opportunity to work on their intrapersonal and interpersonal goals and to develop effective group interpersonal engagement skills.

Finally, when speaking about the ways in which leaders can use groups to teach students new interpersonal skills, leveling is a great way to promote interpersonal awareness among students who may tend to dominate conversations. One way to do this is to invite these students to engage in a silent role during a group session. This not only promotes awareness but also allows them to practice a new way to engage with others.

Limits

Charles (2011) defined limits in the noun form as "the boundaries that separate acceptable behavior from unacceptable behavior" (p. 13). They are the parameters for what can and cannot be done. When thought of as a verb—what one does—we come to the action of setting limits. Counselors working with youth typically set limits to provide safety, increase students' sense of control (the paradox is that when there are parameters or boundaries that limit what can and can't be done, children have an opportunity to control what they do within those parameters), and provide an opportunity for students to increase personal and social responsibility (Vernon & Shimmel, 2019).

Limits help students control their impulses and behaviors in ways that are prosocial and respectful of others. They also provide safety for group members so that they can take risks to learn and change. To accomplish this kind of group climate, leaders should always be prepared to enforce limits in response to physical threats, aggression, sarcasm, teasing, and breaches in confidentiality. This is because these behaviors may be dangerous, or at the very least, they are likely to create anxiety and thus interfere with productive group process dynamics. In addition to these limits on doing harm, play therapists (Kottman, 2011; Kottman & Meany-Walen, 2016; Landreth, 2012) typically include rules and are prepared to intervene in situations related to damage to materials or physical property in the playroom. Finally, group leaders in schools also typically set limits on time (i.e., when the group begins and ends), appropriate engagement in the content or purpose of the group (i.e., limits about staying on task), and, sometimes, on particular situations. For example, if the group is being conducted in a room near where others are working, there might be limits on noise levels.

The need for setting limits is potentially heightened in group work with youth where the peer "gaze" is particularly strong; everything that group members do and say is under peer scrutiny. Youth tend to be sensitive to the perceptions of their peers, and this often leads to perceived (real or unreal) pressures to think, feel, and behave in certain ways. Students sometimes need the extra help of group leaders to navigate these complex social systems with all of their nuanced rules about social behavior.

Our point is that it is the group leader's responsibility to ensure that group rules are established so that the group members adhere to healthy and appropriate norms, and it is the responsibility of the group leader to enforce those rules as needed. This is done through leader-initiated limit setting. Borrowing from the work of counselors and teacher educators (e.g., Bear, 2005; Charles, 2011; Kottman, 2011; Kottman & Meany-Walen, 2016), we offer the following steps for setting limits/enforcing rules in groups:

1. Be sure that the *expectations for member participation are established early*—at the start of the group—and in a clear norm- and rule-setting process (which we discuss in the next chapter). Group rules should be clearly articulated and sometimes even posted so that all members understand them.

2. When a norm has been violated or a rule has been broken, the leader should *restate the rule*. For example, "Let's remember the rule that we do not speak for others in the group." "The rule in here is to keep our hands to ourselves." "Our rule in this group is to not talk about others who are not in the group."

3. It may be helpful (although not always necessary) to briefly *remind students why this rule was initially set—why it is important*. "We set that rule so we could be sure that everyone has the opportunity to express their own opinion." "We decided that was important because we learn from others when they share their experiences and their opinions."

4. The leader may need to *offer a directive* to help enforce the limit. For example, "Zelia, I am going to interrupt you now so that Merka can have an opportunity to speak for herself. Thank you for understanding and making space in this group for others. Merka, would you like to add something now or at a later time?" Another simple example is: "Joshua, you need to put that down now."

5. *Return to the activity or discussion* that was occurring prior to the problem as soon as possible so that the interruption does not further derail the group. For example, after Merka and another student had an opportunity to speak, the group leader continued the discussion by asking who else wanted to comment on the topic that they were discussing. After Joshua put the stick down, the group leader thanked him, put the stick behind his back (the group leader's back), and then seamlessly continued to read the story that he had been reading in the group.

When setting limits in regard to staying on task, the process might unfold in a slightly different way. In these situations, limit setting typically involves redirection and monitoring. For example, the leader of the test-taking strategies group intervened when the conversation digressed by saying, "It looks like we've lost our focus in here. Can we please come back to testing skill number five?"

In another example, members of a high school counseling group were moving off task and began to express frustration about a student who was not in the group. This was problematic because the group was off topic and the members were breaking a rule about not talking about others who are not in the group. The leader intervened by saying, "I know that we all like to have an opportunity to vent, but when we started this group, one of the rules we identified was to not speak about others who are not in the group. In this group, we have been talking about how we can respond to injustice when we witness it. Without focusing on who out there said and did what, let's talk about what kinds of appropriate responses we ourselves could use in this situation." This kind of response requires self-discipline by the group leader—the leader has to avoid falling into the pattern of processing every event and/or soliciting input into every decision-making process. As this example illustrates, this may best be done by not focusing on the distracting event or behavior but instead focusing on the desired behavior, group process, and/or outcome.

Linking, Joining, Connecting

We use the terms linking, joining, and connecting interchangeably here in reference to interventions that invite students to engage with each other in the group. The purpose of these skills is to call attention to commonalities among group members and their ideas, to foster a cohesive group climate, and to generate meaning making.

An example of linking or directing engagement between students is when a group leader said, "Javier, I wonder if you would turn to Adam and say that to him directly?" An example of using linking to draw students together around commonalities is when, in another group, the group leader pointed out, "Zenab, you and Cathy both spoke about feeling isolated, even if your isolation seems to be related to very different things." This latter intervention also served to begin to encourage cohesion among group members who may have been thinking that their concerns were not shared by others.

This final example is of a group leader who used linking to encourage meaning making and to invite students to brainstorm solutions. "Matt, I hear you speaking about being frustrated with

yourself about being silent when you have to speak in large groups. I know that others have also talked about this." The leader paused and looked around the room. After noticing a few students nodding in agreement, he said, "I am thinking that we sometimes use silence as a time to gather our thoughts. I mean, maybe silence isn't something we should feel bad about—maybe it is something that actually helps us. Maybe silence is sometimes productive." This was an attempt to help students understand silence in a different way—as it might also be functional. After the students embraced this idea about productive silence, the leader then added, "Of course, it is very real that silence can also just grip us—that we can get stuck in that silence. Then it may be more about anxiety than helpful thinking." After a brief discussion with a few members about the tension between these two ideas, the leader decided to shift the group into potential solutions but connecting to some things that were discussed in previous group sessions. "Adam talked last week about how he was using some deep breaths to help him calm down when he was starting to get nervous about public speaking. Perhaps Adam's idea about deep breaths can help us here. What are some other ways we can move from helpful to not-so-helpful silence? Ideas?"

Meaning Making

Meaning making refers to creating possibilities for members to make sense of what they are experiencing in the group. This is something that was discussed in detail in Chapter 6 (so we will not review the concept of meaning making in detail again here). Here we identify meaning making as a skill to remind group leaders to intervene in the group whenever possible and appropriate to encourage students to consider an idea at a deeper level or to encourage metacognitive thinking skills. This can be accomplished by pausing and creating spaces for members to take time to think, by asking focused questions, and by inviting students to share their understandings with each other. For example, "Let's take a few silent moments to see what we will take away from group this morning." Or, "Damion, when we consider this example of bullying, can you talk about why the bystander role is particularly troubling?" "Who can talk about why it is so hard to not be a bystander when bullying happens?"

Microgrouping

Microgrouping is when a group leader divides group members into smaller groups. It is an example of a structural intervention discussed in Chapter 8. Group leaders use microgrouping to increase student participation in a particular topic or to bring focus to an activity. It is a strategy that is often used as a classroom management technique in large classroom groups. Before moving forward, we want to differentiate microgrouping as an intervention from systemic subgrouping that sometimes happens in groups. Subgrouping refers to when a small group of members within a group align strongly together (and sometimes against other group members) in ways that have a negative effect on the group's overall functioning (Kline, 2003). Subgrouping typically emerges in group process dynamics; microgrouping is a leader intervention.

Sometimes leaders arrange microgroups by matching students according to a salient variable. This is usually done for particular pedagogical reasons. For example, leaders may want to put students who have a similar level of knowledge or work style together to work on a particular task or project within a larger group. Sometimes leaders form microgroups to save time on a particular task (i.e., having students work on different parts of a larger project), to set up a situation where some students help others, or in response to (or to avoid) exclusionary behaviors—to interrupt status hierarchies that may be present in the larger group. Group leaders can organize microgroups by having students count off by numbers, by using creative prompts that gather students together, or by assigning students to particular subgroups based on student and/or task characteristics.

Modeling

Modeling refers to the example that is set for others to follow. We have talked about modeling (based on social learning principles) in earlier chapters of this text. We list it here, again, to remind leaders of the power of using modeling as a specific intervention skill. With this reminder, we want to highlight some key points already discussed related to the use of modeling.

First, be sure that group members are attending to the model. For example, to garner attention, a leader might say, "Can I have everyone's attention while I try to show you what this might look like." Or, "Maya, can you please look up here?" Second, be sure that the desired behavior is modeled in a way that is accessible to group members. This may mean that complex ideas should be divided into clear and small sound bites and larger actions into smaller pieces. For example, Mr. Jahn divided a learning task into three steps and had the students watch and practice each step separately before they put them together. Third, be intentional about selecting models. As mentioned in earlier chapters, perceived similarity, social capital, desirability, or prestige of a role model are important factors in determining if a modeled behavior will be imitated or tried by others (Bandura, 1971, 1986). Finally, Bandura pointed out that an expectation of a reward or punishment for performing a modeled behavior is a significant influence affecting imitation (Bandura, 1971). So, group leaders should provide positive reinforcement after the behavior is modeled. For example, "Thanks so much for doing that so well, Joel. Great job! I saw you do X, as we discussed, and then you did Y in a slow and deliberate way. I think that is why it worked so well." In this latter example, the leader called attention to the specific behaviors that were demonstrated instead of offering vague praise. This helps concretize what the leader is hoping students will learn.

Process Observations

Process observation entails the use of an invited person outside of the group or one of the group members to observe group process dynamics and to offer their observations to the group (Zieman et al., 1981). Groups may benefit from process observations when they are engaged in conflict or when it seems that an "objective" or outside perspective might be helpful.

Process observers are usually asked to sit quietly in the room and not actively participate in the group. Later, they offer their observations or comments when called upon by the group leader. For example, a school counselor worked in an often rowdy classroom where the teacher typically remained present—often grading papers at his desk—as the counselor conducted their developmental guidance lessons. Just before one such group, the school counselor decided to ask the teacher if he would be willing to observe the group and to make comments about what he saw. At a few points during the group, the counselor stopped the conversation and asked everyone to take a minute and listen to the teacher's observations. One such observation was, "It seems that the students are a little lost. They are walking around as if they are unfocused, and I heard a few of the students asking each other 'what are we supposed to be doing now?'" The counselor asked the students to comment on what they heard the teacher say, and they agreed that they were confused. The counselor thanked the teacher and the students who spoke up and then reviewed the task instructions, one step at a time. In this case, we can see that the process observer was able to provide insight into a group dynamic that the group leader was unaware of. Doing so helped the students gain clarity and helped the leader better manage the group.

We point out that process observers usually do not participate in the group, but in some situations, the group leader may also ask a group member who was not specifically assigned to be a process observer to make a comment about the group. Case Study 7.1 offers another example of using a process observer in the group. In this case, the group is normed to have a different student serve in the process observer role each week. The school counselor in this case study uses the process observer to help the group move through an impasse. (Case Study 7.1 is located after our discussion of questions a little later in this chapter.)

According to Yalom et al. (1975), using process observers in therapy groups may lower group member anxiety, enhance cognitive processing or meaning making, and provide an opportunity for group members to receive feedback. As demonstrated in our example with the teacher offering the school counselor comments on what he observed happening in the group, process observers can also provide valuable feedback to the group leader. In fact, using process observers in group work is a technique that is traced back to Kurt Lewin's work in the late 1940s when he made use of process observers to help group leaders analyze and talk about group dynamics after their sessions (Kislev, 2015). Hulse-Killacky et al. (2001) promoted the use of process observers in task groups, as well, pointing out that process observers can help members reflect on the group's work, focus attention on group members' interactions, and help members think about the extent to which the task is being addressed in the group. While our discussion here is meant to focus on the ways in which process observers can be used in their groups, school counselors can also serve as process observers in school classrooms, helping teachers better understand their classroom dynamics and thus improving the learning environment (Fazio-Griffith & Curry, 2008).

Finally, we take notice of Kislev's warning (Kislev, 2015) that a group process observer may be perceived by members as someone who is "policing" the group and thus constitute an expression of power. This point is important—consider the effect of having a silent member or other adult in the room who has the job of attending to, recording in some way, group process dynamics and then making comments about what they see in the group. Group leaders should consider, then, that process observers may not be appropriate for all groups or in all settings. Also, it reminds us that leaders should be transparent about the purpose and role of a process observer before using them in their groups.

Protecting

Protecting requires being ever watchful to ensure that all members of all groups are safe. Here we talk about the role of the group leader in attending to psychological, as well as physical, safety. Group leaders offer protection through interventions such as setting limits, cutting off, shifting the focus, and leveling. A large aspect of the role of executive functioning serves the purpose of protecting group members.

Questions and Probes

Whether working with students one-on-one or in groups, counselors use questions to initiate discussions, gather information, clarify, focus on an important topic, explore an issue in-depth, solicit input, check out understandings, and prompt meaning making (Geroski, 2017, 2019). Here we will identify some basic question types that can be used in school groups. These question types are outlined in Figure 7.4.

Closed Questions

A closed question is used to prompt a yes or no response or to elicit specific information. For example, "When did you learn that?" "Do you want to talk about that?" "Are you okay?" These kinds of questions provide direction and focus; they point to certain topics and invite the student to add specific information. Using a closed question such as "Is that right?" is a good way to check out or verify understandings. These examples of closed questions are focused on one member: the person who is being asked to provide the information. However, they can also be asked at a group level—meaning that they can be asked more generally inviting anyone (but no one in particular) in the group to respond. For example, "Does anyone remember what time the bell rings this period?"

Open Questions and Open-Ended Focused Probes

Open questions are used to invite exploration, and they allow students considerable freedom to decide how they want to respond. This type of question invites a *paragraph response*—responses articulated in a few or more sentences on a particular theme. For example, "What should we talk about today?"

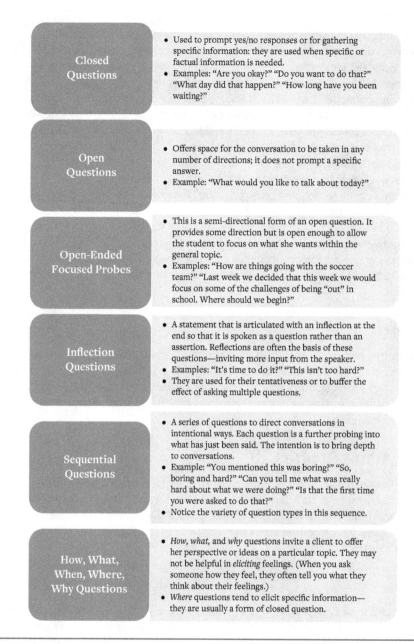

Closed Questions
- Used to prompt yes/no responses or for gathering specific information: they are used when specific or factual information is needed.
- Examples: "Are you okay?" "Do you want to do that?" "What day did that happen?" "How long have you been waiting?"

Open Questions
- Offers space for the conversation to be taken in any number of directions; it does not prompt a specific answer.
- Example: "What would you like to talk about today?"

Open-Ended Focused Probes
- This is a semi-directional form of an open question. It provides some direction but is open enough to allow the student to focus on what she wants within the general topic.
- Examples: "How are things going with the soccer team?" "Last week we decided that this week we would focus on some of the challenges of being "out" in school. Where should we begin?"

Inflection Questions
- A statement that is articulated with an inflection at the end so that it is spoken as a question rather than an assertion. Reflections are often the basis of these questions—inviting more input from the speaker.
- Examples: "It's time to do it?" "This isn't too hard?"
- They are used for their tentativeness or to buffer the effect of asking multiple questions.

Sequential Questions
- A series of questions to direct conversations in intentional ways. Each question is a further probing into what has just been said. The intention is to bring depth to conversations.
- Example: "You mentioned this was boring?" "So, boring and hard?" "Can you tell me what was really hard about what we were doing?" "Is that the first time you were asked to do that?"
- Notice the variety of question types in this sequence.

How, What, When, Where, Why Questions
- *How, what,* and *why* questions invite a client to offer her perspective or ideas on a particular topic. They may not be helpful in *eliciting* feelings. (When you ask someone how they feel, they often tell you what they think about their feelings.)
- *Where* questions tend to elicit specific information—they are usually a form of closed question.

FIGURE 7.4 Question Types

The *open-end focused probe* is a semidirectional version of the open question. This question type is directional in that it invites a student to talk about a particular issue or topic, but it is open in that it invites that student to respond to that topic however they want. For example, notice that the question, "What would you like to say today about how last week's group project went?" invites group members to decide what they want to say about a particular thing: last week's group project. This is a particularly useful question structure for engaging students in a discussion about a particular topic. Open-ended focused probes can be directed to an individual or offered at the group level, as shown in the following examples: "Emma, what did you want to say about that test?" is an invitation for one student to respond. The question, "Let's all of us think about that incident that happened last week on the soccer field. What thoughts do you have about why it happened?" is aimed more broadly, inviting anyone in the group to respond. This second question is an example of a group-level intervention and will be discussed in more detail in the following chapter.

How, What, When, Where, and Why Questions

Keep in mind that the first word in the introductory clause of a question frames a particular response. *How*, *what*, and *why* questions can be helpful in eliciting group member's perspectives or thoughts. They tend to invite members to offer an explanation. For example, "Why do you think that happened?" "What do you think will happen next?" "How will that unfold?"

While these questions do a great job of eliciting the perspectives or thoughts of group members who chose to respond, they are not often helpful in eliciting feelings. When we ask students *how* they feel, they often respond with a thought about how they are feeling. If a group leader wants to learn how a student is feeling, they will probably need to use a combination of skills, such as sequential questions, along with empathy, feeling reflections, immediacy, and, sometimes, interpretation. For example, when working with a group of students who had just lost a peer to suicide, Ms. K asked the group, "How are all of you feeling right now?"

After a long silence, Kyle responded, "I think we are trying to figure out how it happened. What we missed."

Ms. K paraphrased Kyle's thoughts and then offered a tentative interpretation: "So, everyone is a little confused. I'm guessing that there is also a lot of sadness and feelings of guilt in the room as well?" This latter interpretation and question were intended to refocus the group members on some of the feelings they seemed to have.

When and *where* typically initiate a closed question, and they also are not usually good for eliciting feelings. For example, wanting to get a sense of who students were talking to about the suicide that happened over the weekend, Ms. K later asked the group members, "When did you find out about the suicide?" "Who told you about it?" As you can see, these questions invite a narrow and information-based response. They are helpful to elicit specific information or details.

Inflection Questions

Inflection questions are statements offered as a question. They are articulated as a statement but include a slight inflection at the end. For example, "You feel that it was unfair?" Inflection questions offer an alternative to the more typical question structure (e.g., when did ...?, where do ...?, and why is it that ...?) and are useful to alter the conversational flow, especially when the group leader is trying to use a series of questions to draw out group members and engage them in a discussion.

Inflection questions are helpful in keeping a conversational flow since they are easy to insert in a conversation. But, group leaders should be careful when using them, as they, like all of the other question types, are directive; they prompt a particular response. Sometimes group members need a specific prompt, but sometimes the suggestivity or directiveness of inflection and other directional questions can make students feel that they have little control over the conversation and thus prompt silence or defensiveness. Using immediacy or transparency (making it clear what your intentions are when asking questions) can help diffuse these situations. For example, "Hmm, maybe I am pushing a little too much here when this is hard to talk about. I guess I was a little eager to get to the solution without getting input from all of you. Let's try a different approach." This comment was made by one group leader who observed the members of the group shut down as she pushed for more information using directive questions.

Sequential Questions

The caution often given to counselors working with youth is to be careful not to ask too many questions. This is because multiple questions can make a person feel interrogated. This caution is particularly relevant when working with youth who may already feel disempowered in other aspects of their lives. However, we also point out that sometimes students do not answer our questions because they do not understand them, because they do not know or cannot think of an answer, or because they need help putting their thoughts, feelings, or experiences into words. These situations are ones that may call for sequential questioning. Sequential questioning is an intervention that uses a variety of question types in a conversation for the purpose of scaffolding understandings or inviting depth.

Asking sequential questions is not just about firing off random questions. It is a skill that is used to direct conversations in intentional ways. When questions are selected carefully based on the student's response to the preceding question and offered from a position of curiosity, they can communicate to a student that they are being heard, that the counselor is interested in what the they are saying, and they also can offer focus and direction when there is a lack of clarity. The practice of sequential questioning entails using a variety of question types in combination with reflections and paraphrases. Again, it is used for a particular purpose: to promote conversational depth or understanding. Consider the example of sequential questions used in Case Study 7.1 to help a group member navigate a conflict that arose in a task group.

CASE STUDY 7.1 **Sequential Questions**

Mr. Cordera, a high school counselor, is the "adviser" for a group of students who are working together in a task group. The task is to plan the junior prom event at the school, which will happen later in the spring. Mr. Cordera missed the last group meeting because he was away at a conference, but the group had decided to meet in his absence. When he returned, two students came to him (separately) to tell him that the group was a disaster the week he was away. He informed both students that whatever had happened was a group issue, and, as they had all agreed, they needed to address group issues during the next meeting. He reminded them to be careful to avoid rumors in the larger school community, and both students assured him that as far as they knew, none of the group members had been discussing "the issue" with others outside of the group.

The following Tuesday when the group was scheduled to meet, Mr. Cordera walked into the classroom where he found four students sitting together near the front of the room, but not engaging with each other. Another three students were slouched in their seats listening to music on headphones. Two students were in the corner completing a math assignment together. This was unusual, as the students were usually sitting together and talkative when he came to the room and they always seemed eager to get started on their group task. The following dialogue unfolded in the group.

"Abie," Mr. Cordera asked, "are you the process observer for the group today?" (closed question)
"Yes," Abie replied.

Mr. Cordera thanked him for taking his turn in this role.

"So, what happened?" (open question) Mr. Cordera asked the group. The question was met with silence. Mr. Cordera waited and there was still no answer. The two students in the back closed their math books and moved to seats closer to the front of the room. That seemed to prompt others to put their headphones away and look up at Mr. Cordera.

"Who can start us off in a conversation about what happened last week when you all met?" (open-ended focused probe) Mr. Cordera asked, quickly adding that he was aware that something had happened, but he had no idea what it was. He waited.

"I guess you could say a fight broke out," Sylvia stated, adding quickly, "well not a physical fight but an argument."

"So, an argument?" (inflection question) Mr. Cordera asked.

"Yes," Crystal added. "It was about the prom queen and king discussion."

"Thanks, Crystal and Sylvia," Mr. Cordera said. "Let me step back for a second and remind the group of something. Remember how we talked about the importance of using conversation to get through hard things?" (closed question). A few students nodded.

"I am going to ask us to dig deep and do that now," Mr. Cordera continued. "But first, I wanted to remind us of the ground rules for communication that we all discussed during our first meeting. Who can help me with this?" (closed question). The students, familiar with the norms they had decided on, slowly called out the rules as Mr. Cordera wrote them on the board. He thanked them.

"Who will start?" (focused probe) Mr. Cordera asked. As the students began to explain the argument about whether prom queens and kings needed to be binary gendered, Mr. Cordera prompted them to speak calmly, address the person they were talking to directly, and use I-statements, as per the discussion rules on the board.

At one point in the conversation, Matt raised his voice and accused Crystal and Tiffany of "being too politically correct."

Crystal shot back, "Shut up."

The group went silent; it seemed that tempers were simmering—almost ready to boil over. Mr. Cordera waited but the group was stalled.

"Abie," Mr. Cordera said, "can you help us here with a process observation? I am asking for a group-level observation, however, not a comment about any specific individual in the group."

"Well," Abie began, "I see that everyone has stopped talking, and it sounds like everyone is pissed off right now."

"Okay. Yes, that helps. Who can comment on how they are feeling right now?" (focused probe/ who question).

"He's right. I am pissed" Tiffany began. "When we're—okay I'll just talk about myself," she added with a slight smile before Mr. Cordera could get the words out to invite her to talk about her own experience and not speak for the group. She continued, "When I am accused of something and when I hear my friend being accused of something in that tone, it makes me want to ... to ... to just say, 'Shut the F up.'"

"Help me understand, Tiffany. I know that you were—and perhaps still are—mad. Can you help us understand what made you angry? What was said? How it was said? Or was it something else that made you angry?" (open-end focused probe/choices) Mr. Cordera asked.

"All of that," she responded and then she elaborated a bit.

"Me too," Crystal jumped in when Tiffany was done. "What she said."

"Which part of what she said was particularly troubling for you, Crystal?" (open-ended focused probe).

As the conversation slowly advanced, Mr. Cordera invited other voices in and continued to set limits when the students were disrespectful. He later gently invited the group to figure out a solution to how they might repair the damage that had happened in the group so that they could get back to the issue at hand.

Redirecting or Shifting the Focus

Group leaders use redirection, or they shift the focus of the group toward or away from a particular issue, topic, or student to keep the group on task and to ensure that all of the members of the group have "airtime" (Gladding, 2003). For example, "Mathais, I think Eric has said that he doesn't want to talk about that right now. Do you mind telling us what *you* were thinking after that last activity?" In another group, the leader commented, "Nahima, we are not going to focus on that today. Can you help us by offering one temper-taming tip that you learned from someone in the group?" In another group, as the leader walked around the room, she redirected students who were off task and talking about a Netflix series by saying, "Can we have everyone's focus on question number three please." In this way, she also used proximity control (discussed in chapter 9) to facilitate on-task behavior.

As with cutting off and blocking, redirecting and shifting the focus are nuanced skills. If, for example, a student in a group feels unheard, or, conversely, if a student is allowed to overshare or is the focus of too much intensity, they may feel vulnerable, angry, or discouraged. These are situations that may call for cutting off or shifting interventions that can help students participate productively and safely in the group. Group leaders must also be mindful of how group members observe redirecting or shifting the focus being used with their peers. If students in a group believe that a peer is being targeted or singled out unfairly by the group leader, for example, because the leader cuts them off or shifts attention away from that student, they may rush to the group member's defense. (This is particularly true if the "attacked" member is one who enjoys much social capital in the group.) So, leaders must be careful to redirect or shift the focus in respectful and not shaming ways and to monitor group member responses after using this intervention.

Reflections and Paraphrases

Reflections and paraphrases are two of the most basic skills used in counseling conversations. We offer our discussion about these skills under one heading as they are often used interchangeably in the counseling skills literature (Geroski, 2019). Having said that, noticing the nuanced difference in these skills will allow group leaders to use them with more intentionality.

Reflections

Reflections involve repeating, almost verbatim, what the student has communicated; they are like a mirror. *Content reflections* illuminate words, phrases, or the gist of what has been said. For example, Henry says, "I have had it up to here," holding his hand to his forehead. Wanting to give emphasis to what Henry has said, the leader says, "You have had it."

A *behavioral reflection* is the mentioning—reflecting—of a behavior that has been communicated in the group. For example, "I noticed your leg tapping," a leader says. The purpose of a behavioral reflection is to call attention to a behavior as a way of opening a conversation in a particular direction. For example, in this comment, the leader might want to address the topic of being nervous or being impatient.

A *feeling reflection* is focused on student affect. It may be a feeling mentioned by the student or one that the counselor believes is implicit. For example, a student says, "I am really sad." The leader may respond, "You feel sad." Or the leader can simply echo the student's word, "sad," to focus on this feeling. Feeling reflections can also be used as a group-level intervention to focus in on a tone or sentiment among the members. For example, noticing that many students in the room appear angry or agitated, a counselor might say, "It seems like there is a lot of anger—or maybe frustration—in the room today." Offering feeling reflections with tentativeness or curiosity helps avoid defensiveness and invites students to amend the reflection in a way that is more accurate.

In general, and when used with intention, reflections provide focus and can deepen thinking processes and engage students in meaningful conversations. At a more basic level, all of these reflection types communicate to the group member(s) that they have been heard.

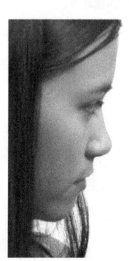

image 7.6

Before we move on, we want to offer a few words of caution about the use of feeling reflections. First, we can never know how others feel. So when reflecting a feeling, we must also recognize that we might be incorrect. Given the power differential between adults and youth, this caution is particularly important, as our influence may cause students to believe something that is not accurate or true for them. Second, it is helpful to remember—and to remind students—that most people typically experience multiple feelings simultaneously. So in selecting one feeling to focus on, we may inadvertently be oversimplifying a student's complex and nuanced affective state. For this reason, we invite group leaders to use the language of "*one* feeling I hear you sharing is ..." or "*one* feeling I observe you expressing is ... although there probably is more going on here" to imply that there are likely multiple feelings. Also, it can be helpful for the group leader to talk about the complexity of feelings and the concept of primary and secondary feelings (where the primary feeling, for example, of hurt, is sometimes more visibly expressed as anger). This kind of psychoeducation can help students begin to think about and make sense of their complex feelings in different situations.

Finally, we want to point out that many children do not have a well-developed feeling vocabulary. So asking them how they feel or reflecting a feeling may have little effect or significance to them. Many school counselors working with youth, and especially younger students, offer "evidence," choice, and psychoeducation when they invite students to focus on their feelings. In terms of choice, a counselor might say, "I wonder if its worries, being scared, or maybe just a little bit of confusion? Or maybe a little of all of these?" This offering of choice also shifts the conversation from a singular dimension of feeling to a nuanced collection of feelings that might be present. It also helps students use names for feelings that they may not be able to come up with themselves. In terms of evidence, prior to starting a psychoeducational classroom group with Jason, the counselor commented, "I saw you slam your book down earlier, and now there is silence. I might be wrong, but it seems like there might be a little frustration here?" Notice, too, that this articulation *externalizes* the hypothesized emotion, locating it in the room rather than in Jason and providing a little distance between the student and the feeling. Externalizing a feeling invites a student to examine an emotion more objectively as something that is in the room with us all. Lowering the intensity around emotion is sometimes needed to calm reactivity and for engagement in thoughtful conversations around emotions.

Paraphrases

Paraphrases are an articulation or summary of something that a group member has communicated. As such, paraphrases are not verbatim reflections; instead, they are an articulation of the *group leader's understanding* of a particular message. This is an important point, as what is included in and what is left out of a paraphrase is shaped by its speaker. For example, a group leader summarized the input of three students in a paraphrase aimed at directing further conversation on a particular topic. However, the paraphrase left out the contribution of a fourth student—a contribution that was different than what the others had said. This prompted that fourth student to feel unheard and become less participatory in the ensuing conversation. Our point is that paraphrases are a form of interpretation; they are shaped by the ears and lens of the speaker. So group leaders must listen for multiple messages and ensure that their paraphrases sufficiently capture what needs attention in the group.

Paraphrases are used to clarify, summarize, slow down, and focus a discussion on an idea or in a particular direction. This is important as sometimes students think out loud as they speak without fully hearing what they are saying; a paraphrase can help them hear themselves. Group leaders should remember that emotional messages are typically a part of communication between people, and these are sometimes communicated nonverbally or in other subtle ways. So, when appropriate, leaders should be sure to include these emotional communications in their paraphrases as well. This will help bring these sometimes subtle but nonetheless important aspects of a message to the forefront, and it also communicates to students that their complete message has been heard. For example, a counselor was working with a group of students who were processing an incident that had happened in their school. Her paraphrase of the conversation was, "So I hear that some of us are feeling 'talked out' about this while others are feeling that they still have questions and comments. For most of us, too, there is a lingering uncertainty and perhaps fear about whether this kind of thing will happen again. Does this capture what we've been talking about and feeling in here today?" Paraphrases can hold the gist of what is happening in a discussion in a way that everyone can hear it, and they also communicate that a student—or a number of students—have been heard.

Because paraphrases are sifted through the lens of the speaker, and thus, they include an element of interpretation, they may easily be inaccurate or capture only part of a message. We recommend, then, that paraphrases be stated with an appropriate level of *tentativeness*. For example, introducing a paraphrase with "I may have missed something, but what I am hearing is ..." invites group members to amend the paraphrase to include missing information or to reword it from another perspective. Following a paraphrase with a *check-in*—an invitation to correct what has been said—also invites input from group members. For example, a group leader can ask, "Is that correct?" It also may be helpful to offer *evidence*, such as key words or phrases used by the student, as this may clarify the paraphrase. For example, a task group leader offered the following paraphrase in an attempt to summarize what some of the group members had said about their work in the group: "We have been talking about how this schedule is not working for some of you. Some of you used the word 'exhausted' and others said 'spent.' I also want to acknowledge that some of you have not said these things. I am not sure if that means agreement or not? Am I picking up on what people are saying? Is there more?" As a rule of thumb, the more interpretative a paraphrase becomes and the more personally invested or biased a group leader is on a particular topic, the more important it is to use tentativeness, to offer evidence, and to check out understandings.

Reframing

Reframing is offering an "alternative lens" or explanation about something that has happened in the group or the topic under discussion (Toseland & Rivas, 2005). Reframing is used to prompt thought, stimulate conversation, and facilitate meaning making—to invite other possibilities or understandings.

Reframing may be used to move a group through complex dynamics when members seem to be misunderstanding each other, for example, or in response to aggressive or potentially aggressive statements made in the group. Reframing can also be used to prompt more expansive thinking about a particular topic. For example, in a sixth-grade classroom psychoeducational group focused on communication skills, Rosa commented, "People are rude because they are uneducated." The group leader reframed this by saying, "Sometimes we make assumptions about others who behave in ways we don't agree with. Here I think that rude behavior happens for lots of reasons: people are tired, angry, they speak before they think. ... How about we take a minute to think about a time when we were rude to someone. I know that we have all said things that we later realize were rude, and I am guessing that for many of us, our rudeness was probably unintentional. Take a minute to recreate that scene for yourself and think about what prompted that rudeness. What was happening for you that prompted a rude response?"

Restatement

A restatement is a paraphrase or substitute language that ensures that what has been said is what was heard or understood. For example, the principal announces something on the school intercom, and the students all groan. The teacher, realizing that the principal's message was misunderstood, restates what was said in another way.

Self-Disclosure

Self-disclosure is when the group leader shares their own experience (when doing so is relevant) of what is currently transpiring within the group. For example, when working with a group of high school students on job-seeking skills, a group leader revealed that he had "blown" a job interview one time because he did not come adequately prepared with information and knowledge about the job he was applying for.

In this example, the purpose of the self-disclosure was to communicate a critical point about job interviewing. If the leader had left the self-disclosure with only the mention of his failure (without explaining what he had neglected to do) or if he had talked in more detail, on and on, about his blown job interview, it likely could have derailed the focus of the group. This latter situation could have morphed into a conversation about the leader and shifted the focus from the task at hand. Also, this is a risky self-disclosure, as a professed failure on the part of the group leader may potentially alter the students' perceptions of him. Of course, on one hand, it might make him seem more human or real, but it also may cause students to think less about his skills and abilities as a leader. If the group leader had revealed repeated job-seeking failures and ultimately having to use connections to secure his current job, this, obviously, would have been inappropriate and quite damaging to his credibility. This discussion, then, reminds us that caution is advised when using self-disclosure in the group.

Sometimes group leaders encourage self-disclosure among group members. That is, they may invite members to share something about themselves that is personal but relevant to the group. In a captain's leadership training group, for example, the group leader asked a student that she knew fairly well if the student would be willing to share one of the struggles she had experienced the previous year as a team captain. In this example, the group leader had asked the student in advance if she would talk about the struggle in the group, and the leader monitored the student's brief personal self-disclosure so that it was focused on her own experience and did not mention others who were not in the group. In this particular group, the self-disclosure, as intended, led to a valuable discussion about the extent to which team captains might be involved in other students' conflicts with their coaches. As a result, group members talked about how they could be both supportive and serve as advocates to their peers, as well as maintain healthy boundaries. The extent to which the group leader structured the self-disclosure in this group underscores our point that while encouraging student self-disclosure can be beneficial in groups, leaders must be thoughtful when inviting a group member to be vulnerable in front of peers.

The notion of inviting students to be vulnerable among their peers is part of a larger nuanced discussion. It touches on important philosophical positions regarding the nature of learning: How much personal investment in a topic is needed for students to learn, change, or grow? It also invites us to reflect on power differentials inherent in the roles of teacher/school counselor/group leader and students, which, of course, are situated in larger contexts of adult-child and related power dynamics. When we ask youth to offer something personal of themselves in the group, do they have (or do they realize that they have) agency or power to decline? Do they have the personal self-regulation abilities to monitor themselves and know when to stop their own sharing so as to not become inappropriately vulnerable in the group? Take, for example, a young child who reveals his parent's alcoholism or abusive behavior by sharing—even unprompted sharing—in a classroom group studying the topic of substance use. Our point is that it is always the responsibility of group leaders to monitor student self-disclosure so that it is appropriate to the type and the topic of the group, and it does not leave children vulnerable or unsafe.

Summarizing

A summary is a form of paraphrase. It can also be thought of as a repackaging of something that was said or that happened in the group. Sentence stems that signal summary may include the following: "What I am hearing is ..." "Here's what I think you're offering us ..."

Alternatively, group leaders can ask members to summarize what they have seen or heard in a group. Using a closing round—asking each person to offer a "takeaway" or to share what they have learned in the group—is an alternative way to summarize learning in a group. In rounds, a group leader may also add something that was not mentioned by one of the students or may emphasize something that they think is of particular importance. Summarizing learning that has happened in a group is a good way to end a session, as it promotes the transfer of learning.

Reflection Questions

1. The authors mentioned that it can sometimes be important to include an emotional communication in a paraphrase. What circumstances might make it particularly important to do this?
2. If a reflection is merely a restatement of what a student has said, why is it helpful in a group?
3. How does a group leader know when to use leveling, cutting off, and shifting the focus, especially if these skills can potentially change the direction of the group and may inadvertently offend a student group member?

CHAPTER EIGHT

Group Leadership Skills and Practices

Introduction

Learning and personal growth do not just happen in groups because students are together in a room engaged in an activity or working toward a common goal; learning happens in groups as a result of intentional planning and facilitation. We also know that groups do not always go as well as hoped, even when careful planning has been put in place.

In this chapter, we invite group leaders to consider a variety of structures and strategies for responding early to problems before they build. All of these require group leaders to step into their executive function role to create a safe and productive group climate for learning. We begin with a discussion about group norming and rule-setting processes. These elements form an important foundation for creating and reinforcing the group climate. We also highlight strategies for starting groups, and we finish with a model for conceptualizing leader interventions that focus on both group process dynamics and content goals. All of the discussions in this chapter build on the philosophical foundations outlined in the early chapters of this book and make use of the important group leader skills identified in Chapter 7. In the next chapter, Chapter 9, we will focus on specific interventions that can be used in a group to address stubborn challenges or problematic behaviors.

Definitions

Group *norms* refer to the informal rules and unwritten code of behavioral expectations that set a tone for member interactions and task completion within groups. They are not typically discussed or negotiated directly among group members and often develop out of the awareness or purposefulness of the group leader (Kline, 2003). Group *rules*, on the other hand, are the explicit or articulated expectations of group engagement. Gladding (2008) refers to these as the "guidelines by which groups are run" (p. 117). Rules establish the boundaries within which the group will function. In effect, rules make group norms explicit.

Group Norms

Feldman (1984) defined group norms as "informal rules that groups adopt to regulate and regularize group members' behavior" (p. 47). Although group norms can sometimes be a bit opaque, he and other group workers remind us that group norms do have a powerful and often consistent effect on group functioning. Group norms that are particularly relevant to work with youth in school contexts include norms regarding safety, challenge, caring, and cohesion to support the development

Image 8.1

of student competencies. Here we discuss why these norms are important and how group leaders can work to establish these appropriate norms in their groups. In the next section, we will move into a discussion about how rule-setting processes and enforcement shape and support appropriate group norms.

Safety and Challenge Norms

Group climate refers to the group conditions that are facilitative (or not) of growth, learning, and change. The importance of creating a group climate characterized by trust, support, and safety is underscored in the group work and teacher education literature (see Corey & Corey, 2006; Kline, 2003; Larrivee, 2005; Luckner & Nadler, 1997). The broad consensus across these fields is that the group leaders, whether they are teachers or counselors, are responsible for establishing the tone of safety in the group.

We want to emphasize, however, that safety *alone* is not a sufficient condition for learning. We also know that learning happens in a safe environment that also *challenges* individuals to grapple with new material and ideas that are just beyond their current level of understanding (Bateson, 1994; Douthit, 2008; Vygotsky, 1978). As you will recall from Chapter 2, this is what Vygotsky referred to as the *zone of proximal development* (ZPD). So, partnered with the concept of safety is also the notion of challenge. Students must feel safe in a group so that they can thrive within the challenge of learning something new.

While Vygotsky's concept of the ZPD reminds us of the importance of introducing students to new material and challenging them to extend toward new growth and learning, it is also true that doing so tends to create a sense of disequilibrium and anxiety (Kline, 2003). This is particularly evident in groups where the gaze of others is apparent and influential—something we especially see when working with youth. Gladding (2003) pointed out that "too much or too little anxiety inhibits the performance of the group and its members" (p. 116). Gladding's point is important, as it highlights both the importance of or need for and also the potentially inhibiting effect of anxiety, discomfort, or challenge in the learning process.

Circling back to the idea of safety, the task of the group leader, then, is to encourage members to take appropriate risks in a way that is safe for them, despite their feeling anxious. It is a process of push and hold by working in what Gerstein calls the *growth zone* (as cited in Luckner & Nadler, 1997, p. 20). Working in the growth zone happens when group norms encourage and support appropriate interaction and risk taking and when these norms are fortified by clearly articulated and enforced rules. This pushing and holding process must be established and maintained by the group leader.

Even with norms and rules around risk in place, some group members may be—and in some cases should be—reluctant to take risks in the group. For example, as discussed in Chapter 1, students who identify in marginalized social locations may be reluctant to share experiences that they believe will isolate them or bring scorn from peers. Students who have difficulties with self-regulation, on the other hand, may share too much information that then leaves them potentially vulnerable among their peers. For example, the potential effect of one child's classroom group disclosure that he has witnessed domestic violence at home may be that peers are reluctant to socialize with the child (given the stigma of domestic violence) or are not permitted to go to that student's home. We can see how discourses and stigma about domestic violence, as well as other topics, such as poverty, religion, sexual orientation, and gender identity, can easily slip into outside-group social interactions. So, norms about sharing must always be structured around choice and monitored by the group leader to assure appropriate safety for group members.

Basic group leadership skills, such as reflection, paraphrasing, immediacy, shifting the focus, cutting off, and confrontation, can be used by the group leader to manage members' anxiety and also to facilitate healthy risk taking in the group. We reiterate that it is the group leader's responsibility to facilitate the group so that all students are engaged and taking appropriate learning risks, and it is also the leader's responsibility to monitor group member safety.

Caring Norms

There are many reasons for creating caring norms in schools. Noddings (1992), for example, pointed out that "perhaps the most important thing children can learn from us [educators] is how to interact with people and other living things" (p. 163). That is, caring experienced translates into caring demonstrated; children learn to care for others when they themselves are cared for. Caring is communicated when children *extend toward others*, when they *engage in the lives of others* (by noticing, asking, being with), and when they *respond to or acknowledge the caring efforts of others* (Noddings, 1992, 1996). Noddings (1992, 1996) reminded us that getting along with others and engaging in caring connections are at the core of what it means to foster caring in schools; these are some of the most basic characteristics of healthy interpersonal relationships and fundamental to healthy school and group climates.

This idea of caring goes beyond what happens in the social-emotional curriculum in schools; it also includes the everyday encounters between children and adults in schools. Palmer (2003) suggested that the very essence of the student-teacher relationship must "be deeply human for real learning to occur" (Palmer, 2003, p. 380). For him, the classroom is a place where teachers safeguard "a space where the soul feels welcome to show up" (Palmer, 2003, p. 384). It is, perhaps, part of a moral obligation that teachers have toward their students (Velasquez et al., 2013). Indeed, research seems to suggest that teacher caring (as perceived by students) may be an important part of school effectiveness, impacting student evaluations, retention, self-efficacy, motivation, social and moral development, and general learning outcomes (Ramberg et al., 2019; Velasquez et al., 2013).

While on this topic, we want to briefly reference a related concept of *hospitality* in education. This notion emerges in the work of educational scholars who were influenced by early Christian interpretations of hospitality as a "mandate to welcome the stranger" (Burwell & Huyser, 2013). Using the metaphor of teacher as a host to children in a classroom, Marmon (2008) pointed out that good hosts believe "their guests have value, good hosts listen. They are eager to hear other people's stories, look at pictures, and ask questions that call for thoughtful reflection" (p. 35). In this way of reaching out and providing good hospitality, teachers encourage learning. Palmer (1993), characterized educational hospitality as providing a place where students and teachers are "receiving each other, our struggles, our newborn ideas, with openness and care" (p. 73–74). "Hospitality is not only an ethical virtue," he adds, "but an epistemological one as well" (Palmer, 1993, p. 74).

Image 8.2

A second reason for caring norms comes from the work of Bear (2005), who emphasized the important role that a positive and caring environment has on the correction and remediation of behavior problems. Here Bear cites evidence indicating that when students perceive that a teacher, group, or classroom is fair (as a marker of caring), they are less likely to engage in resistant, argumentative, or aggressive behaviors. According to Bear (2005), *empathy* is one component of being interpersonally responsible to others. *Guilt*, he proposed, is another. Bear suggested that guilt or the anticipation of guilt reminds children to be respectful of each other and compels them to engage in relational repair if they have demonstrated hurtful behavior. Caring environments where students feel connected to others foster this combination of empathy and restrictive guilt that help children behave responsibly toward one another.

Caring brings a sense of belonging in groups and in school communities (Lindwall & Coleman, 2008). When students feel that they belong in a group, intermember cohesion and a sense of universality can flourish. Grounded in the research of Lieberman et al. (1973), Hulse-Killacky et al. (2001) pointed out that caring is one of the critical leadership characteristics associated with group success (in all group types). They point out that caring is communicated through leader *authenticity*, *approachability*, and *accessibility*. Group members feel cared for when leaders *recognize and acknowledge group member needs* and when they *provide structures that move the group* toward its intended goals. This latter point is also emphasized in the work of Hulse-Killacky et al. (2001), who reminded us that caring is also represented in actions that enable the group to be focused on student learning. Table 8.1 includes suggestions of what group leaders can do to promote caring norms in their school groups.

TABLE 8.1 Caring Norms

- Be explicit about the importance of embracing a caring norm in the group.
- Scaffold and structure student engagement so that it is communicated from a base of empathy and caring. This means that you may need to actively intervene in some discussions to ask students to talk to one another and to respond to each other with empathy and respect.
- Plan your groups around topics that are engaging and relevant to the lives of the students. This will stimulate meaningful thought and conversation, and it communicates interest in the lives of the group members. As students come to know more about the real lives of their peers, they form a foundation that will develop into meaningful relationships.
- Help group members become self-reflective about their own efforts and experiences of caring.
- Be committed to expressing care to students in the group and be mindful of the ways in which you demonstrate this care. Attend to the language and tone you use when communicating with students. Remember that the tone that is set by the group leader will become a norm in the group.
- A caring community has no tolerance for hurtful or disrespectful behavior. It is the group leader's responsibility to monitor the group, and the leader should always intervene against potentially hurtful or disrespectful interactions in the group.

Cohesion

Cohesion refers to the establishment of a place of belonging for all members of the group (Corey & Corey, 2006; Gladding, 2008; Kline, 2003). It is one of Yalom's therapeutic factors (Yalom, 1995, 2005; Yalom & Leszcz, 2005) of group work—one of the conditions that make groups productive. Group cohesion enables students to be accepting of one another, to be open to risk taking, and to engage in some degree of self-disclosure (Corey & Corey, 2006; Gladding, 2008; Kline, 2003). It develops from having a sense that a group is relevant or purposeful and from healthy interpersonal relationships among group members. That is, feeling understood and respected by others in the group and feeling purposefully connected to the content of the group (i.e., when students are clear about why they are in a particular group) promotes a sense of belonging. This sense of belonging breeds investment in one's own learning and in the well-being of others in the group.

Group leaders can facilitate group cohesion by using the basic counseling skills outlined in Chapter 7. For example, paraphrasing, reflecting, and probing questions can be used to help students identify feelings, express empathy, and share their own experiences in the group. Linking, focusing, shifting the focus, and cutting off can be used to help group members listen and respond to each other respectfully, as well as to shape member contributions so they are purposeful. Immediacy can be used to shift conversations to what is happening in the group, which will increase interpersonal authenticity and bonding among group members. Immediacy can also be used to shape conceptual conversations into personally relevant real-life discussions. Case Study 8.1 demonstrates how group cohesion can be fostered to engage group members in powerful and meaningful discussions that foster group authenticity and trust.

CASE STUDY 8.1 Cohesion

Ms. Martinez was working with a high school classroom advisory group that was interested in forming a school-wide Gay-Straight Alliance. This topic was put on the agenda by the advisory group members (all of the students in the group expressed interest in discussing the topic) to be discussed in the group after a recent LGBT-related bullying incident at the school.

As the students began to discuss their perspectives on the need for the Gay-Straight Alliance, Ms. Martinez noticed that a small group of students was involved in a separate discussion in the back of the room. Apparently, this was also noticed by Juan, who was actively involved in the Gay-Straight Alliance discussion. Before Ms. Martinez could intervene to redirect the students, Juan commented loudly, "I guess this is a topic that people who aren't affected by it don't care about. Reminds me of our 'privilege' discussion" he said, referring to the topic of discussion in the group over the past few meetings.

Carmen jumped in saying, "Sounds like some people are trying to closet our Gay-Straight Alliance."

Seeing that the off-task group of students had caused others who were more involved in the Gay-Straight Alliance discussion to feel defensive and, perhaps, even insulted, Ms. Martinez decided that she needed to have the group address this dynamic to regain a sense of cohesion among the members and to help the group be productive. Using immediacy, Ms. Martinez said, "Let's just stop here for a minute and look at how we're doing as a group. I notice that there is a large group of students who are involved in the Gay-Straight Alliance discussion—bringing up pros and cons and trying to figure out what to do in response to the incident that happened last week on campus. I also notice that there is another group of students who seem to be involved in a separate discussion in the back of the room. I'm not sure why there are two discussions in here, but it worries me that this is causing students to feel unsafe."

"You got that right," Emma called out.

"We're not talking about you," Felicia responded from the back of the room. "As a matter of fact, we're trying to help Marc get his homework done."

"Thanks, Emma and Carmen and Juan for letting us know how you feel, and to you, Felicia, for letting us know what's going on back there. That helps avoid misunderstandings. I'd like for all of you in the back to stop what you're doing and listen to what I'm about to say [she stops and waits until all eyes are on her]. It can feel really unsafe in the group when students form their own smaller group and talk about something else, especially when the larger group topic is something as sensitive as LGBT issues. Whether you intend to or not, it gives the message of disinterest and disrespect. Do you see that?"

"We weren't trying to dis anyone" protested Marc, "they're just helping me with my homework."

"I hear what you're saying about not trying to make people feel bad, Marc, and I appreciate you saying that. But, as you know—as we talked about last week—hurt happens, even when intentions are good. I just want everyone to think about the topic we're discussing and how easily mispercep-tions can develop. Do you see what I'm saying?"

"Yeah," conceded Marc.

"Can anyone offer a solution for how to get us to a better place?" Ms. Martinez asked.

"No. But I didn't mean to dis you, Emma and Juan and Carmen," Claudia offered from the back.

"Yeah, man. Let's move on," Juan said.

"No, I'm pissed off," said Carmen. "This is the kind of silencing that happens to LGBT people all the time."

"Anger is going to be a pretty present feeling when we start talking out loud about forming a Gay-Straight Alliance," Ms. Martinez offered. "What do we want to do with it when we see it in here ... and how should we deal with it if we form an alliance? These are important questions."

"Well," said Claudia, "we got to make sure that we don't hurt people when we get mad. I mean. Okay, anger ... yeah, we all get that ... but that stuff that happened last week in school—I mean, peo-ple—I think probably even Juan and Carmen—really got hurt because they were friends with, you know, TJ, who got beat up. That's where it's bad."

"So, you're thinking that it's okay to be angry but not to hurt people," Ms. Martinez paraphrased. "Others?" she asked, inviting perspectives from other members in the group.

By focusing on the incident that arose in the group and using the basic counseling skills of imme-diacy, paraphrasing, drawing out, and inviting students into dialogue, Ms. Martinez was able to redi-rect some of the students who were not engaged in discussion with those who were offended. Part of her success lay in her ability to make parallels between the incident that happened in the group and the larger topic of LGBT issues happening in their school community, which the whole group had earlier agreed was important. This intervention focused on helping the group to be cohesive while engaged in difficult conversations, and it provided a structure for navigating them.

We close with the reminder that in all groups, regardless of group type, students are always seeking connection—how to be together—and their ability to do so constructively will dictate the success of their groups. Early on, group leaders will want to work toward establishing a sense of cohesiveness in their groups and monitor it throughout the life of the group. This is particularly important during and after critical incidents and difficult conversations that emerge in the group.

Learning, Development, and Competency Norms

School counselors conduct groups as part of their role in promoting the academic, career, social, and emotional development of students and to carry out their efforts in being responsive to the immediate needs and concerns of students, especially those needs that impede academic success (ASCA, 2014, 2019). In short, groups conducted by school counselors are intended to promote stu-dent development and/or learning in some way.

Providing instructional content to students via the format of groups is one important way in which group leaders promote competency. This, we would say, is the "teaching" mission of school group work. The important discussions about identifying appropriate group goals in Chapter 4, planning appropriate strategies for achieving those goals in Chapter 6, and assessing whether those instructional goals have been met at the end of instruction in Chapter 5 identify practices that group leaders use in planning groups to address learning goals. Beyond this, learning unfolds when students are actually engaged in the important work of the group, which is predicated, largely, on what group leaders do. This reminds us that group leaders should never lose sight of the learning objectives for each group session. We argue that group norms that support the expectation that students will learn something in the group help group members and leaders stay focused on the learning goals and objectives of the group.

We also want to emphasize the role of competency beliefs and engagement in learning processes. While students can gain content knowledge through group instruction, the experience of being successful is also critically important in enabling students to develop beliefs about their own abilities and successes in the future. For example, domain-specific, self-efficacy beliefs—students' ideas about their ability to carry out particular actions toward success—are also linked to domain-specific areas of academic achievement (for more on domain-specific self-efficacy, see Bandura, 1977; Bandura, 1986; Lane et al., 2004; Multon et al., 1991; Parker et al., 2014). This link between self-efficacy and achievement may be because students with higher levels of academic self-efficacy tend to persist longer when faced with task challenges, and they apply more sustained effort toward tasks (Parker et al., 2014). Similarly, educational research suggests a positive association between domain-specific self-esteem (i.e., the belief in one's value or ability) and student motivation, learning, and achievement (Bong & Skaalvik, 2003). Student engagement is also associated positively with academic achievement, prosocial, and pro-academic behaviors and may ameliorate student boredom and disaffection (Fredricks et al., 2004).

Educational research in the areas mentioned earlier reminds us of the important ways in which learning is linked to social experiences and self-perceptions—all of which can be enhanced through the group experience. We know that self-efficacy beliefs, for example, are constructed from performance accomplishments or direct mastery experiences, vicarious or observational experiences, verbal or social persuasion, and physiological or bodily and somatic states (Bandura, 1977, 1989). Group experiences and group norms that allow students to perform and succeed, then, and norms and experiences that allow students to witness the success of their peers, and norms that invite encouragement and praise can foster self-efficacy beliefs. Anything-goes (but-nothing-really-happens) group norms, on the other hand, are more likely to leave learning up to chance. In the words of Bear (2005),

> Unfortunately, many educators purchase a wealth of materials that espouse the popular and misleading belief that simply telling kids that they are wonderful, terrific, nice, and so on builds self-esteem. Seldom do any of these materials work (Bear, Minke, Griffin, & Deemer, 1997). Recent theory and research show that self-esteem is much more complex. (p. 180)

This discussion brings us back to intentionality. Norms that create and maintain group leader support for students, that facilitate cohesion and respectful relationships among group members, and norms that promote task-clarity and work orientation, promote student competency, engagement, and goal achievement.

Establishing Culturally Appropriate and Culturally Responsive Norms

A major difference in approaching diversity issues in schools from a culturally responsive rather than a tourist curriculum (i.e., just noticing the customs and celebrations of a particular culture; Derman-Sparks, 1993) or a tolerance perspective, centers on valuing difference, understanding social context, and taking up the need for action, when appropriate. This is work that happens in school classrooms, hallways, meeting rooms, and in all of the different types of groups conducted by school counselors.

In enacting their executive function role of ensuring that groups are spaces where students have the opportunity to learn in the context of safety, caring, challenge, and focus, it is up to the group leader to establish and monitor group norms that are both culturally appropriate and responsive. This is because we know that students from diverse backgrounds come to school with various perspectives and experiences that affect their learning. For example, students are exposed to a variety of perspectives and expectations in regard to academic achievement, personal and social behavior, and even in regard to permission about what can and cannot be discussed in public (including in school and in school groups). Youth are also shaped by social discourses and normative practices that regulate their social and academic success perceptions and experiences; these are discourses that closely align with social location categories. The social ordering that is the undercurrent in school communities in regard to social identities is organized according to unspoken rules with powerful implications. It influences how students are perceived and treated by peers and teachers, academic opportunities and outcomes, development of self-competency and self-efficacy beliefs, and future aspirations. For youth who identify in nondominant and/or marginalized social locations, the challenges are immense.

In groups, youth with less social capital may feel silenced by their peers, or they may silence themselves to stay safe. Those with nondominant cultural identities may feel conflicting loyalties—whether to honor home versus school norms and expectations—they may lack the engagement skills and strategies that are used by their peers in the group, and the group activities and larger learning goals may seem irrelevant to their experiences, hopes, and values. All of this underscores the need for counselors to be familiar with the subgroups in the school community, to embrace multiple perspectives and have connections across the diverse communities represented in the school, and to have the skills needed for guiding sensitive conversations and advocating for appropriate diverse educational and counseling practices.

Classroom and counseling groups offer an opportunity for students to acquire a window into the lives of others and, importantly, also for attacking social status norms and perceptions. Importantly, however, this should <u>never</u> happen at the expense of those who are already located in marginalized or nondominant locations. This important windowing and deconstruction work can happen in groups when the group norms ensure that every student in the group has access to learning goals and objects; when all students perceive that their perceptions, experiences, and contributions are valued within the group; and when the group is engaging, interesting, and organized in ways that are responsive to a variety of student interests, experiences, and learning styles. It can only happen in groups that have no tolerance for hurt and hate. No tolerance for hurt norms must be firmly in place in each and every group, and they must be supported by rules that are enforced by the group leader. Finally, windowing discussions must be facilitated carefully by culturally competent group leaders so as to avoid unintentional harm caused by a lack of competence.

Image 8.3

An important first step in making a group relevant and engaging for all is to get to know the students early on. Spending time in classrooms in advance of group planning offers a view into existing group dynamics and can inform ideas about what works best for which students. We realize that visiting the regular classroom for an observation is not a regular practice of most school counselors, but we still hold firm that it can be extremely helpful, especially for planning classroom groups. Group leaders can also ask teachers to share their knowledge about particular group dynamics, trouble spots, and strategies for managing difficult behaviors. Finally, group leaders can be prepared to use tools, such as name tags, icebreakers, and other getting-to-know-you activities in some of the early larger group sessions. It is appropriate to let students know that it will take a little time to get to know everyone.

Rules

Rules provide a structure for maintaining group norms; they offer clarity around the parameters for student participation and behavior in a group. Group leaders have an important (although often unnoticed or underused) role in making group norms explicit through rule-setting processes. Here we will talk very generally about the types of rules that are relevant to group work in schools and identify helpful processes for establishing and enforcing rules. This discussion leads into Chapter 9, where the focus is more specifically on responding to challenging student behaviors.

Establishing Rules

Educational research indicates that having well-articulated rules and procedures in classrooms increases student behavior, motivation, and academic achievement (Bear, 2005; Marzano, 2003). Bear (2005) pointed to research indicating that a salient marker of effective teaching is the ability of teachers to use antecedent-focused interventions—that is, to establish and enforce appropriate classroom rules. Here we are talking mostly about *general rules*—rules that identify broad guidelines and expectations for group participation. Typically, a classroom or group would have only a small number of these types of rules (Charles, 2011; Marzano, 2003). *Specific rules* relate to procedures, routines, or particular activity requirements and are often taught and practiced within a group as needed per a particular activity or circumstance (Charles, 2011). Marzano (2003) referred to this latter group of specific rules as *procedures*.

Group norms and the rules that structure these norms will vary considerably across group types, learning objectives, activities, and group member and leader compositions (Marzano, 2003). They need to be tailored to the needs of the group. Thus the rules that are selected as relevant for a particular group will vary according to the age and developmental, communication, and social abilities of the students in the group and according to group size or type. For example, younger children typically benefit from explicit rules on interpersonal behavioral expectations and for managing transitions (Bear, 2005; Marzano, 2003); teachers tend to spend a great deal of time explaining expectations and rules to students in younger grades (Brophy, 1999). Older students, on the other hand, sometimes feel disrespected if too much attention is given to rules and consequences and if the rules are imposed on the group rather than generated from student input. These older students, however, may need frequent reminders about rules related to task attention and completion (Bear, 2005; Marzano, 2003).

Must-Include Rules

Bear (2005) suggested limiting the number of general classroom rules to five or six. This is because offering students a long list of what can and cannot be done can set a harsh tone in a group, and it is impossible to anticipate all of the potential eventualities that may unfold throughout the course of a group. It is usually a good idea to provide students with some key general rules and then add other rules if and when necessary. As a bottom line for all groups, we recommend establishing rules around safety, no tolerance for hurt and hate, confidentiality, and task orientation.

First, as mentioned, group leaders should always be prepared to introduce *rules related to member safety*—typically articulated as respect for others and for property. Safety rules are never negotiable by group members, and they should always be strictly enforced by the group leader, regardless of group type or the age of the group members. Keep in mind that safety is not limited to physical safety; group members must also be assured that they will be tended to in spaces were their emotional or psychological safety is also respected and monitored by the leader. When students are pushed to take risks that are too far beyond their growth zones, learning is compromised and the leader's ethical responsibility for group safety may be breached. Group leaders must take their cues regarding risk and safety from each individual in the group, as well as from their own knowledge and experience.

Related to group member safety, we want to call specific attention to the need to set and enforce rules that firmly establish a stand against hurt and hate; this is something that should happen in all groups conducted in schools. These *no tolerance for hurt and hate* rules are important because, as mentioned in Chapter 1, schools are replete with subtle and overt messages about marginalization, and the biases and hurtful actions related to social group status are often reenacted in school groups. To address this problem of bias and marginalization, group leaders must explicitly establish no-tolerance norms, and they must reinforce these norms by developing concrete rules that they will then enforce. This also requires leaders to have discussions in their groups about inclusion and exclusion and how it exists in many overt and subtle forms.

School personnel, unfortunately, are not immune to the far-reaching effects of larger social discourses. In schools, bias takes on many overt and nuanced forms. For example, bias looks like regular enactments of microaggressions that go unaddressed (these are sometimes also committed by school personnel), parallel standards set for parallel sets of students, a curriculum that lacks multicultural perspectives and/or is foreign to the lived experiences of some of the students in the room, and a lack of role modeling (mirrors) for students of color and those who locate in nondominant social locations. School counselors are well positioned to address the needs of students who locate in historically marginalized and/or nondominant social group locations. To this end, the profession is calling on us to act as leaders and advocates in our schools (ASCA, 2019). This work includes what school counselors do in their own group work practices.

The actions of group leaders are a model for the students in their groups. This means that they must be sure that they are engaging appropriately and fairly with all of the students in their groups. Group leaders will have to check their own implicit biases and ensure that these biases are not causing them to act in unfair or hurtful ways. This includes ensuring that they are offering support and challenge to *all* of the students in the group fairly, that they use activities and encourage discussions that are relevant to *all* of the students in the group, and in situations where behavior challenges surface, they must be vigilant about enacting punishments and rewards fairly.

A third issue that should be broached by leaders in most groups, even if it is not raised by students in the rule-generating discussion, is that of *confidentiality* (see Chapter 1 for a more detailed discussion about confidentiality). Confidentiality is related to group member safety. In group work, however, confidentiality is quite complicated. While we would expect that what students say in a group is held confidentially by their peers (as well as the group leader), we can never completely ensure that this will happen. The truth is that rules around confidentiality are more easily stated than upheld.

Students should know that group leaders must break confidentiality in situations related to harm (this includes suspicions of abuse or neglect). This caveat should be explained in advance, especially in small counseling group situations, and in language that is understandable and at an appropriate developmental level. Also important is the point that group leaders are not able to control what students say and do in and outside of the group; they do not have the power to completely ensure that confidentiality will be maintained in a group. This means that no student should be promised that what they share in the group will stay in the group—despite our very best intentions. This issue of confidentiality in groups with youth is particularly problematic because some students may not have adequate self-censoring capabilities to limit what they say. Inappropriate self-disclosure may leave some students vulnerable and may unknowingly spawn subsequent breaches in confidentiality (i.e., students in the group tell others what was said). For example, a classroom psychoeducational group discussion on substance use may not be the most appropriate setting for an individual student to disclose details of substance misuse in their home. So, leaders are reminded of their responsibility to oversee the ways in which students are invited to participate in classroom and counseling groups. The executive function of the group leader includes assuring that the content and the level of personal sharing in the group is appropriate.

We recommend that the topic of confidentiality be broached during initial rule-setting conversations in groups. At this time, leaders can engage students in a discussion about what confidentiality means. In our experience, students—even the very youngest of group members in classroom and counseling groups—comprehend the limitations of confidentiality when these are discussed in developmentally appropriate language. Keep in mind that "what is said in group, stays in the group" is a difficult concept for younger children to understand, and it may be too simplistic for older and more sophisticated group members. Instead of using simple catchy statements (or, perhaps, in addition to using them), we suggest focusing on the intent of confidentiality. When we offer youth the opportunity to define what will make the group a safe place to explore feelings, to share beliefs and thoughts, and to feel supported through the process, confidentiality is usually beautifully defined. Rules around confidentiality typically flow rather naturally from clear understandings about why it is so important. We do not support the use of words like "secret" or "private" to connote confidentiality, as these terms are laden with discursive baggage that would likely not be helpful in these discussions, and they suggest an inaccurate and misleading notion of what confidentiality really means.

Group rules around confidentiality also need to be monitored and enforced; this is ultimately the responsibility of the group leader. This means that in addition to intervening to break confidentiality in cases of harm, group leaders must also be prepared to intervene if a student appears to be disclosing information that is potentially inappropriate for the setting. That is, leaders will need to help some students make judicious decisions about what they say in the group. If confidentiality has been breached in a group, it is also the responsibility of the group leader to work through this situation with the group members. Here the adage "what happens in the group must be dealt with in the group" can be a helpful guide in addressing these kinds of breaches within the group. Case Study 8.2. offers an illustration of how a group leader might engage in a conversation with group members after a peer breach in confidentiality.

CASE STUDY 8.2 Peer Breaches of Confidentiality

Ms. Achieng, a new school counselor engaged in running multiple groups in her school, received a report from one of the teachers that group confidentiality was breached during a fourth-grade class hiking trip. A number of students on the hiking expedition were members of a counseling group facilitated by Ms. Achieng. The following is what the teacher reported:

During the picnic lunch break, Sally, one of the group members, apparently solicited peer support in figuring out how she could raise funds to donate to Michelle's family, who were going through a hard time since her parents' divorce. John, another student in the same group, quickly interrupted the discussion stating, "Isn't that information supposed to be discussed *only* in the group?" Michelle who had been sitting quietly nearby, broke out into tears and went and sat by herself far away from the others in the class.

We start with the point that a breach of confidentiality by one group member not only affects the member who was the subject of the breach, but it can also create fear and resentment among others in the group and will likely disrupt the group's process of developing group cohesion.

Ms. Achieng had a responsibility to engage group members in a discussion about this incident. She did this in the next group meeting. It was, of course, her responsibility to address the issue whether Sally owned up to the breach or not, and whether Michelle directly reported the breach or whether it was relayed to her by someone else, as was the case in this situation. Ms. Achieng began the next group meeting by telling students how the information related to the breach of confidentiality had come to her attention in the first place. She also reminded the group about the rules that the group had established about confidentiality. Next, she carefully invited the group members to discuss the incident. In this conversation, Ms. Achieng offered Michelle an opportunity to discuss how the breach had affected her. She also worked with Sally to recognize the effect of her actions (albeit well intended, they were still hurtful, and they disrespected the group rule regarding confidentiality). As the conversation moved along, Ms. Achieng invited Sally to think about how she could repair her relationship with Michelle and regain the trust of the other group members.

The goal of Ms. Achieng's intervention was to help all of the students in the group understand the importance of group confidentiality. This extended to understanding the damaging effect that a breach of confidentiality can have not only on one individual but also on one's relationships with many others in the community (in the group, in this case). She also hoped to help Sally—and others who were witnesses in the group—to acquire the interpersonal skills needed to repair relationships when a betrayal has occurred. Using this incident as a learning opportunity (as opposed to a punitive one), was a great step in teaching valuable interpersonal skills to the students in the group.

Finally, group leaders often find that they will need to establish and enforce group rules related to *task orientation*. This has to do with setting the expectation that the group will be focused on learning goals. This may be particularly relevant in classroom groups because they tend to be large and may require more self-regulation on the part of the group members, in task groups where outcome expectations are often articulated as defined products, and in groups with younger children. Here again, group leaders should articulate specific rules linked to specific behaviors that are manifestations of task orientation so that students are clear about this expectation. For example, at the start of a classroom group, Mr. M reminded students of the lesson objective; here he explained what students were expected to accomplish at the end of the lesson. He also reiterated the rules of sitting in their seats until instructions were given, using "inside voices," and being careful to respect others and classroom property.

Rule-Setting Processes

Discussions about group rules allow students to understand why rules are needed, to develop a sense of ownership of the rules, and to feel more accountable to the group. When students are actively engaged in the process of identifying and establishing group rules, they are able to create rules that represent their ideas, values, and interests.

It is best to initiate rule discussions at the beginning of the year, semester, or first time together as a group, and to involve all of the group members in the rule-setting process (Marzano, 2003). When these conversations are well managed by the group leader, the tone of cooperation and engagement is already being set in the group. It is important to give this rule-setting process the time it deserves; it has implications on student investment, participation, and, later, group processes. Keep in mind, however, that explicitly naming every rule and every behavior that is expected from group members is impossible, and having too many rules can be off-putting (Marzano, 2003); initiating a group with a long list of "do's and don'ts" does not facilitate a positive group climate. Instead, these conversations can begin by asking students how they want to be treated by others in the group (Charles, 2011).

As students introduce suggestions, the leader should clarify the various ideas that are offered and engage students in a discussion of the relative merits of each suggestion. It is important to respect student input during these early discussions, even if the leader does not necessarily agree with all of the suggestions offered. As the list of potential rules is culled, the leader can help students articulate the proposed rules in clear, concrete behavioral terms (Bear, 2005) and in grade/age-appropriate, positive language (i.e., what students should do rather than what not to do), as much as possible.

This will help them to understand the behavioral manifestations of the rules—providing a clear sense of what the rules mean and how to comply with them. This point is especially important when working with younger children and students who may have difficulties understanding how concepts look in practice. Group leaders can further cement understandings by having students practice the rules early on in the group. Of course, group leaders will be offering prompts, cues, positive reinforcement, and direct instruction throughout the course of the group, as needed, to ensure that the rules are maintained (Charles, 2011).

Once an appropriate list of rules has emerged, it should be documented in written form, as this serves as a clear reminder of the rules for later sessions (Bear, 2005; Charles, 2011). This is particularly helpful in situations where the rules for a particular group are slightly different than those of the regular classroom. For example, in many classrooms, teachers require students to raise their hands before talking; school counselors may not have this requirement, especially in their small counseling groups. Documentation is also helpful when rules are established early in the school year and are likely to have been forgotten, in groups with younger children who may need frequent reminders, and when the leader anticipates that some of the group members may challenge or break the rules. If having a poster of the rules is not feasible in a particular setting, a quick reminder of the rules at the start of the group may be more appropriate. These rule-setting tips are summarized in Table 8.2.

TABLE 8.2 Group Rule Setting

1. Initiate a discussion about group rules during the first group meeting.
2. Involve all group members in the rule discussion.
3. Begin with a brief discussion about why rules are important.
4. Invite students to brainstorm their hopes for the climate of their group (explaining the connection between climate and rules).
5. Develop a list of group rules based on students' suggestions and group discussion.
6. Be sure that the list includes rules related to member and property safety, no tolerance for hurt and hate, confidentiality, task orientation, and any additional non-negotiable parameters of the group experience.
7. Construct a visual document that lists the rules articulated in simple language.

There will likely be circumstances in the group that give rise to a need for temporary rule changes. For example, a few students may need to leave a group early on one occasion because of an unforeseen circumstance. Also, sometimes particular activities in a group warrant the creation of specific rules. For example, a rule of "raising your hand before speaking" was established for a particular group activity in a classroom group with younger students who were having difficulties waiting their turn to speak. The group leader may initiate these types of rule changes. Also, at times, it may be appropriate for leaders to encourage students to make rule additions or changes. Rule changes are easier to navigate when they are firmly grounded in an articulated set of beliefs and expectations that are perceived by group members to be fair. The time and attention spent on the group process dynamics that underlie critical rule changes often yield positive benefits in terms of later group goal accomplishment.

Enforcing Rules

Group rules are designed to structure a facilitative group climate that provides safety for and supports student learning. Of course, even with solid and well-established rules in place, most groups require

TABLE 8.3 Steps for Enforcing Rules

1. *Stop What Is Happening and Address the Problem Early and Directly.* For example, "Folks, we need to take a time-out here to talk about something." "Helena, I'm going to ask you to stop for a moment."
2. *Call Attention to the Group Rule That Needs to Be Enforced.* For example, "We have a rule about respecting others in this group."
3. *Point Out the Incident That Represented the Rule Breach.* For example, "I just heard someone tell someone else to 'shut up.' When we decided on the rule of respect, we talked about the words that communicate disrespect, and, clearly, 'shut up' was one of them." This helps students make clear connections between behavior (i.e., the breach) and concept (i.e., the rule).
4. *Redirect the Students to More Appropriate Behavior and Move On.* For example, "If someone does not like what someone else says in this group, please give them direct feedback using I-messages. Do not tell them to 'shut up.' Does anyone need help using I-messages?" "Okay, let's all get back to what we were working on and remember to be respectful of everyone in this group."
5. *Reinforce Appropriate Behavior as Soon as Possible After the Redirection.* For example, "Wow, I'm hearing some very rich conversations in the small groups now. Nice work!"

group leader intervention from time to time to ensure that the group rules are followed. Next, we offer general guidelines for enforcing group rules. They are summarized in Table 8.3.

First, *intervene early* when a group norm is in danger of being disrupted or when a rule is being broken. As Bear (2005) pointed out, it is always best to catch problematic behavior "before the misbehavior escalates or becomes 'contagious'" (p. 202). This is best done by *calling attention to the rule infraction* and *offering a directive* for remedy. For example, "Jonah," Ms. Faya said, "remember that the rule in this group is to respect others' space. Please put George's paper down and return to your seat. Thanks." Closely monitoring student interactions and behaviors within the group—what we refer to later in this chapter as *withitness*—helps group leaders identify potentially problematic behaviors before they become disruptive to the group.

Second, remember that tone is critical when enforcing group rules. Rules should always be enforced in a *respectful, fair, matter-of-fact,* and *instructive* rather than punitive manner. "Please" and "thank you," for example, go a long way in communicating respect and do not diminish group leader authority. We realize that it can sometimes be difficult to remain calm and centered when students in a group need repeated reminders and interventions to follow the rules; this can be very frustrating for group leaders. But when students perceive that they are being respected and treated fairly, even if they are receiving corrective feedback, they will be more willing to conform to behavioral expectations. This helps defuse mounting power struggles. Also, consider the powerfully instructive role of role modeling. When group leaders can center themselves in respectful calm during challenging moments in the group, they are offering themselves as a model for how students can similarly self-regulate during challenging times.

Along these lines and following from our earlier discussions about group dynamics, social status, and bias, here again is the reminder about fairness. Because of the obscure nature of implicit bias, group leaders need to be self-vigilant. A good way to audit yourself in this area is through self-reflection. We recommend asking yourself these questions: Am I calling on all of the students equally? Do I single out some students for misbehavior more than others? If so, why is this happening, and what changes are needed to make the group more successful for these particular students? Is there something happening in this group that I am not aware of that is causing difficulties for some students? Other ways in which group leaders can monitor their own biases are to invite a peer to observe their groups and to periodically seek feedback from the students in the group.

In terms of misbehavior in the group, the leader should also be certain that they are not inadvertently seen as taking the whole group to task for individual student misbehaviors. For example, students will quickly recognize the injustice of all of them missing recess because of the behavior of two students in their group. This kind of punishment may also yield unintended consequences if students feel compelled to retaliate against the two "offenders" for this perceived injustice. Remember that students are measuring their willingness to participate in a given group based on their perceptions of fairness, safety, and benefit. Students who perceive unfair treatment—directed against them or against another group member—will make decisions about future engagement in the group.

Third, so as to avoid having small misbehaviors build and take over the group, we suggest intervening early in some minimally invasive ways. *Withitness*, which refers to continuously scanning and monitoring group member activity (Brophy, 1999), helps leaders to be on the lookout for potential problems and to intervene quickly and early on should infractions occur. Cueing and redirection, discussed in Chapter 7, are two additional leader interventions that can prohibit minor challenges from escalating. When students are consistently off task, when their behavior is causing disruptions for others, or when student behavior is dangerous or grossly inappropriate, more assertive rule enforcement is obviously appropriate. Chapter 9 offers additional extensive response strategies for the more serious rule breaches that may occur in the group.

Finally, when repeated rule infractions occur in a group, it is important for the group leader to consider whether the intended norms and identified rules, structure, learning goals, or particular students are appropriate for the group. This may require revisiting the group plan and reassessing whether the members have the adequate prerequisite group readiness skills to be able to benefit from the group in question or whether the behavioral demands of the group are appropriately commensurate with group members' abilities. In some situations, it may be most appropriate to move students who do not have these prerequisite skills into a more appropriate group learning experience.

Unique Consideration Related to Classroom Group Norms and Rules

While group norms (and rules) will, of course, vary according to many variables, the unique setting of working in school classrooms calls particular attention to norms that should be established in regard to personal sharing, using shared physical space, and, more generally, working in the school context. We discuss each of these here.

When met with a welcoming and caring environment, given appropriate structure, and presented with engaging and meaningful group activities, students are likely to want to talk and participate actively in groups conducted by school counselors. However, in classroom settings, there are some important variables that should be monitored by the group leader. First, time is a factor. If every child in a large group was invited to offer a personal story about a particular topic, everyone would be sitting for hours. Second, since these groups are designed for all students in the classroom (and group screening is not possible), the instructional content will not always seamlessly match the needs and interests of all of the students in the room. As a result, student interest, investment, and experience with the topic will vary considerably among group members. Further, those students who are heavily invested in a particular topic may be apt to engage in discussions and disclose personal information more freely than their peers. For example, when beginning a lesson on the effects of bullying, Sarah, who had previously spent time in individual counseling with her school counselor, wanted to share with the class how she had firsthand experience with bullies. When Sarah began to speak, it seemed that what she was about to share would turn into a personal airing of her own (very real) pain. Had this been a counseling group in which Sarah was a member, her willingness to disclose would have been welcomed as a vital catalyst for the group. But in the classroom group, this level of sharing was likely to shift the focus away from the intended instructional content and inadvertently leave Sarah feeling vulnerable and potentially unsafe in the large group.

It is sometimes difficult to find an appropriate norm regarding personal sharing in classroom groups. We cannot always anticipate what students will say, and in large groups, the leader's ability to provide individual attention to students who may need additional care and attention during tender conversations is limited. It is also difficult to enforce norms regarding confidentiality, as mentioned, especially in larger groups. It follows that norms related to personal sharing in classroom groups, then, should be somewhat conservative. What is meant by *conservative*? It has to do with the function and purpose of the group. We recommend that group leaders talk directly with students about appropriate participation in their groups. These discussions may happen in the moment in the group or in a more private conversation at a different time. Here, especially, we emphasize the importance of helping students begin to think about their own personal boundaries regarding personal sharing. Leaders can support the development of these boundary and self-regulation skills by paraphrasing, cutting off, shifting the focus, and using joining skills (as discussed in Chapter 7).

Conversely, there will be students in classroom (and counseling) groups who are judicious about personal engagement and sharing with others. While the intent of all group work conducted in schools is to engage students in new learning experiences, this, as already discussed, requires a delicate mix of challenge and safety. It certainly does not happen through forced self-disclosure. For many of us, learning to trust others takes time. An important norm that should be supported in all groups, then, is that students are allowed to make decisions regarding their own investment and sharing in the group. Reminding students that they have an option to pass (i.e., they can elect to not speak) helps to ensure member safety and shapes appropriate self-regulation in regard to self-disclosure.

Other pertinent issues concerning norms and rules—especially in classroom groups—has to do with the ownership of the physical space in the room and limits related to activity and noise level. In many schools, classroom groups are conducted in the physical space of a teacher's classroom. As we know, classroom spaces come with implicit and explicit expectations for how they will be used and how people in those spaces are to behave. Teachers establish norms and practices in their classrooms that reflect their own teaching styles, preferences, content of instruction, and what they know about working with their particular group of students. Sometimes, however, the norms and rules that are appropriate for a particular teacher do not fit the kinds of experiences that school counselors want to create in their classroom group work. For example, a teacher's math curriculum may require students to work individually and quietly during the lesson, and thus student desks are arranged accordingly in the classroom. In walks a school counselor with a curriculum that is focused on helping students acquire interpersonal skills, giving feedback, or being assertive—curricular goals are much better met through active and spontaneous engagement. The challenge becomes working this curriculum around the physical arrangement of desks in the room.

In response to physical space and activity level discrepancies, we want to point out, first, that common curtesy suggests that the rightful owner of the classroom space (i.e., the teacher) should always be respected when others are using their room. This should be a guide for negotiating the use of shared space. It is also important to remember that noise tends to fill space quickly when there are many students in a room, and classrooms are typically located in close proximity to one another. Although a group leader may want students to feel comfortable talking and moving about the room freely, the teacher and the students next door who are taking a biology quiz may not appreciate the noise. This requires us to be flexible and remember that our group goals and delivery plans need to suit the school setting. Little goodwill is fostered between school counselors, teachers, and building administrators when group activities disrupt others in the school community.

To navigate some of the norm and rule differences that can surface when using shared instructional spaces, we recommend starting with what is already in place. Review the existing regular classroom expectations and rules in juxtaposition to the goals that you have for your classroom group. If the norms and rules for your work in the classroom need to differ significantly from those of the teacher's, they can be modified by using the rule-setting process or discussion with the students. When making these modifications, be explicit about the changes (and the reasons for the changes) and be clear that the classroom rules will revert back to the standards already set by the classroom teacher when you leave the room. Most students can be flexible in dealing with different expectations when they understand the reason for them.

It is also sometimes a good idea to communicate with the regular teacher about norm and rule differences that might occur throughout the year as you work in their classroom. This is particularly important in situations where the teacher feels uncomfortable with the fact that you have changed the classroom rules, if they are not particularly happy about having you use their space, or if problems have occurred as a result of you being in their room. It can be especially helpful to reiterate your commitment to respecting the classroom space and the teacher. Finally, we recommend that school counselors work closely with the administration in the school so that the administration fully understands the range and nature of the work that happens in school counselor-led groups. Be prepared to explain the purpose of your group, as well as the methods you will be using to accomplish clearly identified learning, social, emotional, academic, and career-related goals. It is helpful to speak in language that is clear, informative, and understandable (but that does not, of course, compromise student confidentiality). Remember that the theory behind some counseling approaches (particularly the use of play media) is often misunderstood by those who are not professional counselors.

Starting the Group

With norms and rule-setting processes in place, we now turn our attention to a number of strategies that teachers and group leaders use to start each group session and manage minor distractions.

Attention and Interest

It is always helpful to start a group in a way that awakens or captures students' interest. This is especially important when working with youth who are not motivated to be in the group and in groups with mandated participants (such as the case with students in classroom groups since developmental guidance groups are not optional in most schools). Interest breeds motivation to be in the group; boredom can lead to misbehavior.

This begins with cueing students' attention—letting them know that the group is starting. Some counselors do this by raising a hand and inviting students to raise their hands when they are focused and ready to begin. Others play music, engage in a group stretch, flicker the lights, start with a countdown, or use a simple statement such as, "Ready, set, okay let's start." We recommend that you develop your own creative way to cue students' attention and to establish this as a routine for the group so that the students will always know when to be ready to start. This is especially helpful when working with younger children, with students who are distractible, and when working in a classroom, as it is not uncommon for the school counselor to enter a classroom that is still engaged in a prior task or for some reason is not quite ready for a change of task. After you have the attention of the students in the group, you can generate further interest by making a provocative statement, asking a question related to the topic, or unveiling an interesting (and relevant) object. You can also play music, read a short essay, or show a short video clip related to the topic. Your opening action welcomes students into the learning mode.

Learning Map

After capturing students' attention, it is a good idea to offer a brief preview of what will happen in the group that day. This *learning map* situates the current topic in a learning landscape. This can be done by linking the current topic or activity to a goal, to a previous lesson or discussion, or by briefly mentioning how the topic for the day is relevant in the students' lives in some way. These strategies of contextualizing learning help establish relevancy. Case Study 8.3 offers an example of using learning maps.

CASE STUDY 8.3 Learning Map

Mr. Padden, who was conducting a psychoeducational group with ninth-grade literature teacher, Mrs. Dvorshak, began the group by saying, "Today, we are going to spend some time talking about 'silencing behaviors.' This fits in with our discussion last week about discrimination and the book *Warriors Don't Cry* (Beals, 1994) that you have been discussing in this class.

"Mrs. D and I noticed last week that some students dominated the discussion and others did not say very much, and we wondered about this, especially after a few students wrote in their group reflection journals that they felt that they 'weren't allowed' to speak their minds in the class. Mrs. D and I have a sense that these things did not happen intentionally but that they were a product of what sometimes happens in big groups and sometimes what happens in schools, too, when people get used to participating in certain ways and that just becomes a norm.

"Today, we want to start by talking about some of the ways in which Melba and the other students of color who were integrated at Little Rock High in *Warriors Don't Cry* were silenced in their school. Who can help us start off the discussion by being the scribe on the board as we come up with a community definition (i.e., classroom definition) of 'silencing' others?"

This learning map was used to help establish the relevancy of the discussion and provided a context for the direction that the leaders wanted to take in the group that day. Remember to keep the introductions and learning map clear and concrete but also brief; spending too much time on the introduction means having less time for the task at hand.

Instructions

Another important aspect of facilitating a group has to do with the way in which task instructions are communicated to students (Brophy, 1999). Something as simple as being clear when delivering task instructions has a huge effect on the group process. When students are unclear about task requirements, they may become disengaged and disruptive as they scurry to figure out what to do.

When giving instructions, first *minimize distractions*. For example, "Okay, everyone, stop what you're doing, please, and listen carefully to these very important directions for what we will be doing today." Be sure to *speak clearly and slowly*, and whenever possible, *offer information sequentially*. Sequential cues offered one at a time, such as "first do this ...," "okay, now that you are done with that, the next step is ..." are particularly helpful when presenting a task that requires many steps, when working in big groups, and when working with younger children. As this alludes, it is important to adjust the way in which you provide instructions so that they are developmentally appropriate and sensitive to the variety of learning styles represented in the group. *Asking a student to repeat the instructions* or *inviting questions* are ways to reveal misunderstandings; a question spoken by one student is often an unvoiced concern of another. Also, providing *written task instructions* is often helpful.

Managing Distractions

Misbehavior often starts with a distraction that then leads to more significant off-task or acting out behavior. Addressing minor problems early on goes a long way toward creating a productive group. Also keep in mind that group leaders can unintentionally cause distractions in the group when they are sidetracked or through their responses to problems that arise in the group, which we will discuss more in the next chapter.

We offer the following recommendations for avoiding or responding to distractions when they arise in a group:

- *Be Mindful of Not Creating Distractions.* Be sure to come to group prepared to go.
- *Be Sure to Provide Instructions Clearly and Introduce Materials at an Appropriate Time.* Keep in mind that showing students fun materials or breaking them into smaller groups before sufficiently providing instructions can easily lead to a distraction. This is especially true when working with young children or youth who have attentional difficulties.
- *Have a Plan for How You Will Manage Transitions and Maintain a Flow in the Group.* This kind of plan typically initiates with being sure that all students are informed of instructions or next steps before the transition occurs. Routines can also be very helpful for managing transitions.
- *Be Firm About Not Being Drawn Into Individual and Private Conversations During Group Time.* It is always appropriate to tell teachers, parents, students, or administrators that this is not a good time to talk, and you will schedule a time to meet with then as soon as possible. Do not answer your telephone when facilitating a group.
- *Be Flexible.* Schools are busy places and antecedent events in the lives of students can easily derail even the best-laid plans. Leader flexibility is a must. There will be times when distractions are largely out of the control of the group leader, such as interruptions from the school intercom, someone walking in the room, or students playing on the playground just outside the window. If students are antsy from sitting too long, group plans may need to be adjusted to allow the students an opportunity to move around. If an incident has happened prior to your entrance into the group, you may need to directly attend to what happened before students are ready to focus and move on. However, leaders must also be careful to keep their learning objectives in mind and be prepared to shift the focus back to the group task as soon as possible. "Clinical judgment" guides leader decision making about when to stick with the lesson plans or when to shift the focus and address the here and now in the group.
- *Be "Withit."* As mentioned earlier, Brophy (1999) used the term *withitness* to describe a kind of teacher presence in the classroom that is key to effective classroom management. Withitness refers to an aware and monitoring presence in the group—a kind of group surveillance that provides the leader with feedback about how things are going. Specific withit group leader behaviors include regular scanning to monitor attention, interest, and progress on a task; intervening promptly and appropriately when students are disengaged; and attending to multiple activities and events simultaneously. Good group management cannot happen without group leader withitness—the group leader must always be aware of what is happening in the center and at the perimeters of the group.

Managing Group Process Dynamics

Recall from Chapter 3 that group *process* refers to interpersonal dynamics within the group (Geroski & Kraus, 2002). Group process explains how learning occurs through group member interactions and dynamics that happen during a group session. Group *content*, on the other hand, refers to what the group is about and is typically reflected in the written goals, topic, theme, and work plan of the group (Geroski & Kraus, 2002). Together, group process and content are the *how* and *what* of a group; a focus on both of these is important. According to Hulse-Killacky et al. (1999), "Process facilitates content, and process needs to be balanced with content or a group will fail to attain its objectives" (p. 114). So, while it may seem that shifting focus from group content to address group process dynamics would take a group off topic, these authors remind us that they really are very much interconnected. Both affect group success. For this reason, we offer a model of some helpful ways to navigate complex group process dynamics within groups. We return to this important idea of using process to facilitate content goals more directly at the end of this discussion.

Intervention Cube

Cohen and Smith's (1976) *intervention cube* offers a conceptual model and practical tool for helping group leaders manage group process dynamics to better enable the group to achieve its intended goals. Here we begin with an explanation of the model and then move into a discussion of how leaders can use this model to guide their work.

In the intervention cube, intervention options are organized into three dimensions: (1) level, (2) type, and (2) intensity, as illustrated in Table 8.4.

Type of intervention refers to the ways in which members are asked to engage with the content of the group. A leader intervention type that focuses on helping members conceptualize or make meaning around a significant issue or idea is a *conceptual* intervention. An intervention type that focuses on a member's experience (feeling, thoughts, or behaviors) in the group is an *experiential* intervention. Intervention types that make use of planned activities, exercises, structured tasks, or interventions that change the physical movement patterns of members in the group are *structural*. Very generally, conceptual interventions provide opportunities for meaning attribution or meaning making. Experiential type interventions invite members to be aware of their experience in the group and tend to stimulate emotional awareness or arousal. Structural interventions typically introduce a change to the group functioning and are often used to stimulate or change group member engagement patterns.

Level of intervention refers to who is addressed by a particular group leader intervention. An *intrapersonal*-level intervention focuses on an individual, an *interpersonal*-level intervention invites two or a few members to interact with each other, and a *group*-level intervention addresses any or all of the individuals in the group (but no one in particular).

This brings us to the third dimension in the model: *intensity*. Group intensity refers to the effect of a particular group intervention in terms of stimulating group members' sensitivity, emotion, or thought. This is presented as a continuous variable: low, medium, and high.

When a group leader is clear about what they want to accomplish in a group, then group level, type, and intensity can be manipulated to accomplish this intended objective. The ways in which a group leader selects and combines the various components of this intervention cube (intervention types, levels, and intensity) allow for a wide range of intervention possibilities in the group.

TABLE 8.4 Level and Type of Group Interventions

Type of Intervention	Level of Intervention	Intensity of Intervention
Conceptual	Intrapersonal	Low →← High
Experiential	Interpersonal	
Structural	Group	

Adapted from: Cohen, A. M., & Smith, R. D. (1976). The critical incident in growth groups: Theory and technique. La Jolla, CA: University Associates.

Type and Level Interventions

Case Study 8.4 describes two groups: one classroom and one counseling group. This case study is offered as a reference for our discussion on the application of the intervention cube (Cohen &

Smith, 1976). Looking at both groups concurrently offers the opportunity to compare and contrast how two different counselors may use level and type interventions in two different circumstances and in two different groups types.

CASE STUDY 8.4   Two Cases for Study—The Intervention Cube

Psychoeducational Classroom Group

The goal for Mr. Jaramillo's fifth-grade classroom group is to expose students to work and career options. In the second session, Sebastian disrupts the group by tapping his pen during a discussion. Shortly afterward, Sebastian talks with two peers who are sitting near him, and they continue to whisper with each other while Mr. Jaramillo and other students are participating in the group discussion.

Counseling Group

Giana is in Mrs. McAllister's fourth- and fifth-grade counseling group for girls, which focuses on divorce. The goals of the group are for the members to develop strategies for managing the stress around the divorce, to support one another in their experiences, and to have the opportunity to grieve the change in their families that have resulted from the divorce. The six members of this group recently experienced divorce in their families (within the last 6 months) and their parents and/or teachers had concerns that the divorce was affecting school performance. All of the children elected to participate in the group, and they all have parental consent. This particular session is the fourth of 8 weekly sessions. In this session, Giana becomes very emotional when she tells the group about a fight she witnessed between her parents. As she talks about it, she also mentions that she believes it was her fault that her parents were fighting.

Mr. Jaramillo will want to keep his classroom group engaged in the content, while also managing the disruptions from Sebastian. In the counseling group, Mrs. McAllister will want to manage the intensity so that Giana can get the support she needs from group members and so that all of the group members can benefit from the concern that she brings to the group (which they probably also share).

Structural Interventions

In response to the disruption in Mr. Jaramillo's classroom group, a *structural-type* intervention might be used to break the large group into smaller subgroups so that students are more personally engaged with the material and less likely to be distracted by others. For example, Mr. Jaramillo might ask students to pair up, read five items from their learning style inventory to their partners, and have them guess about the style profile. Notice that this structural type intervention has an *interpersonal-level* focus since it requires students to engage in pairs. Alternatively, Mr. Jaramillo could make a *structural-type, intrapersonal-level* intervention by asking Sebastian to move his seat, take out his learning inventory, and complete the questions. This would be an intrapersonal-level intervention because it is focused solely on one student (Sebastian).

In Ms. McAllister's counseling group, a *structural-type* intervention might be used as the group begins to wind down toward the end of the session. In this case, she might direct group members to engage in a structured activity, such as deep breathing or a progressive relaxation exercise to help lower the intensity of the emotion and promote self-regulation. This activity serves to regulate the intensity that surfaced in the group and prepares students to return to their instructional classrooms in a more regulated state. It would be a *group-level* intervention because it requests that all of the group members participate in the activity together; it is not aimed at one single individual nor at an exchange between two group members.

Conceptual Interventions

Mr. Jaramillo and Ms. McAllister may opt to use *conceptual* interventions to manage their situations. *Conceptual-type* interventions, again, are aimed at helping members to focus on thinking about an idea or a concept. They may be delivered at the *intrapersonal, interpersonal,* or *group level.* In Mr. Jaramillo's group, the students might be asked to take a minute to think (*conceptual*) by themselves (*intrapersonal*) about which style seems to fit them based on the ranking they received after taking the learning style inventory. Afterward, students could be assigned to work in small groups (*structural-type, interpersonal level* intervention) to share their profiles with one another and to provide feedback regarding the characteristics they display that are illustrative of a concept in the profile. For example, if Jairo's profile indicated that he was artistic/creative, the students in his small group might offer Jairo an example of when they saw him being artistic or creative. As a way of summarizing at the end of the group, Mr. Jaramillo might ask, "What did we learn today?" Because this comment is not directed at a specific group member, it would be a *group-level* intervention. This kind of *conceptual-type, group-level* intervention is often used at the close of groups to refocus the members on what they have learned as they prepare to leave.

In the counseling group example, Ms. McAllister may want to assist Giana with developing a cognitive understanding or framework to help her think about her assertion that she is responsible for her parents' anger at each other. To accomplish this, she could use a *conceptual-type* intervention: She could express wonder about Giana's statement of feeling responsible for her parent's fight. Notice that this type of intervention is still focused on Giana (*intrapersonal*). When moving the focus from a feeling to a cognitive state, Ms. McAllister must move slowly so as to be careful not to give the impression that expressing emotions is not safe in the group and not to abandon a group member when she is emotional. Moving a group member from a feeling to a cognitive state is likely to lower the intensity in the group, so the leader is always thinking about moderating intensity so as to draw members in but not scare them away.

Experiential Interventions

In the counseling group, Ms. McAllister would probably be looking for interventions that would validate Giana's experience and feelings, provide her with the support of other group members, and draw other students into the experience. Leaders want to be sure that the needs of one member do not dominate the group but also in this example it is likely that other students in the group also feel responsible for their parents' conflicts. So, Ms. McAllister will want to intervene in a way that invites all of the students to benefit. Initially, Ms. McAllister might choose to use an *experiential-type, intrapersonal-level* intervention so as to immediately validate Giana's feelings. For example, expressing empathy for Giana's dilemma, she could ask Giana how it felt to think she was responsible for the fight or how it felt to overhear the fight between her parents. She would, of course, want to remind students in the group about confidentiality, and she would also want to remind Giana that she can share as much or as little as she wants. While this intervention would not focus on Giana's feelings *in* the group, it would be intended to elicit feelings, thus fitting with the *experiential type.* Ms. McAllister would probably use basic counseling skills, such as empathy, reflection, and paraphrasing, as a part of this intervention.

Ms. McAllister might also consider using a combination of responses to bring other group members into the experience so they can both support Giana and explore their own related experiences and feelings. Caution is advised here as moving too quickly from an intrapersonal to an interpersonal or group focus can leave the original student feeling that their concerns are not important. To make this shift from intrapersonal to interpersonal, Ms. McAllister could ask if others in the group (*group level*) have sometimes had thoughts (*conceptual type*) that they were responsible for their parents' anger at each other. To promote meaning making, she could add a statement such as, "Sometimes when we do not understand why things are happening, we assume that they are happening because of something we did, when that might not be the case at all." This intervention invites other group members into the discussion by sharing their thoughts or stories of similar experiences, and it also offers students a conceptual framework for understanding their experiences, but it does not raise the intensity by singling out an individual student who has not already self-identified. Monitoring intensity is also important here. The trick is to raise the intensity enough to stimulate engagement but not to make it too high—emotional intensity can be frightening for children and adolescents, especially when they are with peers.

Intensity Variations

The group leader is always aiming for a level of intensity that will stimulate meaningful engagement but also provide safety for student members. When students feel that participating in a group is too risky (i.e., it is too intense, perhaps leaving them feeling too uncomfortable or vulnerable), they are not likely to benefit from the group. On the other hand, groups that lack significant intensity can lead to nonparticipation, acting out behaviors, or fail to accomplish their learning goals. In this model, group leaders vary intensity through the type and level of interventions.

Group-level interventions, in general, tend to be rather low in intensity and are often used to stimulate discussion without leaving members feeling singled out. *Conceptual-* or *structural-type*, *group-level* interventions invite group members to respond by thinking, noticing, listening, talking, or answering a question. Notice how inviting the group (rather than a specific individual) allows students to be self-reflective but to make their own choices about what, when, and how to verbally participate in the group. Since these interventions do not call upon any one student directly, they afford students an opportunity for self-censoring—students have the power of deciding how and when to participate. They may be helpful when a group is populated with students who tend to feel reluctant to speak, particularly in classroom groups because of the larger number of students.

Some group leaders use *rounds* (i.e., when each group member is asked to say something in response to a particular prompt) for group-level interventions. Rounds are helpful, as they invite all members of a group to participate in a discussion or weigh in on an issue. For some students, however, rounds do generate a bit of anxiety (and thus raise intensity) since they communicate the expectation that all students will respond. So, it is important that rounds always include an option for students to pass (i.e., not respond). But for other students, rounds actually mediate the anxiety that comes from having to make a decision and speak in front of the group because they set the expectation that everyone will say something. In addition, they offer a predictable order for when students respond, giving students time to prepare their thoughts. When using rounds, it is advisable to be selective in determining which group member talks first and to be mindful of the round direction. The first to speak in the round will set the response and tone for others, so it is a good idea to initiate the round with a student who is likely to approximate your expectation for a response or who can set a good tone. It is also helpful to set the direction of the round away from a student who may need more time to think about a response and toward a student who has difficulty waiting. These are in-the-moment group leader decisions that will have an effect on the intensity of the group.

Inviting students to speak in pairs or dyads (*conceptual-type, interpersonal-level* intervention) also tends to be less intense for some students who are uncomfortable speaking in the larger group. However, dyads may arouse anxiety for students who are concerned about who they are paired with and what they should or should not say. Social status hierarchies are set into motion when students are invited to select their own partners for paired participation. So it is advisable for the leader to select dyad pairings rather than leave it to the students to pick partners. Also, providing students with explicit instructions for dyad activities helps these interventions run more smoothly. Finally, when appropriate, the leader should remind students of and enforce a standard for confidentiality before they begin speaking in pairs.

Experiential-type group interventions facilitate the expression of feelings or emotionality. Because of the focus in schools on cognitive learning tasks, we find that *experiential* interventions tend to be used less frequently than other intervention types in school groups, particularly in classroom groups. This is unfortunate. There is no reason to avoid experiential interventions in schools, as they offer many rich and powerful learning opportunities for youth. Factors to consider in regard to experiential type interventions include timing and student safety. For example, group leaders need to be careful to provide students time to regain the composure needed to go back to their academic classes if they become emotional in a particular group. Helping students decompress at the end of group by facilitating mindfulness or other coregulation activities is a good routine for managing any transitions. Doing this especially after a particularly emotional group is important. We also caution group leaders to refrain from using any moderate- to high-level intensity interventions with students they are not familiar with. In groups where screening is not possible (i.e., in classroom groups), *experiential-type* interventions should be used only after leaders are familiar with all of the members in the group. Keep in mind that it is the responsibility of the group leader to monitor and alter the intensity in their group, so all members are meaningfully and safely engaged in learning. Working in the growth zone requires that students be stimulated to work at a level that is within reach but just beyond where they are currently functioning. Altering intensity and using experiential interventions judiciously are two excellent ways of stimulating risk within a context of safety.

In general, *conceptual-type* responses are likely to feel a little less intense than feeling or experiential responses. These interventions, however, may cause some anxiety for students who are concerned that others will judge what they say. This is particularly true if students are asked to consider something that is difficult to understand, if the topic is presented as a competition, or in cases where students may experience less social capital in the group than their peers. Asking students what they might have thought in the *past* (or how they might have felt in the past) rather than how they think (or feel) in the *present* provides a cushion of distance to mediate the anxiety around the possibility of saying something "stupid" or having an emotional reaction in the group.

Finally, *structural-type* interventions typically have the effect of lowering the intensity in groups because they offer explicit parameters for engagement. This is probably why teachers and counselors like to use activities, exercises, and games when working with children and adolescents in groups—the rules for engagement are explicit. However, because of their potential for lowering the level of intensity in the group, an over-reliance on group activities—both in classroom and counseling groups—may dilute or detract from the goals or objectives of a group. So while it is nice when learning is fun, we emphasize that it is the responsibility of the group leader to assure activities are used as a means to specific learning objectives or goals. Our discussion of planning group activities in Chapter 6 highlights the importance of the employment of processing questions when using structural group interventions. Processing questions are designed to intentionally bring a meaning-making component into group activities.

Finally, we point out that while *structural* interventions typically lower the intensity in groups, the idea of doing an activity can feel very threatening for some students, especially for those who may not have high levels of self-esteem or who are not comfortable among their peers in the group. Providing students with clear rules for engagement and structuring the ways in which students will be asked to interact in activities are important strategies for mitigating the intensity of structural group interventions.

Using Process to Facilitate Content

Counselors working in schools are charged with providing services that focus on meeting or supporting the academic, career, personal, and social needs of students (ASCA, 2019), and much of this happens in classroom and counseling groups. We maintain that an excellent way to teach a psychoeducational curriculum in classroom and counseling school groups is to use the group as a laboratory for learning. This is particularly true when the purpose of the group—the content—is for students to learn social, interpersonal, or communication skills. For example, if the goal of a middle school counseling group is to develop assertiveness skills, then it is probably not enough to talk about and study those skills; the students in the group should probably be directly engaged in using these skills with each other in the group. Focusing on the interaction among members—group process—allows students to explore, practice, and integrate these interpersonal skills rather than just talk about them. In this way, group process facilitates group content goals.

Group leaders usually will need to have a plan—often an activity—to spawn group member interaction. Obviously, intended learning goals do not always spontaneously arise through group process dynamics. For example, we can't wait for a conflict to arise in order to teach conflict mediation skills. So group plans should outline how students will be stimulated to engage with each other in ways that promote the learning goals. What structuring interventions—discussion points, questions, activities—will be used?

In some groups, group process dynamics may actually run parallel to content objectives or larger group goals. That is, group process dynamics exist among group members—dynamics that potentially offer a "teachable moment" related to the learning objective of the group—but remain unaddressed. For example, students in an elementary school classroom group were learning about decision making through a structured activity intended to teach particular decision-making concepts. During that activity, a few students became engaged in a conflict, and they could not decide on how to go forward with the activity. But this dynamic remained unaddressed by the group leader. In this example, students were talking about good decision making, but they were not asked to actually engage with each other on a decision they had to make in the moment. Unfortunately, potential learning from the group process dynamics in this example was missed; we might say that the group process ran parallel to the content (i.e., it never truly had an effect on the students' experiences) and failed to support the content goals in this group.

So while structuring group activities to advance content goals and objectives is important, group leaders should also be alert to opportunities to harvest critical incidents or spontaneous situations in the group for their learning potential as they arise. In group work circles, we refer to similar phenomena as *working in the here and now* (for more on working in the here and now, see Carroll & Kraus, 2007). We close with the point that moving with teachable moments in the group does not mean that there is no agenda or plan for the group. Nor does it mean that the desired group process is leaderless. On the contrary, the agenda for the leader when working with group process dynamics *is* to manage the process skillfully and to keep it focused on the intended learning goal and objectives.

Shifting the Focus Between Group Process and Content

Decisions about shifting the focus from content to process dynamics (and shifting back again) should be made with intentionality, considering the purpose of the group. Decision making can be guided by asking the following questions: "What is the purpose of this group?" "Is what's happening in the group right now related to that purpose?" Put simply, if what is happening in the group is related to the objectives or goals of the group, then it might be a good idea to shift the focus to group process dynamics. When what is happening in the group is clearly not related to the intended tasks for the group, then refocusing the group away from distracting dynamics should be the priority. These decisions must also take into account the group context (i.e., in a school with youth) and the individual needs and abilities of group members. Here the questions group leaders can ask themselves are as follows: "Will shifting the focus (to or away from a particular direction or intensity) benefit this student?" "What are the needs of this student (and the other students) in this moment?"

Again, as mentioned, using group process to facilitate content requires a certain degree of risk taking on the part of the group members; it is risky to move from talking about something conceptually to talking about one's own experience in the group (which is what a focus on process typically entails). The extent to which students will engage in this kind of risk taking will depend on the level of safety and trust felt in the group. The basic counseling skills listed in Chapter 7 are the tools that group leaders use to shift the focus between process and content in a group, especially paraphrasing, summarizing, questioning (focused open-ended probes), cutting off, and immediacy. But these tools require a baseline group climate of safety, trust, caring, and cohesion.

We end by pointing out that moving from a focus on content to group process dynamics may also engender some anxiety for group leaders. Relinquishing a tight hold on the reins of the agenda and purposely inviting spontaneity into the group through engagement in group process dynamics can be very threatening for even the most seasoned group leader. It is hard to predict how such in-the-moment discussions will evolve if we are not holding on tightly to what we had planned in advance. However, we encourage group leaders to welcome such opportunities as they present themselves. The dimensions of Cohen and Smith's intervention cube (Cohen & Smith, 1976) offer a sound model for doing so.

Reflection Questions

1. Can you identify specific moments in Case Study 8.1 where there are hints that group cohesion is starting to develop? Can you identify any obvious risks to cohesion? If so, discuss additional steps the leader could take to build cohesion in this group.
2. Discuss the role of trust in cohesion. How do cultural phenomena "play out" in group formation? How might you use members' diverse cultural experiences to build cohesion? Brainstorm several examples.
3. When, if ever, is it appropriate to dismiss a student from a group in response to their disruptive behavior patterns? What circumstances might warrant such an action? What alternative actions could a group leader take instead of dismissing a student?

CHAPTER NINE

Responding to Challenges in the Group

Introduction

"The least intrusive and most natural behavior management strategies are, of course, good teaching practices" (Kerr & Nelson, 1998, p. 158). We agree. The most effective way to manage groups with youth is to create an environment in which everyone is meaningfully engaged and where students feel safe to take the kinds of risks that are required for learning within the growth zone. Having said this, challenges seem to find their way into even the best-planned and most carefully managed groups. For example, in a 2017 study conducted in an urban school district, 75% to 80% of teachers polled said they had students who either failed to comply with classroom rules or refused to complete work (Willert, 2017). More than half of the teachers who participated in a 2012 study released by Scholastic and the Bill & Melinda Gates Foundation indicated that they wished they could spend less time during their school day disciplining students (Scholastic, n.d.). While teachers express concerns about classroom behavior management, students, too, suffer. Problematic behaviors that disrupt instruction affect student learning, social development, and classroom climate (Adamson et al., 2019; Marchant & Anderson, 2012).

Most agree that establishing and carrying out systems of discipline is not the sole responsibility of individual teachers. In fact, many schools use a multitiered school discipline framework that begins with providing academic and behavioral instruction and skills (in a variety of ways) to all students and then shifts to providing increased academic, behavioral, and social-emotional support to students who require higher levels of assistance (Adamson et al., 2019). Even within these school-wide discipline practices, however, teachers (and school counselors when running groups) really are the "first line of defense for discipline problems" (Marzano, 2003, p. 27). This means that teachers and school counselors need immediate response strategies to address challenges that arise in their classrooms and groups. This is the focus of this chapter.

Before moving on, a few comments about wording. We grappled with the term "problem" as we wrote this chapter. By offering suggestions for how to deal with problems in groups, we do not want to convey that we see individual group members as problems, even when their behaviors are problematic. Labeling a child as problematic—explicitly or implicitly—is dangerous. Even identifying a *behavior* as problematic can lead to the creation of a narrative about a child that can be damaging. Thinking or speaking about children as problems or even thinking about them through the lens of diagnostic categories and related concepts can easily lead to a downward spiral of problematic behaviors and equally problematic responses. The result is that children may be isolated, sometimes targeted by others, and restricted in their ability to benefit from instruction and see themselves in more positive ways. Clearly, this is not a recipe for healthy human development. We all have multiple ways of being. Moving away from reductionist labels and diagnoses allows us to understand challenges as resulting from multifaceted and complex factors, including, it is important to say, limitations in group leader skills. This broader perspective invites us to be more creative and effective in responding to problems that emerge in our groups.

General Principles for Responding

Marzano (2003) called for a "balanced approach" (p. 28) to responding to problems in classrooms. The challenge is to implement an intervention that most effectively addresses the disruption and that also allows the group to get back on task as seamlessly as possible. This is not always easy to do. One challenge here is to determine which behaviors should be tolerated and which ones require intervention. A general rule of thumb we recommend is to intervene when (1) it is clear that a student's behaviors interfere with learning—whether it is that student's learning or learning opportunities for others, or (2) when a student's behaviors are disrespectful or dangerous to others in the group. A second challenge is be sure that our intervention does not cause further disruption nor inhibit further student participation. As Jones and Jones's (2001) pointed out, "The disruptive influence of the teacher's intervention [to misbehavior] should not be greater than the disruption it is intended to reduce" (p. 301). The converse is also important—an intervention that is too passive can be equally ineffective. The nature of the disruption should inform the response needed. The point that Jones and Jones make is that leaders should not respond to every disruptive behavior, only those that really need intervention.

   Some use a hierarchy approach to describe potential responses to classroom or group disruptions. This is often referred to as a *discipline hierarchy*. The Educational Research Service (ERS, 2005) suggested that this hierarchy ranges from disengagement, to interruption, and, in more severe situations, to de-escalation. *Disengagement*, they suggested, should be used for minor disruptions. Strategies within this category include, for example, taking a deep breath (rather than responding to the disruption) or offering a brief correction without attending to the problematic behavior and then swiftly moving on. Lower level *interrupting* tactics include redirection or inviting an agitated student to take a break or step away from their activity for a few minutes so that they can calm down or become regulated. When these lower level responses are not effective, more visible and assertive interrupting strategies may be required. *De-escalation* may be needed to address intensifying emotions and defensiveness or to avert danger. However, de-escalation is a response that really is malleable to a variety of situations. For example, de-escalation may be used to address a situation where a student actively refuses to participate in an activity with their peers; when a student has an emotional breakdown in the group; when a student angrily lashes out at other group members repeatedly, is actively defiant, or issues physical threats to others in the group; and in situations where a student is out of control and unable to self-regulate (Charles & Senter, 2002). It is important to remember that higher level responses such as interruption and de-escalation do have the potential to generate reactivity and intensity in the group, so they should be used judiciously. Key to maintaining a balanced response, regardless of which level in the hierarchy, is the leader's ability to stay in control of their own reactivity when a student is disruptive and avoiding a situation where a student and/or problem receive more (negative) attention than is needed (ERS, 2005).

   The first principle for group leader intervention in response to behavior concerns is to always respond in a manner that is *calm, fair,* and *respectful*. Inappropriate anger and reactivity increase tension, disobedience, and disruption; calmness breeds composure and responsiveness from students. Second is the principle of *minimal response*. Leaders should attempt to respond by stopping the problematic behavior, maintaining their position as the one in charge, and then get back on task as soon as possible (ERS, 2005; Mendler, 2005). When doing this, leaders should speak to students in *clear, authoritative, and respectful language,* and they should be mindful of speaking *to* rather than *about* students. Group leaders should *intervene privately* whenever appropriate (so as to avoid situations where a student loses face in front of their peers), and interventions should *focus on present rather than past behavior*. However, when a student's behavior is meant to influence group behavior, an intervention within the group can be effective in interrupting the behaviors taking root within the group.

Next is the principle of *consistency*. Group leaders should attempt to be as consistent as possible when responding to disruptive behaviors—that is, being sure that they are responding similarly to students who exhibit similar behaviors (ERS, 2005). However, at the same time, it is important to realize that different students respond differently to behavioral interventions. Some students will respond best to one kind of intervention, whereas other students may require different kinds of interventions. So, *fairness* is key; this requires thoughtful intentionality rather than reactivity in the moment.

Group leaders should *refrain from interpreting the meaning* of a given behavior, especially in the moment when the behavior is occurring. Instead, they should *focus on concrete observable actions*. In the heat of the moment, leaders should also *avoid long discussions* and *not engage in conversations*—these tend to interfere with the effectiveness of an intervention, distract the group from its task, and may provide undue reinforcement to a student who is displaying disruptive behaviors.

For example, Mr. Mescell told Franc, "Franc, I need you to sit down in your seat right now."

When Franc asked, "Why do I need to sit down?"

Mr. Mescell responded, "We can talk about that later, Franc. Right now, I need you to sit down in your seat."

If an intervention that focuses on making interpretations is indicated, leaders should first de-escalate the emotional response and then move into meaning making. If they are working within the group and a group intervention is more appropriate, this should not occur until everyone is calm enough to engage in a processing discussion about the problematic behaviors and their effect on the group.

Leaders can also *provide options and choices*. For example, Mr. Mescell could have said to Franc, "Franc, you have two options: You can sit down with your group and wait your turn to share your concerns—there will be time to do that in a few minutes, or you can sit up here with me and quietly observe others address their concerns within the group."

Finally, after any of these interventions, the leader should always *refocus the group on the intended learning task* as smoothly as possible: "Okay, let's start by checking in on the concerns that we would like to bring to the group today and then we can get started." These general principles are summarized in Figure 9.1 and, you will notice, support the intervention strategies reviewed in this chapter.

Ignoring

Ignoring can be an extremely effective disengagement strategy for extinguishing minor behavioral disruptions. It can be used when attention to a particular problem is likely to be more disruptive than the problematic behavior itself (ERS, 2005). The efficacy of ignoring lies in how it limits the power and reinforcement potential that sometimes happen with misbehavior. As Larrivee (2005) wrote, "Student misbehavior carries its own limited power and will soon exhaust itself if is not fueled, especially if the behavior is done primarily to annoy the teacher" (p. 52). Ignoring also offers an opportunity for a student to self-correct and save face after a small mistake. Here the idea is to ignore behaviors that are ignorable; respond to behaviors that warrant higher level responses.

We know that ignoring misbehavior can sometimes be very difficult to do, and it also can be easy to take a student's misbehavior personally (Kauffman et al., 2002). Intentional ignoring requires monitoring one's own responses, avoiding blame, and not making interpretations about student intent (because these interpretations typically entail placing blame and may generate anger). Ignoring requires letting go.

FIGURE 9.1 General Principles for Responding to Disruptive Behaviors

While ignoring can be very effective, we also caution that some misbehaviors will escalate when they are ignored. So the aftereffect of intentional ignoring needs to be monitored carefully, and leaders will probably need to move into more assertive responses quickly if ignoring does not produce the desired result. The bottom line for considering whether to ignore misbehavior rests on the issue of safety: if misbehavior is interfering with the emotional or physical safety of others, it must be stopped immediately. It cannot be ignored.

Quiet Attention and Proximity Control

Quiet attention refers to the response of calling attention to a minor disruption in a way that does not interfere with the group process and does not switch the focus from the group activity or discussion to the problem. For example, a simple glance, finger to the lips, or some other nonverbal indication that you will respond shortly can help diffuse a problem before it becomes large and noticeable (Emmer & Evertson, 2009). Jones and Jones (2001) also recommended placing a sticky note on the corner of a student's desk to remind them of the behavioral expectations, and they suggest cueing students to appropriate behavior by reinforcing other students who are acting appropriately. These responses are helpful in that they avoid the potential shame that students may feel when their behavior is corrected publicly in the group (ERS, 2005).

Image 9.1

Proximity control is another nonverbal intervention that can interrupt disruptive behavior before it grows (Bear, 2005; Zirpoli & Melloy, 1997). Proximity control is the assertion of a passive physical presence without interrupting the flow of the group (Emmer & Evertson, 2009). This is most easily accomplished by quietly moving near a student who is off task, often not saying anything—just being nearby. The adult presence serves as a cue to the student to get back on task or to change their behavior. Proximity control can be accompanied by redirection, which serves to scaffold more appropriate engagement in the group. When using proximity control with scaffolded redirection, it is important to use minimal verbal and matter-of-fact statements that are focused on limiting the degree to which the misbehavior becomes a focus in the group. In general, group leader movement around the room or space where the group is being conducted, especially when it is a larger classroom group, is a good strategy for minimizing distractions and keeping students on task, thus preventing problems from occurring in the first place (ERS, 2005).

A related intervention is to rearrange the physical placement of students in the room—performing what was referred to in Chapter 8 as a *structural-type* intervention. For example, a student who is displaying some difficulties with staying focused on the group's task can be moved closer to the leader or can be directed (directed, not asked) to sit with specific students who will not encourage or join in the misbehavior.

Hurdle Help and Interest Boosting

Sometimes misbehavior surfaces when students are having difficulty understanding or following a group activity or task. When a group leader notices that a student is in the early stages of agitation or behavioral dysregulation because of task challenges, they can help the student over the task hurdle by offering simple interventions, such as asking a key question to shift the student's thinking, offering a suggestion or explanation to help the student understand a concept, reminding the student to stay on task since they are close to getting a concept, or reminding the student that the leader is there to help if needed. These small interventions are what Larrivee (2005) called *hurdle help*. Case Study 9.1 offers an example of how hurdle help can be used to redirect a student in a classroom group.

Interest boosting (Larrivee, 2005) is a similar intervention of reengaging a student in a task that they have lost interest in, especially if the student finds it particularly challenging. Here the leader may call on the student, use an animated voice or unique tone, or point to a prompt that will help the student refocus. For example, a school counselor reading a story in a first-grade classroom group used a variety of character voices to go along with each of the characters in the story. In a middle school group, the leader pointed to the task list on the board as he explained instructions. An important advantage of using hurdle help and interest boosting interventions is that they do not draw too much attention to a particular student who is having difficulties, thus avoiding unwanted attention or potential shame.

CASE STUDY 9.1 Hurdle Help

In an elementary classroom group, Ming was challenged to draw a picture of himself. He complained out loud that he did not know how to draw, and even threw the crayon on the desk in frustration.

The counselor saw that Ming's behavior was escalating and decided to intervene by using hurdle help. He approached Ming and asked if he could help him start his picture. Ming responded with a "yes" and handed a green crayon to the counselor. The counselor then asked what shape he should draw to start off the picture. When Ming said, "A circle," the counselor asked him to point to where it should go on the paper and then, quickly asked Ming how big the circle should be. With the instructions from Ming, the counselor drew the circle. He then asked Ming, "What's next?" Taking instructions from Ming again, the counselor drew the neck in blue. Shortly, the counselor stood up and said, "Why don't you take over for a minute. I'll be back. I just want to check to see who else may want help." In this way, the counselor dismissed himself from Ming with the knowledge that he would come back and would help again if needed.

Praise, Rewards, and Positive Reinforcement

The concept of shaping student behavior through positive reinforcement comes directly from the work of behavioral theorists, which we discussed earlier in Chapter 2. *Positive reinforcement* is an intervention that has the effect of increasing the likelihood that a particular behavior will reoccur in the future (Henderson & Thompson, 2011; Maag, 2001). Praise and rewards are two methods of positive reinforcement that are commonly used in schools. For example, a group leader thanked two students for settling down quickly after an activity. A teacher reminded the group that if they completed their work quickly, they would be able to go out to recess sooner. A counselor complimented a student for the "lovely way" he supported another student who was upset. *Punishment*, which we discuss later in this chapter, is intended to reduce the occurrence of a particular (problematic) behavior (Henderson & Thompson, 2011; Maag, 2001). Examples include moving a student's seat to the front of the room after his off-task and distracting behavior or having a student stay after school to complete homework, which is intended to extinguish the behavior of incomplete homework.

Reinforcements and punishments both sit under the larger umbrella category of *consequences*. *Natural consequences* refer to events that occur naturally in the environment and have the effect of

reinforcing or punishing a particular behavior (Larrivee, 2005). Examples of natural consequences are when we feel uncomfortable after eating too much (this would be a natural punishment) or when we feel great after engaging in physical exercise (natural positive reinforcement). Some consider student popularity to be a natural consequence of being nice to others (we would argue that popularity is based on numerous other factors as well). More specifically for a classroom or group setting, praise, recognition, and positive teacher/leader attention are generally considered to be natural consequences that reinforce appropriate behavior (Kauffman et al., 2002), although one might argue that these are under the control of teachers and group leaders and thus fall more easily into the category of logical consequences.

Logical consequences are imposed consequences. They are called logical because they closely and logically relate to the behavior that they are intended to shape (Larrivee, 2005). For example, parents sometimes give their children free time to play as reinforcement for completing their chores. In some high schools, an example of a logical positive reinforcement is when students of good standing have permission to leave the school grounds during a free block. The use of logical consequences in schools is popular because it puts consequence distribution in the control of the teacher (or, in our case, the group leader) rather than at the disposal of natural forces.

The term *reasonable consequences* is used by some to highlight the importance of imposing consequences that (a) make sense, (b) are developmentally appropriate, (c) are related to a personal learning outcome that is student specific, and (d) are focused more on instruction than on punishment (Hoover & Kindsvatter, 1997). Reasonable consequences are based on the premise that most students can be persuaded by reason and fairness to behave in an appropriate way. Teachers often use reasonable consequences to underscore behavioral expectations and to help a student understand their behavioral infraction. For example, Kayla was distracting students in a classroom group by incessantly tapping her pencil when they were supposed to be working quietly. The school counselor asked Kayla to stop tapping her pencil. In response, Kayla broke the pencil and sauntered to the garbage container in the front of the room and threw the pencil away. The school counselor was triggered and told Kayla that she should go to the principal's office immediately. In this example, the school counselor's initial response seemed to be reasonable. But the second intervention—directing Kayla to go to the principal's office—we would argue, was unreasonable. Had the school counselor disengaged by ignoring Kayla's action of throwing the pencil away, the initial problem likely would have extinguished. Or if the counselor had taken the time to assess the purpose of Kayla's distracting behavior or to help Kayla understand why the pencil tapping was inappropriate, then Kayla's response may have been different, and the outcome could have been a valuable lesson about respect rather than an outburst of anger.

Research suggests that affirmative feedback (such as praise) can have strong positive effects on student behavior and performance (Marchant & Anderson, 2012; Tetteris, 2006). This is especially true for younger children (Bear, 2005). Praise is particularly advantageous because it does not cause distress, and it is potentially instructive, especially when it includes specific feedback regarding what exactly the student is doing well (Bear, 2005; Marchant & Anderson, 2012). Bear also pointed out that there are observational learning benefits of positive reinforcement. When students see a peer being reinforced for a particular behavior, they may be inspired to engage in that behavior as well. Thus there is a potential ripple effect of using positive reinforcement to shape student behavior in groups.

There are also a number of valid concerns about the use of praise to manage student misbehavior in schools. One is that offering external rewards such as praise does not cultivate intrinsic motivation. As a result, in the words of Curry and Johnson (1990), "we unwittingly teach children to rely on the judgments of others rather than on their own evaluations based on experience" (p. 92). This concern, then, is that positive reinforcement diminishes intrinsic motivation and children's sense of autonomy, especially in situations where tangible rewards (rather than praise and nonverbal reinforcement) are being used (Bear, 2005). We don't want children behaving in certain ways just because someone told them to do so; we want them to be thoughtful and make their own good judgements about appropriate behaviors. In addition, Kohn (1994) had concerns that shaping desired behaviors through reinforcement techniques can easily be perceived by students as manipulative; he functionally equated positive reinforcement with bribery. Kohn also suggested that a focus on rewards and punishments in a classroom has the potential to damage more important caring relationships between adults and youth in schools.

It is important to point out that using praise and rewards to reinforce desired behaviors is only effective to the extent to which such rewards are actually reinforcing to that student. That is, the success of any particular reinforcement effort really depends on what reinforcement is used for which student. Also, remember that consequences are not just actions imposed by teachers or group leaders; students are reinforced (and punished) regularly through everyday experiences and encounters in and out of school classrooms: groups, hallways, playgrounds, gyms, etc. When a student makes a funny comment in a classroom and other students laugh, for example, this peer attention is likely very rewarding. When a student misses a layup on the basketball court, the disappointment communicated by all of the spectators watching is punishing—that student may be reluctant to try this kind of shot again in the near future. So, group leaders must also be mindful of the ways in which peers in their groups reinforce or punish each other's behaviors. This reminds us that sometimes the best intervention in response to disruptive behavior is to make changes in existing group dynamic patterns. For example, Mr. Long used a structural-type intervention—breaking students into smaller subgroups for an activity—to extinguish the laughing that appeared to be reinforcing the acting out behavior of one of the students in his group. This structural intervention not only improved that student's participation in the group, but it also seemed to help draw out some of the quieter students to participate more actively. The point is that leaders can use a variety of interventions to shape group dynamics so as to shape and reinforce productive student participation in their groups.

I-Messages

An I-message offers a direct communication to a student regarding the effect of their behavior on others (Emmer & Evertson, 2009). The I-message format is as follows:

I feel: _____

when you: _____.

For example, "I feel frustrated when you start talking before I am finished." In some cases, I-messages also include instruction or a specific request for correction. For example, "Please remember to respect the 'talking space' rule."

I-messages can be helpful interventions in situations where a student seems unaware of or has difficulties acknowledging the effects of their actions on others. This mode of offering feedback shifts the level of communication to a human interpersonal level. Most of us are moved when we are able to see how our behavior has affected others. This technique is also effective because it is difficult to argue with someone's testimony about their own personal experience. That is, in the previous example, students would be hard-pressed to argue with the fact that the group leader was frustrated with their talking out.

Returning to Rules

In Chapter 8, we described rules as the articulated behavioral expectations for group participation. We discussed the importance of establishing rules as part of the group norm-setting process, which is typically done in the early stages of a group. Here we revisit this discussion in the context of using rules for responding to disruptive behavior. Reminding students about rules is a fairly common and effective behavior management strategy that is used in many classroom and group settings.

Roughly following the steps for enforcing rules outlined in Table 8.1, leaders can evoke rules in response to problematic behaviors by beginning with a *restatement of the rule*. This should be articulated in clear, simple, nonpunitive language and tone. Next, the leader should issue a *simple instruction*. This instruction may be a simple direction of what the student should be doing at that moment or a declarative expectation that the student should comply with an existing rule. Finally, the leader should *shift the focus* immediately back to the original task or what was happening before the problem emerged. For example, "Michael, remember our rule of listening when others are speaking. Please remember to sit quietly so we can hear Abduliah. Okay, go ahead now Abduliah." If the rule is broken again or the infraction presents a significant distraction or danger to the group, the rule may need to be stated along with consequences for what will happen if the rule is not followed. For example, "This is the second time you have interrupted others in this group, Michael. If this happens again, I will ask you to sit outside of the group for two minutes."

While this type of feedback and correction is not uncommon in schools, we do invite group leaders to be thoughtful about the consequences of using rule reminders publicly in their groups. One benefit of correcting misbehavior out loud is that it also serves as a reminder of group expectations to others in the group. However, doing so can also bring undue attention to the student who is misbehaving, thus reinforcing rather than punishing the unwanted behavior. Worse, this kind of public intervention may also arouse shame, and it can prompt further misbehavior or initiate a power struggle. Decisions regarding public versus private intervention will depend on a number of variables, including the specific student(s) in question, existing group dynamics, the purpose of the group, the level of seriousness of the behavior problem, and the extent to which others in the group may likely benefit from the public restatement of the rules.

We suggest using the intervention cube model (Cohen & Smith, 1976), outlined in Chapter 8, to guide rule reminder interventions. A lower intensity group-level intervention may sound like this: "I just wanted to remind *everyone* that we do not talk when others are talking. We'll let you continue, Abduliah, just as soon as everyone is in the listening position." This intervention does not singularly name any one offender but clearly delivers the message. Alternatively, the leader could offer private feedback to the student who is breaking the rule (intrapersonal-level intervention), probably evoking some intensity but with less scrutiny from peers. This might look like a quick whisper, a nonverbal cue, or it may entail calling the student outside the room to discuss a behavioral infraction. Calling the student out of the room, of course, raises the intensity. But it delivers a strong message and provides an opportunity for more conversation or direction if needed. Either way, responding in a matter-of-fact, fair, and respectful manner—whether it is in public or private—is critical.

Sometimes disruptions happen that do not constitute a breach of a stated group rule, per se, but, nonetheless, are problematic. In these cases, using a group-level intervention is usually sufficient. For example, students in a seventh-grade counseling group were involved in an activity that used clay. When three of the students began to throw the clay at each other, the counselor intervened by stating a new rule: "Listen up, folks. A basic rule here is to respect property, so no throwing clay." While this rule of respecting physical property was never explicitly stated in the group, it was clearly an appropriate request.

A second concern related to correcting misbehavior by restating rules is that it typically does not allow for any exploration of the underlying problem that may have caused the misbehavior or rule infraction in the first place (Kline, 2003). Sometimes, of course, misbehavior is not connected to a significant underlying problem, and a long discussion and exploration is not necessary; the student just needs a cue or a reminder. But when rule infractions occur with frequency, when the offending student struggles with dysregulation, or when we know that there is an underlying trigger that should be addressed, cues and rule reminders will need to be part of a more complex intervention plan that may include instruction and support. We would add that when there are multiple students breaking the rules or misbehaving in a group, a group discussion about the situation is probably warranted. This kind of discussion can elicit a good understanding of what is happening in the group (or what is not happening in the group) that is causing such problems. The group problem-solving intervention outlined later in this chapter is a good model to use for facilitating these kinds of discussions. When issues related to bullying or microaggressions emerge in a group, we recommend a two-tiered response of (1) clearly stating rules (with consequences) and (2) a group discussion to confront the discrimination, intolerance, or bullying behaviors that occurred in the group. This is important as a simple "reminder of the rules and move on" approach can silence important issues (such as bullying) and send the message to group members that there are no significant consequences for students who are disrespectful or aggressive toward others.

Finally, it is important to point out that most students have a good general sense of school norms and expectations, and they also know when rules are being broken. Even in situations where a group leader is encouraging students to develop personal agency and to be assertive when their peers engage in inappropriate behaviors, it is ultimately the responsibility of the group leader to enforce rules and respond to misbehavior in their groups. It is also essential that the group leader is consistent in how they manage disruptive behavior across group members. Inconsistency in responding to group members' behaviors may lead to accusations of favoritism (i.e., that the leader is targeting some students), a perception of leader incompetence, or a loss of leader credibility.

Humor

Humor has a way of putting people at ease, and for this reason, it can be a very useful way of interrupting disruptive behavior and defusing tension before it escalates in a group (ERS, 2005; Larrivee, 2005; Zirpoli & Melloy, 1997). Humor can be especially effective when working with older students (Sprick, 2006). Some examples of using humor to diffuse problems include telling a funny story, retelling a funny incident, making a joke, making a play on words, or using a funny nonverbal behavior or expression. Larrivee's (2005) example of offering a student the "High Flyer Award" when her kite flew off into space during a kiting activity is a good illustration of how humor can be used to diffuse tension.

There are many appropriate cautions around the use of humor as an intervention, however. Humor can be problematic if it is insulting, causes discomfort or shame, is confusing, and, of course, if it compromises safety. Also, it is important to remember that humor sits in cultural and social contexts. What may be funny in one context may make no sense or even be offensive in another. The following guidelines offer important considerations for using humor in response to a problem in the group:

- Humor is sometimes appropriate in response to minor disruptions, but it is not an appropriate response to major disruptions.
- Because it is socially and contextually situated, a humorous statement affects students in different groups differently. For example, a joke about a current TV show will not have meaning to students who have not watched that show. A humorous comment about a material object may be lost on individuals who are not familiar with that object (e.g., a dream catcher or a worry stone). Mention of a particular snowboarding maneuver in a joke will not have meaning to those individuals who have never snowboarded. These comments, then, may unintentionally leave out some individuals and inadvertently underscore social and cultural capital and status hierarchies that are likely already operating in the group or larger school community. The point is to be thoughtful about how you use humor as an intervention.
- Humor can be effective in distracting a problem in the making or in helping a person "lighten up," but there may be an incendiary effect of using humor if it is used

Image 9.3

in response to an individual who feels unheard, unacknowledged, or disrespected. Therefore, think carefully about who is the "target" of the humor and be sure to check that the intent (or the humor itself) was not misunderstood.

- Do not mistake cynicism or sarcasm for humor—they are not. Although sometimes considered witty, cynical remarks often feel like put-downs, and because they are typically ambiguous, they may be confusing to some students. Similarly, sarcastic remarks can be confusing and are easily misinterpreted. Thus, both can have the unintentional effects of making individuals feel excluded and create or reinforce divisions within a group. In short, cynical and sarcastic comments really do not contribute positively to a group in any way (ERS, 2005; Sprick, 2006).

- Humor should *never* be used at the expense of any one student in a group. Collusion with one student against another is always inappropriate and very damaging; this can happen in subtle ways, often through humor. Always be aware of group dynamics prior to joining with a student in humor.

- Humor should not be encouraged when a student uses it to belittle or undermine themselves, their identities, or their abilities. For example, a comment such as, "I am just a girl, what do you expect?" may have a long-lasting damaging effect on how this student sees herself and how she is viewed by others, and these perceptions are easily transferred to other women as well.

- Group leaders should be on the lookout for attacks that are cloaked as humor, and they must be clear that these comments are not welcome in the group. Of course, this means that the group leader should resist using humor in this way as well.

In summary, while humor can be a helpful way to diffuse small potential problems, it is a deceptively challenging intervention, and leaders should be careful when using it as an intervention in response to problems in their groups.

Unhooking From Power Struggles

The need for power—for both children and adults—is not an inherently bad thing. In fact, most educators and counselors would agree that a sense of empowerment is critical for child development—it helps students develop a sense of mastery in their environments (Larrivee, 2005). Indeed, Glasser (1998a) identified gaining power as a basic human need. However, he pointed out that "our needs [e.g., gaining power] push for fulfillment; whether in our attempt to satisfy them we do right or wrong is up to each of us to decide" (Glasser, 1998a, p. 29). So a need to feel powerful is not a bad thing, but sometimes the ways in which individuals seek to fulfill their power need can cause problems.

Charney (1991) described a *power struggle* as a "deliberate desire to challenge the teacher with defiance and insurgence, rather than an unwitting provocation or imperfect impulse controls" (p. 111). As she pointed out, a power struggle is less about not having self-control than it is about struggling with someone to gain power and control; it is a statement of defiance not a show of deficit. Implicit in Charney's description of a power struggle is that two or more individuals are always implicated; it is not an individual behavior.

While power struggles can happen between students or between a group leader and student in a group, we will focus our discussion here on group leader–student power struggles. These kinds of power

Image 9.4

struggles typically transpire in some variation of this scenario: a student refuses to follow a group rule. This disrupts the group, and the leader responds in a way that asserts power—perhaps telling the student to sit down. This furthers the disruption. Perhaps the student refuses to sit down or makes an offensive comment while slowly finding his seat. This action, then, is typically followed by the leader's response that asserts power—a threat, perhaps, that the student will be told to go to the "planning room" if "this keeps up." This assertion is then countered by the student's assertion of power—another comment, perhaps. You get the point.

Working with power struggles such as the one illustrated in the previous example requires that both the leader and the student unhook from the struggle over power. Ironically, often the best way to unhook from a power struggle is to engage in the relationship and to offer an opportunity for the student to experience power. With this in mind, we offer the following recommendations for responding to power struggles:

1. When a student is casting a power hook, listen to their words, feelings, and experiences *without* agreeing or disagreeing.

2. Validate the student's feelings, experiences, and/or concerns—understanding that they are real for that student. For example, if Marissa complains that she should get another turn in an activity because she had less time than the others, listen carefully to her concern and validate it. You might say, "You really feel that it wasn't fair for you and that you should have an extra turn."

3. Be sure not to accuse the student of anything. We recommend discussing the event as an external interaction between the two of you (i.e., a conflict between you rather than a student's problem). For example, "You thought you had less time than the others, and I thought that the time was about equal. So, we have a different perspective about this."

4. Tentatively label what is happening as "a power struggle" or "a conflict" and suggest that the issue be dealt with at another time when tensions are not high. Using these kinds of labels locates the problem as external rather than as something the student has done wrong or as something that is wrong with the student. For example, Junior was not able to meet his goal in a rope challenge and refused to return to the group for the processing activity. This had become a pattern for him and frustrating for the leader. The leader's frustration was exacerbated by the observation that when Junior was successful, he had no trouble joining the group, engaging in the present discussion, and even frequently bragging to his peers about his success. In an effort to avoid being hooked into yet another power struggle with Junior about his participation, the leader said to him privately, "I hear that you think this is unfair, Junior, and it seems that we may even be in a bit of a power struggle about this. Since we're both a bit hotheaded right now, how about we find a way for you to be in the group right now, and then we can spend some time afterward talking about what happened. Okay?"

5. Whenever possible, respond to power requests by granting power. Choices allow for power. When legitimate options are available and students are able to make their own choices, they will have less of a need to assert power over others. The key here is that options offered must be safe, valid, and available, and the decisions that the student makes must be honored as long as they do not endanger themselves or others. So, group leaders need to be sure to structure the choices they offer to be commensurate to the situation. In the example, if Junior continued to refuse to join the group, the leader might say, "Junior, at this point you have two choices: You can join the group now, and we can talk about this later, or if you decide to remain apart from the group, you will not be allowed to join the group later when we get our final reward activity." Weighted choice options such as these (i.e., where one option is clearly more desirable than the other) help structure student responses. But again, it is important that even if the options are weighted, all of the choices must be fair and implementable. Weighted choice options are discussed in more detail later in this chapter.

6. It is usually a good idea to step away from the group to deal with the power struggle, especially if it appears that an audience is reinforcing the problem. If other group members are beginning to exhibit similar behaviors, however, it is probably better to use a group resolution strategy.

7. In situations where a student's behavior is likely to result in additional consequences (in or outside of the group), it may be important to point that out in a nonthreatening and matter-of-fact way. Students must be held accountable for their behavior and fairness dictates that they should have advanced knowledge of what those consequences might be. For example, reminding Coco that she will have to replace any books she destroys is fair. But again, this warning should not be issued as a threat.

8. Sometimes having a specific known language, terminology, or word for behaviors that have a history of being problematic can sidestep prolonged and public conversations about an individual's behavior in the group. For example, the group leader and Loni had begun to use the term "blowout" to describe Loni's behavior outbursts. This kind of language externalized the problem outside of Loni, thus tamping the potential for reactivity. With this common language in place, the group leader could quietly warn Loni that "it looks like we're on the verge of a 'blowout' here," adding "let's not let that happen. I know we can keep a 'blowout' from happening; we've done it before." This language attempts to conjure a partnership; the message is that we can figure this out together.

9. Accusations, interpretations, and judgments are inflammatory to power struggles; these tend to distance people from potentially available constructive solutions. If discussing the situation that *caused* the power struggle is something that should happen, this discussion should happen only after parties are calm and respectful—when the power struggle is over.

10. Keep in mind that ultimately no one can force a student into a meaningful conversation about a problematic behavior or situation. For some students, attempts to do so will have the effect of extending the life of the power struggle. In our earlier example with Junior, allowing him the choice of whether to have a conversation about the problem is an excellent way to give the power back to him. If the leader had insisted that he talk about the problem, this insistence would have robbed him of power and may have even caused an escalation of the power struggle. Of course, there are times when it might be important to have a discussion about a particular situation, even if the student does not want to. But keep in mind that these conversations are rarely constructive when the power struggle is in full effect. The best option is to save the conversation for a later time when both parties are calm and in a position to talk, learn, and/or change.

11. Always communicate your belief in the student's ability to handle difficulties. In the previous example, the counselor pointed out that she and Loni had been able to handle potential blowouts together in the past. This statement communicated confidence and offered evidence of past successes. When and if the current difficulty is resolved without a blowout, it would be a good idea for the counselor to highlight this additional success. Students should get credit and be appreciated for their hard work in solving problems and avoiding power struggles. Prevention is always the best intervention.

Figure 9.2 offers suggestions for how to avoid power struggles from emerging in a group.

Group Problem Solving

When a challenge that emerges in a group—whether it is the behavior of one student, a conflict among members, or a tone, lack of investment, or behavioral challenges displayed by a few students in the group—it has an impact on the functioning of the group and thus becomes a group problem. Typically, group problems warrant group solutions.

Group problem solving refers to the process of having all of the group members working through a problem together. It is premised on the idea that all members of a group have a role to play in how problems are addressed and resolved since the outcome of problem resolution will affect each and

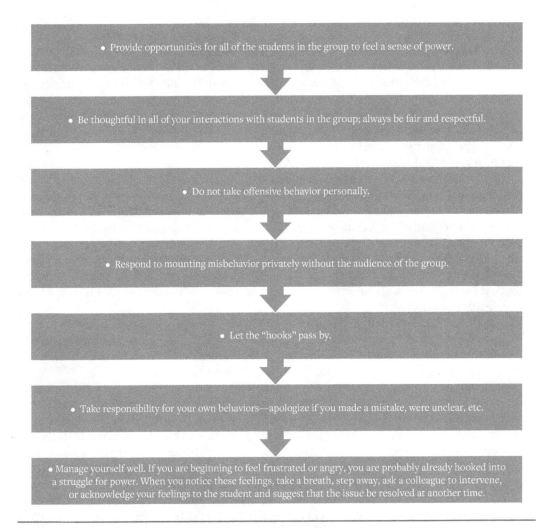

- Provide opportunities for all of the students in the group to feel a sense of power.

- Be thoughtful in all of your interactions with students in the group; always be fair and respectful.

- Do not take offensive behavior personally.

- Respond to mounting misbehavior privately without the audience of the group.

- Let the "hooks" pass by.

- Take responsibility for your own behaviors—apologize if you made a mistake, were unclear, etc.

- Manage yourself well. If you are beginning to feel frustrated or angry, you are probably already hooked into a struggle for power. When you notice these feelings, take a breath, step away, ask a colleague to intervene, or acknowledge your feelings to the student and suggest that the issue be resolved at another time.

FIGURE 9.2 Preventing Power Struggles

every member of the group. Group problem solving also has the educational function of teaching and modeling how students can resolve difficulties with others outside of the group; it can foster trust and genuineness among members; it can also help the group move into the working stage, ultimately fostering group cohesion (Corey & Corey, 2006; Gladding, 2003).

Most models of group problem solving tend to follow a conflict mediation process whereby the leader directs students in identifying the problem and brainstorming solutions. In some groups, students themselves can actually facilitate this process under the direction of the leader. We have adapted Luckner and Nadler's (1997) problem-solving/conflict mediation steps and Popkin's (1994) active problem-solving models in these suggested steps for group problem solving:

1. *Identify the Problem.* Invite students to share their understandings of the problem. Be sure to listen to and respect each member's perspective and insist that all individuals respect each other's contributions and perspectives.
2. *Attempt to Reach Consensus on the Identification of the Problem.* It can be helpful to point out that there will likely be competing perspectives in identifying the problem and that all members can learn from listing to each other's perspectives.

3. *Generate Alternative Solutions.* Attempt to generate a list of possible solutions from all members of the group. Include all of the suggestions offered, even if you do not agree with some of them. Creating a generous list of potential solutions stimulates further thought and communicates openness and respect for the contributions of each student in the group. It is best to display this list visibly (i.e., on a board/chart paper) so that all of the students can see the various options.

4. *Evaluate the Suggestions.* Invite students to discuss the potential solution options. Help them use critical thinking skills to evaluate the various solutions, identifying the potential benefits and drawbacks of each option. This should not be a conversation about the person who offered a potential solution; the focus is on the options on offer.

5. *Help the Students Find a "Best Fit" Solution to the Problem.* Optimally, the group will come to a consensus regarding the solution, but this may not always be possible. It is important to remind students that solutions to problems that affect many people are complex, and compromise is sometimes needed. So, instead of finding "the best" solution, they may need to find a solution that they can live with. This is a time to teach and model flexibility.

6. *Implement the Agreed-Upon Solution by Identifying Specifically How It Will Be Carried Out.* This is the action phase of the model. It is important to involve all group members—those who are and those who are not affected by the problem, those who are enthusiastic about the identified solution, and those who are not as enthusiastic and supportive. This helps generate a variety of suggestions for the action plan. Group members who are part of the decision-making process are more likely to commit to the actions that have been decided on, and when all members are involved, the responsibility is shared. Leaders may need to intervene to help students commit only to actions that are realistic, and they may need to offer specific ideas and offer coaching to help students follow through.

7. *If No Solution Has Been Achieved, Discuss With Members How the Group Can Move On.* Sometimes, group members may decide that the conflict cannot be resolved, but that they can continue to work together, despite the disagreement. This then becomes the solution to the problem.

8. *Follow Up With an Evaluation of the Solution at a Later Date.* Sometimes solutions that have been selected as remedies for a particular problem do not work as planned. If this is the case, be willing to revisit the discussion about the problem and work with students to deconstruct what has gone wrong and to find new solutions.

9. *Intervene Individually With Some Students if Needed.* Even after engagement in a constructive group problem-solving process, some students may not be able to or may decide not to honor the decisions made in the group. If this poses a challenge that disrupts the group or prohibits that student from meaningfully engaging or reaping the benefits of the learning opportunities available in the group, individual follow-up is likely needed. In these cases, the group leader should talk with the student privately outside of the group. This conversation may involve discussing ways to make the group work for this student, bringing attention to the student's behavior and its effect on self and others in the group, and discussing the opportunity for growth and learning provided by the conflict that occurred in the group.

10. *Any Decision to Have a Student Dismissed From a Group Because of a Group Conflict Should Be a Last Option Decision.* Group problems are best resolved when all of the members of the group are part of the solution. When a group problem is solved by removing a group member, the message to students is that the leader has the power to eliminate dissenting voices and, possibly, disrespects student input and ability to change. Leaders must be aware of the power dynamic that exists within their relationships with students, how this dynamic influences their interactions with students, and how it affects decisions about leaving a group. We emphasize that leaving the group decisions should be actual discussions rather than unilateral group leader decisions. Group leaders need to remember that their behavior—in all of their interactions in the group, outside of the group, and in the hallways of the school—serves as a role model for

students. Successfully navigating difficult conversations and solving problems together is a learning experience that is critical for all students. Group leaders have much to offer students when they model effective engagement around conflict and problems.

Choice Options

Used as an intervention, *choice options* involves offering students options from which they can select an appropriate or constructive alternative to their current behavior. Responding to student misbehavior by offering choice options communicates to the student that they are responsible for their behavior and, since they have choices, it also helps them feel less controlled by others (Emmer & Evertson, 2009; Jones & Jones, 2001).

There are a number of ways to offer choice options. An *open choice option* is when the group leader invites students to come up with their own behavioral alternatives. For example, a leader noticed that a some students were off task, discussing an incident that had happened earlier in the day rather than attending to the group activity. He said, "You guys seem to be off task. Please find a way to get back on task" This open choice option can be used when the behavior of concern is not hugely problematic, immediate action is not needed, and students have the ability to make appropriate decisions about their behaviors.

Limited choice options offer students a few options for adjusting their behavior. For example, in a third-grade classroom group, Juana wandered around the room and was disruptive to other students. The counselor said, "Juana, you have two choices: You can join the group you were with, or you can go with Alaya's group over there. Either way, you need to be in a group." This response offered Juana two clearly articulated options for her continued participation in the classroom group. Limited choice options are helpful in providing structure around choices for students who cannot locate appropriate behavioral options in the moment and when the leader wants to minimally respond to the misbehavior and quickly shift back to the task at hand.

Weighted choice options are the provision of options that range in their appeal—some clearly more desirable than others. The point of weighted options is to encourage a decision in a particular direction. For example, a teacher proposed that a student could finish his work by the end of the class time or that he could make it up after school. Weighted choice options are helpful in situations where few real options are available or when, as mentioned, the leader wants to encourage a particular course of action. In the moment in a busy group, it makes sense that a leader might want to use weighted choice options to encourage a student to make a choice that is beneficial to them and the rest of the group.

It is important for the leader to present choice options in a calm and nonpunitive way and to be sure to offer students real and appropriate choices. In the previous example, the options offered

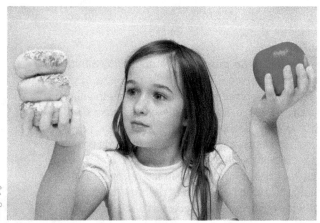

to Juana assume that Juana is fully capable of making a decision about which group to join. If Juana really was not able to follow through on being with a group, the leader would find herself needing to intervene again. So the option of her choosing between two groups would not have been realistic or appropriate in that situation. Of course, there are subtle differences between appropriate and realistic choices. Some options might be *possible* for a particular student but not *appropriate*. For example, Meaghan is a student who prefers to work on her own, who often isolates herself, and who has few friends. Inviting her to choose

Image 9.5

whether or not to participate in a group activity may not be a choice that is in her best interest. In this case, better options might be for Meaghan to participate in a particular activity with or without assistance rather than not at all. In terms of being *possible* but not *realistic*, inviting Juana to join Alaya's group would not be realistic if Alaya's group was conducting their small group discussion in a language that was not understandable to Juana. So in this case, the second group option for Juana would need to be one that she could realistically participate in.

Options that invite students to work in the hallways or after school also warrant caution. These kinds of options are not appropriate if they require supervision that is not available. Keep in mind that when impossible or inappropriate options are offered to students, they are not *real* choices. Offering such options (and then later recanting them) is likely to lead to additional problems for the leader and may leave students feeling manipulated. Also, not following through on the selected option sends the wrong message to students and endangers the effectiveness of this intervention in the future. Finally, choice-option interventions may not be particularly effective when used in response to misbehavior that occurs repeatedly, when the misbehavior seriously compromises learning opportunities for others in the group, or when misbehavior puts individuals in danger. In those cases, a clearer articulation of what is expected—with no options—is probably more appropriate.

Finally, the tone of choice-option discussions deserves important consideration. As with most disciplinary actions, having a private choice-option conversation with an offending student is probably best. This avoids public (in the group) embarrassment and resulting power struggles. Also, it is important to remember that some students may be reluctant (or unable) to actually *verbalize* to the leader what option they have decided on, but they respond behaviorally instead. For example, Meaghan may not *say* that she has decided to join the group, but her *action* of moving her desk back into the group with her peers and raising her hand in response to the next question signals the option she has selected. We suggest that group leaders recognize and be respectful of the various ways in which students may communicate their selection. If a group leader feels strongly that a verbal acknowledgment must accompany a nonverbal choice that is clearly being carried out, the leader can provide this verbalization themselves by naming what the student is doing and validating that the student has followed through on the choice. For example, "I see, Felix, that you have decided to put your papers away. Thank you. Remember that making this choice was also agreeing to sit quietly until everyone else is done." Leaders can also communicate their belief that the student will make good on their decision: "I know that you will be able to follow through on your decision. I have seen you be able to sit quietly when you start to get bored, so I am sure you will be able to do that today."

Punishment

As mentioned earlier, *punishment* is a consequence that is theoretically intended to reduce the occurrence of an undesired behavior (Henderson & Thompson, 2011; Maag, 2001). For example, in response to a student's off-task behavior, a teacher may frown, move the student to a different part of the room, or issue a warning—often called "a friendly reminder"—or some other mild reprimand (Bear, 2005). We emphasize that the purpose of punishment is to reduce the occurrence of a particular behavior, not to hurt, damage, or shame. Punishment can be very effective when used properly, especially if it occurs immediately after the undesired behavior (Leach & Helf, 2016; Marzano, 2003).

The use of punishment to shape student behavior is somewhat controversial in educational and lay-public communities for a variety of reasons. Some philosophical-based arguments against the use of punishment center on the point that punishment is a form of control over students (Moberly et al., 2005). While it is true that punishment and other forms of behavior management are aimed at changing and controlling student behavior, one might argue that there is nothing inherently wrong with controlling, shaping, or changing student behavior at times. In fact, we all experience consequences in our everyday lives that control our behavioral decisions; some of these consequences are reinforcing and others are punishing. Bear (2005) suggested that this concern about punishment is at least in part because of differing definitions of punishment, confusion, and disagreement about what constitutes "appropriate" punishment, and he pointed out that these concerns are also related to larger debates about the role of punishment in classroom management practices. Interestingly, Bear pointed out that many schools use the term "discipline" or "consequences" instead of "punishment" when what they are doing is actually using mild forms of punishment. These alternative terms, while perhaps not theoretically proper, do tend to attenuate concerns about punishment because they sound less foreboding. Of course, when punishment is unfair, harsh, or abusive, it is obviously not appropriate for any setting. We know that excessive use of punishment can cause trauma and result in a variety of mental health problems.

A second concern is that punishment may result in undesired consequences, such as a power struggle or escalated problematic behaviors; students may respond to punishment by exacting revenge or disengagement (Larrivee, 2005; Zirpoli & Melloy, 1997). This is what Patterson (1975, as cited in Maag, 2001) referred to as a "negative reinforcement trap" (p 176) between teacher and student—when punishment results in a power struggle rather than a change in behavior. In the words of Moberly et al. (2005), punishment may lead to the "calculation of risks, blind conformity, or revolt" (p. 360), especially if a punishment leaves a student feeling ashamed, singled out, or unfairly treated. These cautions underscore the important point that group leaders must always be thoughtful (not impulsive), fair, and respectful when using punishment to shape student behavior.

Others point to research that indicates punishment is usually effective for managing minor behavior problems and often has immediate results, but it is less effective for managing more complex and challenging behaviors (Leach & Helf, 2016; Maag, 2001). This may be because, in the words of Skinner (1971), "the trouble is that when we punish a person for behaving badly, we leave it up to him to discover how to behave well" (p. 66). That is, punishment delivers the "no" message, but it does not teach the "yes." It does not help students learn more appropriate alternative behavior. This reminds us that punishment must be used in tandem with other behavior management strategies. This is why we highlight the importance of "catching the student being good" in the recommendations that follow. It is important to think of punishment as only one part of a response package; reinforcement and shaping desired behavior is the other part.

A final point is that punishment does not easily discriminate between appropriate and inappropriate behavior. That is, appropriate behaviors may be unintentionally punished if they occur at or around the same time as inappropriate and punished behaviors (Zirpoli & Melloy, 1997). An example of this is when a student was put in school detention for a self-reported behavioral infraction of engagement in underage drinking on campus after school with his peers. In this example, the student was punished, as per the school policy, for the drinking behaviors. But since he self-reported those behaviors, the punishment also risked deterring him from making an honest confession about his behavior in the future.

Given all of the cautions discussed here, we end with two important points. The first is about tone: How a group leader issues a punishment will affect how it is received, whether it is effective (particularly in the longer run), and how it affects interpersonal group dynamics moving forward. Second is about intentionality. Punishment should never be an impulsive response to problematic behaviors. Group leaders must be intentional in how they use punishment so that it is not only effective in extinguishing a problematic behavior but also teaches students how to engage in behaviors that will allow them to be successful in the group.

Recommendations for Using Punishment

- *Intervene Privately (and Use a Soft, Calm Tone).* Intervening privately helps minimize potential shame and embarrassment, and it also reduces the audience for further misbehavior. For example, when a student was misbehaving in his group, Mr. J said, "We will take a few more minutes to work on these pictures—everyone please continue to work in your small groups for five more minutes. Zoey, can you please come here for a minute?"

- **_Name the Problem Directly._** Begin with a clear statement that identifies the problem or behavior of concern. This should be stated in understandable language, using concrete observations whenever possible. For example, "Zoey, I see that you broke three colored pencils and threw them on the ground."

- **_Provide Feedback Regarding the Effect of the Behavior on You or the Group._** Use I-statements. For example, "I feel a little angry that you're breaking my materials, and I can see that your group members are spending a lot of their work time trying to talk you into not breaking pencils."

- **_Identify the Rule That Was Broken (if One Was Broken)._** This should be stated simply and directly. For example, "In this group, we have all agreed that we would respect school property."

- **_Identify the Consequence of the Behavior (if Appropriate)._** Whenever possible, use choice options. "Zoey, you have a choice: You can pick up the pencils you have broken and put them in the garbage and then get back on task, or you can finish your work during the after-school callback period." Mendler (2005) recommended that students not be permitted to remain in the classroom if they are unable to accept the consequences of their behaviors or if they are unable to come up with respectful or responsible alternative behaviors. So, if Zoey were to become more escalated at this point, an exclusionary time-out (discussed in the next section) would probably be the next appropriate response.

- **_Do Not Require a Student to Verbalize That a Choice Has Been Made: Accept Action as a Response._** The adage "actions speak louder than words" is helpful here. For example, if Zoey begins to pick up the pencils without saying anything, accept that this is her way of indicating that she has made a choice about her behavior. She may also need prompting to rejoin the group after the pencils are thrown away, but do not insist that she verbalize to you what action she has chosen (if her actions obviously indicate her decision). For example, after Zoey picked up the pencils, the group leader commented, "Great. Do you want to join Heather and Maxie now? It looks like they have lots of room at their table over here."

- **_Stay Focused on the Problem and the Solution. Implement Solutions Respectfully._** Do not shame students. Consequences should never insult a student's dignity, nor should they impede a student's engagement or motivation to learn. Avoid moralizing, do not use put-downs, and be sure that the particular consequence is in proportion (in intensity) to the behavior that it is intended to correct (Albert, 1996). Also, it is best to avoid offering interpretations of the reasons for the misbehavior and avoid predictions of the long-term consequences for the student if the behavior continues. Be consistent and fair, and do not allow whining, bargaining, etc.

- **_You May Need to Impose a Time Frame for When a Choice Needs to Be Made._** Indicate that a nonresponse is a choice that also has a consequence. For example, "Zoey, I see that you have not decided which option you will take. I will give you one more minute to make a choice, and then I will have to make the choice for you. My choice will be for you to sit out now and join me after school. You can make a different choice, but you need to make it now."

- **_Always Follow Through on Implementation of the Consequences._** Everything that happens in schools happens in a fishbowl; students are always watching how adults behave. If you do not implement the consequences that you have articulated, the message to students is that you are unreliable. This message can erode trust and invite future behavior infractions.

- **_Return to the Group as Quickly as Possible._** The purpose of a particular group should always be the focus of that group. Do not let a problem hijack a group's agenda.

- **_Communicate Confidence That the Student Will Be Able to Get Back on Track or Select an Appropriate Behavior._** For example, "I know that this is not a great situation for you right now, but I have confidence that you will be able to pull it together and finish this activity. I would be happy to talk with you about what caused all of this, but we'll have to do that at another time. Right now, it's important to get back on track. I think that you can do it."

- *Catch the Student "Being Good" as Soon as Possible After Their Behavior Has Been Corrected.* For example, the counselor offered Zoey a thumbs up immediately after the pencils were thrown away, and she rejoined the group.

These action steps are not necessarily sequential, and they are not easy for all group leaders to perform. For many of us, engaging in these tough conversations requires our own self-regulation. The key, we think, is to allow yourself to slow down and respond thoughtfully.

Time-Out

Time-out is an effective behavior management strategy that is based on the principles of *negative punishment* (Lerman & Toole, 2011). Negative punishment is the removal of a stimulus or reinforcement with the intent of decreasing an undesired behavior. Along these lines, time-out entails removing a student's opportunity to earn positive reinforcement for a specified period of time (Kostewicz, 2010). Everett (2010) pointed out that a time-out "is not a singular 'one-size-fits-all' intervention" (p. 159); there are a variety of types of time-out with "interconnected procedural variables" (p. 159). *Exclusionary time-out* is accomplished by moving a student to a less reinforcing environment—to another room, for example, or a partitioned space within a room (Lerman & Toole, 2011). In schools, we sometimes see time-out rooms, detention, and in-school or out-of-school suspensions. *Nonexclusionary time-out* entails removing the reinforcement that stimulates the undesired behavior but not moving the child out of the environment altogether. For example, turning off music that the student enjoys for a period of time (Lerman & Toole, 2011), planned ignoring (ignoring for no more than about 30–60 seconds), and removal of specific reinforcers (e.g., toys, papers, pencils) for a short period of time. All of these time-out situations should be enforced within a specified and reasonable time frame.

Time-out can be effective in addressing extremely disruptive behaviors, particularly when no other options are available and in life-threatening or critical situations when immediate intervention is required (Lerman & Toole, 2011). In fact, time-out is one of the most commonly and successfully used disciplinary strategies in the United States (Kostewicz, 2010; Lerman & Toole, 2011), particularly in school classrooms (Everett, 2010; Tetteris, 2006). In schools, time-out is typically used when a student chooses not to follow the rules or makes poor choices, and it is clear that an adult needs to intervene to help the student regain control or make another decision (Charney, 1991). Two prerequisites for time-out effectiveness are (1) the current environment (the group) is reinforcing for the student in question and (2) removal from that environment will be perceived as undesirable for the student (Kostewicz, 2010). That is, time-out can effectively shape a student's behavior when that student truly wants to be in the group, and removal from the group is perceived to be aversive in some way. Also, time-out is more effective when it is implemented immediately after the undesirable behavior (Kostewicz, 2010; Lerman & Toole, 2011). Charney (1991) reminded us that there should be an established, predictable, and consistent rule and behavior system in place in the group prior to using time-out.

Image 9.6

Time-out has a secondary benefit for students, as it gives them an opportunity to get away from a situation in order to cool down, reflect, and/or to get composure (Jones & Jones, 2001). Used in this way, time-out is a relief for some students rather than a punishment. This can be helpful for when a student is triggered by others, after a critical incident, and for students who have difficulties with overstimulation and emotional self-regulation.

There are a number of valid concerns about the use of time-out in school settings, and anyone considering using time-out as a behavior management strategy should take these concerns seriously. First, because the implementation of time-out involves giving students attention for their misbehavior—either through the actions of removing a reinforcer or physically guiding a child to a new environment (i.e., walking the child to time-out)—time-out can have the paradoxical effect of reinforcing rather than punishing or extinguishing misbehavior (Kostewicz, 2010). A second concern is that separating students from their educational experience by putting them in exclusionary time-out means that these students lose valuable educational time (Kostewicz, 2010). Third, Kostewicz warned that time-out procedures have "heightened detrimental effects when used ineffectively by inexperienced people" (p. 95). When this happens, children may be at an increased risk of abuse and isolation. Finally, Lerman and Toole (2011) cautioned that in some cases, time-out may result in an escalation of behavior or heightened aggression. In fact, all of the concerns discussed earlier in regard to the use of punishments are also relevant to the use of time-out. The important point is that time-out be used appropriately and only when lower level responses are not effective.

We emphasize that time-out is an intervention that should be used for a specific reason, with purposefulness and intentionality, and with respect and care. It should not be a vague threat that may or may not be implemented appropriately. Also, keep in mind that time-out will not be appropriate nor effective for every student and in every situation. Finally, remember the point mentioned earlier that students who are in time-out will likely miss important learning opportunities that are happening when they are not in the group. One of these important learning opportunities is the opportunity to make amends—to repair the damage caused by their actions. Providing a forum for students to discuss the wrongdoing that has occurred in their group, including who and how it has affected others, can be transformative for youth. Restorative justice practices offer an effective alternative to exclusionary behavior management practices, such as time-out (Kline, 2016). We encourage group leaders to learn more about restorative practice, as it is currently gaining momentum in schools across the country.

Implementing Time-Out

The effectiveness of using time-out as a response to behavior problems rests on how well the procedure is implemented. We emphasize again that the time-out experience is intended to remove the student from stimulation not to hurt, humiliate, or exert control for the sake of enacting power. It is a procedure that must be implemented in a way that is fair, respectful, appropriate, and safe. Also, time-out should be presented as a directive, not a negotiation (Charney, 1991)—this means with no additional discussion—and it should be implemented immediately following the misbehavior. We recommend the following steps:

1. Identify the misbehavior.
2. Articulate the time-out conditions (where the child should go or what will be taken away and the time frame). For example, a timer can be set or instructions provided, such as, "You are to sit here in silence for one full minute." The expectations for time-out behavior should be articulated explicitly at the start of the intervention and consistently enforced. Keep in mind that vague conditions (e.g., "When you're ready …") detract from the intent of time-out and can lead to misuses, yielding the intervention ineffective.

3. Once the time-out is completed, the student should return to an environment that offers immediate access to reinforcers. This should occur without fanfare and as soon as possible. Appropriate behaviors should be promptly reinforced, and efforts should be made to reengage or redirect the student to a more appropriate behavior.

Exclusionary time-out should occur in a space that is *not* reinforcing to the student (Emmer & Evertson, 2009). That means no toys, papers, games, conversations with counselors or peers, or attention of any kind should be permitted while the student is in time-out. These reinforcements can be returned to the student after time-out has ended (preferably after the student has demonstrated a positive behavior). Also, an adult should carefully supervise all time-out spaces. It goes without saying that time-out should occur in a physically and emotionally safe space; students should never be locked in a room and never placed in scary and dark places.

Students should not be released from time-out for inappropriate behaviors (e.g., cursing, shouting, pleading). Two response options for dealing with inappropriate behaviors are to ignore them or give the student a reminder with a choice option. For example, a student can be told that she can remain in time-out quietly until the time is up and if she does not do this, she is choosing to move into a more restrictive time-out situation. Keep in mind that if a long string of time-out reminders and punishments are needed, time-out is probably not an effective strategy for the situation and another response strategy may be needed.

Behavior Contracts

Behavior contracts, sometimes called *contingency contracts*, are behavioral interventions that are sometimes used in a variety of settings in response to disruptive or unproductive student behaviors. They typically include a draft of behavioral expectations, as well as an outline of consequences that will occur if a student is unable to conform to these expectations (Bowman-Perrott et al., 2015; Hawkins et al., 2011; Mruzek et al., 2007). Behavior contracts have been shown to be effective in addressing school tardiness and truancy, academic performance, personal hygiene, and isolation or withdrawal, as well as to promote effective transitions between special education and regular classrooms in schools (Mruzek et al., 2007). Contracts are also used to decrease aggressive behavior; improve attention and school-related, on-task behaviors; and even with clinical issues, such as eating disorders or weight gain (Bowman-Perrott et al., 2015). Most often in schools, we see contracts being used to address repeated problematic behaviors that impede group functioning or when a problem is so severe that immediate intervention is required (Emmer & Evertson, 2009). For example, if a student has difficulty regulating behavioral outbursts when triggered by other students, a contract may be drafted that outlines specific expectations for the student and how the teacher will respond when outbursts happen in class. It may say, for example, that the teacher will cue and remind the student to "take three breaths" when they appear triggered. Sometimes these contracts include a progression of stipulations or contingencies, such as stating that if the student is still having difficulties after the reminders, they will be asked to go directly to the time-out room, etc.

While contracts can be used with students of all ages and to address a wide variety of concerns with modest to good results, it should be mentioned that not all students are responsive to behavioral contracts (Bowman-Perrott, et al., 2015). Also, behavior contracts that are aimed at decreasing undesirable behaviors do not typically have the effect of teaching or shaping desired behaviors (Bowman-Perrott et al., 2015). For this to happen, reinforcement strategies should be used immediately after desired behaviors are displayed (Bowman-Perrott et al., 2015; Henderson & Thompson, 2011). Contracts are more likely to be successful when they are partnered with other intervention strategies (Bowman-Perrott et al., 2015), when students have an active voice in crafting the terms of behavior contracts (Henderson & Thompson, 2011; Mruzek et al., 2007), and when there is home-school collaboration regarding the articulated behavioral expectations and consequences (Hawkins et al., 2011). That is, when a student's caregiver is involved in supporting the goals of the behavior contract and reinforcing its principles at home, the student is more likely to be successful in changing their behavior. In addition, Henderson and Thompson reminded us that the language of behavior contracts must match that of the student's developmental ability; the goals should be written in clear and concrete terms; there should also be a minimal number of steps or contingencies in behavior contracts. Keep them simple!

Some additional benefits of using behavior contracts in schools are that they prompt teachers and others to reinforce prosocial behaviors or skills; they provide an opportunity for a teacher/counselor/group leader and student to regularly discuss and asses a student's behavior as well as group expectations. Contracts can be implemented in a minimally intrusive way, and they are easily modifiable and flexible to use (Mruzek et al., 2007). With all of these benefits, however, it is important to note that behavior contracts are not drafted in the moment of a behavior problem in a group; they are written individually with the student at another time. So, it is not an immediate solution to here-and-now problems that surface in a group.

Drafting the Contract

As mentioned, behavior contracts typically include a clear statement that outlines the expectations for a student's behavior, as well as rewards (i.e., reinforcements) that the student will receive upon meeting the behavioral expectations and any punishments that will result if the problematic behavior continues. They should always be drafted privately between the student and the group leader and at a time when both are calm—not in the heat of the moment. When possible, parents/guardians should also be involved in drafting contracts so that the major premises or goals of the contract are also reinforced at home.

Once drafted, the implementation of a contract often happens in classrooms or other school groups. An example of a contract drafted between Mr. Weaver and Ismael (in response to the problem outlined in the examples below) is included in Figure 9.3. We recommend the following are the steps for drafting a contract.

Step 1: Clearly Articulate the Problem to be Resolved

To help the student understand the problem, offer a clear description of the behavior you observed and a nonblaming account of how you are affected by the behavior. You can invite the student to comment on your observation or perspective.

This conversation will likely be more productive if you approach it from a problem-solving position: as someone who is working *with* the student to eliminate a problem and to promote success. Be sure not to sideline this conversation by lecturing, hypothesizing the intent behind the behavior, or shaming the student. As much as possible, be clear, concise, and specific.

Example
Ismael repeatedly disrupted the counseling group by running into the hallway, and once he even ran outside of the school building during group. The counselor, Mr. Weaver, met privately with Ismael to set up a behavior contract in regard to the running away. He started the meeting by saying, "Ismael, the reason we are here is that I am concerned about you running out of the room when we are in group. I want you to know that I worry when you run out because I don't know where you are going, and I'm not even sure what triggers you to run like that. Also, you need to know that this running is very disruptive to the group." After a pause, he asked, "What are you thinking, Ismael, as you hear me say this?"

Agreement
Ismael R. and Mr. Weaver
1/24/2020

I, ___Ismael R____, agree that I will participate in group by:
        Doing all of the activities
        Working with my friends in group
        Dealing with anger and nervousness by centering
    myself by taking a breath, counting to 10, or asking Mr.
    Weaver if I can sit in the time-out chair.

I, ___Mr. Weaver,___ agree to help Ismael in the group, especially
        when he seems to be having a hard time with anger and
        nervousness by offering to help and reminding him that
        "it's time to get centered."

We both understand that if Ismael runs from the group, he will make
up all missed group time after school in Mr. Weaver's office. He will
have to sit silently for the total amount of time and Mr. Weaver will
not talk to him during any of the make up time.

Also, we both understand that Ismael will not be allowed to go on any
school field trips until he can show that he is able to be safe. This
means that he will need to participate in three groups without running
away before going on a field trip.

Signatures:

_____   _____   _____

Ismael   Mr. Weaver   Mr. R [Ismael's dad]

FIGURE 9.3 Behavior Contract

Step 2: Goal Setting

Once the problem has been identified and briefly discussed, it is time to move on to goal setting. The purpose of goal setting is to create a plan for how to manage the problem in a more constructive way. A good way to set goals, particularly when the student is unable to identify constructive goals themselves, is to talk about what would be different if the problem behavior did not exist: What would the student be doing if they weren't engaging in the problematic behavior? This helps identify a desired behavior.

Once identified, the next task is to articulate this more appropriate behavior as a goal, described in clear, specific, and behavioral language. It is sometimes tempting to write a contract about what the student should *not* do, but basing the contract on expectations for desired behaviors is far more constructive. This helps to create win-win goals (i.e., goals that both the student and group leader agree on) and provides concrete information on what behaviors are expected. It is important to engage the student in this goal-setting process. To this end, we suggest that you offer only as many suggestions as generated by the student. That is, do not hand the student a long list of suggestions—generate that list together. Second, it is important to refrain from discussing the consequences of misbehavior at this point. Here the focus is on getting the student involved in productive discussions about their behavior and identifying clear and achievable behavioral expectations.

Example

Mr. Weaver worked with Ismael to clarify the behavioral expectations and goals for future participation in the group: "You say that you won't run tomorrow. Can you describe what you will be doing in the group if you are not running?" Ismael identified that he will be sitting and listening to others when they are talking and that he will be patient for his turn to talk.

Step 3: Articulate Expectations and Outline Contingencies or Consequences

As you are discussing with the student how you will be involved in helping them reach the identified goals, also be clear about general expectations for group behavior. This can lead to a discussion about how these expectations will be enforced. Balance is helpful here: When identifying the punishments that will occur as a result of continued problematic behaviors, also include the rewards that result from appropriate behavior. Here the reinforcements motivate compliance, while punishments are designed to extinguish disruptive or inappropriate behaviors.

Example

After the behavior expectations were fully discussed, Mr. Weaver told Ismael that he wanted to talk about what he would be doing to help Ismael stick to the contract—the specifics. First, he asked for input from Ismael: "I hear you saying that you won't run out of the room, Ismael, but it sounds like you don't have many strategies for staying when things get really tough. I wonder if we could try to identify one or two specific strategies that you could try that might help you sit and listen, be patient, and stay in the room when things are not working for you?"

After Ismael indicated that he didn't have any ideas, Mr. Weaver offered some: "How about if I help you, Ismael, by pointing out when I notice you starting to get wound up. I will use the phrase 'it's time to get centered' to help you remember. I will also remind you to use the time-out chair if you need to—when I notice that things are still difficult. For each group that you can successfully manage yourself, you'll get a smiley face card. Remember that you can turn smiley face cards in at the school office for a prize when you get ten."

"Okay," Ismael agreed, getting antsy to go back to his class.

"But," Mr. Weaver added emphatically, "because it is so very disruptive to the group when you run, Ismael, I also need to let you know that I will be asking you to make up any group time you miss after school—that is, only if you do end up leaving without permission. This makeup time will happen after school in my office, where I will ask you to sit silently for the total amount of time you missed."

Mr. Weaver asked Ismael to repeat these contingencies so that he could be sure that Ismael clearly understood the consequences he outlined. He wanted Ismael to know how serious the situation was and why it warranted this consequence. Ismael nodded that he understood as he began to doodle on a piece of paper. Mr. Weaver took this as a sign understanding and realized that they were coming near the end of Ismael's attention span.

When contracting with students, it is important to listen carefully and determine the student's motivational level. This will help you to be clear about what, specifically, the student is willing to commit to. Students are more likely to commit to working on goals that seem appropriate and attainable to them. Equally important, the group leader should not agree to conditions or actions that they are not comfortable with or that are not easily implementable.

Step 4: Documenting (Writing) the Contract

While contracting *discussions* are important, contracts are more effective when they are drafted in writing. This allows everyone to be clear about the expectations and contingencies, and documentation adds an air of formality to the process. Written contracts should include the following components:

- the behaviors that are problematic and the desired goals that the student is working toward;
- the specific ways in which the leader, teacher, and/or parent/guardians will support the student (this may include offering cues and prompts, reinforcement, and identifying locations and conditions for time-out);
- the agreed-upon rewards that will be given for contract compliance and the punishments that will be issued for noncompliance;
- the plan/time line for reassessing the terms of the contract; and
- signatures from all parties involved.

Example

Because the school administrator decided that Ismael's running away behavior was dangerous, Ismael was not permitted to go on a walking field trip in school unless he committed to a contract regarding his running away behavior. Also, the administrator decided that Ismael would not be permitted to go on any field trips until he was able to remain in the group without running for three subsequent sessions. The contract that was drafted and signed by Ismael and Mr. Weaver in Figure 9.3 included these contingencies.

Working With the Contract in the Group

Once the contract is drafted, the group leader should always follow its agreed-upon terms. While some students will need little prompting to uphold their contract agreements, others may need more reminders and direction. In these situations, we recommend using a reality therapy wants, doing, evaluation, and planning (WDEP) (Wubbolding, 1988; Wubbolding & Brickell, 1999) approach. Reality therapy is the therapeutic application of Glasser's choice theory (Glasser, 1998b), and WDEP is a specific method of applying the principles of reality therapy. The premise of choice theory is that all behavior is purposeful and directed toward satisfying basic fundamental needs, and it stresses responsibility and action (Glasser, 1998a; Wubbolding, 1988; Wubbolding & Brickell, 1999). A WDEP intervention aims to help students develop insight and take responsibility for their behaviors. We describe how WDEP can be used to help students follow the terms of their contracts when they are back in their groups. In our example here, Selina had agreed to a contract to keep focused on her work in class.

- The W stands for *wants* (including needs and perceptions; Backler et al., 1994). When the contract is based on what the student wants to achieve, then responding with a W response can redirect the student to focus on her contract goals. For example, "Selina, what were your goals—the ones we talked about?"
- The next step in the process is D: *doing*. In this step, the group leader asks the student what she is doing in the moment (Backler et al., 1994). This line of inquiry invites the student to be aware of the problematic behavior, implicitly drawing attention to how it deviates from the contract: "What are you doing?"
- Next is the E: *evaluation*. Here the student is asked to evaluate her behavior with regard to her wants and goals (Backler et al., 1994). That is, the student is asked whether her particular behavior is consistent with her contract/goals and/or with her wants and needs. For example, "Selina, is talking to Carlos going to help you get your work done? Will it help you finish so that you don't have to miss field hockey practice after school?"
- Finally, we have the P: *plan*. Here the student is invited to think about a plan for getting refocused on what needs to happen to meet their goals. In the example, the counselor might ask, "What do you need to do next, Selina?"

A variation of this process can be used in response to problematic group behaviors, even in the absence of a drafted behavior contract. Simply ask the student to name the particular problem that is happening in the group. After the problem has been identified, the student can be asked to evaluate whether what they are doing is helping the group. Next is the prompt asking the student what they will do next to get back on task.

Behavior De-Escalation

Fortunately, most student behavior in schools can be managed through proper planning, overall good group management approaches, and using many of the disengaging and interrupting strategies outlined in this chapter. When the lower level disengaging and interrupting strategies are not successful and problematic behaviors continue to rise to the point of concern, we can say that the student is in a crisis state, and de-escalation is probably needed (ERS, 2005). Behavior de-escalation is called for when a student begins to spin out of control or when a student engages in potentially harmful actions (Damiani, 2006; ERS, 2005). The fundamental purpose of de-escalation is to ensure safety, provide support, and help restore the student's personal equilibrium and self-regulation capacities.

Most out-of-control behaviors are preceded by a trigger that prompts a state of anxiety or agitation (Cavaiola & Colford, 2006; ERS, 2005). This underscores the importance of attending to the warning signs of a mounting crisis whenever possible (Damiani, 2006). Signs that a student might be getting significantly agitated and potentially out of control include a refusal to participate in an activity or discussion; facial expressions that indicate frustration or anger (i.e., a glare); rude, loud, threatening, or inappropriate comments; or physical behaviors, such as pacing or a confrontational stance with others (i.e., looming over others, clenched fists). Group leaders are advised to intervene at these earlier stages of agitation using some of the disengaging and interrupting strategies already discussed in this chapter. Damiani (2006) cautioned, however, to be careful not to escalate these situations by responding to every minor behavior infraction, and she suggested using problem solving rather than blaming or an accusing tone. Also, counselor self-management during these escalations is critical. Do not take dysregulated student behavior personally.

Our response model outlined next is adapted from Roberts's (2005) seven-stage crisis intervention model, which has shown to be effective in responding to adolescents who are in an acute suicidal crisis (Jobes et al., 2005), young adolescents who have experienced loss (O'Halloran et al., 2005), and children and adolescents who are experiencing an acute psychiatric episode (Singer, 2005). As we discuss each of the steps, we invite you to reflect on Case Study 9.2. In this case study, middle school counselor Ms. Grover intervenes with Jake at the very closing moments of their fifth counseling group session.

CASE STUDY 9.2 **De-escalation**

As the other group members are leaving group for the day to go to their next class, Ms. Grover notices that Jake, who has been uncharacteristically quiet and unwilling to participate fully in group for the last 30 minutes, does not get up to leave. He seems to be stewing about something. In general, it seems that Jake likes Ms. Grover, and they have had a positive relationship since sixth grade. Ms. Grover approaches Jake.

"Jake it's time for class, come on—I doubt that you want to be late."

Jake responds, "Shut the f—up, I'm not going anywhere. This group pisses me off. It is a waste of my time—whole bunch of stupid-ass wimps sitting around for an hour wasting my time."

With this outburst, Jake stands abruptly; his chair flips back, and several of the remaining students look alarmed and unsure of what to do. Jake appears startled by the chair and perhaps even by his uproar and language.

Ms. Grover, speaking to the other students says, "Folks, please give Jake some space. You can head to class. Jake will be okay." Then to Jake she says, "Jake, I can see how frustrated and angry you are, and I want you to help me understand what is going on with you right now. But, first, I need to be sure we're in a safe space to talk. Can you show me that you can sit down and talk with me?"

Jake says, "I didn't mean to throw that f—ing chair! I don't want to go to class. I hate this damn place—I'm too wound up. And now I'm screwed—knocking that chair down."

Ms. Grover responds, "I understand that you didn't mean to tip over the chair and that you didn't mean to say what you said. But, Jake, for us to talk about what is going on, I want you to take a seat. Could you take a few deep relaxing breaths, open and relax your fists? I see how tight and clenched your whole body appears right now."

"I should just leave," Jake says. "I'll be suspended anyway. What the hell difference does it make if I'm in this much trouble?"

"Jake we are not talking about consequences now," Ms. Grover responds. "I want to talk with you about what is happening. I want to know what has triggered all this, and I want to support you in making the best decisions that you can now. Leaving, we both know, is not going to benefit you. Can you sit down, breathe, calm yourself?

At this moment, two teachers who have been alerted to the problem in Ms. Grover's room appear at the door. For an instant, it looks like their presence will further escalate Jake.

"Thank you for checking on us," Ms. Grover says to both teachers. "Jake, I'm hopeful that you will make the decision to sit down so that Ms. Rodrigues and Mr. Spruill can leave us knowing you and I will be okay. It is clear that you are really upset right now, and we want you to be okay."

Jake walks to another upright chair, sits, and puts both hands up in front of his face to hide his tears. He says, "This is so messed up. I can't do anything right. I didn't mean to do this."

Ms. Grover again speaks to the two teachers standing near the door, purposefully out loud so that Jake can hear that she is not talking about him behind his back.

"Thanks, it looks like Jake is working to calm himself down. Can you come back to check on us in a minute?"

She turns her attention to Jake. "Jake, thank you for sitting down and beginning to relax—I can see how powerful these feelings are for you right now, and you have begun to do a good job of dealing with them. I know this requires a lot of control and skill. You're taking much better care of your feelings now than a few moments ago." Wanting to telegraph her movements and give him a sense of control, she asks, "Is it okay for me to pull over a chair and sit across from you so that we can talk when you are ready?"

Jake replies, "I guess so."

Mr. Spruill reappears at the door again and asks if everything is okay. Ms. Grover asks Jake to respond to Mr. Spruill, who is wondering if he is calm enough to be safe.

Barely lifting his head, Jake quietly says, "Yes. I'm okay." He appears absolutely exhausted, and his breathing has returned to normal.

Slowly, Jake begins to regain his composure and focus as Ms. Grover sits across from him calmly. It feels like a crisis is diverted, but there is still a lot of work to be done. Ms. Grover then asks him to talk about the problem, and they will work together on developing a plan. Part of the plan that Ms. Grover will introduce is for a debriefing in the group the next time they all meet.

Step 1: Assessment

De-escalation begins with conducting a brief assessment of the student and the situation (James & Gilliland, 2001; Roberts, 2005). In the context of a school setting, we are referring to a nonclinical brief assessment conducted in the moment to determine the extent to which the student is able to manage their affective, behavioral, and cognitive states. Students who are physically assaultive to others, who appear to be in a suicide crisis, or who are engaged in self-harm will require immediate intervention from a clinical professional and, perhaps, law enforcement. In these cases, the group leader should call for assistance immediately. If, however, the student appears to be in a heightened state of agitation but not at this high level of dysregulation, de-escalation can help.

When assessing the student's *affective state*, pay attention to overemotionality or, on the other end of the spectrum, withdrawal or detachment. Extremes in either of these areas may indicate a level of self-regulation that might prohibit the student from benefiting from or participating appropriately in a conversation. Assessment of the student's *behavioral functioning* focuses on what the student is doing. If the student is fidgety or unable to sit still, these may be early signs of agitation. Asking the student to engage in a brief concrete task when in this state, such as putting a book away or taking a deep breath, is a good way to assess their level of self-control and will help determine if more extensive intervention is required. Also, this simple request may actually serve to refocus and de-escalate the student in the moment.

Assessing the student's *cognitive state* refers to determining the extent to which the student is thinking rationally. This is important, as irrational thinking often leads to irrational behavior. Assessing the student's cognitive state can happen by asking the student to calmly tell you what happened. It is important to ask this question in a calm and clear voice and, especially, to listen attentively to the student's response (Damiani, 2006). Gaining an understanding of how the student is thinking about the problematic incident not only helps you assess how the student is making sense of the situation but will also be helpful in later steps of determining how to move toward resolution. In clinical settings, the initial assessment would also include a mental status exam—determining whether the student is able to locate themself in current time and space (e.g., is the student aware of who they are and where they are?), but this would typically be conducted by a clinical mental health professional if needed.

Conducting a brief assessment also requires an examination of the group—how the whole group is responding to the problem or incident. Under the gaze of peers, a student who is out of control may feel humiliated and worry about losing peer respect. Conversely, undue attention from peers may reinforce disrespectful behavior, further escalating the situation. So, it is important to consider how the other students in the group are affected by and how they may be triggering or reinforcing the student who is struggling (Damiani, 2006). If students are sympathetic to their peer who is agitated, they may be able to help by offering support or assistance (at the direction of the group leader). For example, a student who is in a low level of agitation because she does not understand a group task can be paired with another student in the group who understands the task and is empathetic to the need for help. Of course, when a student is moving into a critical crisis stage, peers should *not* be asked to assist; it is not their role to defuse an out-of-control student.

In situations where a student is out of control and potentially poses a danger to others, the leader should call for help and dismiss the other students immediately. Leaders should always seek assistance if the level of danger is high enough to warrant this type of response, and they should never work alone with a student who is dangerous and out of control. Physical restraint should never be used by school personnel who have not been trained in using proper restraint procedures, and this intervention should only be used in situations where restraint is appropriate and deemed a necessity.

Step 2: Engage and Establish Safety

Establish an immediate connection with a student who is starting to spiral out of control (Roberts, 2005). Group leaders can draw on the relationship they have with the student to try to secure a sense of trust and invite the student to see them as someone who is there to help rather than a threat. Damiani (2006) recommended using a calm and clear voice with a medium level of tempo and loudness. She also recommended avoiding confrontational gestures, such as finger-pointing, standing a little to the side of the student (so that the student doesn't feel blocked in) and at about 1½ to 3 feet distance, and trying to find a place where both adult and student can sit. Damiani also underscored the importance of intervening privately, out of view and earshot of others in the group, so as to help the student save face. Added to this, ERS (2005) recommended being careful not to engage in humiliating practices, such as writing the student's name on the board for all to see: not labeling the student by the problematic behavior—for example, don't call a student the "out-of-control student"; and avoiding the use of idle threats (e.g., "if you don't do x, than …"). When working with students who are extremely agitated and somewhat out of control, be careful to move slowly and telegraph your movements (i.e., tell the individual what you are doing and why), do not use threats or ultimatums, be aware of any potential throwable objects in the room near the individual, avoid being cornered, and always have assistance nearby (Cavaiola & Colford, 2006).

Step 3: Explore the Problem

Again, we offer the reminder that most conversations about a student's misbehavior are personal and should be conducted in private. So, as the leader begins to explore the problem with the student privately, they should shift the group to work independently for a few minutes. This is particularly critical when the group is having a reinforcing effect on the student's behavior.

Having an understanding of what happened to cause the problem, especially the student's perspective on the situation, is important. If you have not yet asked, then this is the time to invite the student to articulate their perspective and express their feelings (Damiani, 2006). We recommend treating the problem as the problem (the student is not the problem) and positioning yourself (figuratively) as someone who is standing alongside the student against that problem. For example, "let's see how we can figure this out" signals cooperation against a problem rather than "you need to pull yourself together." "Let's talk about what happened" is different than "what is wrong with you?" This practice, called *externalization*, is used by Michael White (White & Epston, 1990) and other narrative practitioners as a way of reducing defensiveness and blame when talking about problems (Freeman et al., 1997). It frees the student up to be more engaged in problem solving.

Listening is the key here for exploring the problem. Leaders should avoid distractions and give the student their full attention. ERS (2005) added that it is important to exude a calm presence with a confident, professional, and positive demeanor, as these traits communicate that the leader is able to contain the situation, especially when the student is out of control. Paraphrases and reflections are excellent skills for letting a student know that they have been heard, and they also help the student hear what they, themselves, are saying.

It is important to validate the student's experience, even if you do not agree with the events or perspectives that the student has articulated; this stage of de-escalation is not about debating facts and perceptions. In this discussion, it is appropriate to agree with the student when you do agree and to apologize for any wrongs, mistakes, and miscommunications you may have committed. Finally, it is critically important to acknowledge injustices that have been experienced by the student, even if you are not yet sure when or how they happened. For example, "As I listen to you, Reggie, I hear your perspective that the principal was not fair to you when she accused you of taking the money from the classroom last week. You think that you have been singled out because you are Black. I get what you are saying—this is not the first time you have had this experience in school—and I agree that we really need to get to the bottom of this."

Listening includes focusing on more than just the concrete facts and time lines; it also includes listening to the student's emotional experience. For example, when a student appears to be agitated, a comment such as "this looks like it might be very frustrating" signals to the student that you hear them on an emotional level. Of course, caution is appropriate here. De-escalation is not psychotherapy—at least not in the long-term, self-exploration sense of therapy; do not confuse attending to emotion with offering psychotherapy. De-escalation is about stabilizing and providing safety. So, group leaders must listen and validate but also be careful not to invite a student—especially a student who is spiraling out of control—into a therapeutic space that is beyond what they can attend to in the school setting and beyond what is appropriate for their role and relationship with the student. The point of attending to emotion, then, refers to slowing things down, listening, respecting, and supporting. This is best accomplished through the communication of empathy.

At times, it may be helpful for the group leader to articulate their own understandings and experiences into the problem exploration discussion. But this should happen only if the student is in a position to hear the perspective of others and is seeking input, suggestions, or help. If you decide that introducing your perspective would be productive, be sure to limit it to concrete observations that are free of interpretation and delivered with respect and sincerity. For example, "I know that you are angry about what Alana said to you, and that makes sense. But I am thinking that this argument may have even started before class. I'm not sure what happened, but I remember that you walked into the room saying you didn't want to be friends with her anymore." Comments such as these should be delivered with an appropriate level of tentativeness; the idea is not to *impose a* contradictory perspective but instead to merely *offer* another one.

Once you have listened carefully and are beginning to grasp the situation, it can be helpful to offer a clear summary of what has been discussed. For example, "You came to school already having a difficult morning, and then it felt like the teacher was picking on you. I'm so sorry, Kim, that must have been hard. And then that fight with Maya was the last straw. Did I get that right?" This presentation of the problem should be delivered with appropriate tentativeness and include an invitation for the student to clarify or add to what you have presented. This is also a good time to help the student recognize or remember their strengths and past successes—particularly those successes or abilities that have enabled them to overcome similar challenges in the past. It may also be helpful to normalize without trivializing the student's feelings. For example, "I know that it is your first day back, Leo. Sometimes it can be hard to get back into things when you have been away for so long. Things have changed, and it looks like all of us will need to adjust a bit. Huh?"

If students in the group have been adversely affected by the behavior of one group member, they need to be aware that the group leader is attending to and managing the situation. For example, a leader may say, "I am going to continue this conversation in private with Jane so as not to disrupt the group any further," or "I would like the rest of the group to complete today's task while I talk privately with Jane." This lets students know that opportunities exist for student issues to be discussed and resolved with the group leader, even when it's not always done publicly. It also communicates that the leader will protect the privacy of students who are having difficulties (by speaking to them privately). Group leaders do need to be aware, however, that addressing group issues privately with members—without the rest of the students' knowledge—can at times take away from the value, impact, and power of the group to create change for an individual and the group as a whole.

Step 4: Develop a Plan

The next step in de-escalation is helping the student move through the situation toward a livable resolution. Beyond de-escalation, this entails assessing the effect of what has happened and making things right again. For example, if the physical space in the room has been altered, restoring it to its previous condition may be a part of reaching resolution. If the student said some hurtful things to others when she was angry, those relationships will need attention. The student will likely need help thinking about how to regain face, repairing the damage done in their relationships, and reentering appropriate relationships, especially with her peers. It is important that this step focused on resolution not be omitted in the hope that a "forgive and forget" strategy will make everything work out okay. However, none of this can happen until the student is in a fairly regulated emotional state and able to think rationally and engage in appropriate perspective-taking behaviors. Moving into this step prematurely may cause a slip back into emotional agitation and dysregulation. So, it is important to take the time needed to explore the problem and help the student become fairly regulated before moving toward resolution.

We recommend starting by asking the student what they think needs to happen for them to go back into the group or what still needs to be resolved. This invites the student into a relative position of agency. Of course, many students will need help with identifying the issues that remain unresolved or the relationships that need repair. So the group leader will probably also need to contribute to this important discussion.

In this part of the process, the leader should work from a firm, consistent, fair, and empathic position—understanding how hard it is to make amends to people we have hurt. The leader should be careful not to overwhelm the student with a long list of what they have done wrong, how it has affected large numbers of people, and what the student needs to do to make amends. The keys are to keep it simple, promote agency, remember the educational value of restitution, and try to build in opportunities for the student to experience success during this process. To this end, the plan will probably be an outline of specific steps or actions and may also include rehearsal of what the student can say or how they can carry out the plan. For example, Sheri broke another student's iPod when in a rage about something the student said to her. Later, Sheri felt bad about what she'd done and said that she really wanted to replace it or at least make a good faith effort to do so. To this end, the counselor and student needed to create a plan for talking to the student whose iPod was broken, determine the cost of the replacement, and decide if replacing the iPod was even possible, given how expensive it was. The two of them talked about this for a while, and Sheri realized that it was not likely that she could actually replace the iPod (because of the cost), but she knew that it was important to apologize for what she had done. Sheri anticipated that this would be a difficult conversation, so she rehearsed with the counselor what she would say to her peer.

In some cases, a student who has acted out of control at school will face additional school-related disciplinary consequences (punishments) for their actions. For example, most schools have articulated policies around breaking school rules, especially when student behavior has caused harm or destruction to others or school property. These may be imposed by the leader of the group, by the teacher of the class, by a school administrator, by parents, or by legal or law enforcement authorities. In many situations, the student may or may not be fully aware of the impending consequences, and they were most certainly not thinking about them when they were spiraling out of control. Some group leaders may feel that discussions about these issues are not appropriate for their role and that disciplinary actions should be left to whomever in the school is responsible for enforcing them. But we believe that it may be helpful to alert students to these potential consequences so that they are better prepared to hear them, thus serving as a preemptive intervention to avoid further escalation. If rule infractions occurred within the group without spilling over into the larger school community, the group leader is the person who is ultimately responsible for monitoring group safety and ensuring that the rules are followed. This may entail issuing small consequences for improper behavior. Avoiding this duty may run the risk of sending a message to group members that the rules are not important, will not be enforced, or that some students do not have to follow the rules.

All of these conversations, of course, should happen at a time when the student has gained composure—the student is in a regulated state with clear and rational thinking capacities. The leader should use clear, matter-of-fact language and validate the student's perceptions and feelings (i.e., "I know that this is hard to hear." "I understand that this is upsetting") but also be firm without backing down if the student argues, denies, and blames (ERS, 2005). As with all disciplinary actions, these conversations should happen privately and not involve any shaming, blaming, or humiliation.

Step 5: Follow-Up

It is important to see the de-escalation process through by monitoring the student after the incident to provide continued support. For many students, follow-up may also entail drafting long-term plans to help avoid future difficulties. In fact, helping students develop a sound repertoire of affect management and coping skills is likely going to be one of the most important follow-up measures that many students will need. In addition, if any consequences were implemented as a result of the incident, those should be included in the follow-up as well. This is because some students may need help understanding, accepting, and adhering to consequences, especially if they believe that the consequences were unfair, if they lack insight into the impact of their actions, or they continue to struggle with emotion or behavioral self-regulation.

In situations where a student has not been able to calm themselves fully and/or when issues of harm to self or others remain, even remotely, appropriate duty-to-warn protocols must be followed (James & Gilliland, 2001) as per the code of ethics in the counseling profession (ACA, 2014; ASCA, 2016; ASGW, 2007). Cobia and Henderson (2007) pointed out that most schools have policies regarding reporting threats of harm. They remind us to take every threat seriously and for school counselors to consult and document all actions involving protection from harm. Even if questions of harm to self or others do not surface, the issue of informing parents and school administrators about even milder forms of these incidents warrants careful consideration. School counselors are required to operate under the policies of the school in which they work (Linde, 2007), and parents and legal guardians have the right to be informed of what is happening in their child's experience at school. The *Ethical Standards for School Counselors* (ASCA, 2016) indicates that school counselors have a duty to "provide parents/guardians with accurate, comprehensive and relevant information in an objective and caring manner, as is appropriate and consistent with ethical and legal responsibilities to the student and parent" (Code B.1.h). Most schools have policies and protocols related to informing parents and caregivers about student disciplinary actions.

In terms of notification to other staff and personnel in the school, the ASCA (2016) Code of Ethics clearly states in Standard A.2.e that school counselors should

> keep information confidential unless legal requirements demand that confidential information be revealed or a breach is required to prevent serious and foreseeable harm to the student. Serious and foreseeable harm is different for each minor in schools and is determined by students' developmental and chronological age, the setting, parental rights and the nature of the harm. School counselors consult with appropriate professionals when in doubt as to the validity of an exception.

This means that informing administrators about incidents that require de-escalation, as well as seeking their input on appropriate consequences, is appropriate so long as administrators also respect the confidential nature of a school counselors' role and treat consultations as confidential interactions. In many schools, these kinds of incidents warrant immediate referral to instructional support teams or services. At the very least, an incident serious enough to warrant de-escalation should prompt coordinated action plans among teachers, administrators, and counselors to determine a plan of support and prevention against further incidents. Coordinated efforts with school personnel and parents or guardians assure that consistent and adequate supports will be put into place. Working as a team composed of multiple players increases the likelihood of implementation and success.

Final Comments

Tatum (1997) powerfully pointed out that many of us have early memories of race relations that are shrouded by emotions such as anger, confusion, sadness, surprise, and embarrassment. These memories are typically rooted in our observations of the world around us, beginning in early childhood. Little discussion or meaning making about these observations sends a loud and powerful message: This is unspeakable. In Tatum's words, "Children who have been silenced often enough learn not to talk about race publicly. Their questions don't go away, they just go unasked" (Tatum, 1997, p. 36). When observations and curiosities about race are not silenced, Tatum argued, opportunities for learning how to spot and resist racism, strategies for responding to injustice, and occasion for critical thinking are possible.

We call attention to Tatum's point about children's observations and the learning that is gleaned from these observations because it has relevance here in our final chapter on responding to problems in groups. We want to raise awareness of the issue of what others see and subsequently learn when a peer is being disciplined in a group. The group experience is a public experience—all of the members of the group are watching, and they are learning something when they see us intervene in response to problems in the group. So, we must ask, Who are the children who "get in trouble" in the group (and at school)? Are intervention practices distributed widely among children in our groups (and in our schools)? What messages about race, gender, sexual orientation, socioeconomic class (and other nondominant group membership) are unintentionally promoted, and what subtle social practices are reinforced through the discipline interventions in our groups (and in the larger school community)? What do others see when they look at what is happening in our group? In our school?

A new paragraph here is intended to give pause to our previous comments and then follow up with some quick clarifying points on this discussion. First, we must clarify that our intent is *not* to advocate for not intervening when the behaviors of children from under-represented minority groups are disruptive to the learning goals of our groups. Let us be clear: If there is a problem behavior in the group, it must be addressed—no matter who has exhibited the problematic behavior. What we do want to point out, however, is that research shows that racial minority children are the target of discipline in schools at higher rates than white students and that their punishments, especially for African American children, are often more severe than that of their white peers (see Petrilli, 2017; Steinberg et al., 2017; Townsend, 2000; U.S. Department of Justice Civil Rights Division & U.S. Department of Education Office of Civil Rights, 2014). The actions of counselors, teachers, staff, and administrators in schools do not go unnoticed by students. When students become aware that some children in the group always seem to be the ones in trouble, the messages to all students in the school are powerful, damaging, and may take a lifetime to repair.

More to the point, if it is the children who are from minority or marginalized groups who always seem to be getting in trouble, then perhaps the individual discipline problem is more symptomatic of a larger issue that is institutional and community based. And so, while intervention must address the individual, it must also be a part of an effort to combat the larger issue that creates problems unequally for some students in the school. For example, Shella, a fifth-grade student who moved to a suburban elementary school a year ago, was initially popular but over the last year appeared to have few friends. With her popularity in decline, teachers noticed an increase in her disruptive classroom behavior; soon it was characterized as "attention-getting" behavior. The school counselor began to worry, as she noticed an edge of anger in Shella's behavior. After talking to Shella's mothers, she learned that Shella's family had been maligned by some in the community because the mothers are in a same-sex relationship. So, while Shella's disruptive and angry behavior is of concern and needs to be addressed, the context of that behavior is of equal concern. In another example, a number of parents came to the school counselor because a popular young man on the football team (whose parents were, by the way, very active in the school athletic booster club) was caught at an underage drinking party and was not penalized by being prohibited to play in the next football game, which was school policy. These concerned parents were outraged because only a year before, a similar incident happened with a student on the team whose parents were not involved at the school, and he was suspended for the next 2 weeks of practices and games.

We would be naïve to believe that such inequities do not exist in our educational system at large. Just as the profession of school counseling has asked that school counselors take action on such inequities, such as these within their schools (see ASCA, 2016; Dahir & Stone, 2012; Holcomb-McCoy, 2004; Paisley & Milsom, 2006/2007; The Education Trust, 2009), we ask you here, at the close of our book, to pay attention to these issues in your groups, in your schools, in your communities, and in the larger society. Simply put, our point is this: Context does matter and intervention sometimes needs to extend beyond the individual.

Reflection Questions

1. What are some strategies that a group leader can use to manage other students in a group when an individual student is spiraling into a dysregulated state?
2. What are some of the important variables that should be considered when deciding whether a student should be removed from a counseling group (permanently)?
3. What are some strategies that group leaders can use to address issues of inequity that exist in the larger school community and are being enacted within their groups (i.e., the group dynamics)?

Credits

APPENDIX A: ELEMENTARY-LEVEL SAMPLE CLASSROOM GROUP PLAN

Identity Expression *Unit* Plan

Topic: Identity expression (part of bullying/harassment curriculum)

Grade/Class: First grade

Approximate Number of Students: 18 students

Rationale: One of the social-emotional learning curricula in the district aims to promote openness and understanding of marginalized identities within school systems. A second goal within this curricula focuses on developing anti-bullying and anti-harassment behaviors. The district school counselors believe that to achieve these aims, students must be exposed to conversations about difference, be encouraged to be curious, and develop compassion for others; this starts with the very youngest children in the district.

District plan competencies addressed in the group: Elementary-Level Social Competencies 2, 3, and 8 and Elementary-Level Personal Competencies 5 and 8.

Goals for Unit:

1. Students will explore concepts of personal identity development.
2. Students will explore concepts of personal identity expression.
3. Students will explore differences within their classroom community.
4. Students will embrace differences within their classroom community.

Unit Lessons: Five total (35 minutes per lesson)

Assessment Plan:

- Students will explore concepts of personal identity development.
  - ° Observation of students' participation in and reactions to classroom discussions (Lessons 1-5)
- Students will explore concepts of personal/identity expression.
  - ° Observation of students' participation in and reactions to classroom discussions (Lessons 1-5)
- Students will explore differences within their classroom community.
  - ° Observation of students' participation in and reactions to classroom discussions (Lessons 1-5)

- Students will embrace differences within their classroom community.
  - ° Observation of student engagement with each other in classroom discussions (Lessons 1-5)

Source: Adapted from Santacross, G. (2020, February). *Informal case presentation.* Class assignment for EDCO 389 Counseling Internship. University of Vermont.

Identity Expression Classroom Group *Lesson* Plan

Lesson: Two (of five)

Grade/Class: First grade

Approximate Number of Students: 18 students

Plan:

- Seat students in a circle around the leader (who will sit on the chair)
- Mindfulness moment (with chimes)
- Learning map:
  - *Today, we will be reading the book Bunnybear by Andrea Loney.*
  - *After that, we will play a little game called "The Wind Blows For ..." as we discuss the book.*
  - *Has anyone read this book before?*
- Ask students to sit "story style" on the floor. Offer reminders about "hands in lap" and "respectful listening."
- Read *Bunnybear*, stopping for understanding checks or clarifications.
- Processing questions:
  - *Why do you think that the other bears did not understand Bunnybear?*
  - *Do you think it's important that all bears act the same? Is it okay to be different? Why do you think so?*
  - *Why do you think Bunnybear has a difficult time making friends?*
- "The Wind Blows For ..." activity:
  - The counselor calls out "*the wind blows toward the side of the room where _____.*" Everyone who matches up with what was said has to get up and move to the side of the room where the counselor is pointing with the plastic candle.
  - Prompts:
    - *Like recess*
    - *Like school*
    - *Like to get up in the morning*
    - *Like to eat vegetables*
    - *Like to play soccer*
    - *Like to dance*
    - *Like to read*
  - Processing questions:
    - *Was it hard to make a decision about whether you liked something or not?*
    - *What was it like when some of your friends didn't move where you were going?*
    - *Do you think this is what happens for Bunnybear when hard to be different from the other bears?*
    - *Were you in a small group? Big group? How was that?*
- Summary:
  - *Today, we talked about Bunnybear and what it was like for him to be different than the other bears. We also talked about some of the ways all of you are the same and different from each other.*

º *The important thing we want to remember—and we will talk about this again next week—is that there are lots of ways of being, and it's okay to be the same as others in some ways and different from others in other ways. It's okay to be different.*

Materials:

- Mindfulness chimes
- *Bunnybear* by Andrea Loney (ISBN-10: 0807509388, Pub: Albert Whitman & Company, 2017)
- Plastic candle (for "The Wind Blows For …")

Source: Adapted from Santacross, G. (2020, February). *Informal case presentation. Class assignment for EDCO 389 Counseling Internship.* University of Vermont.

APPENDIX B: ELEMENTARY-LEVEL SAMPLE COUNSELING GROUP PLAN

Friendship Group *Unit* Plan

Topic: Friendship group

Grade/Class: Second grade

Approximate Number of Students: Four to six

Rationale: Through peer groups, children develop many personal, social, and academic skills, such as leadership, empathy, and teamwork. Children also develop cultural awareness, such as race, gender, and socioeconomic status, among others. Children who struggle to form friendships sometimes become passive, aggressive, isolated, disengaged, and nonparticipatory in their academic learning. This group is designed to help students develop social skills that are facilitative of healthy friendship development and that have positive implications for their academic learning.

Goals for Unit:

- Students will learn and identify the characteristics of a *good friend*.
- Students will learn strategies for and practice cooperation, turn-taking, and working with peers.
- Students will learn strategies for and practice assertiveness.

Number of Sessions: 6 weeks—35 minutes per session

Group Assessment Plan:

Goal 1: Students will learn and identify the characteristics of a *good friend*:
- List generated in friendship brainstorm (Session 2)
- Content of friendship collage (Session 5)

Goal 2: Students will learn strategies for and practice cooperation, turn-taking, and working with peers:
- Counselor observation of student behaviors:
  ○ Name Game (Session 1)
  ○ Cooperation Game (Session 2)
  ○ Friendship Group Activities (Sessions 3 and 4)
- Student report in final checkout (Session 6)
- Teacher report (use the teacher feedback form)

<u>Goal 3</u>: Students will learn strategies for and practice assertiveness:
- Student participation (observation by the counselor) in the following:
  ° Assertiveness training/practice I (Session 5)
  ° Assertiveness training/practice II (Session 6)
- Student report in final checkout (Session 6)
- Teacher report (use the teacher feedback form)

Source: Adapted from Lewis, N. (2007, May). *Developmental guidance small group counseling plan: Friendship group.* Class assignment for EDCO 340 Developmental Guidance in Schools. University of Vermont.

Friendship Group Teacher Feedback Form

Teacher Name: _____ Student Name: _____

One of the goals for this group was for students to learn strategies for turn-taking, working with peers, and appropriate assertiveness. Please comment on any changes you have noticed that this student has made in these areas.

_____

_____

_____

_____

One of the goals for this group was for students to learn about friendship. Do you notice any changes in how this student is approaching peers or in how this student is making or acting with friends? If so, please explain.

_____

_____

_____

_____

Comments, suggestions, additional needs for this student:

_____

_____

_____

_____

Thanks for taking the time to respond to this survey!!!!!

Elementary-Level Counseling Group Session Plan

Friendship Group: Second grade

Group Session: Four

Session Objectives:

- Students will identify the characteristics of a *good friend*.
- Students will work cooperatively.

Plan:

1. Welcome students back and review the last session's topics/activities:
   - Quick review of group rules
   - Quick review of the first three sessions:
     - We worked on listening to each other as we got to know each other.
     - We worked on taking turns: why it is important to and how it sometimes is hard to take turns.
     - We talked about *what is a friend* (characteristics). Take out the poster created last week.
2. Today, we are going to talk about *what being a friend* looks like.
   - Take out sample picture 1 (does not illustrate friendly behavior) and show students:
     - *Does it look like these two people are friends in this picture?*
     - *What do you see that says so? Not?*
     - *How do you think these children feel when they are together in this picture?*
   - Take out sample picture 2 (illustrates "friendship"):
     - *What do you see that says "friendship"?*
     - *How do you think the children in this picture feel when they are together?*
3. Now we are going to work on creating a friendship collage. Explain what a collage is if students don't know. Here are the rules:
   - You must create one collage for the group. This means that you will need to work together to select which pictures to put onto the collage.
   - You must decide who gets to cut out which pictures.
   - You must decide how to arrange the pictures on the poster board and how to use the markers to create a message on the board about the pictures (show example).
   - After you make these decisions, let me know, and I will pass out the glue so that you can glue the pictures in the spots.
4. Questions?
5. Place magazines on the table with scissors (the leader will probably have to help with the cutting).
6. While students work, structure their group behavior in order to highlight the friendship skills they are using. Scaffold inappropriate behaviors if necessary. If students are not acting appropriately, process in the group by reviewing the rules for the group and the friendship characteristics mentioned last week.
7. At 10 minutes remaining: Give a time warning and start to pick up.

8. At 5 minutes remaining: Ending round/processing question:
   - *What actions in the group did you notice that your classmates were using that were good friendship skills (add observations)?*
   - *What did you have to do yourself to be a friend to others? Was this hard sometimes? How did you manage to be a friend and share when you really didn't want to?*

Materials:

- Group rules list
- Sample pictures and example poster
- Friendship characteristics list from the last week
- Magazines
- Scissors
- Glue
- Poster board
- Markers

Source: Adapted from Lewis, N. (2007, May). *Developmental guidance small group counseling plan: Friendship group.* Class assignment for EDCO 340 Developmental Guidance in Schools. University of Vermont.

APPENDIX C: MIDDLE-LEVEL SAMPLE CLASSROOM GROUP PLANS

Media Influences on Body Image *Unit* Plan

Topic: Media influences on body image

Grade/Class: Sixth grade (health classes)

Approximate Number of Students: 18–25 per class

Rationale: Unhealthy eating and dieting behaviors often lead to eating problems, which are increasingly prevalent in preadolescence. While there are many causes of eating disorders, research suggests that one of the major influences is negative body image. Research indicates that one of the most effective ways to confront problems in body image is to have students critically examine the link between body image and the media. This unit is designed to help students develop "media literacy" or to critically examine the ways in which the media influences our ideas about our bodies and body image.

District developmental guidance plan standards addressed in the lesson:
- 2.14 Critical Thinking Skills
- 3.4 Healthy Choices
- 3.7 Decision Making
- 3.1 Personal Health

Goals for Unit:

1. Students will critically examine the ways in which men's and women's bodies are portrayed in the media and society in general.
2. Students will understand the ways in which ideas about body image are socially and culturally constructed.
3. Students will distinguish between healthy and unhealthy body images.
4. Students will determine an appropriate "body type" for themselves. (This is also a health class goal.)
5. Students will develop "refraining from comment" skills for not engaging in body image comments and self-perceptions.

Unit Lessons: Six total
- Lesson 1: Let's Get Real Part 1 (school counselor and health teacher)
- Lesson 2: Let's Get Real Part 2 (school counselor and health teacher)
- Lesson 3: Body Mass Indicators Part 1 (health teacher)
- Lesson 4: Body Mass Indicators Part 2 (health teacher)

- Lesson 5: Refraining From Comment (school counselor)
- Lesson 6: Refraining From Comment (school counselor and health teacher)

Assessment Plan:

Goal 1: Students will critically examine the ways in which men's and women's bodies are portrayed in the media and society in general.
- Student participation in "Let's Get Real" and "Refraining From Comment" discussions/activities (see processing questions in the lesson plans)
- Reflection question written at the end of each week (as per the weekly reflection prompt)
- Body image questionnaire pre (Lesson 1)/post (Lesson 6)

Goal 2: Students will understand the ways in which ideas about body image are socially and culturally constructed.
- Student participation in "Let's Get Real" discussion questions (see processing questions in Lesson 1 and 2)
- Reflection question at the end of Lessons 1 and 2 (see prompts in the lesson plans)
- Body image questionnaire pre (Lesson 1)/post (Lesson 6)

Goal 3: Students will distinguish between healthy and unhealthy body images.
- Student participation in "Let's Get Real" discussion questions (see the processing questions in Lesson 1: "Let's Get Real")
- Reflection question written at the end of each week (as per the weekly reflection prompt)
- Body image questionnaire pre (Lesson 1)/post (Lesson 6)

Goal 4: Students will determine an appropriate "body type" for themselves (Sessions 4 and 5 conducted by the health teacher).
- Body image questionnaire pre (Lesson 1)/post (Lesson 6)
- Body mass assessment (see the health class assignment/assessment for Lessons 4 and 5)
- Participation in the body mass assessment and discussion (see the processing questions)

Goal 5: Students will develop "refraining from comment" skills to avoid engaging in body image comments and self-perceptions.
- Participation in the discussion of cognitive reframing: unhelpful self-talk
- Participation in discussions/class list of "no comments"
- Reflection question written at the end of Lessons 5 and 6 (see the reflection questions)
- Body image questionnaire—post (final lesson)

Source: Adapted from Dickerson, K. (2006, May). Individual project: Developmental guidance unit plan and small group counseling session outline. Class assignment for EDCO 340 Developmental Guidance in Schools. University of Vermont.

Middle-Level Classroom Group
Sample *Lesson* Plan

Media Influences on Body Image—Week 2: "Let's Get Real" (Part 2)

Grade/Class: Sixth grade (health classes)

Time: 45 minutes

Learning Objectives:

1. Students will distinguish between healthy/unhealthy media images.
2. Students will become aware of how body image is socially and commercially constructed.

Plan:

1. Review last week's lesson (video/TV/magazine extravaganza, clips of men/women) and discussion points (5 minutes).
2. Present the video clip from "Extremely Perfect" (CBS 48 *Hours* news documentation about how media makes celebrities perfect; Stahl & Maher, 2003) (20 minutes). <u>Note</u>: Although this is an older documentary, the ideas are still relevant, so it would be good to mention this to students/or include in discussion below.
3. Discussion. "Let's Get Real" Lesson 2 processing questions (15 minutes):
   * *Why do you think advertisers change the way people look?*
   * *How do standards of beauty become determined?*
   * *How might media and social images/words affect how people feel about their bodies? Do they affect you personally?*
   * *What are some ways in which teens can have healthy bodies and healthy body images?*
   * *How can teens develop healthy bodies and healthy body images?*
4. Closing round: *What stands out for you from today's discussions?*
5. Exit card (prompt on handout—students submit this at the end of the group—for discussion later [anonymous responses]).

Materials:

* *48 Hours* "Extremely Perfect," (Stahl, L. (Host) & Maher, M. (Special Correspondent). (2003, April 30). Extremely perfect [TV series Season 16, Episode 35]. In S. Zirinsky, (Executive Producer). *48 Hours*. New York: CBS News.)
* Reflection Question #2 (handouts—attached MAKE COPIES!!)

Source: Adapted from Dickerson, K. (2006, May). *Individual project: Developmental guidance unit plan and small group counseling session outline. Class assignment for EDCO 340 Developmental Guidance in Schools.* University of Vermont.

"Let's Get Real" Reflection Question #2:
What kinds of thoughts and feelings do you have about your body that may be influenced by others? Are these thoughts/feelings helpful/healthy?

APPENDIX D: MIDDLE-LEVEL SAMPLE COUNSELING GROUP PLAN

Stress Management Group Unit Plan

Topic: Stress management

Grade/Class: Seventh or eighth grades

Approximate Number of Students: Approximately six

Rationale: Middle school is a time of great social and academic stress for many students—compounded by physical and hormonal changes in their bodies. An inability to manage stress appropriately can lead to inappropriate behavior, with effects on students' social, personal, and academic lives. The focus of this group is to help students who have been identified as having difficulties with anxiety acquire helpful stress management strategies.

Goals for the Group:

- Students will recognize the signs of stress.
- Students will gain an understanding of how individuals are affected by stress.
- Students will develop skills for managing stress.
- Students will identify support systems in school that can help them with stress.

Number of Sessions in Unit: 6 weeks—30 minutes per session

Group Assessment Plan:

1. Students will recognize the signs of stress.
   - Student participation in discussion (all sessions)
   - Student participation in "Where Is the Stress?" activity (Session 1)
   - Student responses on the "What I Learned" questionnaire (Session 6)
2. Students will gain an understanding of how individuals are affected by stress.
   - Student participation in group discussion (all sessions)
   - Student responses on the "What I Learned" questionnaire (Session 6)
3. Students will develop skills for managing stress.
   - Student participation on the "Healthy/Unhealthy Expression Worksheet" activity
   - Student responses on the "What I Learned" questionnaire (Session 6)
   - Referral teacher to report at follow-up
4. Students will identify support systems in the school that can help them with stress.
   - Participation in the discussion (Session 6)
   - Student responses on the "What I Learned" questionnaire (Session 6)

Source: Adapted from Kearns, L. (2007, May). *Six week small group counseling lesson plan.* Class assignment for EDCO 340 Developmental Guidance in Schools. University of Vermont.

Middle-Level Counseling Group Session Plan (Week 4)

Topic: Stress management

Grade/Class: Seventh or eighth grade

Session: Week 4 (of 6)

Session Objective:

- Students will develop strategies for managing stress (Part 1).

Plan:

Check-in questions (whip rounds):
- *Where did you notice your stress this past week (refer back to week 2 exercise)?*
- *Did the stress you felt correspond to a particular event (referring to last week), or was it general stress?*
- *Did anyone notice the thoughts they had that might have increased their stress levels (reflecting back on last week's discussion on "unhelpful thoughts")?*

Introduce the agenda:
- Ways to get a handle on stress. Today, we will talk generally about some helpful tips. Next week, we will talk about using your thoughts to control your stress feelings.

Anything to add to the agenda?
- Do students have any particular stress-related incidents that they need the group to help them with?

"Getting a Handle on Stress" worksheet (see attached):
- Read through each item. Have the students comment or give examples and discuss how the strategies may help.
- Have students check in blue the items they feel that they're pretty good at already. Check in red those that they would like to use more.
- If the discussion is fluid, allow the group to talk.

Commit to trying one of the following suggestions this week:
- Circle an item on the "Getting a Handle on Stress" worksheet to try.
- Discuss: *What might get in the way of you being able to use this strategy?*
- Discuss: *How will you push through the resistance?*

Closing:
- *What are you taking from the group today that will help you with stress this week?*

Backup plan (or do before closing if there is time):
• Move directly to the progressive relaxation exercise planned for Group 4.

Materials:

• "Getting a Handle on Stress" worksheet (copies for all)
• Red and blue fine-point markers
• Progressive relaxation script (just in case!)

Source: Adapted from Kearns, L. (2007, May). *Six week small group counseling lesson plan.* Class assignment for EDCO 340 Developmental Guidance in Schools. University of Vermont.

Getting a Handle on Stress

1. *Work Off Stress.* Blow off steam in a constructive way through physical activity.
2. *Talk Out Stress.* Find someone to talk to who will listen, support, and help you. Don't worry about burdening this person—the person to talk to is someone who really cares. Be clear with the person on whether you just want a sounding board or if you want help. Be open to help if you ask for it.
3. *Learn to Accept What Can't Be Changed.* If the problem is out of your control, recognize this. Always look for aspects of the problem that are within your control. Problems rarely are all or nothing.
4. *Get Enough Sleep.* Not getting enough sleep can make it harder to deal with stress. If you're having trouble sleeping, try to increase your exercise routine and be sure to eat well.
5. *Take It Easy and Have Fun—and Get Your Work Done.* Balance work and play. You will get stressed if you haven't done your work, and playing will help you relax. Schedule time for work and time for fun. Both are important.
6. *Do Something for Others.* Sometimes when we are stressed, we get too focused on ourselves and our problems. Reaching out to help someone else can help *us* too!
7. *Take One Thing at a Time.* Doing too many things at once is a setup for stress—and for failure. If you're stressed, take something off your "to-do" list, figure out what needs to be done first (prioritize), and do one thing at a time.
8. *Take a Stand.* Sometimes stress is about not asserting yourself. If that's the case, think clearly (sometimes it helps to talk it through with someone else) and then assert what you need or assert your preference. Others will cope, and they'll probably also appreciate your clarity and your honesty. Be careful to assert yourself with respect and the appropriate self-restraint, of course!
9. *Know Your Abilities and Your Limitations.* When you can't: Don't. When you can: Do.
10. *Get Organized.* Come up with a plan and follow it.
11. *Avoid Perfectionism.* Allow yourself to make a mistake. Attend to those things that shouldn't be done erroneously and let the others go.

APPENDIX E: HIGH SCHOOL-LEVEL SAMPLE CLASSROOM GROUP PLANS

Career Exploration *Unit* Plan

Topic: Career exploration

Grade: Ninth

Approximate Number of Students: 16 (advisory period)

Time Allotment for Each Group Session: 45 minutes

Rationale: Research suggests that school counselors are in a position to assist students in the postsecondary planning process and that doing so helps students feel more ready and prepared for postsecondary plans. This unit is used to aid students in their career exploration while also helping them form a greater understanding of themselves in the process.

As a result of this unit, plan for and make a successful transition from school to postsecondary education and/or the world of work and from job to job across the life span (ASCA, 2014).

District School Counseling Program Standards:

- Students will understand the importance of their academics as connected to future life planning.
- Students will identify academic, personal, and career interests, strengths, and skills.
- Students will identify long- and short-term academic, career, and social-emotional goals.

Goals for the Unit:

1. Students will identify academic, personal, and career interests, strengths, and skills.
2. Students will identify postsecondary options that align with their interests, personal characteristics, and skills.

Assessment Plan for Unit Goals:

1. Students will identify academic, personal, and career interests, strengths, and skills.
   - "Career Cluster Finder" worksheet (Lesson 1)
   - Holland Code Assessment (Lesson 2)

2. Students will identify postsecondary options that align with their interests, personal characteristics, and skills.
   - "Top Three" worksheet (Lesson 3)
   - "Training/College Options" worksheet (Lessons 4 and 5)

Source: Adapted from Zuckerman, J. (2018, March). *Group assignment.* Class assignment for EDCO 340 Developmental Guidance in Schools. University of Vermont.

High School Level Classroom Group Sample *Lesson* Plan

Career Exploration Lesson Plan—Week 1

Objectives:

- Students will understand the concept of a *career cluster*.
- Students will identify career clusters that match their personal (and academic) interests, strengths, and skills.

Plan:

- Introduce the students to the concept of career clusters (career cluster PowerPoint)
- Give students directions on accessing the career cluster assessment through the Naviance website.
- Direct students to take the career cluster assessment on Naviance.
- After the assessment has been completed, students are provided the "Career Cluster Finder" worksheet to guide them in exploring their results.

Differentiated Instruction Consideration:

Give students extra time to complete the assessment or assignment. If students have difficulties with the assessment or worksheet, they may receive help from a peer or their group leader.

Materials:

- Career cluster PowerPoint
- "Career Cluster Finder" worksheet
- Laptops
- Access to/log-in information for Naviance
- "Naviance Task Guide" (instructions)

Source: Adapted from Zuckerman, J. (2018, March). *Group assignment.* Class assignment for EDCO 340 Developmental Guidance in Schools. University of Vermont.

APPENDIX F: HIGH SCHOOL-LEVEL COUNSELING GROUP (OVERALL) PLAN

Topic: "What, Me Worry?" (anxiety reduction strategies)

Grade/Class: Sophomores and juniors

Approximate Number of Students: Four to eight

Rationale: The purpose of this group is to help students acquire anxiety reduction strategies. This group was requested by teachers in the math and English departments, based on observations of their honor's students who were anxious about midterm exams and the upcoming SAT exam, which would be taken later in the year. Member selection will be based on teacher recommendations and self-referral. The group will implement a cognitive-behavioral model for reducing test anxiety.

Goals for the Group:

- Students will recognize their personal signs of stress.
- Students will gain an understanding of how their feelings of stress may be triggered by real-life events and experiences, some of which they can control and some which they cannot control.
- Students will gain an understanding of how their feelings of stress may be triggered by thoughts—many of which are unrealistic and distorted.
- Students will identify distorted thoughts and apply strategies for restructuring their thoughts.
- Students will acquire additional relaxation and anti-anxiety strategies—lifestyle and in-the-moment strategies.

Number of Sessions in Unit: 4 weeks—30 minutes per session

Group Assessment Plan:

1. Students will recognize their personal signs of stress.
   - Participation in signs of stress discussion (Session 1)
   - "What I Learned" questionnaire (Session 4)
2. Students will gain an understanding of how their feelings of stress may be triggered by real-life events and experiences, some of which they can control and some which they cannot control.
   - "What I Learned" questionnaire (Session 4)

3. Students will gain an understanding of how their feelings of stress may be triggered by thoughts—many of which are unrealistic and distorted.
   - Participation in a discussion prompted by (CBT) strategies/worksheets/instruction (Sessions 2 and 3)
   - "What I Learned" questionnaire (Session 4)
4. Students will identify distorted thoughts and apply strategies for restructuring their thoughts.
   - Participation in a discussion prompted by CBT strategies/worksheets/instruction (Sessions 3 and 4)
   - "What I Learned" questionnaire (Session 4)
5. Students will acquire additional relaxation and anti-anxiety strategies—lifestyle and in-the-moment strategies.
   - Participation in discussion after relaxation training (Session 4)
   - "What I Learned" questionnaire (Session 4)

High School Level Counseling Group Session Plan

"What, Me Worry?" Group Session 4

Session Objective:

- Students will acquire additional relaxation and anti-anxiety strategies. These will be *lifestyle* and *in-the-moment* strategies.

Plan:

- Begin with a review of last week's discussion on distorted thoughts and restructuring strategies. Round:
  - *Did anyone use any of the strategies we discussed last week?*
  - *What distorted thought did you notice?*
  - *What was the distortion (refer to the list—have the student point it out)? What did you do to correct the distortion? What was the result?*
- We have focused a lot on changing your thoughts to manage your stress reactions. Today, we are going to focus on some other things you can do to manage stress. These are more of the lifestyle kinds of things that you learned in health class (if you took that class); they are healthy lifestyle actions that help manage stress.
- In general, what are good action strategies you can do to manage stress?
  - Prompt students to think about exercise, recreation, quiet time, and diet.
- Teach students progressive relaxation exercises (see the book), building on Session 1—Where We Feel Stress. Have students tighten and then loosen parts of their bodies to feel relaxation.
- Discuss how this can be adapted to be used "in the moment" in class.
- Closing round:
  - *Think back over the past 4 weeks. What have you learned about how stress affects you?*
  - *What have you learned to do to manage stress that has been particularly helpful?*
- Handout: "What I Learned" (explain the purpose of this to students).

Materials:

- Book: *The Relaxation and Stress Reduction Workbook* (in the counseling office)
- "What I Learned" questionnaire (attached)
- Davis, M., Eshelman, E. R., & McKay, M. (2008). *The relaxation and stress reduction workbook*. New Harbinger Publications.

What I Learned ... What Happens With You That Tells You That You Are Probably Stressed?

Besides the deadlines and events that happen in our lives, what else causes stress?

How does the way you think affect stress (positively and negatively)?

What have you learned in terms of managing stress? What can you do to manage stress?

How was this group for you? What was and wasn't helpful?

REFERENCES

Adamson, R. M., McKenna, J. W., & Mitchell, B. (2019). Supporting all students: Creating a tiered continuum of behavior support at the classroom level to enhance schoolwide multi-tiered systems of support. *Preventing School Failure: Alternative Education for Children and Youth, 63*(1), 62–67. https://doi.org/10.1080/1045988X.2018.1501654

Agazarian, Y., & Gantt, S. (2005). The systems perspective. In S. A. Wheelan (Ed.), *The handbook of group research and practice* (pp. 187–200). SAGE Publications.

Akos, P., Hamm, J. V., Mack, S. G., & Dunaway, M. (2006). Utilizing the developmental influence of peers in middle school groups. *Journal for Specialists in Group Work, 32*(1), 51–60. https://doi.org/10.1080/01933920600977648

Albert, L. (1996). *Cooperative discipline.* American Guidance Service, Inc.

Alexander, A., & Hulse-Killacky, D. (2005). Childhood memories and receptivity to corrective feedback in group supervision: Implications for group work. *Journal for Specialists in Group Work, 30*(1), 23–45. https://doi.org/10.1080/01933920590908642

American Counseling Association (ACA). (2014). *ACA code of ethics and standards of practice.* Retrieved April 20, 2019, from https://www.counseling.org/docs/default-source/default-document-library/2014-code-of-ethics-finaladdress.pdf?sfvrsn=96b532c_2

American Group Psychotherapy Association. (2007). *Practice guidelines for group psychotherapy.* Retrieved November 20, 2017, from http://www.agpa.org/home/practice-resources/practice-guidelines-for-group-psychotherapy

American School Counselor Association (ASCA). (2014). *Mindsets and behaviors for student success: K–12 college- and career-readiness standards for every student.*

American School Counselor Association (ASCA). (2016). *ASCA ethical standards for school counselors.* Retrieved November 22, 2016, from https://www.schoolcounselor.org/asca/media/asca/Ethics/EthicalStandards2016.pdf

American School Counseling Association (ASCA). (2019). *The ASCA national model: A framework for school counseling programs* (4th. ed.).

Anderson, M. L., & Collins, P. H. (2004). *Race, class, and gender. An anthology* (5th ed.). Wadsworth/Thompson Learning.

Arnett, J. J., & Tanner, J. L. (2009). Toward a cultural-developmental stage theory of the life course. In K. McCartney & R. A. Weinberg (Eds), *Experience and development* (pp. 17–38). Psychology Press.

Armstrong, P. (n.d.). *Bloom's taxonomy.* https://cft.vanderbilt.edu/guides-sub-pages/blooms-taxonomy/

Arredondo, P., Toporek, R., Brown, S., Jones, J., Locke, D., Sanchez, J., & Stadler, H. (1996). Operationalization of the multicultural counseling competencies. *Journal of Multicultural Counseling and Development, 24,* 42–78.

Ashdown, D. M., & Bernard, M. E. (2012). Can explicit instruction in social and emotional learning skills benefit the social-emotional development, well-being, and academic achievement of young children? *Early Childhood Education Journal, 39*(6), 397–405. https://doi.org/10.1007/s10643-011-0481-x

Askew, S., & Lodge, C. (2000). Gifts, ping-pong and loops-linking feedback and learning. In S. Askew (Ed.), *Feedback for learning.* Routledge.

Association for Specialists in Group Work (ASGW). (2000). *Professional standards for the training of group workers.* Journal for Specialists in Group Work, 25(4), 327–342, https://doi.org/10.1080/01933920008411677

Backler, A., Eakin, S., & Harris, P. (1994). *Managing the disruptive classroom: Strategies for educators* [Video]. Agency for Instructional Technology.

Bandura, A. (1971). Analysis of modeling processes. In A. Bandura (Ed.), *Psychological modeling* (pp. 1–62). Aldine/Atherton.

Bandura, A. (1977). Self-efficacy: Toward a unifying theory of behavioral change. *Psychological review, 84*(2), 191–215.

Bandura, A. (1986). *Social foundations of thought and actions. A social cognitive theory.* Prentice Hall.

Bandura, A. (1989). Regulation of cognitive processes through perceived self-efficacy. *Developmental Psychology, 25*(5), 729.

Bandura, A. (1993). Perceived self-efficacy in cognitive development and functioning. *Educational Psychologist, 28*(2), 117–148.

Bandura, A., Ross, D., & Ross, S. A. (1961). Transmission of aggression through imitation of aggressive models. *Journal of Abnormal and Social Psychology, 63*(3), 575.

Bandura, A., & Walters, R. H. (1980). Adolescent aggression: A study of the influence of child-training practices and family interrelationships. Ronald Press (Original work published 1959)

Banks, T., & Obiakor, F. E. (2015). Culturally responsive positive behavior supports: Considerations for practice. *Journal of Education and Training Studies, 3*(2), 83–90. https://doi.org/10.11114/jets.v3i2.636

Barnett, J. E., & Johnson, W. B. (2015). *Ethics desk reference for counselors* (2nd ed.). American Counseling Association.

Baron-Cohen, S. (2011). *Zero degrees of empathy: A new theory of human cruelty.* Penguin UK.

Bateson, C. (1994). *Peripheral visions. Learning along the way.* HarperCollins.

Beals, M. P. (1994). *Warriors don't cry.* NY: Washington Square Press

Bear, G. G. (2005). *Developing self-discipline and preventing and correcting misbehavior.* Pearson Education.

Beebe, S. A., & Masterson, J. T. (2015). *Communicating in small groups* (11th ed.). Pearson Education.

Begun, R. W. (Ed.). (1995). *Ready to use social skills lessons and activities for grades preK–K.* The Society for Prevention of Violence with the Center for Applied Research in Education.

Bemak, F., & Chung, R. C. (2005). Advocacy as a critical role for urban school counselors: Working towards equity and social justice. *Professional School Counseling, 8*(3), 196–202.

Bennett, R. (2010). *Formative assessment. A critical review.* Education Testing Center Presentation at the Hong Kong Institute of Education, Hong Kong, SAR, China. Retrieved March 6, 2019, from https://www.researchgate.net/profile/Randy_Bennett/publication/228836856_Formative_assessment_A_critical_review/links/00b7d5225d29ea6958000000/Formative-assessment-A-critical-review.pdf

Bergen, D. (2008). *Human development. Traditional and contemporary theories.* Pearson/Prentice Hall.

Berk, L. E. (2014). *Exploring lifespan development* (3rd ed.). Pearson.

Berman-Rossi, T. (1993). The tasks and skills of social worker across stages of group development. *Social Work with Groups, 16*(1–2), 69–81. https://doi.org/10.1300/J009v16n01_07

Bernard, H., Burlingame, G., Flores, P., Greene, L., Joyce, A., Kobos, J. C., Leszcz, M., Semands, R.R.M., Piper, W. E., Slocum McEneaney, A. M., & Feirman, D. (2008). Clinical practice guidelines for group psychotherapy. *International Journal of Group Psychotherapy, 58*(4), 455–542. https://doi.org/10.1521/ijgp.2008.58.4.455

Bigge, M. L., & Shermis, S. S. (1999). *Learning theories for teachers* (6th ed.). Longman.

Birnbaum, M. L., & Cicchetti, A. (2005). A model for working with the group life cycle in each group session across the life span of the group. *Groupwork, 15*(3), 23–43. https://doi.org/10.1921/0951824X.15.3.23

Black, P., & William, D. (2009). Developing the theory of formative assessment. *Educational Assessment, Evaluation and Accountability, 21*(1), 5–31. https://doi.org/10.1007/s11092-008-9068-5

Bloch, S., Crouch, E., & Reibstein, J. (1981). Therapeutic factors in group psychotherapy: A review. *Archives of General Psychiatry, 38*(5), 519–526.

Bloom, B. S. (1956). *Taxonomy of educational objectives, handbook I: The cognitive domain.* David McKay Co Inc.

Bloom, M., Fischer, J., & Orme, J. G. (2009). *Evaluating practice* (6th ed.). Pearson.

Bong, M., & Skaalvik, E. M. (2003). Academic self-concept and self-efficacy: How different are they really? *Educational Psychology Review, 15*(1), 1–40.

Bowman-Perrott, L., Burke, M. D., de Marin, S., Zhang, N., & Davis, H. (2015). A meta-analysis of single-case research on behavior contracts: Effects on behavioral and academic outcomes among children and youth. *Behavior Modification, 39*(2), 247–269. https://doi.org/10.1177/0145445514551383

Boyd, D. G., & Bee, H. L. (2015). *Lifespan development* (7th ed.). Pearson.

Brenner, M. H., Curbow, B., & Legro, M. W. (1995). The proximal-distal continuum of multiple health outcome measures: The case of cataract surgery. *Medical Care, 33*(4), AS236–AS244.

Brophy, J. (1999). Perspectives of classroom management: Yesterday, today, and tomorrow. In H. J. Freiberg (Ed.), *Beyond behaviorism; changing the classroom management paradigm* (pp. 43–56). Allyn & Bacon.

Brown, D., & Trusty, J. (2005). The ASCA national model, accountability, and establishing causal links between school counselors' activities and student outcomes: A reply to Sink. *Professional School Counseling, 9*(1), 2156759X0500900104.

Brown, S. D., Brack, G., & Mullis, F. Y. (2008). Traumatic symptoms in sexually abused children: Implications for school counselors. *Professional School Counseling, 11*(6), 368–379. https://doi.org/10.2156759X0801100603.

Bruner, J. (1966). *Toward a theory of instruction.* Harvard University Press.

Bruner, J. (1983). Play, thought, and language. *Peabody Journal of Education, 60*(3), 60–69.

Bruner, J. (1990). *Acts of meaning.* Harvard University Press.

Burr, V. (1995). *An introduction to social constructionism.* Routledge.

Burwell, R., & Huyser, M. (2013). Practicing hospitality in the classroom. *Journal of Education and Christian Belief, 17*(1), 9–24.

Caper, R. (2001). The goals of clinical psychoanalysis: Notes on interpretation and psychological development. *Psychoanalytic Quarterly, 70*(1), 99–116. https://doi.org/10.1002/j.2167-4086.2001.tb00591.x

Carroll, M. R., & Kraus, K. L. (2007). *Elements of group counseling: Back to the basics* (4th ed.). Love Publishing.

Cavaiola, A. A., & Colford, J. E. (2006). *A practical guide to crisis intervention.* Lahaska/Houghton Mifflin.

Champe, J., Okech, J. E. A., & Rubel, D. (2013). Emotion regulation: Processes, strategies, and applications for group work training and supervision, *Journal for Specialists in Group Work, 38*(4), 349–368. https://doi.org/10.1080/01933922.2013.834403

Charles, C. M. (2011). *Building classroom discipline* (10th ed.). Pearson.

Charles, C. M., & Senter, G. W. (2002). *Elementary classroom management* (3rd ed.). Allyn & Bacon.

Charney, R. S. (1991). *Teaching children to care. Management in the responsive classroom.* Northeast Foundation for Children.

Ciulla, J. B. (2006). Ethics. The heart of leadership. In M. Thomas & N. M. Pless (Eds.), *Responsible leadership* (pp. 17–32). Routledge.

Claiborn, C. D., Goodyear, R. K., & Horner, P. A. (2001). Feedback. *Psychotherapy, 38*(4), 401–408. https://doi.org/10.1037/0033-3204.38.4.401

Cobia, D. C., & Henderson, D. A. (2007). *Developing an effective and accountable school counseling program* (2nd ed.). Pearson.

Cohen, A. M., & Smith, R. D. (1976). *The critical incident in growth groups: Theory and technique.* University Associates.

Cohen, E. G. (1994). *Designing group work. Strategies for the heterogeneous classroom* (2nd ed.). Teachers College Press.

Cohen, H. S. (Executive Producer). (2002). *That's a family. A film for kids about family diversity* [Video]. Women's Educational Media.

Collins, S., & Arthur, N. (2010). Culture-infused counselling: A fresh look at a classic framework of multicultural coun-selling competencies. *Counselling Psychology Quarterly, 23*(2), 203–216. https://doi.org/10.1080/09515071003798204

Connors, J. V., & Caple, R. B. (2005). A review of group systems theory. *Journal for Specialists in Group Work, 30*(2), 93–110. https://doi.org/10.1080/01933920590925940

Cook, A., Spinazzola, J., Ford, J., Lanktree, C., Blaustein, M., Cloitre, M., DeRosa, R., Hubbard, R., Kagan, R., Liautaud, J., Mallah, K., Olafson, E., & van der Kolk, B. (2005). Complex trauma in children and adolescents. *Psychiatric Annals, 35*(5), 390–398. https://doi.org/10.3928/00485713-20050501-05

Corey, M. S., & Corey, G. (2006). *Groups: Process and practice* (7th ed.). Thomson Brooks/Cole.

Council for Accreditation of Counselor Education and Related Programs (CACREP). (2019). *2016 CACREP standards.* Retrieved April 20, 2019, from http://www.cacrep.org/wp-content/uploads/2018/05/2016-Standards-with-Glossary-5.3.2018.pdf

Curry, N. E., & Johnson, C. N. (1990). *Beyond self-esteem: Developing a genuine sense of human value.* (Research monograph, Vol. 4, Publication No. 143). National Association for the Education of Young Children.

Dahir, C. A., & Stone, C. B. (2012). *The transformed school counselor* (2nd ed.). Brooks/Cole.

Damiani, V. B. (2006). *Crisis prevention and intervention in the classroom.* Rowman & Littlefield.

Dann, R. (2018). *Developing feedback for pupil learning: Teaching, learning, and assessment in schools.* Routledge.

Darvin, J. (2018). Becoming a more culturally responsive teacher by identifying and reducing microaggressions in classrooms and school communities. *Journal for Multicultural Education, 12*(2), 2–9. https://doi.org/10.1108/JME-03-2017-0020.

Davis, M., Eshelman, E. R., & McKay, M. (2008). *The relaxation and stress reduction workbook.* New Harbinger Publications.

Day, S. X. (2007). *Groups in practice.* Houghton Mifflin.

Day-Vines, N. L., Wood, S. M., Grothaus, T., Craigen, L., Holman, A., Dotson-Blake, K., & Douglass, M. J. (2007). Broaching the subjects of race, ethnicity, and culture during the counseling process. *Journal of Counseling & Development, 85*(4), 401–409. https://doi.org/10.1002/j.1556-6678.2007.tb00608.x

De Jong, P., & Berg, I.K. (2008). *Interviewing for solutions* (3rd ed.). Brooks/Cole.

DeLucia-Waack, J. L. (2006). *Leading psychoeducational groups for children and adolescents.* SAGE Publications.

DeLucia-Waack, J. L., & Gerrity, D. (2001). Effective group work for elementary school-age children whose parents are divorcing. *Family Journal, 9*(3), 273–284.

Derman-Sparks, L. (1993). Revisiting multicultural education. What children need to live in a diverse society. *Dimensions of Early Childhood, 22*(1), 6–10.

Douthit, K. (2008). Cognition, culture, and society: Understanding cognitive development in the tradition of Vygotsky. In K. L. Kraus (Ed.), *Lenses: Applying lifespan development theories in counseling* (pp. 83–118). Lahaska/Houghton Mifflin.

Drewery, W. (2005). Why we should watch what we say: Position calls, everyday speech and the production of relational subjectivity. *Theory & Psychology, 15*(3), 305–324. https://doi.org/10.1177/0959354305053217

Drewery, W., & Winslade, J. (1997). The theoretical story of narrative therapy. In G. Monk, J. Winslade, K. Crocket, & D. Epston (Eds.), *Narrative therapy in practice: The archaeology of hope* (pp. 32–52). Jossey-Bass.

Educational Research Service (ERS). (2005). *Effective classroom management to support student learning.* Educational Research Service.

Elkind, D. (1981). *Children and adolescents. Interpretive essays on Jean Piaget* (3rd ed.). Oxford University Press.

Emihovich, C., & Lima, E. S. (1995). The many facets of Vygotsky: A cultural historical voice from the future. *Anthropology & Education Quarterly, 26*(4), 375–383.

Emmer, E. T., & Evertson, C. M. (2009). *Classroom management for middle and high school teachers* (8th ed.). Pearson Education.

Everett, G. E. (2010). Time-out in special education settings: The parameters of previous implementation. *North American Journal of Psychology, 12*(1), 159–170.

Fazio-Griffith, L., & Curry, J. R. (2008). Professional school counselors as process observers in the classroom: Collaboration with classroom teachers. *Journal of School Counseling, 6*(20), 1–15.

Feldman, D. C. (1984). The development and enforcement of group norms. *Academy of Management Review, 9*(1), 47–53.

Fields, J. W., Thompson, K. C., & Hawkins, J. R. (2015). Servant leadership: Teaching the helping professional. *Journal of Leadership Education, 14*(4), 92–104. https://doi.org/10.12806/V14/14/R2

Floyd, R. G., Phaneuf, R. L., & Wilczynski, S. M. (2005). Measurement properties of indirect assessment methods for functional behavioral assessment: A review of research. *School Psychology Review, 34*(1), 58.

Forehand, M. (2005). Bloom's taxonomy: Original and revised. In M. Orey (Ed.), *Emerging perspectives on learning, teaching, and technology.* Retrieved April 2, 2020, from https://cdn.vanderbilt.edu/vu-wpo/wp-content/uploads/sites/59/2010/06/12092513/BloomsTaxonomy-mary-forehand.pdf

Foucault, M. (1972). *The order of things: An archaeology of the human sciences.* Pantheon.

Fox, E., & Riconscente, M. (2008). Metacognition and self-regulation in James, Piaget, and Vygotsky. *Educational Psychology Review, 20*(4), 373–389. https://doi.org/10.1007/s10648-008-9079-2

Frankel, R. M. (2009). Empathy research: A complex challenge. *Patient Education and Counseling, 75*(1), 1–2. https://doi.org/10.1016/j.per2009.02.008

Fredricks, J. A., Blumenfeld, P. C., & Paris, A. H. (2004). School engagement: Potential of the concept, state of the evidence. *Review of Educational Research, 74*(1), 59–109.

Freeman, J., Epston, D., & Lobovits, D. (1997). *Playful approaches to serious problems: Narrative therapy with children and their families.* W. W. Norton & Company.

Garrett, K. J. (2005). School social workers' evaluation of group work practices. *Children & Schools, 27*(4), 247–252.

Geinger, F., Vandenbroeck, M., & Roets, G. (2014). Parenting as a performance: Parents as consumers and (de)constructors of mythic parenting and childhood ideals. *Childhood, 21*(4), 488–501. https://doi.org/10.1177/0907568213496657

Geroski, A. M. (2017). *Skills for helping relationship professionals.* SAGE Publications.

Geroski, A. M. (2019). *Helping skills for counselors.* Cognella.

Geroski, A., & Kraus, K. (2002) Process and content in school psychoeducational groups. *Journal for Specialists in Group Work, 27*(2), 233–245. https://doi.org/10.1080/742848694

Gershon, M. (2013). Classroom practice—Still blooming after almost 60 years. *The Times Educational Supplement Scotland,* 2340, 30–32.

Gitterman, A., & Knight, C. (2016). Curriculum and psychoeducational groups: Opportunities and challenges. *Social Work, 61*(2), 103–110. https://doi.org/10.1093/sw/sww007

Gladding, S. T. (2003). *Group work. A counseling specialty* (4th ed.). Pearson Education.

Gladding, S. T. (2008). *Groups: A counseling specialty* (5th ed.). Pearson Education.

Glass, J. S., & Benshoff, J. M. (1999). PARS: A processing model for beginning group leaders. *Journal for Specialists in Group Work, 24,* 15–26.

Glasser, W. (1998a.). *Choice theory in the classroom* (revised ed.). HarperCollins.

Glasser, W. (1998b.). *Choice theory. A new psychology of personal freedom.* HarperCollins.

Goeke, J. L. (2009). *Explicit instruction. A framework for meaningful direct teaching.* Pearson.

Goldstein, A. P. (1973). *Structured learning therapy: Toward a psychotherapy for the poor.* Academic Press.

Goodman-Scott, E., Hays, D. G., & Cholewa, B. E. (2018). "It takes a village": A case study of positive behavioral interventions and supports implementation in an exemplary urban middle school. *The Urban Review, 50*(1), 97–122. https://doi.org/10.1007/s11256-017-0431-z

Greenleaf, R. K. (1977). *The servant as leader.* The Robert K. Greenleaf Center.

Gresham, F. M., Watson, T. S., & Skinner, C. H. (2001). Functional behavioral assessment: Principles, procedures, and future directions. *School Psychology Review, 30*(2), 156–172.

Gronlund, N. E. (2000). *How to write and use instructional objectives* (6th ed.). Merrill Prentice Hall.

Guerney, L. (2001). Child-centered play therapy. *International Journal of Play Therapy, 10*(2), 13.

Guney, A., & Al, S. (2012). Effective learning environments in relation to different learning theories. *Procedia-Social and Behavioral Sciences, 46,* 2334–2338. https://doi.org/10.1016/j.sbspro.2012.05.480

Guth, L. J., Nitza, A., Pollard, B. L. Puig, A., Chan, C. D., Bailey, H., & Singh, A. A. (2019). Ten strategies to intentionally use group work to transform hate, facilitate courageous conversations, and enhance community building. *Journal for Specialists in Group Work, 44*(1), 3–24. https://doi.org/10.1080/01933922.2018.1561778

Hansen, J. C., Warner, R. W., & Smith, E. J. (1980). *Group counseling: Theory and process* (2nd ed.). Rand McNally.

Harre, R., & Moghaddam, F. (2003). Introduction: The self and others in traditional psychology and in positioning theory. In R. Harre & F. Moghaddam (Eds.), *The self and others: Positioning individuals and groups in personal, political, and cultural contexts.* Praeger.

Harre, R., & Van Langenhove, L. (1991). Varieties of positioning. *Journal for the Theory of Social Behaviour, 21*(4), 393–407. https://doi.org/10.1111/j.1468-5914.1991.tb00203.x

Harris, T. E., & Sherblom, J. C. (2005). *Small group and team communication* (3rd ed.). Pearson.

Hattie, J., & Timperley, H. (2007). The power of feedback. *Review of Educational Research, 77*(1), 81–112. https://doi.org/10.3102/003465430298487

Hawe, P., Shiell, A., & Riley, T. (2009). Theorising interventions as events in systems. *American Journal of Community Psychology, 43*(3–4), 267–276. https://doi.org/10.1007/s10464-009-9229-9

Hawkins, E., Kingsdorf, S., Charnock, J., Szabo, M., Middleton, E., Phillips, J., & Gautreaux, G. (2011). Using behaviour contracts to decrease antisocial behaviour in four boys with an autistic spectrum disorder at home and at school. *British Journal of Special Education, 38*(4), 201–208. https://doi.org/10.1111/j.1467-8578.2011.00518.x

Hazler, R. J., & Banvick, N. (2001). *The therapeutic environment: Core conditions for facilitating therapy.* Open University Press.

Hedegaard, M. (2005). The zone of proximal development as basis for instruction In H. Daniels (Ed.), *An introduction to Vygotsky* (2nd ed., pp. 227–251). Routledge.

Henderson, D. A., & Thompson, C. L. (2011). *Counseling children* (8th ed.). Brooks/Cole.

Hogan-Garcia, M. (1999). *The four skills of cultural diversity competence: A process for understanding and practice.* Brooks/Cole.

Holcomb-McCoy, C. (2004). Assessing the multicultural competence of school counselors: A checklist. *Professional School Counseling, 7*(3), 178–186.

Hook, J. N., Farrell, J. E., Davis, D. E., DeBlaere, C., Van Tongeren, D. R., & Utsey, S. O. (2016). Cultural humility and racial microaggressions in counseling. *Journal of Counseling Psychology, 63*(3), 269.

Hoover, R. L., & Kindsvatter, R. (1997). *Democratic discipline: Foundation and practice.* Merrill Prentice Hall.

Hughes, J. N. (2002). Authoritative teaching: Tipping the balance in favor of school versus peer effects. *Journal of School Counseling, 40*(6), 485–492.

Hulse-Killacky, D., Killacky, J., & Donigian, J. (2001). *Making task groups work in your world.* Merrill Prentice Hall.

Hulse-Killacky, D., Kraus, K. L., & Schumacher, R. A. (1999). Visual conceptualizations of meetings: A group work design. *Journal for Specialists in Group Work, 24*(1), 113–124. https://doi.org/10.1080/01933929908411423

Hulse-Killacky, D., Orr, J. J., & Paradise, L. V. (2006). The corrective feedback instrument-revised. *Journal for Specialists in Group Work, 31*(3), 263–281. https://doi.org/10.1080/01933920600777758

Hunter, R. (2004). *Madeline Hunter's mastery teaching. Increasing instructional effectiveness in elementary and secondary schools.* Corwin Press.

Ingersoll, G. M. (1996). What is your classroom management profile? *Teacher Talk, 1*(2). http://education.indiana.edu/cas/tt/v1i2/authoritative.html

Jacobs, E. E., Masson, R. L., & Harvill, R. L. (2005). *Group counseling. Strategies and skills.* Brooks/Cole.

Jacobs, E. E., Schimmel, C. J., Masson, R. L., & Harvill, R. L. (2016). *Group counseling: Strategies and skills* (8th ed.). Cengage.

James, R. K., & Gilliland, B. E. (2001). *Crisis intervention strategies* (4th ed.). Wadsworth/Thomson.

Javdani, S., & Allen, N. E. (2011). Proximal outcomes matter: A multilevel examination of the processes by which coordinating councils produce change. *American Journal of Community Psychology, 47*(1–2), 12–27. https://doi.org/10.1007/s10464-010-9375-0

Jarvis, P. (2006). Teaching: An art or a science? In J. P. Jarvis (Eds.), *The theory and practice of teaching* (2nd ed., pp. 28–38). Routledge.

Jensen, T. (2010). 'What kind of mum are you at the moment?' Supernanny and the psychologising of classed embodiment. *Subjectivity, 3*(2), 170–192. https://doi.org/10.1057/sub.2009.2

Jobes, D. A., Berman, Al. L., & Martin, C. E. (2005). Adolescent suicidality and crisis intervention. In A. R. Roberts (Ed.), *Crisis intervention handbook. Assessment, treatment & research* (pp. 395–415). Oxford University Press.

Johansson, P., Høglend, P., Ulberg, R., Amlo, S., Marble, A., Bøgwald, K. P., Ulberg, R., Marble, A., Sørbye, O., Sjaastad, M. C., & & Heyerdahl, O. (2010). The mediating role of insight for long-term improvements in psychodynamic therapy. *Journal of Consulting and Clinical Psychology, 78*(3), 438–448. https://doi.org/10.1037/a0019245

John-Steiner, V. P. (2007). Vygotsky on thinking and speaking. In H. Daniels, M. Cole, & J. V. Wertsch (Eds.), *The Cambridge companion to Vygotsky* (pp. 136–154). Cambridge University Press.

Johnson, D. W., Johnson, R. T., & Holubec, E. J. (1994). *Cooperative learning in the classroom.* Association for Supervision and Curriculum Development.

Johnson, M. H. (2005). Sensitive periods in functional brain development: Problems and prospects. *Developmental Psychobiology, 46*(3), 287–292. https://doi.org/10.1002/dev.20057

Johnson, R., & Johnson, D. (2004). *Assessing students in groups.* Corwin Press.

Johnson, S., Johnson, C., & Downs, L. (2006). *Building a results-based student support program.* Lahaska Press.

Jones, K. D., Casado, M., & Robinson III, E. H. (2003). Structured play therapy: A model for choosing topics and activities. *International Journal of Play Therapy, 12*(1), 31.

Jones, V. F., & Jones, L. S. (2001). *Comprehensive classroom management* (6th ed.). Allyn & Bacon.

Kauffman, J. M., Mostert, M. P., Trent, S. C., & Hallahan, D. P. (2002). *Managing classroom behavior. A reflective case-based approach* (3rd ed.). Allyn & Bacon.

Kees, N. L., & Jacobs, E. (1990). Conducting more effective groups: How to select and process group exercises. *Journal for Specialists in Group Work, 15*(1), 21–29.

Kerr, M. M., & Nelson, C. M. (1998). *Strategies for managing behavior problems in the classroom* (3rd ed.). Merrill Prentice Hall.

Kirylo, J. D. (2016). *Teaching with purpose. An inquiry into the who, why, and how we teach.* Rowman & Littlefield.

Kislev, E. (2015). The use of participant-observers in group therapy: A critical exploration in light of Foucauldian theory. *Group, 39*(1), 9–24. http://www.jstor.org/stable/10.13186/group.39.1.0009

Kivlighan Jr., D. M., & Goldfine, D. C. (1991). Endorsement of therapeutic factors as a function of stage of group development and participant interpersonal attitudes. *Journal of Counseling Psychology, 38*(2), 150.

Kleingeld, A., van Mierlo, H., & Arends, L. (2011). The effect of goal setting on group performance: A meta-analysis. *Journal of Applied Psychology, 96*(6), 1289. https://doi.org/10.1037/a0024315

Kline, D. M. S. (2016). Can restorative practices help to reduce disparities in school discipline data? A review of the literature. *Multicultural Perspectives, 18*(2), 97–102. https://doi.org/10.1080/15210960.2016.1159099

Kline, W. B. (2003). *Interactive group counseling and therapy.* Merrill Prentice Hall.

Koester, J., & Lustig, M. W. (2015). Intercultural communication competence: Theory, measurement, and application. *International Journal of Intercultural Relations, 48,* 20–21. http://dx.doi.org/10.1016/j.ijintrel.2015.03.006

Kohn, A. (1994, December). *The risk of rewards.* ERIC Clearinghouses on Elementary and Early Children Education (ED376990).

Kostewicz, D. E. (2010). A review of timeout ribbons. *The Behavior Analyst Today, 11*(2), 95.

Kottman, T. (2011). *Play therapy: Basics and beyond* (2nd ed.). American Counseling Association.

Kottman, T., & Meany-Walen, K. (2016). *Partners in play: An Adlerian approach to play therapy* (3rd ed.). American Counseling Association.

Krathwohl, D. R. (2002). A revision of Bloom's taxonomy: An overview. *Theory Into Practice, 41*(4), 212–218, https://doi.org/10.1207/s15430421tip4104_2

Kraus, K., & Hulse-Killacky, D. (1996). Balancing process and content in groups: A metaphor. *Journal for Specialists in Group Work, 21*(2), 90–93. https://doi.org/10.1080/01933929608412236

Kubiak, S. P. (2005). Trauma and cumulative adversity in women of a disadvantaged social location. *American Journal of Orthopsychiatry, 75*(4), 451–465. https://doi.org/10.1037/0002-9432.75.4.451

Landreth, G. L. (2012). *Play therapy: The art of the relationship* (3rd ed.). Brunner-Routledge.

Lane, J., Lane, A. M., & Kyprianou, A. (2004). Self-efficacy, self-esteem and their impact on academic performance. *Social Behavior and Personality: An International Journal, 32*(3), 247–256.

Larrivee, B. (2005). *Authentic classroom management. Creating a learning community and building reflective practice* (2nd ed.). Allyn & Bacon.

Latham, G. P. (2016). Goal setting: A possible theoretical framework for examining the effect of priming goals on organizational behavior. *Current Opinion in Psychology, 12*, 85–88. http://dx.doi.org/10.1016/j.copsyc.2016.07.005

Latham, G. P., & Locke, E. A. (1991). Self-regulation through goal setting. *Organizational behavior and human decision processes, 50*(2), 212–247.

Leach, D., & Helf, S. (2016). Using a hierarchy of supportive consequences to address problem behaviors in the classroom. *Intervention in School and Clinic, 52*(1), 29–33. https://doi.org/10.1177/1053451216630288

Lerman, D. C., & Toole, L. M. (2011). Developing function-based punishment procedures for problem behavior. In W. W. Fisher, C. C. Piazza, & H. S. Roane (Eds.), *Handbook of applied behavior analysis* (pp. 34–369). Guilford Press.

Letendre, J., Henry, D., & Tolan, P. H. (2003). Leader and therapeutic influences on prosocial skill building in school-based groups to prevent aggression. *Research on Social Work Practice, 13*(5), 569–587. https://doi.org/10.1177/1049731503253404

Leung, K., Ang, S., & Tan, M. L. (2014). Intercultural competence. *Annual Review of and Organizational Psychology and Organizational Behavior, 1*, 489–519. https://doi.org/10.1146/annurev-orgpsych-031413-091229.

Lewin, K. (1944). The dynamics of group action. *Educational Leadership, 1*, 195–200.

Lieberman, M. A., Yalom, I. D., & Miles, M. B. (1973). *Encounter groups: First facts*. Basic Books.

Linde, L. (2007). Ethical, legal, and professional issues in school counseling. In B.C. Erford (Ed.), *Transforming the school counseling profession* (2nd ed., pp. 51–72). Pearson Education.

Lindwall, J. J., & Coleman, H. L. (2008). The elementary school counselor's role in fostering caring school communities. *Professional School Counseling, 12*(2). https://doi.org/10.2156759X0801200211

Locke, E. A., & Latham, G. P. (1984). *Goal setting. A motivational technique that works!* Prentice Hall.

Locke, E. A., & Latham, G. P. (1990). *A theory of goal-setting and task performance*. Prentice Hall.

Logan, J., Chasnoff, D., & Cohen, H. S. (2002). *That's a family. Discussion and teaching guide*. Women's Educational Media.

Luckner, J. L., & Nadler, R. S. (1997). *Processing the experience. Strategies to enhance and generalize learning* (2nd ed.). Kendall/Hunt.

Maag, J. W. (2001). Rewarded by punishment: Reflections on the disuse of positive reinforcement in schools. *Exceptional Children, 67*(2), 173–186.

MacLeod, L. (2012). Making SMART goals smarter. *Physician executive, 38*(2), 68–72.

MacNair-Semands, R. R., & Lese, K. P. (2000). Interpersonal problems and the perception of therapeutic factors in group therapy. *Small Group Research, 31*(2), 158–174. https://doi.org/10.1177/104649640003100202

Marchant, M., & Anderson, D. H. (2012). Improving social and academic outcomes for all learners through the use of teacher praise. *Beyond Behavior, 21*(3), 22–28. https://doi.org/10.1177/107429561202100305

Marmon, E. L. (2008). Teaching as hospitality. *The Asbury Journal, 63*(2), 33–39.

Marogna, C., & Caccamo, F. (2014). Analysis of the process in brief psychotherapy group: The role of therapeutic factors. *Research in Psychotherapy: Psychopathology, Process and Outcome, 17*(1), 43–51. https://doi.org/10.7411/RP.2014.019

Martin, D. G. (2003). *Clinical practice with adolescents*. Brooks/Cole.

Marzano, R. J. (2003). Classroom management that works. Research-based strategies for every teacher. Merrill Education/Pearson (in arrangement with Association for Supervision and Curriculum Development).

Marzano, R., Pickering, D., & Pollock, J. (2001). *Classroom instruction that works* (1st ed.). Association for Supervision and Curriculum Development.

Maslow, A. H. (1967). Synanon and eupsychia. *Journal of Humanistic Psychology, 7*(1), 28–35. https://doi.org/101177/002216786700700104

Mason, C., Griffin, M., & Parker, S. (2014). Transformational leadership development: Connecting psychological and behavioral change. *Leadership & Organization Development Journal, 35*(3), 174–194. https://doi.org/10.1108/LODJ-05-2012-0063

Mayer, R. E. (2002). Rote versus meaningful learning. *Theory Into Practice, 41*(4), 226–232. https://doi.org/10.1207/s15430421tip4104_4

McGinnis, E. (2011a). *Skillstreaming the elementary school child: A guide for teaching prosocial skills* (3rd ed.). Research Press.

McGinnis, E., (2011b). *Skillstreaming the adolescent: A guide for teaching prosocial skills* (3rd ed.). Research Press.

McGinnis, E., & Goldstein, A. P. (1984). *Skillstreaming the elementary school child*. Research Press.

McGinnis, E., & Goldstein, A. P. (2003). *Skillstreaming in early childhood* (2nd ed.). Research Press.

McIntosh, P. (1998). Interactive phases of curricular and personal re-vision with regard to race. In L. C. Nelson & K. A. Wilson (Eds.), *Seeding the process of multicultural education* (pp. 166–188). Minnesota Inclusiveness Press.

Meier, D. (2002). *The power of their ideas*. Beacon Press.

Mendler, A. N. (2005). *Just in time*. National Education Service.

Miller, P. A. (2002). *Theories of developmental psychology* (4th ed.). Worth/Macmillan.

Moberly, D. A., Waddle, J. L., & Duff, R. E. (2005). The use of rewards and punishment in early childhood classrooms. *Journal of Early Childhood Teacher Education, 25*(4), 359–366. https://doi.org/10.1080/1090102050250410

Monk, G., Winslade, J., & Sinclair, S. (2008). *New horizons in multicultural counseling*. SAGE Publications.

Morran, D. K., Stockton, R., Cline, R. J., & Teed, C. (1998). Facilitating feedback exchange in groups: Leader interventions. *Journal for Specialists in Group Work, 23*(3), 257–268. https://doi.org/10.1080/01933929808411399

Mowrer, R. R., & Klein, S. B. (1989). A contrast between traditional and contemporary learning theory. In S. B. Klein & R. R. Mowrer (Eds.), *Contemporary learning theories: Instrumental conditioning theories and the impact of biological constraints on learning* (pp. 1–12). Lawrence Erlbaum Associates.

Mruzek, D. W., Cohen, C., & Smith, T. (2007). Contingency contracting with students with autism spectrum disorders in a public school setting. *Journal of Developmental and Physical Disabilities, 19*(2), 103–114. https://doi.org/10.1007/s10882-007-9036-x

Multon, K. D., Brown, S. D., & Lent, R. W. (1991). Relation of self-efficacy beliefs to academic outcomes: A meta-analytic investigation. *Journal of Counseling Psychology, 38*(1), 30–38.

Nieto, S. (2000). *Affirming diversity: The sociopolitical context of multicultural education* (3rd ed.). Longman.

Nitza, A. (2014). Selecting and using activities in groups. In J. L. Delucia-Waack, C. R. Kalodner, & M. T. Rivas (Eds.), *Handbook of group counseling and psychotherapy* (pp. 95–106). SAGE Publications.

Noddings, N. (1992). *The challenge to care in schools.* Teachers College Press.

Noddings, N. (1996). The caring professional. In S. Gordon, P. Benner, & N. Noddings (Eds.), *Caregiving. Readings in knowledge, practice, ethics, and politics* (pp. 160–172). University of Pennsylvania Press.

Norcross, J. C. (2010). The therapeutic relationship. In B. L. Duncan, B. E. Wampold, & M. A. Hubble (Eds.), *The heart and soul of change* (2nd ed., pp. 113–142). American Psychological Association.

O'Brien, W. H., & Carhart, V. (2011). Functional analysis in behavioral medicine. *European Journal of Psychological Assessment, 27*(1), 4–16. https://doi.org/10.1027/1015-5759/a000052

O'Halloran, M. S., Ingala, A. M., & Copeland, E. P. (2005). Crisis intervention with early adolescents who have suffered a significant loss. In A. R. Roberts (Ed.), *Crisis intervention handbook. Assessment, treatment & research* (pp. 362–394). Oxford University Press.

Okech, J.E.A., Pimpleton, A., Vannata, R., & Champe, J. (2016). Intercultural conflict in groups. *Journal for Specialists in Group Work, 41*(4), 350–369. https://doi.org/10.1080/01933922.2016.1232769

Okech, J.E.A., & Rubel, D. (2007). Diversity competent group work supervision: An application of the supervision of group work model (SGW). *Journal for Specialists in Group Work, 32*(2), 245–266. https://doi.org/10.1080/0193392070143651

Okech, J.E.A., & Rubel, D. (2009). The experiences of expert group work supervisors: An exploratory study. *Journal for Specialists in Group Work, 34*(1), 68–89. https://doi.org/10.1080/01933920802578087

O'Neill, J., & Conzemius, A. (2006). *The power of SMART goals: Using goals to improve student learning.* Solution Tree.

OSEP Technical Assistance Center on Positive Behavioral Interventions and Supports. (2017). *Positive behavioral interventions & supports.* Retrieved April 21, 2019, from www.pbis.org.

Owens, R. G., & Valesky, T. C. (2015). *Organizational behavior in education* (11th ed). Pearson.

Oyum, L. (2007). Dilemmas of confrontation: Challenging the participants while keeping the process going. *Systemic Practice and Action Research, 20*(1), 41–52. https://doi.org/10.1007/s11213-006-9048-y

Padilla-Walker, L. M., & Nelson, L. J. (2012). Black hawk down?: Establishing helicopter parenting as a distinct construct from other forms of parental control during emerging adulthood. *Journal of Adolescence, 35*(5), 1177–1190. https://doi.org/10.1016/j.adolescence.2012.03.007

Paisley, P. O., & Milsom, A. (2006). Group work as an essential contribution to transforming school counseling. *Journal for Specialists in Group Work, 32*(1), 9–17. https://doi.org/10.1080/01933920600977465

Palmer, P. J. (1993). *To know as we are known. Education as a spiritual journey.* HarperCollins.

Palmer, P. J. (2003). Teaching with heart and soul: Reflections on spirituality in teacher education. *Journal of Teacher Education, 54*(5), 376–385.

Parker, P. D., Marsh, H. W., Ciarrochi, J., Marshall, S., & Abduljabbar, A. S. (2014). Juxtaposing math self-efficacy and self-concept as predictors of long-term achievement outcomes. *Educational Psychology, 34*(1), 29–48. https://doi.org/10.1080/01443410.2013.797339

Parris, D. L., & Peachey, J. W. (2013). A systematic literature review of servant leadership theory in organizational contexts. *Journal of Business Ethics, 113*(3), 377–393. https://doi.org/10.1007/s10551-012-1322-6

Patterson, L. E., & Welfel, E. R. (2000). *The counseling process* (5th ed.). Brooks/Cole.

Pearlin, L. I. (1989). The sociological study of stress. *Journal of Health and Social Behavior, 30*(3), 241–256. http://search.proquest.com.ezproxy.uvm.edu/docview/201659323?accountid=14679

Perry, B. D., & Szalavitz, M. (2006). *The boy who was raised as a dog.* Basic Books.

Petrilli, M. J. (2017, November 20). *In search of common ground on school discipline reform.* Thomas B. Fordham Institute. https://edexcellence.net/articles/in-search-of-common-ground-on-school-discipline-reform

Piaget, J. (1972). *To understand is to invent.* Viking Press.

Pieterse, A. L., Lee, M., Ritmeester, A., & Collins, N. M. (2013). Towards a model of self-awareness development for counselling and psychotherapy training. *Counselling Psychology Quarterly, 26*(2), 190–207. https://doi.org/10.1080/09515070.2013.793451

Polcin, D. L. (2003). Rethinking confrontation in alcohol and drug treatment: Consideration of the clinical context. *Substance Use and Misuse, 38*(2), 165–184. https://doi.org/10.1081/JA-120017243

Popkin, M. H. (1994). *Active teaching. Teacher's handbook grades K–6.* Active Parenting Pub.

Price, T. L. (2008). Transformational leadership. In E. Maturano & J. Gosling (Eds.), *Leadership. Key concepts.* (pp. 170–174). Routledge.

Price, K. M., & Nelson, K. L. (2007). *Planning effective instruction. Diversity responsive methods and management* (3rd ed.). Thomson/Wadsworth.

Puddy, R. W., Boles, R. E., Dreyer, M. L., Maikranz, J., Roberts, M. C., & Vernberg, E. M. (2008). Demonstrating support for the formative and summative assessment paradigm in a school-based intensive mental health program. *Journal of Child and Family Studies, 17*(2), 253–263. https://doi.org/10.1007/s10826-007-9164-z

Ramberg, J., Låftman, S. B., Almquist, Y. B., & Modin, B. (2019). School effectiveness and students' perceptions of teacher caring: A multilevel study. *Improving Schools*, 22(1), 55–71.

Ratts, M. J., Singh, A. A., Nassar-McMillan, S., Butler, S. K., McCullough, J. R., & Hipolito-Delgado, C. (2015). Multicultural and social justice counseling competencies. AMCD.

Richardson, J., & Parnell, P. (2005). *And tango makes three.* Simon & Schuster.

Roberts, A. R. (2005). Bridging the past and present to the future of crisis intervention and crisis management. In A. R. Roberts (Ed.), *Crisis intervention handbook. Assessment, treatment & research* (pp. 3–34). Oxford University Press.

Rogers, C. (1951). *Client-centered therapy: Current practice implications, and theory.* Houghton Mifflin.

Rogers, C. (1980). *A way of being.* Houghton Mifflin Company.

Rolfe, A. (2008). 'You've got to grow up when you've got a kid': Marginalized young women's accounts of motherhood. *Journal of Community & Applied Social Psychology*, 18(4), 299–314. https://doi.org/10.1002/casp.925

Runesson, U. (2015). Pedagogical and learning theories and the improvement and development of lesson and learning studies. *International Journal for Lesson and Learning Studies*, 4(3), 186–193. https://doi.org/10.1108/IJLLS-04-2015-0016

Ryoo, J. H., Hong, S., Bart, W. M., Shin, J., & Bradshaw, C. P. (2017). Investigating the effect of school-wide positive behavioral interventions and support on learning and behavioral problems in elementary and middle schools. *Psychology in the Schools*, 55, 629–643. https://doi.org/10.1002/pits.22134

Scaturo, D. J. (2002). Fundamental dilemmas in contemporary psychodynamic and insight-oriented psychotherapy. *Journal of Contemporary Psychotherapy*, 32(2–3), 145–165. https://doi.org/10.1023/A:1020540909172

Schermer, V. L. (2011). Interpreting psychoanalytic interpretation: A fourfold perspective. *Psychoanalytic Review*, 98(6), 817–842. https://doi.org/10.1521/prev.2011.98.6.817

Schmidt, J. J. (2007). *Counseling in schools* (5th ed.). Allyn & Bacon.

Scholastic. (n.d.). *Classroom behavior problems increasing, teachers say.* Retrieved January 25, 2020, from https://www.scholastic.com/teachers/articles/teaching-content/classroom-behavior-problems-increasing-teachers-say/

Schwarz, R. (2002). *The skilled facilitator: A comprehensive resource for consultants, facilitators, managers, trainers, and coaches* (2nd ed.). John Wiley & Sons.

Sciarra, D. T. (2004). *School counseling. Foundations and contemporary issues.* Brooks/Cole-Thomson Learning.

Seaman, M. (2011). Bloom's taxonomy. Its evolution, revision, and use in the field of education. *Curriculum & Teaching Dialogue*, 13(1 & 2), 29–43.

Shechtman, Z. (2007). How does group process research inform leaders of counseling and psychotherapy groups? *Group Dynamics: Theory, Research, and Practice*, 11(4), 293.

Shechtman, Z., (2014). Counseling and therapy groups with children and adolescents. In J. L. De-Lucia-Waack, J. L., Kalodner, C. R., & Riva, M. T. (Eds.), *Handbook of group counseling and psychotherapy* (2nd ed., pp. 585–596). SAGE Publications.

Shute, V. J. (2008). Focus on formative feedback. *Review of Educational Research*, 78(1), 153–189.

Siegel, D. J. (2012). *The developing mind* (2nd ed.). Guilford Press.

Singer, D. G., & Revenson, T. A. (1997). *A Piaget primer. How a child thinks.* International Universities Press.

Singer, J. (2005). Child and adolescent psychiatric emergencies: Mobile crisis response. In A. R. Roberts (Ed.), *Crisis intervention handbook. Assessment, treatment & research* (pp. 319–361). Oxford University Press.

Singh, A. A., Merchant, N., Skudrzyk, B., & Ingene, D. (2012). Association for specialists in group work: Multicultural and social justice competence principles for group workers. *Journal for Specialists in Group Work*, 37(4), 312–325. https://doi.org/10.1080/01933922.2012.721482

Sink, C. A. (2005). The contemporary school counselor. In C. A. Sink (Ed.), *Contemporary school counseling. Theory, research, and practice* (pp. 1–42). Lahaska Press.

Skinner, B. F. (1971). *Beyond freedom and dignity.* Alfred A. Knopf.

Smead, R. (1995). *Skills and techniques for group work with children and adolescents.* Research Press.

Smidt, S. (2011). *Introducing Bruner. A guide for practitioners and students in early years education.* Routledge.

Smith, L. C., Geroski, A. M., & Tyler, K. B., (2014). Abandoning colorblind practice in school counseling. *Journal of School Counseling*, 12(16), 1–30.

Sommers-Flanagan, R., & Sommers-Flanagan, J. (2007). *Becoming an ethical helping professional.* John Wiley & Sons.

Sorrells, K. (2013). *Intercultural communication.* SAGE Publications.

Sprick, R. S. (2006). *Discipline in the secondary classroom* (2nd ed.). Jossey-Bass.

Stahl, L. (Host) & Maher, M (Special Correspondent). (2003, April 30). Extremely perfect [TV series Season 16, Episode 35]. In S. Zirinsky, (Executive Producer). *48 Hours.* New York: CBS News.

Steinberg, M. P., & Lacoe, J. (2017). "What do we know about school discipline reform? *EducationNext*, 17(1). http://educationnext.org/files/ednext_xvii_1_steinberg.pdf

Sternberg, R. J. (2007). Culture, instruction, and assessment. *Comparative Education*, 43(1), 5–22.

Stockton, R., Morran, D. K., & Nitza, A. G. (2000). Processing group events: A conceptual map for leaders. *Journal for Specialists in Group Work*, 25, 343–355.

Stone, C. B., & Dahir, C. A. (2006). *The transformed school counselor.* Lahaska.

Strong, T., & Zeman, D. (2010). Dialogic consideration of confrontation as a counseling activity: An examination of Allen Ivey's use of confronting as a microskill. *Journal of Counseling & Development*, 88(3), 332–339. https://doi.org/10.1002/j.1556-6678.2010.tb00030.x

Style, E. (1998). Curriculum as window and mirror. In L. C. Nelson & K. A. Wilson (Eds.), *Seeding the process of multicultural education* (pp. 149–156). Minnesota Inclusiveness Press.

Sue, D. W. (2010). Microaggressions, marginality, and oppression. An introduction. In D. W. Sue (Ed.), *Microaggressions and marginality. Manifestation, dynamics, and impact* (pp. 3–22). John Wiley & Sons.

Sue, D. W., Arredondo. P., & McDavis, R J. (1992). Multicultural counseling competencies and standards: A call to the profession. *Journal of Counseling & Development*, 70, 477–483.

Sue, D. W., Capodilupo, C. M., Torino, G. C., Bucceri, J. M., Holder, A. M. B., Nadal, K. L., & Esquilin, M. (2007). Racial microaggressions in everyday life: Implications for clinical practice. *American Psychologist*, 62(4), 271–286. https://doi.org/10.1037/0003-066X.62.4.271

Sue, D. W., & Sue, D. (2003). *Counseling the culturally diverse: Theory and practice* (4th ed.). John Wiley & Sons.

Tatum, B. D. (1997). *Why are all the black kids sitting together in the cafeteria?* (5th ed.). Basic Books.

Taylor, E. W. (1994). A learning model for becoming interculturally competent. *International Journal of Intercultural Relations*, 18(3), 389–408.

Tetteris, B. C. (2006). *The nitty-gritty. Classroom and behavior management resource.* Rowman & Littlefield.

The Education Trust. (2009). *The new vision for school counselors: Scope of work.* Retrieved April 20, 2019, from https://edtrust.org/resource/the-new-vision-for-school-counselors-scope-of-the-work/

Thomas, R. V., & Pender, D. A. (2007). Association for specialists in group work: Best practice guidelines 2007 revisions. *Journal for Specialists in Group Work*, 33(2), 111–117. https://doi.org/10.1080/01933920801971184

Thorsten, A. (2015). How teachers' practice knowledge is used and challenged in a learning study using variation theory as a tool. *International Journal for Lesson and Learning Studies*, 4(3), 274–287. https://doi.org/10.1108/IJLLS-08-2014-0030

Three Types of Logical Consequences. (2011). *Responsive classroom.* Retrieved April 21, 2019, from https://www.responsiveclassroom.org/three-types-of-logical-consequences/

Tileston, D. W. (2004). *What every teacher should know about instructional planning.* Corwin Press.

Toseland, R. W., & Rivas, R. F. (2005). *An introduction to group work practice* (5th ed.). Pearson.

Townsend, B. L. (2000). The disproportionate discipline of African American learners: Reducing school suspensions and expulsion. *Exceptional Children*, 66(3), 381–391. https://doi.org/10.1177/001440290006600308

Trotzer, J. P. (2004). Conducting a group: Guidelines for choosing and using activities. In J. L. DeLucia-Waack, D. A. Gerrity, C. R. Kalodner, & M. T. Riva (Eds.), *Handbook of group counseling and psychotherapy* (pp. 76–90). SAGE Publications.

Trusty, J., & Brown, D. (2005). Advocacy competencies for professional school counselors. *Professional School Counseling*, 8(3), 259–265.

Tuckman, B. (1965). Developmental sequence in small groups. *Psychological Bulletin*, 63, 384–399.

Tuckman, B. W., & Jensen, M.A.C. (1977). Stages of small-group development revisited. *Group & Organization Management*, 2(4), 419–427. https://doi.org/10.1177/105960117700200404

U.S. Department of Justice Civil Rights Division and U.S. Department of Education Office of Civil Rights. (2014, January 8). Joint "dear colleague" letter. https://www2.ed.gov/about/offices/list/ocr/letters/colleague-201401-title-vi.html

Velasquez, A., West, R., Graham, C., & Osguthorpe, R. (2013). Developing caring relationships in schools: A review of the research on caring and nurturing pedagogies. *Review of Education*, 1(2), 162–190. https://doi.org/10.1002/rev3.3014

Vernon, A. (2010). *Counseling children and adolescents* (4th ed.). Love Publishing.

Vernon, A., & Shimmel, C. J. (2019). *Counseling children and adolescents* (5th ed.). Cognella.

Vetere, A., & Dowling, E. (2016). Narrative concepts and therapeutic challenges. In A. Vetere & E. Dowling (Eds.), *Narrative therapies with children and their families: A practitioner's guide to concepts and approaches* (2nd ed, pp. 3–23). Taylor & Francis.

Vygotsky, L. S. (1978). *Mind and society: The development of higher mental processes.* Harvard University Press. (Original works published 1930, 1933, and 1935)

Waguespack, A., Vaccaro, T., & Continere, L. (2006). Functional behavioral assessment and intervention with emotional/behaviorally disordered students: In pursuit of state of the art. *International Journal of Behavioral Consultation and Therapy*, 2(4), 463–474.

Ward, D. E., & Litchy, M. (2004). The effective use of processing in groups. In J. L. DeLucia-Waack, D. A. Gerrity, C. R. Kalodner, & M. T. Riva (Eds.), *Handbook of group counseling and psychotherapy* (pp. 104–119). SAGE Publications. http://dx.doi.org/10.4135/9781452229683.n6

Waterman, H. (2011). Principles of 'servant leadership' and how they can enhance practice. *Nursing Management*, 17(9), 24–26.

Weiser, D. A., & Riggio, H. R. (2010). Family background and academic achievement: Does self-efficacy mediate outcomes? *Social Psychology of Education*, 13(3), 367–383. https://doi.org/10.1007/s11218-010-9115-1

Welfel, E. R., Danzinger, P. R., & Santoro, S. (2000). Mandated reporting of abuse/maltreatment of older adults: A primer for counselors. *Journal of Counseling & Development*, 78(3), 284–292. https://doi.org/10.1002/j.1556-6676.2000.tb01909

Wertsch, J. V. (1985). *Vygotsky and the social formation of mind.* Harvard University Press.

Wertsch, J. V., & Toma, C. (1995). Discourse and learning in the classroom: A sociocultural approach. In L. P. Steffe & J. Gale (Eds.), *Constructivism in education* (pp. 159–174). Lawrence Erlbaum Associates.

Wheelan, S. A. (1990). Facilitating training groups: A guide to leadership and verbal intervention skills. Greenwood Publishing Group.

Wheeler, A. M., & Bertram, B. (2012). *The counselor and the law. A guide to legal and ethical practice* (6th ed.). American Counseling Association.

Wheeler, C. D., & D'Andrea, L. M. (2004). Teaching counseling students to understand immediacy. *Journal of Humanistic Counseling, Education and Development*, 43(2), 117–128.

Whiston, S. C. (2007). Outcomes research on school counseling interventions and programs. In B. T. Erford (Ed.), *Transforming the school counseling profession* (pp. 38–50). Pearson Education, Inc.

White, M., & Epston, D. (1990). *Narrative means to therapeutic ends*. Dulwich Centre.

Willert, T. (2017). Survey: Student discipline monopolizes teachers' time. *The Seattle Times* (*Nation & World*). https://www.seattletimes.com/nation-world/survey-student-discipline-monopolizes-teachers-time/

Winters, D., & Latham, G. P. (1996). The effect of learning versus outcome goals on a simple versus a complex task. *Group & Organization Management*, 21(2), 236–250.

Wiseman, T. (1996). A concept analysis of empathy. *Journal of Advanced Nursing*, 23(6), 1162–1167. https://doi.org/10.1046/j.1365-2648.1996.12213.x

Wubbolding, R. E. (1988). *Using reality therapy*. Harper Perennial.

Wubbolding, R. E., & Brickell, J. (1999). *Counseling with reality therapy*. Winslow Press.

Wynn, R., & Bergvik, S. (2010). Studying empathy as an interactional three-part sequence. *Patient Education and Counseling*, 80(1), 150. https:doi.org/10.1016/j.pec.2009.05.007

Yalom, I. D. (1995). *Theory and practice of group psychotherapy*. Basic Books.

Yalom, I. D. (2005). *Theory and practice of group psychotherapy* (5th ed.). Basic Books.

Yalom, I. D., Brown, S., & Bloch, S. (1975). The written summary as a group psychotherapy technique. *Archives of General Psychiatry*, 32(5), 605–613.

Yalom, I. D., & Leszcz, M. (Collaborator). (2005). *The theory and practice of group psychotherapy* (5th ed.). Basic Books.

Yalom, V. J., & Yalom, I. (1990). Brief interactive group psychotherapy. *Psychiatric Annals*, 20(7), 362–367. https://doi.org/10.3928/0048-5713-19900701-06

Young, A., & Kaffenberger, C. (2015). School counseling professional development: Assessing the use of data to inform school counseling services. *Professional School Counseling*, 19(1), 1096–2409. https://doi.org/10.5330/1096-2409-19.1.46

Zieman, G. L., Romano, P. A., Blanco, K., & Linnell, T. (1981). The process-observer in group therapy. *Group*, 5(4), 37–47. https://doi.org/10.1007/BF01456612

Zirpoli, T. J., & Melloy, K. J. (1997). *Behavior management. Applications for teachers and parents* (2nd ed.). Merrill Prentice Hall.

INDEX

ABOUT THE AUTHORS

Anne Geroski, Ed.D., is an associate professor in the Counseling Program at the University of Vermont. She has worked as a school and mental health counselor in a variety of settings in the U.S. and overseas, and has been preparing counselors at the University of Vermont for over 20 years. Her professional interests include child and adolescent counseling, group work, narrative practice, and the study of parenting intentions and practices. Anne lives with her partner, Kevin, in Burlington, Vermont, and they have four young adult children.

Kurt L. Kraus, Ed.D., NCC, ACS, LPC, is a professor in the Department of Counselor Education at Shippensburg University of Pennsylvania. Kurt's career includes school counseling, mental health counseling, and counselor education. His professional interests include child and adolescent counseling, group work, and the implications of human development on the therapeutic alliance. Kurt currently serves on the Commonwealth's LPC Licensure Board and he directs Ship's Ed.D. in Counselor Education and Supervision Program. He is most thankful to be a husband, dad, and grandpa.

Jane E. Atieno. Okech, Ph.D., NCC, is a professor and chair of the Department of Leadership and Developmental Sciences at the University of Vermont. Her research primarily focuses on the advancement of proficiencies in the practice of group psychotherapy and clinical supervision. Her scholarship also examines models of clinical supervision and the development of core supervision intervention proficiencies across various domains of clinical practice. Associated aspects of this scholarship foci is its intersection with counselor training, culturally responsive pedagogy and clinical practice, professional ethics, and standards of practice. She is most thankful for having the opportunity to apply the lessons learned from her academic career to the role of being a mother, leader, and mentor to emerging scholars.

CPSIA information can be obtained
at www.ICGtesting.com
Printed in the USA
FSHW021812040121
77406FS

9 781516 514410